BISMARCK

The Man and the Statesman

BISMARCK

The Man and the Statesman

A. J. P. Taylor

FELLOW OF MAGDALEN COLLEGE, OXFORD

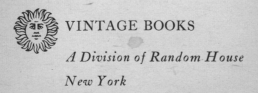

VINTAGE BOOKS

A Division of Random House

New York

CONTENTS

BISMARCK

The Man and the Statesman

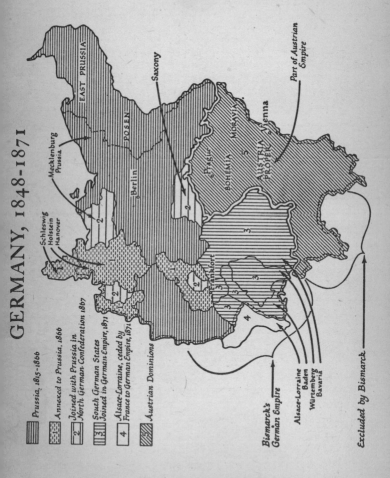

GERMANY, 1848-1871

Prussia, 1815-1866

Annexed to Prussia, 1866

2 Joined with Prussia in
    North German Confederation 1867

3 South German States
   Joined in German Empire, 1871

4 Alsace-Lorraine, ceded by
   France to German Empire, 1871

Austrian Dominions

EAST PRUSSIA

POSEN

Berlin

Mecklenburg
Prussia

Schleswig
Holstein
Hanover

Saxony

Prague

BOHEMIA

MORAVIA

Vienna

AUSTRIA PROPER

Part of Austrian
Empire

Frankfort

Bismarck's
German Empire

Alsace-Lorraine
Baden
Wurtemberg
Bavaria

Excluded by Bismarck

Map by Robert Galvin, from A HISTORY OF THE MODERN WORLD, *by R. R. Palmer*

THE BOY AND THE MAN

OTTO VON BISMARCK was born at Schönhausen in the Old Mark of Brandenburg on 1 April 1815. Both place and date hinted at the pattern of his life. Schönhausen lay just east of the Elbe, in appearance a typical Junker estate —some sheep and cattle, wheat and beetroot fields, with woods in the background. Life seemed to follow a traditional rhythm, far removed from the modern world. Yet if Bismarck had been born two years earlier, the kingdom of Westphalia, ruled by Jerome Bonaparte, would have been just across the river. French troops had occupied Schönhausen during the wars; French revolutionary ideas lapped to the edge of its fields. The true Junkers lived far away to the east, in Pomerania and Silesia. These Junkers were a Prussian speciality—gentry proud of their birth, but working their estates themselves and often needing public employment to supplement their incomes. They looked with jealousy at the high aristocracy with its cosmopolitan culture and its monopoly of the greatest offices in the state. We may find a parallel in the English country-gentry with their Tory prejudices and their endless feud against the Whig magnates; but the Junkers were nearer to the soil, often milking their own cows and selling their wool themselves at the nearest market, sometimes distinguished from the more prosperous peasant-farmers only by their historic names.

Schönhausen was an estate of this kind, but the winds of the modern world blew round it. Though Bismarck was born a couple of miles on the Junker side of the Elbe, he was always the Junker who looked across it—sometimes with apprehension, sometimes with sympathy. The date of his birth was also significant. A fortnight earlier Napoleon had arrived in Paris for his last adventure of the Hundred Days. The old order had a narrow escape. Bismarck, despite his appearance of titanic calm, was always aware of the revolutionary tide that had threatened to engulf the antiquated life of Schönhausen. The kingdom of Prussia, of which he was a subject, had risen again into the ranks of the Great Powers, but it had been almost snuffed out by Napoleon. Her statesmen feared that the same fate might come again. It became their dogma: 'Unless we grow greater we shall become less'. This was no basis for a confident conservatism.

The very geography of Schönhausen also shaped Bismarck's character and political outlook. It was unmistakably in north Germany, in a district entirely inhabited by Protestants. Bismarck never came to regard the south Germans as true Germans, particularly if they were Roman Catholics. Yet Schönhausen also lay far from the sea. Its inhabitants looked to Berlin as their metropolis; and the connexion which Bismarck later established with Hamburg was always rather artificial. If Germany was to expand at all, he preferred that it should be overseas rather than down the Danube; yet both were alien to him. The eastern expansion of Prussia, which had shaped her history, was equally remote for him. Unlike the Junkers of Silesia or West Prussia, he never had a Pole among his peasants. The Poles whom he denounced from personal experience were educated revolutionaries, not workers on the land; it was because of them that Bismarck disliked intellectuals in politics.

There was a similar contradiction in his family heritage. His father Ferdinand was a typical Junker, sprung from a family as old as the Hohenzollerns—'a Suabian family no better than mine' Bismarck once remarked. Schönhausen itself symbolized their humiliation; for they had received it as compensation for their original family estate, which a Hohenzollern elector had coveted and seized. The Bismarcks had done nothing to gain distinction during their long feudal obscurity. Ferdinand did not even exert him-

self to fight for his king. He left the Prussian army at 23;
and missed both the disastrous Jena campaign in 1806 and
the war of liberation against Napoleon in 1813. The efficient
management of his rambling estates was beyond him, and
he drifted helplessly into economic difficulties. It needed a
vivid imagination for the son to turn this easy-going, slow-
witted man, with his enormous frame, into a hero, representing all that was best in Prussian tradition.

Wilhelmine, the mother, was a different character. Her
family, the Menkens, were bureaucrats without a title, not
aristocrat landowners. Some of them had been university
professors. Her father was a servant of the Prussian state,
prized by Frederick the Great and later in virtual control of
all home affairs. His reforms and quick critical spirit
brought down on him the accusation of 'Jacobinism'.
Wilhelmine was a town-child, at home only in the drawing
rooms of Berlin. She had a sharp, restless intellect, which
roamed without system from Swedenborg to Mesmer. At
one moment she would be discussing the latest works of
political liberalism; at the next dabbling in spiritualist experiments. Married to Ferdinand von Bismarck at sixteen,
she developed interest neither for her heavy husband nor in
country life. All her hopes were centred on her children.
They were to achieve the intellectual life that had been
denied to her. Her only ambition, she said, was to have 'a
grown-up son who would penetrate far further into the
world of ideas than I, as a woman, have been able to do.'

She gave her children encouragement without love. She
drove them on; she never showed them affection. Otto, the
younger son, inherited her brains. He was not grateful for
the legacy. He wanted love from her, not ideas; and he was
resentful that she did not share his admiration for his father.
It is a psychological commonplace for a son to feel affection
for his mother and to wish his father out of the way. The
results are more interesting and more profound when a son,
who takes after his mother, dislikes her character and standards of value. He will seek to turn himself into the father
with whom he has little in common, and he may well end up

neurotic or a genius. Bismarck was both. He was the clever, sophisticated son of a clever, sophisticated mother, masquerading all his life as his heavy, earthy father.

Even his appearance showed it. He was a big man, made bigger by his persistence in eating and drinking too much. He walked stiffly, with the upright carriage of a hereditary officer. Yet he had a small, fine head; the delicate hands of an artist; and when he spoke, his voice, which one would have expected to be deep and powerful, was thin and reedy —almost a falsetto—the voice of an academic, not of a man of action. Nor did he always present the same face to the world. He lives in history clean-shaven, except for a heavy moustache. Actually he wore a full beard for long periods of his life; and this at a time when beards were symbols on the continent of Europe of the Romantic movement, if not of radicalism. In the use of a razor, as in other things, Bismarck sometimes followed Metternich, sometimes Marx. Despite his Junker mien, he had the sensitivity of a woman, incredibly quick in responding to the moods of another, or even in anticipating them. His conversational charm could bewitch tsars, queens and revolutionary leaders. Yet his great strokes of policy came after long solitary brooding, not after discussion with others. Indeed he never exchanged ideas in the usual sense of the term. He gave orders or, more rarely, carried them out; he did not co-operate. In a life of conflict, he fought himself most of all. He said once: 'Faust complains of having two souls in his breast. I have a whole squabbling crowd. It goes on as in a republic.' When someone asked him if he were really the Iron Chancellor, he replied: 'Far from it. I am all nerves, so much so that self-control has always been the greatest task of my life and still is.' He willed himself into a line of policy or action. His friend Keyserling noted of his conversion to religion: 'Doubt was not fought and conquered; it was silenced by heroic will.'

He felt himself always out of place, solitary and a stranger to his surroundings. 'I have the unfortunate nature that everywhere I could be seems desirable to me, and dreary and boring as soon as I am there.' He loathed the intellectual circles of Berlin to which his mother introduced him, and in 1848 said to a liberal politician: 'I am a Junker and mean to have the advantages of that position.' But the years he spent as a Junker, managing his estates, were the most miserable of his life; and when, as Chancellor, he retired to his beloved countryside, he was happy only so long as the state papers continued to pour in on him. He spent the twenty-eight years of supreme power announcing his wish to relinquish it; yet no man has left office with such ill grace or fought so unscrupulously to recover it. He despised writers and literary men; yet only Luther and Goethe rank with him as masters of German prose. He found happiness only in his family; loved his wife, and gave to his children the affection that he had been denied by his mother. He said in old age that his greatest good fortune was 'that God did not take any of my children from me.' Yet he ruined the happiness of his adored elder son for the sake of a private feud, and thought nothing of spending a long holiday away from his wife in the company of a pretty girl; indeed he was so self-centred that he boasted to his wife of the girl's charm and good looks. He claimed to serve sometimes the king of Prussia, sometimes Germany, sometimes God. All three were cloaks for his own will; and he turned against them ruthlessly when they did not serve his purpose. He could have said with Oliver Cromwell, whom he much resembled; 'He goeth furthest who knows not whither he is going.' The young Junker had no vision that he would unify Germany on the basis of universal suffrage; and the maker of three wars did not expect to end as the great buttress of European peace.

Bismarck was not brought up as a Junker, despite his constant assertions of this character in later life. The family moved soon after he was born to the smaller estate of Kniephof in Pomerania. Here there was a smaller house with no architectural pretensions and hard practical farming. The Junkers, unlike the English gentry, did not live on rents. They worked the land themselves, and their peasants

were, in reality, agricultural labourers, many of whom did
not cultivate any land of their own. Bismarck experienced
this idyllic existence only till he was seven. Then his
mother set up house in Berlin, no doubt much to her own
satisfaction, but ostensibly to send her sons to school in the
capital. This exile from the country gave Bismarck a lasting
grievance against his mother. The education which she
chose for him was another. A Junker's son usually went into
a cadet corps and, later, joined a cavalry regiment, even if
he was not destined for a permanent military career.
Wilhelmine, however, insisted that her children should have
an intellectual education suited to the grandsons of the
great Menken; and Bismarck went to the best Berlin
grammar school of the day where he mixed with the sons
of middle-class families. His mother revived her connexions
with the court; and Bismarck led a privileged existence,
mixing on intimate terms with the younger Hohenzollerns.
This counted in his later career. Despite his sturdy affectation of independence, he was always inside the royal circle
and was treated as one of the family.

The spirit of the Enlightenment still dominated Prussian
education; and Bismarck left school 'as a Pantheist and if
not as a republican, with the belief that a republic was the
most reasonable form of state.' His mother once more imposed her intellectual standards by sending him out of
Prussia to the university of Göttingen in Hanover, the
greatest liberal centre of the day. Bismarck at first took a
radical line. He defied university discipline both in behaviour and ideas. What was more, he joined the *Burschen-
schaften*—students' unions which tried to keep alive the
revolutionary spirit of the war of liberation. He soon
turned the other way. It was one thing to pose as a young
radical in the court circles of Berlin; quite another to accept
these ill-bred students from the middle class as his equals.
Personal relations changed Bismarck's political outlook, as
was often to happen in his later life. He suddenly discovered
pride of blood and joined an aristocratic students-corps. He
still led a disorderly existence. He drank a great deal; had

some passionate *affaires*; and, like the young Disraeli, wore fantastic and colourful clothes. He was always ready for a duel, though the only time he was injured he characteristically alleged that it was a foul blow—an allegation which he maintained unforgivingly even thirty years later. After three terms, debts drove him back to Berlin, where he could live at home; and here he put in a second academic year. In May, 1835, when he was just twenty, he scraped through the examination which qualified him for entry into the Prussian civil service.

Though Bismarck was never a great scholar, his years at the university left their mark. He read widely, despite his boasts of idleness, though he read more history than the law that he was supposed to be studying. He liked Schiller, admired Goethe, and ranked Shakespeare and Byron above either of them—tastes characteristic of the Romantic movement. Scott was his greatest favourite of all, romance and history blended in the right proportions. Bismarck's classical learning was scanty; his scientific knowledge almost non-existent. All the historical references in his speeches are to the three hundred years since the Reformation; his occasional echoes of Darwinianism only what he could pick up from a newspaper. Philosophy never interested him; and he was one of the few Germans to escape the influence of Hegel. People were always more important to Bismarck than books; and he made at the university the only two lasting friendships of his life, both with men who were—like him—in a strange environment, fish out of water. Alexander Keyserling was a German baron from the Baltic and later a distinguished naturalist. John Motley was a budding American diplomat, who became the historian of the Dutch republic. Bismarck trusted himself only to these strangers. The ties of affection between these three never weakened, despite years of separation. Bismarck was writing to 'dear old John' with undiminished enthusiasm forty years later; and even when he became Imperial Chancellor would throw aside the cares and dignity of office to make Motley welcome. Keyserling was less demonstra-

tive; but he, too, was faithful. After Bismarck's fall from
power, Keyserling, though nearly eighty, left his Baltic
retreat to console his old friend; and his visit gave Bismarck
a last experience of quiet happiness.

Bismarck grew up into the Germany of reaction. The
great storm of the Napoleonic empire had been followed by
'the quiet years'. Germany was divided into thirty-nine
states, the survivors after much Napoleonic reconstruction.
Most of them were tiny; half a dozen were of medium rank;
and, overshadowing them, the two great states, Austria and
Prussia. The congress of Vienna had tied them all together
into a loose confederation, which was supposed to settle
internal disputes and even to provide a federal defence
force in case of foreign war. In practice its only function
turned out to be the suppression of German liberalism; and
it did even that ineffectively. Austria was the presiding
Power in the confederation. She had the greater historic
prestige—an emperor as ruler, and Metternich, the most
famous statesman of the day, as chancellor. She had the
army of a Great Power, supposedly capable of challenging
that of France, as it had often done—unsuccessfully—
during the Napoleonic wars. But the Austrian empire was
in decay—its finances shaky, its administration rigid and
out-of-date, its very existence menaced by the rise of
Italian and German nationalism.

Prussia had been the more severely mauled by Napoleon;
and remembrance of this kept her policy safely on the conservative line with Austria. She hardly counted among the
Great Powers. In 1815, there were only ten million Prussians, as against thirty million Frenchmen and almost
thirty million subjects of the Austrian emperor. Her army
was not of much esteem. The other Powers relied on con-
scripts chosen by lot, who served for fifteen or twenty years.
Prussia made up for her weakness in manpower by giving
all, or most, of her subjects a three-year training and re-
calling them for service in time of war. Though this was to
be the pattern of all subsequent military development, it
was despised by contemporary experts as providing little

more than a civilian militia. Frederick William III, who reigned until 1840, was timid and unimaginative, clinging anxiously to Metternich's coat-tails for protection. During the excitement of the war of liberation he promised his people a constitution. But he soon repented of his promise and did not carry it out. All that remained of it was a promise that the Prussian state would not incur any new loan without the consent of some sort of popular assembly. The eight provinces of Prussia had diets elected on a class basis and with few real functions. For all practical purposes Prussia continued to be run by a narrow bureaucracy, its standards of efficiency and honesty higher than any other in Europe, but remote from popular feeling.

Germany was still overwhelmingly rural, even Berlin only an overgrown garrison-town. The French had begun to develop the coalmines of the Ruhr when they controlled the Kingdom of Westphalia. But the few great capitalists of Germany drew their wealth from commerce and banking on the artery of the Rhine. The customs-union (*Zollverein*) which Prussia had organized by 1834 got rid of most internal tariffs, but trade was on a modest scale—mainly the import of British manufactured goods in exchange for German wool and wheat. There was some intellectual stir in Germany, despite this economic stagnation. The German universities were at this time the best in Europe. The Prince Consort rightly took them as his model when he attempted, somewhat ineffectually, to reform Oxford and Cambridge. Most of the students affected a hazy radicalism. Even Bismarck did not escape this influence. He jeered at the bureaucracy and said to Keyserling: 'A constitution is inevitable. This is the way to honour in the world.' Like most of his generation, he thought that Prussia would come to dominate Germany by her liberalism, not by her strength.

His short career in the civil service was not a success. In 1836, after a few weeks of training at Potsdam, he was sent to Aachen in the Prussian Rhineland. This territory had been acquired by Prussia only in 1815, as compensation for the Polish lands which Russia insisted on retaining. The inhabitants had no attachment to Prussia. They were Roman Catholics, much influenced by French liberalism and impatient with reaction. They had been included in France for twenty years and indeed retained the Napoleonic code until 1900. The Prussian administrators were despised and disliked. But Bismarck did not trouble himself much with the inhabitants. Cosmopolitan travellers passed through Aachen on their way to more fashionable spas; and Bismarck neglected his official duties to mix with this wealthy crowd. He imagined himself in love with one rich English girl after another, allegedly flying as high as a niece of the Duke of Cleveland. Soon he claimed to be engaged to a young lady from Leicestershire. Taking a fortnight's leave, he followed his betrothed across Germany. He ran heavily into debt and overstayed his leave by three months. The affair came to nothing, and he was left only with a knowledge of colloquial English. He was too proud to return to Aachen with a request for forgiveness. It is easy to guess what he would have said, as Chancellor, of a subordinate who slipped off in this way. Bismarck merely replied to complaints: 'He by no means intended to give the government an account of his personal relations.'

He found a simple means of evading Aachen. Prussians with a secondary education had to serve for a year in the army as officers; and Bismarck still had this hanging over him. He tried to escape by pleading a muscular weakness: 'I have told them I feel pain when I raise my right arm.' The plea did not work, and Bismarck joined the garrison at Potsdam. He found it tedious and, never having been to boarding-school, railed fiercely against the hardships of life in barracks. Yet he led a privileged existence, constantly invited to the royal palace, where he strengthened his acquaintance with the crown prince—soon to be Frederick William IV—and perfected the arts of a courtier. His only achievement in the field was to rescue a corporal who had fallen into a ditch; he received a medal for life-saving—the only military decoration that he ever earned. His later admiration for the military virtues was certainly not based on personal experience or taste; and when his sons did their military service, he lamented their fate with civilian bitterness.

In 1839, when his year of service was completed, he resigned from the Prussian bureaucracy. He found high grounds for his action. The Prussian official, he said, was only a member of an orchestra. 'But I will play music the way I like, or none at all.' His ambition was to have 'the career of a statesman in a free constitution, such as Peel, O'Connell, Mirabeau, etc.' A strange trio! Peel, seeking a compromise between the old England and the new, one can understand; even Mirabeau, struggling to create a strong constitutional monarchy in the storm of the French Revolution. But how did Bismarck hit on O'Connell, the radical tribune of Irish nationalism? Evidently principles did not matter to him. The important thing was to take part in 'energetic political movements'.

Bismarck was now 24, at a loss for a future. His mother died the same year, with her hopes for her son disappointed. The family fortunes had fallen into disorder through his father's incompetence and neglect. Bismarck and his elder brother established the old man at Schönhausen and took over the Pomeranian estates themselves.[1] Here was the Junker life which had always been Bismarck's ideal; and he anticipated an idyllic existence. 'I shall be happy in the country surroundings of my family; car tel est mon plaisir.' It soon turned to dust and ashes. He confessed later to his wife: 'I learnt only from experience that the Arcadian life of a dyed-in-the-wool landowner with double book-keeping and chemical experiments was an illusion.' The eight years that he spent as a working landowner were the most wretched and barren of his life. Unlike Cavour in similar circumstances, he never tried to take the lead in agrarian improvements. As he showed later, country life was for him

[1] In 1845, when Ferdinand von Bismarck died, Otto moved to Schönhausen and left the Pomeranian estates in the hands of his brother. He later sold his share, insisting on the full market price.

a matter of display, not of genuine economic activity; and he would overspend on his estate at the slightest excuse. In these years he and his brother restored the family finances by plodding economy, not by any striking initiative. This vegetating life was not enough to satisfy Bismarck's energy. He was driven crazy with boredom and with the futility of his existence. He found the society of his Junker neighbours intolerable; and they in turn distrusted him. His only public achievement was to become keeper of dykes on the Elbe—symbolic, perhaps, but trivial. He read enormously—history for the most part and classical English novels. *Tristram Shandy* especially took his fancy; and he saw himself as the same sort of eccentric. He rode hallooing through the woods at night and seduced the peasants' daughters. He released a fox in a lady's drawing-room. These wild escapades won him the title of 'the mad Junker'. When money ran to it, he travelled—once to England, where he saw the new industries of Lancashire. He thought of joining the British forces in India; then asked himself, 'what harm have the Indians done to me?', and refrained.

In 1844 he returned to the Prussian civil service, only to leave it again after a fortnight. His simple explanation was: 'I have never been able to put up with superiors.' By now he was 30, bitter, cynical and neurotic, his gifts running to nothing. New life came unexpectedly with religion, a wife, and a revolution. Bismarck learnt religion from the only neighbours for whom he cared—devout Lutherans who developed a quietist religion in a Quaker spirit. He was impressed by their content and peaceful confidence. Hoping to discover their secret, he spent much time in their company; and he found there a wife, Johanna von Puttkamer. His open avowal of religious belief was, no doubt, made partly to win her hand. After baring his soul to his prospective father-in-law, he wrote lightheartedly to his sceptical brother: 'I think I am entitled to count myself among the adherents of the Christian religion. Though in many doctrines, perhaps in those which they regard as

essential, I am far removed from their standpoint, yet a
sort of treaty of Passau has been silently established between us.[1] Besides, I like piety in women and have a horror
of feminine cleverness.' This letter, too, was a piece of
diplomacy, with its repudiation of their mother in the last
sentence. Yet there can be no doubt that, whatever re-
serves he might have for his brother, Bismarck's faith
became strong and sincere.

His religion was far removed from Christianity, or rather
from the humanitarian Christianity of the twentieth century. There was in it little love, except for his own family.
He believed in the God of the Old Testament and of the
English puritans, the God of battles. Luther or Oliver
Cromwell would have understood Bismarck's religion,
though it is less easily grasped by those for whom religion
is simply a high-flown form of liberalism. Bismarck certainly used war as an instrument of policy and exercised
secular power to the full. Anglo-Saxon sentimentalists are
therefore inclined to suggest that his religion was sham.
Yet the overwhelming majority of Christians have agreed
with Bismarck in both theory and practice for nearly two
thousand years. Lutheranism especially never claimed to
lay down moral principles for public policy. It taught that
service to the state and to the appointed ruler was a high
religious duty. Bismarck felt this himself: 'I believe that I
am obeying God when I serve the King.' His religion gave
to his unstable personality a settled purpose and a sense of
power. He said just after Sedan: 'You would not have had
such a Chancellor if I had not the wonderful basis of
religion.' He believed that he was doing God's work in
making Prussia strong and in unifying Germany. The belief
itself brought power. God was on his side; therefore he
could ignore the opposition of men. Like others who have
had this belief, he easily persuaded himself that whatever
suited him at the moment was God's purpose and, indeed,

[1] The treaty of Passau, made in 1552, first allowed Lutheranism and Roman
Catholicism to exist side-by-side in Germany. It symbolized a grudging and
resentful religious toleration.

that he understood this purpose a great deal better than did God Himself.

Marriage brought to Bismarck lasting and secure happiness. Unlike most men, Bismarck did not marry his mother, but her opposite—a simple, devoted woman, endlessly patient and ready to put up with anything. Under his rough exterior, he was deeply emotional, a man of the romantic movement. He had grown up just when the Byronic legend dominated the continent. He was the contemporary of Heine and Wagner. Like Gladstone, he was much given to tears at any public or private crisis; no doubt he too would have wept over *East Lynne*. He broke down sobbing after his first public speech and again after the battle of Sadova. He wept when he became Prime Minister and even more when he left office. William I and he often sobbed together, though Bismarck always got his way. Music affected him deeply, the more because he could neither play nor read it. And by music he meant a soft glow of feeling when the sonatas of Beethoven were played with more expression than accuracy. He agreed with his wife's verdict on Anton Rubinstein, the greatest pianist of the age: 'The playing was masterly both in control and attack and in everything you like, and yet "the heart, the heart remains homeless".' Johanna gave him a home for his heart, and it was very homely indeed. Though he played high drama on the public stage, his private setting resembled a Victorian boarding-house. Even in that tasteless age contemporaries commented on the banality of Bismarck's surroundings.

When Bismarck proposed marriage to Johanna von Puttkamer, he supposed that he was offering her a life in the country. But political activity called him even before the wedding, and the Bismarcks never knew uninterrupted country life until his retirement at the age of 75—and then much to his regret. Frederick William IV, who succeeded his father as King of Prussia in 1840, was far removed from the usual Hohenzollern stamp. He had an intellect above the average and a fine gift of phrase. Though he asserted his divine right, he strove also for popularity and dreamt of restoring the glories of an imaginary middle age, as described in the novels of Sir Walter Scott, when the King was surrounded by his loyal vassals. He thought to ward off a parliament by reviving the Estates of the Realm—estates which had never existed in Prussia and had long perished elsewhere. This would get round his father's promise of a constitution and, as a more practical point, allow him to raise a loan for a railway to the eastern provinces of Prussia. In 1847 he summoned the provincial estates to meet as a 'united diet' in Berlin. Bismarck had little prestige among his fellow Junkers, and they had not made him a member of his local diet, only a substitute in case any regular member fell ill. He did not receive the call to Berlin. But in May a regular member retired, and Bismarck took his place. Only the illness of Herr von Brauchitsch launched him into history. Bismarck said so himself in 1881: 'No one would ever have heard of me in my rural retreat, if I had not become a member of the united diet by chance.'

Bismarck had often expressed his dislike of the absolutist bureaucrat state; and he might have been expected to join with those who were demanding a modern constitution for Prussia. But those who demanded control over the public accounts and regular meetings of the diet were themselves bureaucrats. Indeed in a community without political experience, it would have been impossible to provide a quorum for the diet if state servants had been excluded from it. Thus, when Bismarck attacked the liberals he was attacking his old enemies. He was a true rebel, though for himself, not for others—always better at destructive criticism than at creation, and never willing to co-operate. Now he found himself, somewhat to his surprise, the champion of 'historic' Prussia, asserting what were in fact the very recent rights of the Crown and the nobility. He liked nothing better than to face a hostile assembly; and he got his wish in full measure.

Bismarck resisted every liberal proposal. He denounced the emancipation of the Jews and defended the game laws.

When a speaker argued that the Prussian people had
merited freedom by their services during the war of liberation in 1813, Bismarck answered: 'He had thought that the
oppression against which they fought then came from
abroad. Now he was taught that it was at home, and he was
not grateful for the lesson.' It did not need Bismarck to
bring the united diet to deadlock. The majority would not
authorize a railway loan without the guarantee of regular
meetings; and Frederick William IV would not make this
concession to liberalism. At the end of June the diet was
prorogued. Bismarck had made a name for himself in a
narrow reactionary circle. He had high Tory principles, yet
a gift of sharp expression that would have become a
Jacobin. Perhaps his gift was a little too striking; slow-
witted squires distrust cleverness even when it is displayed
on their side. With the diet out of the way, he was free to
marry and to go on honeymoon. He met Frederick William
IV at Venice and received the King's approval for his attitude at the diet. His future as a reactionary seemed secure.

But the old world of monarchy was coming to an end.
The continent of Europe had recovered from the exhaustion
of the Napoleonic wars. Everywhere men wanted to take up
the work of the French Revolution and to assert the ideals
of individual and national freedom. The year of revolution
was approaching. In January 1848, revolution stirred in
Italy. On 24 February, the French monarchy was overthrown and a republic established in Paris. The revolution
soon spread to Germany. A group of learned men called for
a German national parliament. On 13 March Metternich,
symbol of the old order, was overthrown in Vienna. Prussia
was more stable than Austria, its army strong enough to put
down any disorder. But Frederick William was not the
man for a stern conflict with the revolution. Street-fighting
in Berlin soon made him lose his nerve. On 18 March he
ordered the army to withdraw; announced that 'Prussia
merges into Germany'; and agreed to call a Prussian parliament. Bismarck's liberal enemies of 1847 had won. He himself was in the country when the revolution broke out. His

first thought was to rescue the king with the aid of his 'faithful peasants'. It was sentimental Jacobitism to suppose that untrained peasants could succeed where the army had failed. .

Bismarck hurried off to Potsdam and even entered Berlin, wearing a national cockade. He tried to persuade the commanding generals to stage a counter-revolution; but, as on many later occasions, the Prussian generals would not meddle in politics without an order from above. Each would act only if the other generals acted first. They were moved, but not to action, when Bismarck picked out the notes of a cavalry-charge on the piano. Finally, he managed to see the king for a few minutes. The queen lamented that the king had been unable to sleep for three nights from worry. Bismarck answered: 'A King *must* be able to sleep.'[1] In desperation he planned a reactionary stroke. Frederick William was childless; his brother William, Prince of Prussia, had gone into exile in England. Bismarck sought out Augusta, William's wife, and proposed that Frederick William should be pushed aside; William should renounce his rights; and their young son should be put on the throne as the figurehead of reaction. A similar manœuvre made Francis Joseph Emperor of Austria in December. In March it was too early; and Augusta in any case too loyal both to her husband and to her brother-in-law. She rejected the idea indignantly and harboured a lasting resentment against Bismarck which was to hamper him throughout his career.[2]

There seemed nothing to be done. Liberalism was in the ascendant. A German national assembly and a Prussian parliament were elected, both by universal suffrage; and the electors did not choose Bismarck for either. As a gesture

[1] But did he really say it? In the first draft of his recollections, the remark appears as: 'A King *must* not sleep.' Perhaps the whole dialogue only occurred to him some forty years later.

[2] Here again Bismarck improved on reality when he came to write his recollections. According to him, Augusta proposed putting her son on the throne with herself as Regent; and he loyally defeated the proposal. But the contemporary record is against him.

of defiance against the revolution, he began to sign himself *von* Bismarck for the first time. This was his only concrete achievement during the revolutionary year. Throughout the summer he drifted round Berlin, attempting to organize the Prussian conservatives and engaging in futile court intrigue. In the autumn Frederick William plucked up courage. He ordered the army to reoccupy Berlin and dissolved the radical parliament. But he did not intend to restore absolutism. He issued a constitution which provided for a parliament with more restricted powers; the electorate was also limited, and the elections were made indirect—the primary electors did not choose their representative, but only an electoral committee. This gave Bismarck his chance. He was elected to the new parliament by 152 votes of the committee against 144. He was still hostile to Frederick William's attempts at compromise. Later on, he claimed to have acted as a secret adviser in forming the conservative ministry. The king's real opinion of him was expressed in the comment; 'red reactionary, smells of blood, only to be used when the bayonet rules.'

Frederick William kept up an appearance of liberalism in the hope of leading the movement for German unity. He was always a German nationalist, though he learnt his nationalism from the romantic movement and not from the French Revolution. Here, too, Bismarck was hostile. He was, he said, 'a decided opponent of the German swindle in every form' and believed only in 'the specifically Prussian'. He denounced the attempt 'to force on Prussia the role which Sardinia had played in Italy'. Instead he wanted a conflict between 'authority by the grace of God' and 'revolution and popular sovereignty'. Frederick William hoped to reconcile the two. While the revolution was at its height, the national assembly at Frankfurt had tried to create a united German state which would include also the German provinces of Austria. At the end of 1848 reaction triumphed in Vienna; and Felix Schwarzenberg, the Austrian prime minister, would have nothing to do with German nationalism. The Frankfurt assembly had to accept a 'lesser Germany' without Austria, whether they would or not; and in April 1849 they offered the Imperial throne to Frederick William IV. The Prussians jumped at this chance of aggrandisement, even with its liberal coating. On 2 April the members of the Prussian parliament appealed to Frederick William IV to accept the Imperial crown; even Bismarck put his name to the letter. But Frederick William stuck to his monarchist principles. He would accept the crown, he replied, only if it were offered to him by the German princes. Bismarck hastily trimmed his sails. He, too, denounced the Frankfurt assembly. Though he admitted that everyone who spoke German, including himself, wanted the unification of Germany, 'yet with this constitution I do *not* want it.'

He did not need to worry. Frederick William's refusal of the Imperial crown ended the Frankfurt national assembly. The moderate liberals, who were in the majority, went home in despair. The radical rump tried to put the imperial constitution into effect without either an army or an emperor. The Austrian forces were still fully engaged against the revolutions in Hungary and Italy. All the German princes clustered under Prussia for protection. The radicals had once planned to capture the Prussian army. Now this army turned them out of Frankfurt and suppressed the risings in Saxony and Baden. There was, in a sense, a Prussian conquest of Germany, but it was a conquest achieved against those who believed in German unification. Frederick William and his intimate adviser, Radowitz, tried to turn the situation to some account. The German princes were dependent on Prussian protection; therefore they could be induced to 'consent' to Prussia's leadership of Germany, yet—with the defeat of the radicals —this could be presented as a respectable, even a conservative, programme. The princes had no choice so long as Austria was without weight in Germany; and Radowitz badgered them into setting up the Erfurt Union, a 'lesser Germany' with a parliament, elected on a limited suffrage, and its armed forces under Prussian control. This was al-

most exactly the Germany which Bismarck created twenty
years later. But at the time he could not denounce it
enough. 'We are Prussians and want to remain Prussian.'
Instead of challenging Austria, they should return to the
system of Metternich—'the agreement of Austria and
Prussia to control the whole of Germany.' Another saying
of his in the Prussian parliament was to read oddly later.
Opposing civil marriage, he declared: 'I hope to see the ship
of fools of the age wrecked on the rock of the Christian
church.' He was always ready to challenge the liberal
politicians with some provocative phrase. Yet in 1849 he
took a step on the road to professional politics and away
from a quiet Junker life. He farmed out the lands at Schönhausen which had come to him on the death of his father
in 1845 and rented a house in Berlin.

The parliament of the Erfurt Union actually met in
April 1850. The liberals from the Frankfurt assembly were
in the majority and Bismarck protested against everything
as usual. But the struggle for mastery in Germany had still
to be fought. The Austrian empire had recovered its
strength. Italy and Hungary were subdued, and despotic
Austria enjoyed the favour of the tsar. Schwarzenberg was
determined to reassert Austria's pre-eminence in Germany.
He revived the diet of the old confederation which had
fallen into oblivion at the beginning of the revolution, and
looked round for a conflict. He soon found one. The Elector
of Hesse, once a member of the Erfurt Union, was at odds
with his subjects. He appealed to the confederation to
restore order, and the diet authorized Austrian and
Bavarian troops to intervene. This was a vital challenge to
Prussia. For, apart from the question of the Union, the
Prussian military road which joined the Rhineland to
Brandenburg ran through Hesse. Frederick William was at
first all for resistance. Radowitz was made foreign minister,
and preparations were made to mobilize the Prussian army.
Shots were exchanged between Austrian and Prussian
soldiers for the first time since 1778. The king's conserva-
tive advisers soon revolted. They shrank from a war in

which they would have to call on revolutionary France and even on Sardinia against the two legitimist Powers, Austria and Russia. The minister of war discovered that the army was not prepared for war; and Bismarck, 'as a lieutenant of the reserve', felt it his duty not 'to raise his voice against a general'. Radowitz resigned; and his successor, Manteuffel, met Schwarzenberg at Olomouc (Olmütz). He agreed to disband the Erfurt Union and to join in restoring the old confederation.

The course of Prussian aggrandisement was temporarily arrested. Even the most conservative felt the 'shame' of Olomouc. When Manteuffel came to defend it in parliament, he said ruefully: 'The efforts of Prussia have not been crowned with success. . . . There is always something sad in the failure of a policy.' Bismarck had no such regrets. He alone defended the settlement of Olomouc without reserve. He repudiated the notion that Prussia 'should play the Don Quixote for offended parliamentary celebrities'. The Erfurt Union would not have united Germany. It 'would have made us shoot and kill our German fellow-countrymen in the South', and he praised Austria as 'a German power which had the good fortune to rule over foreign races'. Bismarck regarded Olomouc as a decisive defeat for the revolution of 1848. Liberal dreams of German unity had been shattered, and the conservative system of Metternich had been restored. Historic right had triumphed over national freedom. Yet at heart Bismarck had no sympathy with this outlook. When one of his conservative friends said that Austria had right on her side, he answered: 'I don't recognize any right in foreign policy.' And he said in his parliamentary speech: 'The only healthy foundation for a great state is egoism, not romanticism, and it is unworthy of a great state to dispute over something which does not concern its own interest.'

There was no doubt a case to be made against Radowitz and the policy of the Erfurt Union. Prussia lacked allies; the tsar would perhaps have supported Austria; the German liberals were strong only in words; the Prussian army

was inadequate.[1] Yet, reviewing Bismarck's arguments, it
is difficult to resist the impression that the policy of uniting
the lesser Germany without Austria had one overriding
fault in his eyes: it was being conducted by Radowitz,
instead of by Bismarck. He declared in words worthy of
John Bright:[2]

> 'Woe to the statesman, who at this time does not seek
> a cause for war which will still be valid after the war. . . .
> Will you have the courage then to go to the peasant in
> the ashes of his cottage, to the cripple, to the childless
> father, and to say: "You have suffered much, but rejoice
> with us, the constitution of the Union is saved!" '

Powerful rhetoric! But could not a critic have said the
same of the wars which Bismarck conducted in 1866 and
1870? Yet Bismarck was not insincere. Like many great
men before they find their vocation, he specialized in
denunciation and harsh invective. The elder Pitt confessed
late in life the injustice of the attacks on Walpole by which
he made his name; Mussolini, who opposed the Italian conquest of Libya in 1911, himself conquered Abyssinia in
1935; Lloyd George, the pro-Boer of one war, was 'the man
who won the war' of the next; and Stalin rejoiced in 1945 at
having revenged the tsar's defeat in what he had once
called the 'criminal' Russo-Japanese war. Men see things
very differently when they are themselves in power.

[1] This opinion was not held by all good judges. The Prussian minister of
war opposed the war on principle and therefore found technical arguments
against it, as soldiers can always do. But Prince William, who was somewhat
of an authority, believed that the army could defeat Austria; and the Russian
general Paskievich, who had seen the Austrian army in action in Hungary,
thought that Prussia could take on both Austria and such Russian forces as
could be spared for a war in Germany.

[2] The parallel is closer than either man would have liked. During the
Crimean war, Bright denounced the quixotic idea of Lord John Russell that
Great Britain should defend the liberties of Germany: 'What a notion a
man must have of the duties . . . of the people living in these islands if he thinks
. . . that the sacred treasure of the bravery, resolution, and unfaltering courage
of the people of England is to be squandered in a contest . . . for the preserva-
tion of the independence of Germany, and of the integrity, civilization, and
something else, of all Europe.'

It did not yet occur to Bismarck that he would ever attain power. After Olomouc he remained the provocative and irresponsible critic. His last words in parliament as a private member were thoroughly in character: 'Be sure, gentlemen, that we shall know how to make the name of Junkerdom honoured and respected.' When parliament adjourned, he puzzled for some means of adding to his income, in order to support his growing family—a son and a daughter, with another son born in 1852. He even thought of returning to the state-service which he had given up so emphatically twelve years before. Opportunity came unexpectedly. With the restoration of the German confederation, Prussia needed a delegate to the federal diet at Frankfurt. It would be a thankless task to acknowledge in daily practice the Austrian supremacy which had been recognized at Olomouc. Who so suitable as Bismarck, the one Prussian who apparently had a genuine belief in co-operation with Austria? He had had only six months' experience of administration and none of diplomacy. In all the history of the Prussian monarchy he was the only man ever appointed to a high diplomatic post without previous service. However, his training might be enough to handle the economic questions, which were the only important German issues for the men in Berlin. If he failed, no one would be the worse for it. Bismarck was not alarmed. 'I shall do my duty. It is God's affair to give me understanding.' For once he could say with truth: 'I have not sought it, the Lord wished it', though the Lord's name was invoked primarily for its effect on his wife. She would have liked him to give up all public affairs and settle down in the country. He, without knowing it, had turned his back on a quiet life for good and all. He was to serve Prussia, Germany, and God without interruption for more than thirty-nine years. In other words, his feet were at last on the ladder of power. He was 36.

THE DIPLOMAT

WITH the meeting of the federal diet at Frankfurt, the old order in Germany seemed to have been restored unchanged. This was far from being the case. Though the great revolution had blown over, the men who ruled in Vienna and Berlin had been shaped by their experiences in it. Frederick William IV went on dreaming of some impossible stroke by which he could make Prussia dominant in Germany with Austrian consent. Though he would never go against Austria, he would also never accept subordination to her. Manteuffel, the foreign minister, knew nothing of foreign affairs. He was an old-style civil servant, who had been pushed into the office on the sudden death of Brandenburg in November 1850, and he had no plan of foreign policy. All he wanted was to keep out of difficulties; but he, too, had a sturdy Prussian pride and would not accept Austrian orders.

There was a greater change on the Austrian side. Her rulers had acquired new confidence from their victories in Hungary and Italy. They despised Metternich's gentle methods and thought that rudeness was the best diplomatic method. Schwarzenberg, who directed Austrian policy until his sudden death in 1852, planned to include the entire Habsburg monarchy in the German confederation; and a conference to achieve this was held at Dresden early in 1851. But the smaller states, who had welcomed Austrian support against Prussian encroachment, were equally opposed to Austrian control and voted solidly against her plans. The confederation had to be carried on unchanged. The federal diet had seventeen members—the larger states one each, the smaller lumped together with five delegates.[1]

---

[1] The *plenum* of all thirty-nine states met only to approve changes of the federal constitution—and none was ever made.

Previously Metternich had run the diet in partnership with Prussia and arranged the business, such as it was, with her delegate beforehand. Now the Austrians asserted their presidential position and planned to control Prussia with the votes of the smaller states. In any international organization it is easy to forget in peacetime the realities of power; and, since Prussia had only one vote, the Austrians assumed that she was on the same level as Bavaria or even Schaumburg-Lippe.

Bismarck, perhaps, went to Frankfurt with the sincere intention of co-operating with Austria. For him, at any rate, the perils and humiliations of the revolutionary year were not forgotten. More probably, he had not thought about his future policy. He always lived in the moment and responded to its challenge. In the Prussian parliament the liberals had been his enemy; and he answered them by preaching co-operation with Austria. Now, at Frankfurt, his opponent was the Austrian delegate; and he reacted at once without thought for consistency. He did not weigh Prussia's strength or her position in Europe. He saw only his immediate opponent and wanted Prussian policy to be subordinated to his own needs. He was always quick to take offence personally; and Austria's airs as 'the presiding power' were enough to offend a less sensitive man. The Austrian delegate arranged the business and often settled matters without consulting his colleagues. Bismarck insisted, like the Russians at the United Nations, on knowing every detail.

A trivial gesture announced the coming struggle for mastery in Germany. Only the Austrian delegate smoked at meetings. Bismarck pulled out a cigar and asked the Austrian for a match. His act showed that he was a man of a new sort. Previous Prussian delegates had been high aristocrats and, like all the men of the old order, non-smokers. Only Austrian aristocrats smoked—a habit they acquired when they inherited the tobacco-monopoly from Napoleon in Lombardy. Bismarck had learnt to smoke from the radical students whom he otherwise despised; and

his cigar was a reminder that he really belonged to the world
of the *Burschenshaft* despite his affectation of sympathy
with the principles of Metternich. The conflict was repeated
in every conversation. Thun, the Austrian, sneered at 'the
legacy of Frederick the Great' and compared Prussia to a
man who, having once won a prize in a lottery, based his
annual budget on it. Bismarck replied: 'If that is what they
think in Vienna, Prussia will have to speculate in the said
lottery again.'

The Austrians did not take Bismarck's complaints
seriously, nor admit that their policy had changed. They
perhaps behaved with more arrogance than in the days of
Metternich; but they had always behaved with much.
Even Metternich did not really regard Prussia as Austria's
equal. He flattered her because flattery was his way; but he
thought of Austria as the only Great Power in Germany.
Bismarck unconsciously confessed that the change origi-
nated in himself, not in the Austrians. He wrote in February
1852: 'Since the month of September of last year, Austria
has abandoned the ground on which we used to meet.' But
nothing had happened in September 1851 so far as Austria
was concerned. The only significance of the date was that
Bismarck then received official confirmation of his appointment as Prussian representative. Once more he changed his
policy simply because of his personal feelings. He had advocated co-operation with Austria when he was attacking
Radowitz. He swung over to Radowitz's programme of a
lesser Germany when he felt that the Austrian representative was not treating him as a social equal; and this
personal resentment was at once translated into high-flown
political terms. 'I conceived the idea of withdrawing Germany from Austrian control, at least that part of Germany
united by its spirit, its religion, its character and its
interests to the destinies of Prussia—northern Germany.'
He made no pretence as yet that this was what the Germans
wanted. He admitted frankly that 'the best thing for the
confederation would undoubtedly be to put ourselves and
all German governments under Austria militarily, politi-

cally and economically'; but 'advantage for the confederation cannot be the guiding-line of Prussian policy'. His aim, in fact, was to divide Germany with Austria, not to unite it.

The conflict on which he set out could not be settled by votes at the Frankfurt diet. The smaller states, with no real strength of their own, went with Prussia against any Austrian attempt to unify Germany; they swung round just as much to the Austrian side if Prussia made any positive proposals. Bismarck wrote to Berlin: 'Only outside Germany can we find the means to strengthen our position in the interest of Germany itself.' He had no faith in public opinion or in liberal support. Foreign alliances, not an appeal to German feeling, would solve the German question. Hence Bismarck concentrated on European diplomacy, not on the intricacies of federal politics. His guiding principle was the aggrandisement of Prussia 'according to the principles of Frederick the Great'; and he acknowledged loyalty neither to legitimacy nor to German nationalism. He never acted as a traditional ambassador, carrying out the instructions of his government. Soon after going to Frankfurt he wrote with becoming modesty: 'the river of history flows as it will, and if I put my hand in it, this is because I regard it as my duty, not because I think I can change its course.' In reality he soon set out to devise the policy which his government ought to follow. After all, he had no experience of the diplomatic service until he stepped into the highest rank; and he never troubled to learn the trade. His notes of conversations with others were unsatisfactory all his life on a technical standard—invaluable for revealing the current of Bismarck's own thought, unreliable as a record of the other man's point of view.

His reports from Frankfurt carried this to extremes. He never troubled to report what was going on there or what the other representatives said. His sole concern was advocacy. He preached to Frederick William IV and to Manteuffel the policy which seemed to him right and criticized them when they rejected it. A Prussian diplomat who behaved like this when Bismarck was in power would soon have run into trouble. Soon after becoming prime minister of Prussia, he wrote to Goltz in Paris: 'Policy can only be made once, and it must be that on which the ministry and the king are agreed.' This was not at all his line when at Frankfurt; and it earned him no rebuke. Frederick William liked contradictory advice. Manteuffel preached timid inaction; Gerlach, his unofficial adviser, upheld legitimism and a struggle against the revolution; Bismarck wanted conflict with Austria; and Bunsen, the King's closest friend, advocated from London a 'liberal' alliance with Great Britain. Frederick William dodged among them all, appreciating their ideas without following them. He commented on one of Bismarck's reports: 'a masterpiece of its kind', though he did not accept its proposals. Bismarck, while ostensibly loyal, was driven to exasperation by his elusive master; and, when written argument failed, would hurry to Berlin in the hope that personal persuasion might succeed. In his own words, he went from Frankfurt to Berlin like the pendulum of a clock—an early instance of the changes brought to diplomacy by the railway train. But, unfortunately for Bismarck, not all his efforts could make the clock strike.

Bismarck scored an early success against Austria— negative, but decisive. The great Prussian advance of 'the quiet years' had been the building of a German customsunion, the *Zollverein*. This included nearly all the German states except Austria; and it inevitably turned German trade from the Danube valley to the ports of the North Sea. Metternich had foreseen the political weakening of Austria that must follow; but he could do nothing so long as the Austrian empire was itself divided by a separate tariffbarrier with Hungary. This barrier was swept away in 1850 after the revolution; and the Austrian government now asked to be included in the *Zollverein*. The demand was justified if the policy of Olomouc had any real meaning. Bismarck took the lead against it. He went on a special mission to Vienna, gave the Austrians many soft words, but held out on the essential point. It was fortunate for him that Schwarzenberg died suddenly just when the negotiations began. Buol, the new Austrian foreign minister, had less grasp of affairs; 'sharp, but neither broad nor deep', was Metternich's description of him. Austria was bought off with a post-dated cheque. The *Zollverein* was maintained unchanged, but the inclusion of Austria was to be considered again when it next came up for renewal in 1863. By then Bismarck had the decision in his own hands. He did not appreciate the full importance of the decision at the time, nor perhaps even later. He considered the German question in political and, to some extent, in military terms. Yet the economic division was the greatest of all. Germany of the *Zollverein*, which was later Bismarck's Reich, became an economic power of the first order as the coalmines of the Ruhr expanded; Austria remained relatively backward. Two Germanies would have come into existence, even if Bismarck had never been born—though their political character might have been different.

Bismarck at Frankfurt was absorbed in 'grand policy', not in economic questions. He recognized that he was on the way to becoming a professional diplomat and in 1852 did not seek re-election to the Lower Chamber. Though he was given a seat in the Upper House, he never spoke there. Indeed, he never spoke again in the Prussian parliament except from the bench of ministers. It was a grave handicap to him later that he had experience of parliament only as a factious critic and none of working with a political group. At Frankfurt, too, he fought very much for his own hand. There was not much sense in his endless petty quarrels with the Austrian delegate so long as Prussia and Austria were forced together by the international situation. European politics seemed to have reverted to a fixed system after the upheavals of 1848. On the one side was revolutionary France, now under Napoleon III; on the other the conservative alliance of Russia, Austria, and Prussia, 'the three Northern courts'. This conservative union had forced Prussia to accept the agreement of Olomouc, and she had no freedom of movement so long as Russia and Austria held together.

In 1853 this rigidity was dissolved. A conflict started in the Near East, first between Russia and France, soon between Russia and the two western Powers, France and England. The tsar assumed that Austria and Prussia would support him unquestioningly for the sake of 'the Holy Alliance'. Both failed him. Austria wished to maintain the integrity of the Ottoman empire and to keep the mouth of the Danube out of Russian hands; indeed, she wanted Russia to be defeated, though without bearing the risks or the blame herself. Prussia, alone of the Powers, had no stake in the Near East. She was concerned neither to defend Russian claims in the Near East nor to thwart them. The Holy Alliance had been all very well so long as it implied Russian aid to Prussia against a possible French threat on the Rhine. It became a danger if it made Prussia face a war against the western Powers for the sake of Russian interests in the Near East. When the Crimean war broke out early in 1854, Russia found herself alone. The Holy Alliance was dissolved.

Frederick William was at the centre of a turmoil which he much enjoyed. Gerlach urged him to fight on the side of Russia; Bunsen on that of the western Powers; Manteuffel sought security by making an alliance with Austria. Bismarck rejected all three lines. He wanted Prussia to remain in isolation and to profit from it. 'Let us frighten Austria by threatening an alliance with Russia, and frighten Russia by letting her think that we may join the western Powers.' With his mind concentrated on the disputes at Frankfurt, he was fiercely opposed to alliance with Austria. He wrote in February 1854: 'I should be alarmed if we sought protection from the approaching storm by tying our neat seaworthy frigate to Austria's worm-eaten old battleship.' He urged Frederick William to mobilize 200,000 men in Silesia, ostensibly as a threat against Russia; then he should demand from Austria the headship of Germany, and neither she nor the other Powers, fully engaged in the Near East, could withstand him. Frederick William replied: 'A man like Napoleon could pull off this sort of stroke, but not me.' On 20 April 1854—three weeks after the outbreak of war—Prussia concluded a defensive alliance with Austria for three years.

Bismarck was in high agitation. He believed that the subtle politicians of Vienna had taken Frederick William prisoner. But the outcome was not very different from what Bismarck had wanted. Frederick William would not join either side in the war, and he calculated rightly that Austria, too, would be more reluctant to enter the war if she had the Prussian alliance behind her. The Crimean war would have led to a gigantic European upheaval if the two Germanic Powers had fought on either side. As it was, their neutrality prevented any real decision. The Crimean war was localized and had to be fought in a detached peninsula of the Russian empire. The Austrians regretted this limited outcome. Time and again they tried to pull Prussia into war; time and again Prussia pulled them back into neutrality. In December 1854 Austria made an alliance with the western Powers, by which she promised to impose peace terms on Russia. She followed this up by trying to involve all the states of the German confederation in her troubles. The diet was asked to mobilize the federal forces in defence of Austria. The lesser states disliked this threatened burden; and Bismarck had an easy time persuading them to remain neutral. This was certainly a score for Prussia, but one without novelty. It had been shown often enough that the smaller states would always vote with whichever of the great Powers wanted to do nothing.

At the end of 1855 Austria was driven into action by pressure from the western Powers. She sent an ultimatum to Russia, threatening to enter the war if Russia did not agree to the allied peace-terms. Russia was exhausted and gave way. A Congress met at Paris, and Prussia who had remained neutral was at first excluded. She entered the Congress only when the rule of the Straits was discussed, and the treaty of London of 1841, to which she was a signatory, had to be revised. This seemed a humiliating outcome. Prussia had been treated almost as though she were not a great Power. This appearance was deceptive. Russia was grateful for Prussia's neutrality, which had given her security in Poland; the western Powers soon forgot their resentment. On the other hand, Russia would not forgive the threats from Austria; while the western Powers blamed her for not fighting on their side. Frederick William and Manteuffel had, in fact, followed the policy of neutrality which Bismarck himself had advocated. He could have taken no different line if he had been in office. Only his later successes enabled him to establish the myth of Manteuffel's timidity and Frederick William's blunders.

In April 1856, when the war was over, Bismarck reviewed the European situation, seeking—though in vain—to dictate policy to the men in Berlin. The German confederation, he insisted, had broken down. Austria and Prussia were rivals. 'Germany is too small for us both.' Prussia must therefore look outside Germany for allies; and it would not be difficult to find them. Tsar Alexander II was anxious to overthrow the peace settlement that had just been made at Paris; Napoleon III was even more resolved to destroy the settlement of 1815. Though they had recently been enemies, the two emperors would soon come together in a revisionist alliance; and Prussia should make a third in the partnership. Alliance with Russia did not shock Frederick William IV's legitimist principles. Alliance with Napoleon seemed to him mortal sin. Bismarck attacked the idea of basing foreign policy on principle in letter after letter. 'My ideal for foreign policy is freedom from prejudice, the independence of our decisions from impressions of dislike or affection for foreign states and their governments.' He jeered at the doctrine of resisting the revolution. All states had a revolutionary origin. The Habsburg monarchy itself was built on conquest. Even the German princes 'cannot find any completely legitimate origin for the ground which they have won partly from the

Emperor and the Empire, partly from their fellow-princes, partly from the Estates.' Again, with characteristic ruthlessness: 'We cannot make an alliance with France without a certain degree of meanness, but in the Middle Ages very admirable people—even German princes—used a drain to make their escape, rather than be beaten or strangled.'

It would be rash to conclude from these arguments that Bismarck had no principles or that he had abandoned the' cause of conservatism. He always concentrated on the task in hand, and when he was following a trail would reject every scent that led away from it. Conflict with Austria was the only thing that mattered to him during his years at Frankfurt; and he judged all international affairs from this angle. Besides, his argument was founded on fact. The 'legitimism' which Austria preached was fraudulent. The Austrians had no objection to an alliance with France so long as this worked against Russia in the Near East, not against themselves in Italy; and they insisted on conservative principles only to ensure that Prussia should trail in their wake. The Russians did much the same. In August 1857 the Tsar Alexander II met Napoleon at Stuttgart with every mark of intimacy. The whole world talked of 'the Franco-Russian entente'. Why should Prussia alone be fooled by principles which others did not practise?

Moreover, Bismarck had grown up when Prussia was the least of the great Powers; the memories of the Napoleonic wars always at the back of his mind. He underrated Prussian strength and overrated that of others. He knew nothing of the industrial revolution in the Ruhr which would in time make Germany economically dominant on the continent. It never occurred to him that the aggrandisement of Prussia or the unification of Germany might come naturally by force of economic circumstances. Rather he expected a new partition of Prussia—such as Napoleon I carried through in 1807—to be the most likely outcome if things were left to drift. He did not suppose in these years that Prussia could defeat Austria unaided. What he

counted on was a war of Russia and France against Austria
in which Prussia would make easy gains. Prussia had
nothing to lose by such a war. It would not matter to her
if Russia controlled the Straits and the mouth of the
Danube. In 1857 Bismarck visited Paris and discovered
Napoleon's aims. Napoleon had little interest in expansion
on the Rhine. He wanted to expel Austria from Italy and
to make the Mediterranean a French lake 'or very nearly'.
These ambitions, too, did not conflict with Prussia's interests, however much they might injure Austria or Great
Britain. On the contrary, Napoleon was prepared to offer
Hanover and Sleswig-Holstein to Prussia in return for her
neutrality. It was a reasonable speculation that Prussia
could achieve the mastery of northern Germany as reward
for assisting a Franco-Russian revision of the map of
Europe, or perhaps even for tolerating it.

The two emperors, Alexander and Napoleon, seemed to
dominate Europe already, despite the Crimean war. Bismarck thought that he was going with the tide. But in
1858 the tide turned against him so far as Prussia was concerned. Frederick William had always listened fascinated
to Bismarck's ideas and, with his incurably speculative
mind, might ultimately have been won for them. In 1858 he
fell hopelessly insane, and his brother William became
regent. William was a simpler and less intelligent man than
his brother, with some understanding only in military
matters. Frederick William once said: 'If we had been born
as sons of a petty official, I should have become an architect,
William an N.C.O.'[1] Though reputed a reactionary in 1848,
William had none of his brother's high-flown conservatism.
In 1854 he had wished to go to war with Russia on the side
of the western Powers. Now he thought it his duty, as a
good German, to co-operate with Austria, especially in the
defence of her lands in Italy. At home, he intended to give
Prussia a more liberal government and so to make her more
popular in Germany; he planned a policy of 'moral con-

[1] Of the other two brothers: 'Charles would have gone to prison, Albrecht
become a drunkard.'

quests'. He dismissed Manteuffel and opened 'the new era' by appointing a liberal ministry.

Bismarck's career seemed to be ended. He could not work with Austria at Frankfurt. He was equally unwilling to return to Berlin as a liberal minister. William regarded him as a wild reactionary. Augusta, the regent's wife, had a deep-seated hostility to him and, at this time, held her husband firmly against him. Schleinitz, the new foreign minister, had been nominated by Augusta and shared her outlook. Still, Bismarck could not be turned loose. He was consoled early in 1859 by being made Prussian minister to St. Petersburg. His final gesture of contempt was to leave the Diet without the customary formalities of farewell. On his way through Berlin, he said to a liberal politician: 'The only reliable ally for Prussia is—the German people.'

St. Petersburg was poor consolation for Frankfurt. At Frankfurt Bismarck had been fighting a diplomatic campaign against Austria, not unsuccessfully; and he had always had the illusory hope that one day his arguments would impress Frederick William. Moreover, he had enjoyed the life. Frankfurt was the nearest thing to an international capital that Germany possessed; and Bismarck liked clever company whatever his Junker affectations. He had always been exuberantly well, despite his energetic way of living. He smoked Havana cigars from morning to night; drank much 'Black Velvet'—the mixture of stout and champagne which he invented; rode in the woods and swam in the Rhine; wrote endless reports. Yet never a day's sickness. At St. Petersburg he was, in his own words, 'put on ice'. There was, as yet, no through railway, and the journey to Berlin took five days. He could no longer argue with the regent and the ministers in person, and he was removed from events while they pursued a 'German' policy of supporting Austria. He tried to console himself by reflecting on the triviality of all human affairs. 'Peoples and men, folly and wisdom, war and peace, come and go like waves and the sea remains. Our states and their power and honour are nothing to God but ant-heaps and beehives,

which are trampled by an ox's hoof or snatched by fate in
the shape of a honey-gatherer.' These reflections did not
restore his peace of mind. He fell desperately ill of a nervous
complaint, sure sign of strain and frustration that was often
to be repeated. Characteristically, he attributed his illness
to poison from an incompetent doctor, whom he imagined
to be in Austrian pay; and he refused to convalesce at Carls-
bad for fear of further Austrian tricks. He disliked the
damp gloom of St. Petersburg, particularly as the Prussian
minister was more poorly paid than other diplomatic representatives and could not hold his own with the Russian
aristocracy. Bismarck always worried about his private
finances, and never more than at St. Petersburg.

Yet curiously enough the years there did not turn him
into an enemy of Russia. This was a unique exception.
The Frankfurt diet had made him hate Austria and despise
the smaller states. A fortnight in Paris was enough to produce revulsion against 'the modern Babylon'; and he never
developed any affection for Napoleon III, despite their
intimacy. He said himself that England was the only foreign
country for which he cared, but this was romantic humbug,
an imaginary longing for the 'old England' of roast beef and
Burke's classical constitution. Bismarck regarded the contemporary British statesmen with special hostility. Yet
Russian arrogance did not offend him. He was flattered by
attentions from the imperial family, and at this time even
got on well with Gorchakov, the foreign minister. He learnt
Russian and grew so fond of it that he used it to record his
most private thoughts. He even claimed to like the Russian
people. Perhaps there was some deep psychological link.
The Russians, despite their emotional instability, present to
the outer world a stolid resolution, which may be peculiarly
satisfying to neurotic Germans. Or perhaps it was simply a
political calculation. Bismarck regarded the Polish lands as
essential to Prussian power and knew that they were secure
only so long as Prussia and Russia were on good terms. At
any rate, the fact is inescapable. St. Petersburg was the
only capital which Bismarck left without hating it and

without resolving to be revenged for his humiliations. He made a good impression on his side. Alexander II, even offered him a high post in the Russian diplomatic service. Accepting this offer would have had curious historical results.

Circumstances made it easy for Bismarck to like Russia, and to be liked. He never had to dispute with the Russian government; he was too busy disputing with his own. Relations between Prussia and Austria reached a crisis just when Bismarck went to St. Petersburg. In January 1859 France and Sardinia made a secret alliance to liberate northern Italy from Austrian rule. In April Austria was provoked into launching war against them. German feeling was deeply disturbed. All the traditions of German nationalism were bound up with the war of liberation against Napoleon; and many Germans drew an analogy between the present war and the Italian campaigns of Bonaparte which had paved the way for his conquest of Germany. The regent William had himself fought as a boy in 1813 and thought that those great days had come again. Even Moltke, chief of the Prussian general staff, wrote: 'The next French step will be against Prussia, just as the campaign of 1806 followed that of 1805.' Prussia, it seemed, must go to the aid of Austria if she were to remain popular in Germany; and those Prussians who were indifferent to German opinion advocated the same course for reasons of self-preservation.

Only Bismarck opposed this course. He wanted to seize supremacy in northern Germany, while Austria was busy in Italy. He wrote on 5 May: 'The great chance has come for us again, if we let Austria get embedded in war with France and then march south, setting up the Prussian frontier-posts either on Lake Constance or where Protestantism ceases to predominate.' And a week later: 'I regard our connexion with the German confederation as an illness of Prussia, which will have to be cured sooner or later *ferro et igni*, unless we take treatment for it at a favourable opportunity.' No one in Berlin took any notice of him. He was

the only important Prussian diplomat who was not recalled to Berlin for advice on the critical situation. The
army was mobilized and the Prussian government proposed
to 'mediate' between the two sides, as a preliminary to supporting Austria. Instead, Bismarck's policy triumphed,
though not from his exertions. The regent William demanded a reward from Austria for his support: Prussia
must be given supreme command over all the German
forces north of the Main. There was not much sense in this
condition from a military point of view. The forces of the
little German states were not worth quarrelling over. But
it had profound political significance. It implied equality
between Prussia and Austria and therewith the partition
of Germany between them—a return to the policy of the
Erfurt Union, which had been discarded at Olomouc.
Francis Joseph, the emperor of Austria, would not pay this
price, even to keep his lands in Italy. In July he made a
hasty peace with Napoleon III and surrendered Lombardy.

Prussia had made the worst of both policies: she had
neither exploited Austria's difficulties nor made 'moral
conquests' by supporting her. The prince regent would not
admit this. He went on striving for partnership with Austria
against France, but always attached the military supremacy over northern Germany as a condition. In July 1860
things got so far that a defensive alliance between Prussia
and Austria was actually drafted. But negotiations broke
down in April 1861 when it came to a military convention.
Yet still neither side realized that conflict was the inevitable
alternative to alliance. Neither understood that the other
was serious in its attitude; and this lack of understanding
went on until the very outbreak of war in 1866. The Prussians, including even Bismarck, could not believe that
Austria would let things come to a war and would risk her
vital interests in Italy and the Near East rather than
concede to Prussia command over the trivial forces of north
Germany—a command which she did not aspire to exercise
herself and which was of no benefit to anyone. Similarly,
the Austrians could not believe that Prussia would refuse

to see the danger from France and would go to war for the sake of this military triviality. The issue was certainly unreal. Austria would have agreed to it at any time if it had not carried with it the implication of her equality with Prussia. But, of course, the Prussians would not have made the demand unless it had carried this implication, however unspoken.

The prince regent was certainly still unconscious of this challenge. Bismarck paraded himself as an enemy of Austria. This ruled him out as a minister in the regent's eyes. But William was driven towards Bismarck for reasons of domestic policy. With his military training and experience, he was anxious to reform the Prussian army, which Frederick William IV had neglected. The population of Prussia had almost doubled since 1815; the annual intake of 40,000 recruits had remained unchanged. By 1859 23,000 young men were escaping military service each year. William and Roon, his minister of war, proposed to increase the number of regiments and the barracks provided for them, so that every Prussian should receive his three years of military training. There was no conflict with the Prussian parliament about this. The Prussian liberals admired the tradition of Scharnhorst and Gneisenau, and regarded universal military service as an enlightened measure. The dispute between William and the parliament was quite other. It had been an essential part of the Scharnhorst system that every Prussian citizen should pass, after three years' active service and two in the reserve, into the *Landwehr*—a sort of territorial army with its own units and its own officers, most of them not drawn from the nobility. The *Landwehr* was a symbol of democratic nationalism. Roon despised it. It was, he said, 'all wrong as a military institution, because it lacked the genuine soldierly spirit and had no firm discipline.' Moreover, now that Prussia was a constitutional country, the members of the *Landwehr*— especially the officers—were also voters. But, as Roon said, 'the armed forces do not deliberate; they obey.' Roon therefore proposed to increase the years spent in the regular reserve and to whittle the *Landwehr* to almost nothing. The liberals, on the other hand, wished to reduce the period of active service to two years and to make the *Landwehr* the core of the Prussian army.

The constitutional conflict which now began was not a conflict over the size of the army. It was a conflict over its character and particularly over the class-origin of the officers. The regular army had exclusively Junker officers; the *Landwehr* officers from the middle-class. Roon introduced his proposals in 1860. The Chamber was mollified by an assurance from the minister of finance that no fundamental changes would be made if it granted the extra money for a single year. The money was granted. Roon went ahead with his plans despite his colleague's promise. In 1861 the Chamber protested. Once more it granted the extra money for the next year, but with a clear warning that it would refuse further supplies if its conditions were again disregarded. 1862 would be the year of crisis. William had to look round for a man who would defy the Chamber and break its opposition. Bismarck was clearly the man. With his reactionary reputation and his unrivalled courage he would not shrink from infringing the constitution. But he cared nothing for this military dispute. Himself without military experience or devotion, he knew that Roon was fighting a class battle, not a technical one, and expected the *Landwehr* to give a good account of itself in wartime—as proved to be the case. He would become minister and give William and Roon the army they wanted only if he could have his own way in foreign policy: challenge to Austria and alliance with France and Russia. William would not stomach this condition, despite his failure to make the Austrian alliance.

The bargaining dragged on for more than two years. It was relentless, though never consciously formulated. Bismarck waited ruthlessly until William was forced to the wall. Time and again Bismarck was summoned to Berlin in order to take office; time and again he demanded a free hand in foreign policy and was sent back to St. Petersburg.

The first call came in May 1860 when Roon put forward his proposals. Bismarck horrified William with the remark: 'If the kingdom of Italy did not exist, we should have to invent it.' He was at once ordered back to St. Petersburg. In July 1861 he appeared again. This time he advocated a German parliament, elected by universal suffrage, to sweep away all the little princes. He spoke of their 'sovereignty-swindle' as 'completely unhistorical, without divine or human right', and said: 'I am loyal to my own prince even to the Vendée, but as for the others I don't feel in one drop of my blood the slightest obligation to lift a finger for them.' William had become king in January 1861 and was now planning his coronation with legitimist pomp; he was outraged by these subversive remarks, and once more Bismarck returned to St. Petersburg. Early in 1862 the Chamber refused to pass the budget. It was dissolved, and Bismarck was summoned again. He was offered the post of prime minister, but without control of foreign affairs. He refused. He said in 1868: 'I was not absolutely sure that the king would go with me through thick and thin.'

Still, William wanted Bismarck near at hand in case of a crisis. St. Petersburg was too remote. In May 1862 Bismarck was appointed Prussian minister to Paris. At once he began to make out that he had been sent to promote an alliance between Russia and France, with Prussia as the third party. William was again alarmed. He said: 'Tell Bismarck that I will never reconcile myself to alliance with France.' Bismarck decided that he would be better out of the way; he would lie low until despair drove the king to accept his terms. In June he visited London and told Disraeli: 'I shall declare war on Austria, dissolve the German confederation, subjugate the middle and smaller states, and give Germany national unity under the control of Prussia.'[1] In July he went to Biarritz. He met there Katherine Orlov, wife of the Russian ambassador at Brussels, and fell passionately in love with her. No doubt

[1] This story, which comes from Disraeli, was perhaps manufactured later, like many of Bismarck's own.

it was innocent in the law-court sense. The men of the nineteenth century had the art, now lost, of displaying violent emotion without carrying it to its logical conclusion. Kathi was with her elderly husband. She was 22, gay, pretty, irresponsible. Bismarck was nearly fifty, his nerves on edge with anxiety, and uncertain of his future. She called him 'Uncle' and sent him sentimental messages. Johanna, in the remote German country, knew the truth. She wrote to a friend: 'If I had any inclination to jealousy and envy, I could be tyrannized to the depths now by these passions. But my soul has no room for them, and I rejoice greatly that my beloved husband has found this charming woman. Without her he would never have known peace for so long on one spot or become so well as he boasts of being in every letter.' Probably Bismarck was as genuinely in love as he was sincere in politics or religion. That is to say, he was sincere and pretended at the same time.

For whatever reason—love or political tactics—Bismarck remained in the south of France and failed to answer letters. In Berlin affairs reached their crisis. The new Chamber had a larger liberal majority than before. It again refused to authorize the additional military expenditure. The ministers declared that they could not carry on without a constitutional budget. All of them, including Roon, were ready to give way on the three-year service if the Chamber would then grant the full estimate. William would not be moved. He had preached universal three-year service from the time when he was a young officer; and he threatened to abdicate rather than yield. Yet abdication would settle nothing. The crown prince, though more liberal in talk, was as firm on the three-year service as his father. The ministers were in despair. They might soon find themselves at odds with the Chamber and repudiated by the king, yet with no alternative government in sight. It is not surprising that some of them hankered after Bismarck, with his boasted strength of will. He might defeat the Chamber, or overcome the king's reluctance; he would break the deadlock one way or the other. On 16 September Bernstorff, who had succeeded Schleinitz as foreign minister in 1861, telegraphed to Bismarck: 'The king wants you to come here, and I advise you to come at once.' There was no reply, no sign of life. On 17 September Roon offered a compromise to the Chamber; on 18 September he withdrew it, on the king's orders. He was at the end of his tether. He wired to Bismarck: 'Periculum in mora. Dépêchez-vous.' This time Bismarck took notice: perhaps in response to the appeal from his friend, perhaps because he had parted from Kathi Orlov at Avignon. She gave him an onyx medallion which he wore on his watch-chain to his dying day. On 20 September he arrived in Berlin.

William knew nothing of this. He was still far from accepting Bismarck's terms. He had promised his wife not to make Bismarck a minister. When he repeated this to his son, the crown prince replied that Bismarck was pro-French as well as anti-liberal. William answered: 'That is another reason for not appointing him.' On 20 September Roon came to the king to explain that the deadlock could not continue. He wanted William to give way. William wanted to force Roon on the path of unconstitutional action and said provocatively that Bismarck would do it. 'But, of course,' he added consolingly to himself, 'he is not here.' Roon called the bluff: 'He is here and is ready to serve Your Majesty.' William had to see Bismarck. But he still intended to tie him down. He prepared a detailed programme of domestic and, more important, of foreign policy to which Bismarck was to pledge himself; and Bernstorff was to remain as foreign minister. William also drafted a deed of abdication. This, too, was bluff. He meant to produce it when Bismarck made difficulties and counted on Bismarck's being swept away by monarchist devotion.

On 22 September Bismarck met William at Babelsberg, a summer palace just outside Berlin. It was their first struggle, a rehearsal for their future relations. Bismarck gave the king no time to read his prepared papers. 'Royal government or the supremacy of parliament' was, he said, the only issue; and he would bring the first to victory.

William was carried away. He tore up both his act of abdication and his political conditions. He consoled himself with Bismarck's promise that 'he would always submit to the king's orders in the last resort even if he disagreed with them.' William supposed that he was still free to forbid Bismarck's wild ideas in foreign policy; but Bismarck had retained the right to put them forward. Both men remained uncommitted. The future would show which 'in the last resort' was master.

Bismarck returned to Berlin as prime minister. A fortnight later he became foreign minister also. He was to remain in supreme power for twenty-seven years.

PRIME MINISTER OF PRUSSIA

BISMARCK was 47 when he became prime minister. No man has taken supreme office with a more slender background of experience. He had never been a minister and had spent only a few months of rebellious youth in the bureaucracy nearly twenty years before. During his short time in parliament he had merely voiced extreme reactionary views; he had not tried to win votes or to work with others. At Frankfurt he had fought Austria, not practised diplomacy in the usual sense. He had no friends or social circle, except for a few sycophants who wrote at his dictation. Where an English prime minister spent the recess going from one great country house to another, Bismarck withdrew to his own estate and saw no one. In later years he was absent from Berlin for months, once for ten months, at a time. He is often called a Junker and certainly he liked to present himself as a landowner. But he had a poor opinion of his fellow Junkers and jettisoned their interests without hesitation whenever it suited his policy. His aim was to succeed in whatever he turned his hand to or, as he called it, 'to accomplish God's purpose'; and he certainly did not think that every Junker prejudice was a divine ordinance. The only check on him was the king's will, but he meant to see to it that the king should will what he wanted.

He was too old to learn political habits. He stood outside party or class, a solitary figure following a line of his own devising. He had no colleagues, only subordinates. The Prussian council of ministers rarely debated policy. It was called together only when it was necessary to pass a unanimous resolution or to force the king on some distasteful course. Bismarck conducted foreign policy in autocratic isolation, easily roused. to anger if some ambassador tried to influence him. He knew nothing of internal affairs or of economics when he became prime minister; and he left these matters entirely to other ministers until some event suddenly drove him to intervene with devastating effect. Even then his policy was the outcome of private reflection, uninfluenced by others. Discussion always brought on a nervous crisis, which ended in tears or the breaking of china; and he preferred to do all his work on paper.

Opposition infuriated him. Bismarck never respected an opponent or listened to his argument. If a minister raised objections, then the critic's position was undermined with the king and he was soon dismissed. To parliamentary critics Bismarck always attributed unworthy motives, jeering at their ambition for office, their financial difficulties, or their personal appearance. One fearless critic, Lasker, was pursued with hatred even after his death. Bismarck developed a petty malignity during his years of office, until at the end of his life he seemed concerned only to carry on his personal feuds. Yet he did not show gratitude for the most unwavering support. Lother Bucher, an extreme radical of 1848 now convinced that Bismarck alone could unite Germany, gave him thirty years of devoted service. He once received a word of praise. All others, including the most responsible ministers, were used so long as it suited Bismarck's purpose; and were then flung casually aside.

Nor did Bismarck take part in parliamentary debates as this is understood in England or France. The Prussian ministers were not members of the Chamber. They sat aloof on the ministerial bench; and Bismarck delivered his Olympian speeches without any contact with the members. He stated his policy. He did not try to argue or to convince. The effect was increased by his thin, high voice, like a professor lecturing his class. Though he admitted the right of members to question him, he refused to listen to their criticism and withdrew ostentatiously to his own room when the debate turned against him.

Yet, on the other hand, he had great personal charm

when he cared to use it. He bewitched Alexander II, Napoleon III and Queen Victoria—all of whom had started out with strong prejudice against him. He had been trained as a courtier in his youth; and those who met him in old age were astonished to find under his rough exterior all the formal grace of a Talleyrand or a Metternich. Foreign statesmen and German radicals alike succumbed to his magic. He would catch a politician in the corridor of the parliament-house or casually in a railway carriage and talk to him as though they were the most intimate friends in the world. Of all the great public figures of the past he is the one whom it would be most rewarding to recall from the dead for an hour's conversation. With all his brusqueness, no man was more skilful at evading a storm. When a member was preparing to move the adjournment of the Chamber owing to Bismarck's absence, Bismarck put his head round the door and said: 'I can hear everything you are saying.' He once caused an uproar by saying that a critic 'was associated with the refusal of taxes in 1848'. The president of the Chamber interrupted him. Bismarck repeated the phrase. The president declared that he would suspend the sitting if the phrase were repeated again. There seemed no alternative between humiliation and defiance. With a disarming smile, Bismarck said: 'It is not necessary for me to repeat my words again. Everyone heard them'; and he went on with his speech. Gladstone could not have managed things better.

Bismarck had no settled views on domestic policy when he became prime minister. It was a matter of indifference to him whether men served for two or three years in the army. His only concern was to have a free hand in foreign policy. For this he had to keep his hold over the king. Therefore the constitutional conflict must continue. If it were once settled, William could get rid of Bismarck or, at the very least, refuse to follow his advice in foreign affairs. Bismarck disliked his dependence on the king; he always feared that Augusta might reassert her influence over her husband. Bismarck had no real devotion to the monarchy, despite his legitimist phrases. As he himself often said, he was 'by nature a republican'; and he accepted the monarchy only as he disciplined himself to accept reality in so many ways. He was quite prepared to use the Chamber against the king if it on its side would back him over foreign policy in return. If the bait of uniting Germany under Prussia would make the Chamber swallow the military programme, then William would be helpless. He, too, would have to follow Bismarck's foreign policy. A parliamentary assembly was easier to manage than the king in the long run, as Bismarck found in later life. With his usual impetuosity, he tried out this idea as soon as he took office. He fell into talk with a leading liberal and compared the king to a horse who 'takes fright at an unaccustomed object, will grow obstinate if driven, but will gradually get used to it.' The unaccustomed object was, of course, a rivalry with Austria.

On his first appearance in the Chamber, Bismarck pulled out of his pocket a leaf of olive and offered it as a gesture of conciliation. It was also, although no one knew it, a gesture of sentiment: Kathi Orlov had plucked the leaf for him at Avignon. So, in Bismarck's life, one hand washed the other. Were his thoughts now on political tactics or on the pretty girl at Biarritz? On 29 September he appeared in the budget commission and tried to brush aside the constitutional dispute. 'Germany does not look to Prussia's liberalism, but to her strength.' And then, in his most famous sentence: 'The great questions of the day will not be decided by speeches and the resolutions of majorities— that was the great mistake from 1848 to 1849—but by iron and blood.'[1] This was a statement of fact, not of principle. The liberals dreamt of uniting Germany by 'moral conquests'. Yet whoever has examined the Austrian records must recognize that the Habsburg statesmen would never have admitted the equality of Prussia except by blood and iron, though it might well have been the iron force of economic power rather than the bloody victory of war

[1] For some reason unknown to me, the accepted version soon became 'blood and iron'.

which forced the decision. All the great questions of our own day, from the defeat of Hitler to the checking of Soviet expansion, have been determined by blood and iron. It is the task of the idealist to put moral clothing on the victor.

Bismarck never acquired this art. He was always inclined to call things by their real names, and when he was excited he found frankness irresistible. Later in life he could afford to enrage the Reichstag; but at this time he had meant to persuade the deputies. He was amazed when even Roon found the phrase too provocative. Bismarck replied: 'I only meant that the king needs soldiers. It was not an appeal to use force against the other German states.' Roon's disapproval was not the worst. William I, who was at Baden-Baden, read of 'blood and iron' in the newspapers; it convinced him that Augusta's view of Bismarck was right, and he took train for Berlin to dismiss his new Prime Minister. Bismarck sensed that he was lost if William I were once firmly back among the Prussian politicians. He went to meet the king, travelling in an ordinary carriage and waiting at a deserted junction with the buildings still unfinished for William I to change trains. It would have been useless to make out to William I that the phrase had meant nothing: the king would reply that he could not afford a prime minister who committed such indiscretions unintentionally. Bismarck, therefore, played things the other way. The phrase, he claimed, had been an assertion of royal authority. William I said mournfully: 'I see how it will end—on the gallows. You will suffer the fate of Strafford and I of Charles I.' Bismarck countered skilfully: 'Better that than surrender.' And the trick was turned. The soldier-king could not run away from a fight. He drew himself up, according to Bismarck's account, like an officer responding to the command of a superior.

William I would have been bewildered if he had known that Bismarck was still trying to settle the dispute by compromise without a fight. Despite 'blood and iron' Bismarck offered the liberals something like a fresh start. He would withdraw the budget of 1863; the army reforms, hitherto carried out by executive action, would be submitted as a parliamentary bill; and the budget for 1863 would be brought forward again before the New Year. This was typical of all Bismarck's compromises. While his opponents would escape humiliation, he would keep open his path to the future. The constitutional crisis would be evaded. The Chamber could, if it liked, amend the army law. But it would have surrendered its fiscal weapon, and Bismarck no doubt hoped to win it over by some stroke of foreign policy. The liberals refused to be caught. On 7 October the Chamber demanded the immediate submission of the budget, pruned of the army estimates. Bismarck answered by carrying the budget in the Upper House. There was now, he said, 'a hole' in the constitution. Money could be spent only with the agreement of the king and the two Houses. They had failed to agree. Therefore the king must spend the money until they reached agreement. This was a tawdry piece of constitutional theory, and Bismarck himself did not take it seriously. The liberals had defied him. Now he defied them. On 13 October parliament was adjourned. Bismarck was securely in power, defending the cause of hereditary monarchy. But he was more dependent on William I than he liked. The hold which the constitutional conflict gave him over the king might be shaken if he moved too fast in foreign policy; and, in fact, it took him nearly four years to break William's reluctance.

It is often said that the Prussian liberals failed at this decisive crisis, but there was nothing they could do. The constitution of 1850, within which they had to work, did not establish parliamentary sovereignty; it was not even undefined, like the English constitution of the seventeenth century. The taxes were not granted annually by parliament; they were laid down permanently in the constitution. Any refusal of taxes would have been illegal. The expenditure of money which had not been authorized by the Chambers was certainly unconstitutional; but not even the most fervent liberal wanted to disband the Prussian state and the Prussian army—just as the Whigs of the British parliament shrank in 1784 from refusing supplies to the younger Pitt. The Prussian liberals desperately wanted a compromise. When the Chamber met in the following year, they offered to agree to the increased army and even to the three-year service if the *Landwehr* kept some of its importance. Roon accepted the compromise. Bismarck was in dismay. He could not allow the constitutional conflict to be ended until either the king or the Chamber accepted his line of foreign policy. He went down to the Chamber and behaved so provocatively that the compromise was withdrawn. It was never in sight again. The Chamber continued to meet regularly, though with occasional dissolutions, which did not shake the liberal majority. It continued to reject the budget. And Bismarck continued to spend the money. Far from the conflict embarrassing him, it was the essential condition of his political existence.

Bismarck did not attempt a *coup d'état*; the liberals did not attempt a revolution. The constitutional struggle was fought within the constitutional framework. The liberals were not solid country squires like the English parliamentarians of the seventeenth century. They were intellectuals from the professional classes—lawyers, journalists, university professors, many of them actually drawing a salary from the Prussian state.[1] In earlier times a revolutionary struggle could perhaps be confined to the established classes. The events of 1789 and 1848 had shown that now the masses broke in when revolution raised its head; and the liberals were further removed from the masses than any other section of the community. Indeed, the only man who thought of calling in the masses was Bismarck himself. He had no more respect for the constitution than for hereditary monarchy and said maliciously to the crown prince, who was himself a liberal: 'I have sworn to observe the constitution conscientiously, but what if my conscience tells me not to observe it?'

[1] Bismarck most outraged the liberals by proposing that civil servants should not receive their salaries while they worked in the parliamentary opposition; and even Bismarck did not carry out the suggestion.

Bismarck had thought of playing off the conservative peasants against the town radicals even during the revolution of 1848. Since then he had watched Napoleon III's success in using universal suffrage to destroy a liberal republic. He agreed with Proudhon: 'universal suffrage is counter-revolution.' He spent long hours during 1863 in discussion with Lassalle, the revolutionary socialist. Lassalle urged that only the educated middle-classes cared for constitutional niceties; the masses wanted material rewards. 'Give me universal suffrage and I will give you a million votes.' These votes would certainly swamp the propertied voters; but Bismarck counted on the peasants in turn swamping the urban proletariat. Both Bismarck and Lassalle wanted to ruin the liberal *bourgeoisie*; then the strange allies would round on each other. In 1863 the idea was too new. A working-class movement hardly existed. As Bismarck said later of Lassalle, 'what could the poor devil offer me?' Besides, universal suffrage was even more abhorrent to William I than conflict with Austria. Bismarck might have been driven to it if foreign affairs had stagnated. As it was they served his turn.

If universal suffrage were ruled out on the one side and revolution on the other, only foreign affairs could break the constitutional deadlock. On this at least Bismarck and his opponents agreed. The liberals calculated that Prussia would have to take a liberal line at home in order to win Germany. Bismarck planned to succeed in Germany so as to drown the liberal opposition at home. In foreign politics at any rate his rule marked the real 'new era'. His first act as foreign minister was to instruct Prussian representatives abroad that they must henceforth write their reports in German—previously they had been in French. This was a formal sign that Prussia now claimed a German national character. Bismarck could not, of course, make a new foreign policy. Though he alleged in 1870 that he had planned the war against Austria from the first day he took office, his contemporary opinion rang truer: 'Events are stronger than the plans of men.' Conflict with Austria had certainly the attraction that it might win liberal support, both in Prussia and beyond. Moreover, there was the strong negative argument that co-operation with Austria offered no concrete reward. In Bismarck's words: 'Even if we are victorious against a Franco-Russian alliance, what should we have fought for?' He certainly did not aspire to more Polish lands and it did not occur to him at this time to take seriously the Romantic national claim to Alsace.

But these arguments and still more the abstract debate between a conservative or a revolutionary course in foreign policy with which his admirers later credited him were remote from the day-to-day facts. What mattered in 1862 was that Austria seemed hostile to Prussia and that the Franco-Russian partnership favoured her. Events were stronger than the plans of men. Francis Joseph of Austria had been trying to work a liberal constitution in his empire since February 1861. He needed the support of the German liberals in Austria for this; and the conflict in Prussia increased the temptation for him to woo German liberalism. Austrian plans for strengthening the German confederation proliferated at the diet; and the Austrian statesmen, who had a clear grasp of economic realities, pressed hard for the fulfilment of the promise made ten years before that Austria should be included in the *Zollverein*. Bismarck defied them by pushing through a commercial treaty between Prussia and France. The low tariffs which followed from this made economic co-operation with Austria almost impossible. But Bismarck did not invent the conflict with Austria. It had been in existence ever since 1849. Every Prussian statesman had insisted that equality was the necessary condition for Austro-Prussian friendship. Manteuffel refused to back Austria during the Crimean war; Schleinitz demanded military supremacy north of the Main in 1859; Bernstorff repeated this demand in 1861. All three shrank from admitting that they could achieve this aim only by war; and Bismarck, too, did not yet face this hard fact. In December 1862 he told the Austrian ambassador that it would come to war between them 'unless Austria shifted her centre of gravity to Hungary'. This was not a demand that Austria be excluded from Germany. After all, Bavaria was nearer to Budapest than it was to Berlin. It was the old demand for dividing Germany at the line of the Main.

In 1862 Bismarck hoped and believed that this demand could be achieved without war. The Austrian empire was having a fairly easy time of it at the moment, after losing Lombardy in the Italian war of 1859. This easy time was not likely to last. The new kingdom of Italy still claimed Venetia; and her claim would be backed by France when Napoleon III had another burst of nationalist enthusiasm. At the other extremity of the Austrian empire, Russia resented the loss of Bessarabian territory at the Congress of Paris and might even revive the claim to dominate the territory at the mouth of the Danube which she had advanced before the Crimean war. This claim threatened Austria's vital economic outlet to foreign markets. Bismarck assumed that one challenge or other would soon blow up—perhaps both. Then he could take advantage of Austria's difficulties, either by aiding or attacking her. Even in the conversation of December 1862, when he threatened Austria with war, he also offered to guarantee her interests in Italy and the Near East if she would divide Germany at the Main. But he talked just as often of making a third in the Franco-Russian alliance.

The reality of this alliance was indeed Bismarck's basic assumption when he took office in September 1862. He had matured as a diplomat during the years of the Franco-Russian *entente*. He prophesied its coming during the Crimean war; he saw his prophecy fulfilled immediately afterwards. There was nothing unique in this. Every statesman in Europe regarded France and Russia as the two dynamic, restless powers, who would turn the continent upside down—Napoleon III driven on by the explosive spirit of the French revolution, Alexander II dominated by resentment against the peace of 1856. The difference between Bismarck and his predecessors lay only in the deduction to be drawn. Manteuffel and Schleinitz had held, as William still did, that the Franco-Russian alliance crippled Prussia; she must stand by Austria and forget the German question so long as this alliance existed. Bismarck took the opposite line. He had always preached, though hitherto in vain, that Prussia should join in revolutionizing the map of Europe. After all, Venetia and the Danubian principalities were not her affair. Control of Germany north of the Main would be cheap at the price. No doubt Bismarck was vague about the ultimate outcome. Sometimes he talked of going to the rescue of the Austrian empire when it had been sufficiently weakened. At other times he suggested that the dismemberment of the Austrian empire would be no great catastrophe. He had no regard for any traditional state except Prussia—perhaps not even much for her.

Bismarck was to establish himself in history as a great conservative statesman, but he was conservative in an unusual way. Though he admired traditional beliefs and institutions, he had no faith in their strength. The revolutions of 1848 gave him a shock from which he never recovered; and he always supposed, like any radical, that fresh, more violent revolutions were only a matter of time. In so far as he had any vision of the future, he held that Europe would not be at peace until her peoples had been sorted out into nationalities or, as he preferred to put it, into 'tribes'. The difference of words is not a triviality. The advocates of nationalism claimed to be preaching a high moral principle—Mazzini equating nationalism and Christianity merely carried this to its extreme. Bismarck did not regard nationalism as high or moral; he merely accepted it as inevitable and wished to be on the winning side. His calculations have proved correct. The 'tribes' have won all over Europe; the sorting-out has even been completed artificially by the compulsory moving of populations; yet politics are no more moral than they were before.

Bismarck's error was in his timing. Dynamic himself, he always overrated the dynamism of others. He could understand the conservatism of high principle; he could not understand the conservatism of inertia. He supposed that men would burn down churches as soon as they lost faith in God, and would cut off the king's head as soon as they substituted the rights of man for the divine right of kings. In practice men are too lazy to act on their convictions, or lack of them, unless driven to it by extreme necessity. Bismarck had intended to be a Cavour on a greater scale. Within a few years he found himself cast for the role of Metternich. The transformation began as soon as he entered office. He came into power with the urgent conviction that the great national upheaval was at hand. He had spent ten years craving to conduct a diplomatic campaign against Austria; and now he planned an immediate challenge at the diet. Against her feeble plans for a stronger confederation, he proposed to launch a German parliament based on universal suffrage—the revolutionary constitution of 1849. Almost his first act was to inquire in Paris what the French would do 'if things grew hot in Germany'. Here was the revolutionary alliance with France which King William had determined to resist. But events did not at all follow Bismarck's programme. Napoleon III was losing his revolutionary zest. The clericals at the French court, led by the Empress Eugenie, had just got rid of Thouvenel, the foreign minister with nationalist sympathies. Drouyn de Lhuys, his successor, wanted a conservative alliance with Austria. Bismarck's inquiry was met with cold indifference; his revolutionary policy had misfired.

Even the Austrians disappointed him. They failed to live up to their aggressive pretensions. In January 1863 the smaller German states voted down the Austrian plans for federal reform; and Austria took her rebuff quietly. Bismarck's career as a statesman begins from this moment, not from September 1862. During his first few months of office, he had been trying to carry out a preconceived plan—a plan formally advocated by him for more than a decade. Now he discovered that events would not conform to his plans; and he began to live with reality instead of trying to force his will upon it. He did not face reality all at once. He continued to exaggerate the aggressiveness of Austria and the revolutionary spirit of Napoleon III; indeed, he exaggerated dangers of every sort to his dying day. But in January 1863 he came to realize that European politics could not be forced into a pattern even by a man of ruthless will, impatient with long years at the federal diet.

There was a more urgent practical reason for Bismarck's retreat from his preconceived plans in January 1863. Revolt broke out in Russian Poland; and this disrupted the Franco-Russian *entente*. Napoleon III had to protest for the sake of French opinion; and he tried to drag the other Powers along with him. The dynamic alliance which Bismarck had hoped to join disappeared; the 'Crimean coalition'—most baleful of combinations for Prussia— threatened to take its place. But Prussia had been indifferent to the eastern crisis itself; this time a vital interest of her own was at stake. The revolt might spread to Prussian Poland; and Bismarck held that, while Russia could still be a Great Power without her Polish lands, Prussia could not. Indeed, with his endless ingenuity in discovering dangers that were largely imaginary, he even suspected that Gorchakov, the Russian chancellor, was planning to liberate both Russian and Prussian Poland in order to recover the friendship of France. Prussia would be dismembered; France and Russia would join hands across the continent. Bismarck had welcomed the Franco-Russian alliance so long as it was directed against Austria; he had to destroy it when it threatened to turn against Prussia. As a final provocation to him, the Prussian liberals—like the radicals of 1848—inclined sentimentally towards Poland. Bismarck goaded them on, so as to discredit them further with the king; and he recognized more clearly than they did that the defeat of Poland would be a crushing blow also against Prussian liberalism.

Bismarck acted with his usual impatience. General Alvensleben was sent to St. Petersburg, and on 7 February concluded with Russia a convention for joint action against the Polish revolution. Bismarck later claimed that by this pact he had defeated Gorchakov as well as Napoleon III; he had played off the 'anti-Polish monarchist against the polonizing Panslav forces' at the Russian court. This was a characteristic exaggeration. Gorchakov had no real plans in favour of Poland; and the anti-Polish party at the Russian court would have carried the day without Bismarck's assistance.[1] As it was, Alexander II felt little gratitude for Prussia's patronage. It reminded him humiliatingly of Russia's protection of Austria against the Hungarian revolution in 1849. Moreover, the convention threatened to turn European resentment against Prussia. France could not act against Russia, even if she would; she could easily move against Prussia on the Rhine. Bismarck had to ask Gorchakov to cancel the convention; and within a month he was assuring the other Powers that it was 'a dead letter'. After March 1863 he kept out of the Polish affair—left Russia to suppress the revolt herself and drew his profit from her ensuing isolation.

The Alvensleben convention showed Bismarck in all his strength and weakness: a lightning grasp of any possible danger, but also excessive haste in meeting it. In later life, though he never lost his speed of vision, he learnt to control his immediate impulse and to let events do the work for him. Even in this case, he recovered from his initial blunder. He kept clear of both sides from March 1863 until the end of the affair. England and France continued to make impotent protests against the Russian treatment of Poland. Austria joined them, even more ineffectually. She was a partner in the partition of Poland, but she could not

[1] Ever resourceful, Bismarck had an alternative policy which he thought of applying if Russia acted weakly towards Poland. In that case, he would proclaim the liberation of Poland and would unite Russian and Prussian Poland under Hohenzollern sovereignty. This was no doubt little more than a sketchy improvisation; but it is a curious thought that, if things had run differently, Prussia, not Austria, would have been 'the Dual Monarchy'. It was not so preposterous as may appear in retrospect. Bucher, Bismarck's closest assistant, had advocated it in 1848; and Bismarck was often ready to steal from the radical programme.

resist the prospect of reviving 'the Crimean coalition'. As in the Crimean war, she ended by estranging everybody. England and France were angry that Austria had not translated her protests into acts; Russia was angry that she had protested at all. The Polish revolt ruined the Franco-Russian alliance. Even more important from Bismarck's point of view, it ended what fragments of monarchical solidarity remained between Russia and Austria. It was certain after 1863 that Russia would tolerate a war between Prussia and Austria if Prussia chose to fight one. Bismarck's gain should not be exaggerated. Prussia performed an inestimable service to Russia merely by remaining neutral; and Russia would henceforth repay in kind. She would not do more. She would not protect Prussia against Austria or France. In fact, like Italy in 1848, Prussia was only free 'to do it herself'. Still, a Power with three strong neighbours has a great advantage when one frontier is firmly neutral; and Prussia enjoyed this advantage between 1863 and 1871.

It did not look much like an advantage in the summer of 1863. Austria, not Prussia, took the lead in Germany. Prussia seemed to need protection, not a free hand. The Polish affair had forced Austria towards a choice between France and Russia; she tried to escape as she had done during the Crimean war, by uniting all Germany behind her. Francis Joseph invited the German princes to meet at Frankfurt, there to consider a reform of the federal constitution. There was to be an executive directory of five (Austria, Prussia and three others) and an assembly drawn from the parliaments of the individual states. It was the last and greatest attempt to unite Germany by consent—the consent of princes who owed their sovereign existence solely to the fact that Germany was not united. Francis Joseph and his advisers might make out that Austria was putting herself on a level with the others. In fact, Austria would be the presiding power; the princes would lose their existing right of veto; German power would be at Austria's beck and call. In particular, the Prussian claim for military supremacy north of the Main would be circumvented. All German forces would be merged in a new federal army; and these troops would be fighting for Austria, one day in Italy, the next on the Danube. The Austrians guessed that Prussia might raise objections. Therefore they concealed their plans and delayed the invitation to King William till the last moment.

William was at Baden-Baden near Frankfurt when the King of Saxony arrived to deliver the invitation in person. William was swept away by his monarchical emotions: 'Thirty reigning princes and a king as messenger? How can I refuse?' Bismarck fought with the king his first and most severe battle. He won the day by arguing that, if William went to Frankfurt, surrender to the Prussian parliament must follow—there would be no point in quarrelling over an army that had no longer an independent existence. When William gave way, Bismarck broke off the door handle as he left the room and then, smashing a jug against the wall, burst into hysterical sobbing. It was worth the effort. Bismarck had ruined the Austrian plan. Without Prussia the Frankfurt meeting achieved nothing. The German princes agreed to surrender their sovereignty only if Prussia did the same—an easy and unshakable excuse. When Francis Joseph left Frankfurt on 22 August 1863, Austria had lost the initiative in Germany for ever.

Bismarck had not yet won it. His first year in office was a watershed in European affairs—the moment when moderate liberalism faltered and began to run backwards. The Prussian chamber had been checked; the Franco-Russian alliance had crumbled; Austria's plans for a liberal Germany had miscarried. European anarchy and confusion was at its height. In November 1863 Napoleon III invited the Great Powers to a Congress which should consider every European problem. No one troubled to turn up. France had certainly lost the leadership of Europe. But Bismarck had not yet discovered how he could take the lead himself. He tried the idea of a German parliament elected by direct universal suffrage. The initiative fell as flat as those of others. The middle-class liberals, who were alone vocal in Germany, would not trust Bismarck so long as he was in conflict with the Prussian parliament. He beat about wildly, consulting Lassalle, the extreme reactionaries, even the liberals, for something that would raise a storm and get things moving. Events came to his rescue. In November 1863 Frederick VII of Denmark died. The question of Sleswig and Holstein was opened; and Bismarck stumbled, without knowing it, through the door that led to victory.

THE DEFEAT OF AUSTRIA

THE affair of the Danish duchies, which opened in January 1864, led by logical steps to the defeat of Austria in July 1866. This is far from saying that Bismarck knew at the outset where he was going, whatever he might claim later on. The future is a land of which there are no maps; and historians err when they describe even the most purposeful statesman as though he were marching down a broad high-road with his objective already in sight. More flexible historians admit that a statesman often has alternative courses before him; yet even they depict him as one choosing his route at a crossroads. Certainly the development of history has its own logical laws. But these laws resemble rather those by which flood-water flows into hitherto unseen channels and forces itself finally to an unpredictable sea. The death of Frederick VII opened the flood-gates; and Bismarck proved himself master of the storm, a daring pilot in extremities. In his own words: 'Man cannot create the current of events. He can only float with it and steer.'

Sleswig and Holstein, the two 'Elbe duchies', had long been a pivot of German national feeling. They had been in personal union with Denmark for many centuries. Holstein, inhabited entirely by Germans, was a member of the German confederation; Sleswig was not, though Germans predominated in its southern half. In 1848 they had risen against the King of Denmark; and all Germany had rallied to their side. Even Prussia fought for them. The non-German Great Powers were then united on the side of treaty-rights. They had threatened to support Denmark. Prussia had given way, much to her discredit in Germany; the revolution had been humiliated; and the duchies were restored to union with Denmark by the treaty of London in 1852. Now times had changed and new legal issues had arisen. Frederick VII was the last King of Denmark in the male line; it was argued that the Salic law applied to the duchies, though not to Denmark itself. Moreover, Christian IX, the new king, opened his reign by confirming a constitution which incorporated Sleswig in a unitary 'Greater Denmark'. This was a breach of the treaty of London. The German liberals thought that their chance had come. They had found a cause which would arouse the enthusiasm of the masses. The German Powers would have to support the Duke of Augustenberg, the rival claimant, and so liberate the duchies from Danish rule. The unification of Germany on liberal lines would surely follow.

Bismarck had no sympathy with this policy: 'It is no concern of ours whether the Germans of Holstein are happy.' He certainly did not wish to help in manufacturing a new small state which would vote against Prussia at the diet. He said from the outset that only annexation of the duchies would justify Prussia's going to war. This was not crude land-hunger on his part; it was an appeal to William I —the only argument that might keep him from succumbing to nationalist feeling. For not only the liberal crown prince, but even William himself, was affected by the prevailing enthusiasm. When Bismarck spoke only of Prussian interests, William asked reproachfully: 'Are you not a German as well?' William looked back with humiliation to the failure of 1848–50 and wished to avenge it. When Bismarck was negotiating his alliance with Austria, he said that the king would not allow a new reference to 'the hated treaty of 1852'. This has usually been regarded as a clever trick by which Bismarck shook himself free of treaty obligations; but the objection was genuine enough. Again and again Bismarck had to hold William back from openly supporting the claim of Augustenberg; and if this had happened, reconciliation between William and the Prussian liberals would have followed at once. Though this might have given Germany a better future, it would also have led to Bismarck's fall—a consideration for him of some importance.

Bismarck therefore had to do something in the duchies—something which would satisfy the king without satisfying the liberals. Yet, with his mind always dominated by recollections of 1848, he feared the other disaster of that year. If Prussia took the lead against Denmark, the Great Powers would unite against her, as they had done in 1848. Bismarck found a way of escape. He would co-operate with Austria to enforce the treaty of London. There should be war against Denmark, but only to destroy the unitary Danish constitution. The other Powers could not object to a war for a treaty which they themselves had made. Moreover, the unity of the Powers would be broken: 'It is better to be two against three than one against four.' Most important of all, Austria would be tied down, taken prisoner for the conservative cause. Bismarck's anxiety may seem surprising. Austria lives in history as the conservative, Prussia as the revolutionary, power. But it did not look like that in 1864. Bismarck was condemned to conservatism by his quarrel with the Prussian chamber; Austria had a liberal constitution, ostensibly in full operation, and Francis Joseph was being strongly urged to bid for the leadership of liberal Germany. Bismarck himself wrote to the king: 'Austria is trying to outbid us in the Danish question.'

His apprehensions were, as usual, exaggerated. Francis Joseph was weary of German liberalism after the failure at Frankfurt in August 1863. Rechberg, his foreign minister, feared that the nationalist arguments used against the Danes could be turned against Austria in Venetia. He wished to restore the conservative partnership of Metternich's time, as Bismarck had perhaps wished to do in 1850. Alliance between Austria and Prussia, previously so difficult, suddenly became easy. Both countries dropped the conditions on which they had hitherto insisted. Austria did not get a Prussian guarantee of Venetia; Prussia did not demand military supremacy north of the Main. These conditions seemed to have become irrelevant. Venetia was not endangered by a war against Denmark; and there was no point in arguing over the federal forces just when they were being brushed aside. The alliance, signed on 16 January 1864, provided only for joint action against the Danish constitution and that the two allies should settle the fate of the duchies together.

This alliance has always been regarded as Bismarck's master stroke. Certainly it prevented either Austria or William I from going over to German liberalism. But in international affairs it increased Bismarck's difficulties rather than lessening them. Even he could not yet appreciate how completely the concert of Europe had been disrupted by the Crimean war. He still went on fearing a united European front against Prussia, when in fact her alliance with Austria was the only thing that offended the three non-German Powers. All three were friendly to Prussia, though for different reasons; all three were hostile to Austria and wanted to see her isolated. Russia favoured Prussian aggrandisement, which she thought would make her more secure; Napoleon favoured the national principle; Great Britain wanted a liberal Germany under Prussia. Prussia's stock went down when she made the alliance with Austria; it mounted again only as it became clear that the alliance would not last. If Prussia had acted alone, she could have acquired the duchies and defeated Austria without the diplomatic alarms of the following years. Bismarck was certainly a political genius. But he often displayed the genius of a pavement-artist who first ties himself up with knots and then brilliantly escapes from them.

Nor was the alliance designed as a trap for Austria. There was no reason to suppose that joint control of the duchies would necessarily lead to a quarrel. Powers usually learn from working together how to work together. The partition of Poland was there to prove it. Poland was the strongest bond between Russia and Prussia; it even enabled Russia and Austria to tide over innumerable crises in the Near East without war. It had been the only cement in the Holy Alliance. Why then should Sleswig and Holstein not be the cement of a new conservative partnership? The alliance was a test for Austria rather than a trap. Bismarck answered the criticism of Goltz, his ambassador in Paris: 'You do not trust Austria. Nor do I; but I think it right to have Austria with us now; we shall see later whether the moment of parting comes and from whom.' This might only mean that Bismarck wished to prove to the king that co-operation with Austria was impossible; it is more likely that he needed also to prove it to himself. After all he—along with others—had been posing the choice for the last ten years: either a revolutionary alliance with France and Russia, or a conservative partnership with Austria. The revolutionary alliance was no longer on offer. Therefore only the conservative alliance remained. No one, not even Bismarck, foresaw a third course—that Prussia should defeat Austria without the help of either France or Russia. But Austria had to show that she was more friendly to Prussia than in the days of Schwarzenberg and Buol. When the Italian ambassador complained: 'You don't need us. You have chosen another,' Bismarck replied: 'Oh, we have hired him.' 'Gratis?' 'Il travaille pour le roi de Prusse.' Here surely was the truth. If Austria would help Prussia to conquer the duchies and would surrender northern Germany to her, then Bismarck would maintain Austria as a Great Power elsewhere—in Italy and the Near East. Though this has often been dismissed as a preposterous dream, it was in fact the ultimate outcome in 1879.

The war against Denmark opened on 1 February. Though the Danes could not withstand two Great Powers, they counted on the others to help them. Not altogether in vain. The signatories of the treaty of London allowed Austria and Prussia to overrun the duchies; but they protested when the invading armies reached the frontier of Denmark itself. An armistice was signed; and an international conference met in London on 25 April. Then the Danes over-played their hand. Still confident that the Great Powers

would support them, they refused to restore the autonomy
of the duchies; and this Danish repudiation of the treaty of
London enabled Austria and Prussia to repudiate it also.
Bismarck has sometimes been given the credit for provok-
ing the Danes into obstinacy; but they needed little
provocation. The conference broke up, and war was re-
sumed. None of the Powers came to Denmark's assistance.
Napoleon III would not go against the national principle;
Russia would not go against Prussia, her only friend; and
British isolationist opinion silenced the feeble attempts of
Palmerston and Russell to repeat their firm stand of 1848.
The Danes, left to themselves, were again defeated. They
made peace at the beginning of August, surrendering the
duchies to Austria and Prussia jointly.

So far the conservative partnership had been successful.
The two German Powers had been able to ignore European
opinion and to have things in the duchies their own way—a
great improvement on the events between 1848 and 1850.
But now Austria and Prussia had to work together in peace.
On 23 August, Bismarck and Rechberg, with their two
royal masters, met at Schönbrunn, the Habsburg palace
just outside Vienna. Bismarck claimed the duchies for
Prussia. Rechberg answered by demanding a Prussian
guarantee of Venetia and, as well, that Prussia should help
to reconquer Lombardy for Austria in case of a new war
against Italy. Bismarck agreed. Perhaps, as most historians
think, he was not sincere. But it is difficult to resist the
conclusion that, with his usual impetuosity, he was now
running full tilt after the conservative alliance, as he had
run full tilt after the revolutionary alliance in earlier years.
At any rate, the scheme was wrecked by the two monarchs.
William said shamefacedly, 'he had no right over the
duchies,' and, with all the stubbornness of his limited in-
telligence, revived the claim for Prussian military supremacy in northern Germany. Francis Joseph would not swallow the German aggrandisement of Prussia which her
annexation of the duchies would involve, for any price short
of the surrender of some Prussian territory. He would not,

in short, compromise in Germany for the sake of his lands in Italy; and as a result lost both.

Rechberg and Bismarck had to drop their proposed treaty. No agreement was reached except that the two Powers should hold the duchies jointly until something turned up. At Schönbrunn the conservative policy reached high-water—and passed it. Bismarck realized this. While still in Vienna, he said to the French ambassador: 'We Berliners do not now look on Vienna as a German city.' The conversation, made sharper by the fact that it took place in Rechberg's own drawing-room, was Bismarck's first approach to France for nearly two years. The tide soon began to run fast the other way. The treaties on which the *Zollverein* were based expired at the end of 1865. Rechberg pressed hard for the fulfilment of the promise to include Austria that had been made ten years ago. Bismarck was ready to meet him or, at any rate, to renew the promise; it was 'an inexpensive act of friendship'. The Prussian ministers in charge of economic affairs objected. They were eager to shake off the conditional promise to Austria and to press further on the Free Trade course. Bismarck did not usually allow his colleagues to dictate policy to him. This time a strange thing happened. He went off to Biarritz, where he once more enjoyed the company of Kathi Orlov; and, though he urged the Prussian ministers to agree to Austria's request, he acquiesced when they turned it down. Was he exhausted? Did he feel economic questions beyond his ken? Or, recognizing that this was a vital decision, did he prefer to place the responsibility on others? We can never know. But certainly the breach over the *Zollverein* made a greater cleavage than any of the political actions in these years. The tariff frontier between Austria and the *Zollverein* became the frontier between two worlds. Austrian trade went down the Danube and into the Balkans. Germany turned to the world market across the North Sea. Political division was bound to follow even if Bismarck's diplomacy had failed.

The check over the *Zollverein* ruined the Austro-Prussian

alliance. Rechberg resigned. Mensdorff, his successor, was
in the hands of his professional advisers; and they were
determined to resist Prussian claims. Biegeleben, the most
outstanding of them, wrote contemptuously: 'Austria
would have to give up the presidential dignity, as she gave
up the Imperial dignity half a century ago, and conclude
an alliance with the Prussian German Reich.' To this
indeed Austria was to come, but only after defeat in war.
The breach was not welcomed by Bismarck. He would have
preferred to let things drift in the duchies until compromise
was forced on Austria by new difficulties in Venetia or the
Near East. As he wrote to Goltz in February 1865: 'I think
it wiser to continue the existing marriage with Austria for
the time being despite little domestic quarrels.' But Russia
and France did not oblige him. Both remained inactive.
Russia was busy subduing Poland. Napoleon III, ill and
dispirited, was playing at imperialism in Mexico. Neither
was in the mood to revolutionize Europe. Austria seemed
free to take the offensive against Prussia.

Mensdorff and his advisers had no clear picture of their
plans for Germany. Conservative in outlook, they disliked
German nationalism; yet equally disliked the upstart
Prussia, and resented the way in which they had been involved in the affairs of the duchies. They took to patronizing
the claim of Augustenberg, more to provoke Prussia than
for any constructive purpose. Bismarck tried to strike this
weapon from their hands. In February 1865 he offered to
recognize Augustenberg as duke of Sleswig-Holstein, but
on condition that Prussia had military control of the
duchies. Augustenberg was confident of German liberal
support; he was encouraged even by the Crown Prince of
Prussia and dreamt of becoming a truly independent ruler.
Bismarck has described their interview. He greeted
Augustenberg as 'Your Royal Highness'; lowered his tone
to 'Your Highness' when Augustenberg proved obstinate;
and saw him off at the door as 'Your Excellency'. The
Austrians approved Augustenberg's obstinacy. Biegeleben
said that he would sooner plant potatoes than be duke on

such terms. Soon afterwards, the Austrian delegate at
Frankfurt voted for a federal resolution supporting
Augustenberg; this was a breach of the Austro-Prussian
alliance in all but name.

Bismarck had to contemplate war against Austria, or at
any rate to threaten it. He asked the general staff for an
appraisal of Austrian strength, and received an encouraging
reply. On 29 May the Prussian Crown Council discussed
future policy. Bismarck described Austria's mounting
hostility and urged William to claim the duchies. He
urged his old line of the revolutionary alliance: 'If war
against Austria in alliance with France is ruled out of the
diplomatic vocabulary, no Prussian policy is possible.'
William saw the trap. If he claimed the duchies, he would
have to pay Bismarck's price and agree to alliance with
France, a course that was abhorrent to him. He therefore
declared that he had no moral claim to the duchies, though
he would accept them if Austria offered them to him. This
was an unlikely contingency. Bismarck had to play a
game of bluff against Austria—not authorized to claim the
duchies, forbidden to negotiate with France, yet giving the
impression that he intended to go to war with Austria for
some reason or other. He talked threateningly and even
proposed alliance to Italy through the Austrian post
office.

The Italians were not taken in. They suspected that Bismarck was not ready 'to play the great game'. The Austrian
ministers, however, drew back. They had no clear-cut plans
for war against Prussia and, besides, wanted to settle their
internal difficulties in Hungary. The lesser states were even
more alarmed; and a Bavarian came forward as mediator.
His mediation was successful; and Austria and Prussia
struck a bargain when Bismarck was on holiday on
Austrian soil. The treaty of Gastein, signed on 14 August
1865, divided the administration of the duchies—Holstein
to Austria, Sleswig to Prussia; Lauenberg, the third fragment of territory, was ceded to Prussia outright. William
was delighted. He exchanged pledges of 'loyal and honest

understanding' with Francis Joseph, and made Bismarck a count for having saved the peace of Germany. No doubt Bismarck was rather less pleased; and yet rather better pleased than is sometimes made out. Though he spoke slightingly of the treaty of Gastein as 'papering over the cracks', he did not seek to widen the cracks himself. After all, Gastein gave some territory to Prussia; it ignored Augustenberg; and the administrative division prepared the way for a more lasting partition if Austria ran into difficulties. Bismarck had a deep sense of moral responsibility—certainly deeper than any other continental statesman of the time; and he would not disrupt the existing order in Europe unless events drove him to it. In his own words to Friedjung many years later: 'I had to try every way one after the other—the most dangerous last.' The treaty of Gastein was a further opportunity—almost the last—for Austria to accept Prussia as an equal. The Austrians did not mean to do so; it was they, not Bismarck, who refused to treat Gastein as a step on the road towards agreement.

It may seem paradoxical to describe Bismarck as having a deep sense of moral responsibility; and certainly it was of an unusual sort. Most statesmen seek to show that they have acted from high-minded motives, but have failed to live up to them. They do not plan wars; they drift into war and think it an adequate excuse to plead that this was unintentional. Bismarck aspired to control events. He would go to war only 'when all other means were exhausted' and then for 'a prize worthy of the sacrifices which every war demands'. This may shock those who judge by motives instead of by results. But Bismarck's planned wars killed thousands; the just wars of the twentieth century have killed millions. Moreover, Bismarck disliked war, though not primarily for the suffering that it involved. War was for him a clumsy way of settling international disputes. It deprived him of control and left the decision to generals whose ability he distrusted. A civilian to the core, he always wanted to back a certain winner; and Moltke, the greatest

Prussian general, told him repeatedly that nothing was certain in war.

Gastein gave Bismarck some hope that he might succeed without war; but only if he could increase Austria's difficulties elsewhere. It was clear to him that Russia would not be stirred to move in the Near East; therefore Napoleon must be roused over Venetia. In September 1865 Bismarck again went to Biarritz—for the last time. Kathi Orlov failed to meet him, much to his annoyance.[1] He even blamed her for his political talks with Napoleon III and for the upheaval that followed. If she had been there, he would have had something better to do—a preposterous example of the way he liked to put the blame on others. Bismarck wished to push Napoleon into action over Venetia so that Prussia could get the duchies peacefully. Napoleon had the opposite aim. He regarded the quarrel between Austria and Prussia as providential—'a stroke of luck which it seems should never arise;' and he wanted to push the two German Powers into war so as to get Venetia peacefully for Italy.

Both men talked vaguely of their future plans; neither succeeded in tying the other down. It is often said that Bismarck cheated Napoleon at Biarritz by hinting at territorial concessions on the Rhine. This is not so. Napoleon was not interested in the Rhine; he was obsessed with liberating Venetia and so, he supposed, distracting Italy from Rome. But he wished to accomplish this miracle without war—at least without war in which France was involved. This was for Bismarck the real importance of the meeting at Biarritz. He realized for the first time that Napoleon wanted to avoid war, not to promote it. Hitherto Bismarck had preached alliance with France in and out of season; now he saw that this alliance was not on offer in any positive form. Instead of the revolutionary alliance, Prussia 'must do it herself'. Napoleon would offer neutrality, no more. Previously Bismarck had believed that this was not enough; now, he had to make do with it, and in any

[1] There was an alarm of typhoid at Biarritz, and Kathi took her children to Sidmouth instead.

case Moltke's assurances had perhaps convinced him. At
Biarritz, not earlier, Bismarck came round to the view
that Prussia could defeat Austria without French assistance. Of course, he still preferred to get his way peacefully
and would have rejoiced at a Franco-Italian attack on
Venetia. Neither Napoleon nor Bismarck committed himself to war at Biarritz. They struck a negative bargain,
which left each free to act if he wished to do so; and of
course, each wished the other to act first. Bismarck
promised not to give Austria a guarantee of Venetia;
Napoleon promised not to make an alliance with her. This
was the agreement of Biarritz. Bismarck kept his word;
Napoleon later repented.

When Bismarck returned from Biarritz, he said to the
Austrian ambassador: 'Either a genuine alliance or war to
the knife.' The Austrians refused the first; they shrank
from the second. They stirred up agitation in favour of
Augustenberg, though without any clear appreciation that
war must follow. This certainly pleased German opinion,
but it also helped to convince William I of Austria's
hostility. Bismarck answered by stirring up Italy in
Austria's rear. His motive was not primarily military,
though Moltke pointed to the obvious advantage of dividing the Austrian army by having Italy on their side. The
advantage was not great; for the Austrians must have kept
on their guard against Italy even if she remained neutral.
Bismarck's main concern was to give a further pledge to
Napoleon. He still feared that Austria might recover
French favour by surrendering Venetia without a war.
The Italians had the reverse fear that Austria might consolidate her position in Venetia by agreeing to Prussia's
demands north of the Main. Both Prussia and Italy, in fact,
wanted to tie the other down without being tied themselves.
Each wanted to bluff Austria into surrender. Napoleon gave
the final push which brought them together. He told the
Italians that alliance with Prussia would make the balance
more even in Germany and so open the road to Venetia.
On 8 April 1866 the Italians gave way. Italy promised to

attack Austria if Prussia went to war within three months; Prussia only promised to continue the war (if it occurred) until Italy gained Venetia.

Italy was caught: she had to go to war if Prussia chose to do so. But others had also lost their freedom of man-œuvre. Austria could no longer buy Italian neutrality by surrendering Venetia; she could only buy Prussian neutrality by giving way in Germany. And no doubt Bismarck had still a faint hope that she might do this. But he could no longer rely on time to do his work for him. He must either settle with Austria or fight her within three months before the alliance with Italy ran out. He had always held that the duchies alone would not justify a great war; for that, he must open the German question. On 9 April— the day after concluding the Italian alliance—he proposed a German parliament elected by universal suffrage. The stroke miscarried once more. Few Germans would take Bismarck seriously as a radical. Public opinion was against him not only in Germany, but even in Prussia itself; and William I, not German nationalists, made the war of 1866 possible. The king had no desire to unify Germany, but he resented Austria's threatening attitude. The Austrians were manœuvred into this by the clumsiness of their military machine. Their army needed six weeks to mobilize; Prussia's needed only three. Therefore the Austrians had to start the race to a war which they feared and did not want. They tried to escape the trap by proposing mutual disarmament. William accepted joyfully. Bismarck saw precious time slipping away. He was saved by the Italians. They began to mobilize, and the Austrians therefore refused to disarm. William was now finally convinced of Austrian hostility.

In May Bismarck offered Austria a peaceful settlement for the last time. It was on the old terms: Prussia to command all German forces north, and Austria those south, of the Main. The Austrians answered with the old condition: Prussia must guarantee Venetia. Earlier Bismarck would have agreed to this. Now his hands were tied by his promise to Napoleon at Biarritz. Napoleon had won the diplomatic competition, or so it seemed: Venetia would be liberated without any French exertion. Bismarck's last negotiations with Austria were abandoned, wrecked on the question of Venetia. The same question barred every way against a peaceful settlement. The Austrians offered Venetia to Italy in exchange for her neutrality; but she was bound by the Prussian alliance. When Napoleon had a pacific qualm and tried to prevent the war by proposing a European Congress, the Austrians insisted that no territorial changes, and therefore no surrender of Venetia, be discussed. The congress failed to meet, much to Bismarck's relief. Finally, the Austrians reached the despairing conclusion that only war with Prussia would end their difficulties—as indeed it did, though not to their advantage. On 12 June they promised to cede Venetia to Napoleon if he would allow them to have their war against Prussia first. Thus both sides paid the same price for a neutrality which Napoleon did not, in any case, mean to abandon.

By the time the Austrians made their treaty with Napoleon, war in Germany had virtually started. On 1 June the Austrians placed the question of the duchies before the federal diet and asked for a federal decision on their future. This was a formal repudiation of the Austro-Prussian alliance, which had provided that the two allies should settle the fate of the duchies between themselves. Bismarck had won the waiting game after all. Austria had made the first open gesture of hostility. Prussia could claim to be acting defensively. William I was at last convinced of Austria's ill-will. Even Bismarck spoke of 'freeing Germany from Austrian domination', and attributed the war to God's inscrutable will, not to his own doing. In one particular Bismarck waited too long. He had intended the war to start in the duchies, so as finally to win the king to his policy; and he answered the Austrian action at the diet by ordering the invasion of Holstein. The Prussian general there moved slowly, and the Austrian troops got away, much to Bismarck's annoyance, before a shot could be fired. However, the Austrians were determined to provide Bismarck with his war. On 14 June they called for federal mobilization against Prussia. The smaller states temporized to the last. Though they agreed to mobilize, they cited the armaments of both Prussia and Austria, and proposed to defend their own neutrality. Bismarck did not respect their nice point. He declared the confederation dissolved and sent an ultimatum to the states that had voted for mobilization. There was no formal declaration of war against Austria. The Prussian armies advanced through Saxony and, when they reached the Austrian frontier their commander sent a message to the nearest Austrian officer that a state of war existed. All wars are a struggle for power, but a practical occasion for their outbreak is usually found. In 1866 there was no disguise; Austria fought for her primacy, Prussia for equality.

The campaign lasted barely a fortnight. On 3 July the Austrian armies suffered catastrophic defeat at Sadova or, as it is called in German, Königgrätz. Prussian policy had to be decided literally on the battlefield. William I accompanied the armies, theoretically commander-in-chief, with Moltke as chief-of-staff; and Bismarck went along with him. Though only a lieutenant in the reserve, he was hastily made a temporary major-general and tried to behave as a soldier during the campaign. His real concern was to keep his hands on the king, and this proved difficult. The smell of powder made William almost uncontrollable. A small incident showed it. William refused to withdraw when under fire; and he was unmoved by the accusation that he was endangering the life of his civilian prime minister. Finally Bismarck gave William's horse a sharp, unperceived kick in its flank; and William obeyed this protest. It was a perfect parable of relations between king and minister—outward obedience, secret kicks. Bismarck was anxious to end the war as quickly as possible. He still could not believe that Russia and France would allow the remaking of central Europe without their participation. Therefore he kept to the modest aims that he had before

the war. He took some steps which might have heralded
the breakup of the Habsburg monarchy; he organized a
Hungarian legion and even talked of a Czech national state
in Bohemia. But these were simply precautions in case
Francis Joseph proved obstinate. Essentially Bismarck's
terms remained the same: Prussian hegemony in Germany
north of the Main. The only advance was that, whereas
previously he would have left Austria supreme south of the
Main, he now insisted that she withdraw from Germany
and leave the south to enjoy 'an independent international
existence'.

The Austrians made little difficulty over accepting these
terms. Francis Joseph was angry with the German states,
which—apart from Saxony—had given him no effective
help. It troubled him little to renounce the last scraps of
Habsburg supremacy in Germany; and he was quite ready
for Prussia to annexe all north Germany, so long as his one
loyal ally, Saxony, was spared. Nor did Russian complaints
prove serious. Bismarck invoked William's family ties with
the tsar, and threatened to raise Poland if Russia tried to
intervene. The Russians acquiesced in sulky silence. France
seemed a graver danger. Napoleon III had got what he
wanted—the liberation of Venetia, the aggrandisement of
Prussia, and the triumph of 'the national principle' in
which he believed. He would have been content to let well
alone. But his advisers insisted that France would be
humiliated and his prestige ruined, unless he imposed himself on the combatants and claimed territorial compensation
for France. Unwillingly he followed their advice. On 4 July
he announced that Austria had appealed to his mediation
and that he had agreed. This was a breach of the neutrality
which he had promised at Biarritz. Bismarck exclaimed:
'I will be revenged on the Gauls when opportunity offers.'
He discussed the possibility of a war on two fronts with
Moltke and prepared to rouse German feeling by resurrect-
ing the revolutionary constitution made at Frankfurt in
1849. The alarm did not last. Napoleon might have been
pushed into action, despite the inadequacy of the French

army, if Prussia had stood alone. But Italy was also in the war. The Italian army had been defeated by the Austrians at Custoza, and occupied Venetia only when the Austrian troops were recalled to defend Vienna after Sadova. Now the Italians wanted a victory of their own and dreamt of conquering south Tyrol. Napoleon could never go against Italy, his own creation. Therefore he swung round to his old line and welcomed the triumph of nationalism. He even pushed Bismarck to make higher claims. Where Bismarck would have been content with military hegemony in north Germany, Napoleon urged full annexation; and thanks to him, four million Germans became 'compulsory Prussians'. Napoleon made two conditions: south Germany should be independent, and there should be a plebiscite in northern Sleswig. Bismarck agreed to both. He had no ambitions south of the Main; and he himself believed in the national principle particularly where the territory concerned had no strategic importance.[1]

A fortnight after Sadova, Austria had accepted Bismarck's terms; France approved of them; Russia did not object. Yet Bismarck's greatest struggle was still to come. The obstacle which almost broke his will was William I. The king had never understood Bismarck's far-reaching plans and had been dragged reluctantly into war. He had given way only when convinced that Austria and her German allies were planning to attack him. Now he regarded them as wicked and insisted that they be punished. For him, as for many lesser mortals, war was a matter of moral judgement, not an instrument of power. It seemed to him immoral that Austria should be allowed to end the war without losing some territory, and even without a march of the victorious Prussian army through her capital. On the other hand, the dethronement of the north German princes seemed to him excessive; it would be a more bitter and more appropriate punishment for them to survive diminished. Bismarck had no scrap of this outlook. Resent-

[1] The plebiscite in northern Sleswig was not held in Bismarck's lifetime; but he was not to blame for this.

ment was no part of his policy—at any rate when the offence was against the king, not against himself. The lesser princes were a nuisance; therefore they should disappear. Prussia would be no stronger for a fragment of Austrian territory; therefore should claim none. He said to William: 'Austria was no more in the wrong in opposing our claims than we were in making them'—an even-handed judgement that will stand as the verdict of history, but not one likely to appeal to a simple-minded Hohenzollern.

The conflict raged for more than two days at Prussian headquarters. The generals, with their simple moral code, supported William. The crown prince, with a vision of a united Germany, supported Bismarck. There has never been a clearer dispute between the moral and the 'real' view of politics; the more fascinating in that William was advocating a more severe peace with Austria and a less severe peace with the princes—but both on moral grounds. Bismarck used all his most powerful weapons—tears, hysterics, the breaking of crockery, even the threat to jump from a high window. On 24 July the crown prince at last talked William round. The preliminary peace with Austria was signed two days later. Austria withdrew from Germany, consented to a new German confederation under Prussia, and surrendered Sleswig to her. Bismarck kept his word to Italy: he stipulated that she receive Venetia. But he did not go an inch beyond this; and when the Italians tried to conquer south Tyrol, he left Austria free to defeat them. She benefited already from a Prussian neutrality that might soon turn into active protection.

Schweinitz, one of Bismarck's assistants, said in 1870: 'You ask what we gave Austria. We gave her life.' But even Bismarck did not appreciate in 1866 that, by failing to carry the war to a revolutionary conclusion, he had committed himself to the maintenance of Austria as a Great Power. He wrote to his wife after the victory: 'There has never been such a decline in so short a time. And all this because Austria would not tolerate Prussia beside her as a Great Power!' Now he had got what he wanted, and therefore was prepared to leave her alone. But he still supposed that she was a power of the first rank. He believed in theory that national frontiers were the final solution; and he advocated them in Sleswig, with France, and later in the Balkans. Ultimately all Germany would be united; and this would mean the dismemberment of the Habsburg monarchy. But Bismarck had ceased to be the man in a hurry that he was at Frankfurt or even when he became prime minister in 1862. Then he had believed that the national reconstruction of Europe could be carried through in a year or two. Now he began to think that it would take generations. He did not even aspire to bring in the south German states. He insisted during the peace negotiations on the impossibility of including 'the German-Catholic-Bavarian element': and he wrote to his wife, with obvious sincerity: 'There is nothing more to do in our lifetime.' If south Germany was beyond his ambition, how much more then the Austrian empire. It would last his time; and he wanted its friendship. He said immediately after Sadova 'We shall need Austrian strength for ourselves later.' It was the mistake of his successors, and perhaps even of himself, to believe that they needed even her weakness.

Even Bismarck did not foresee all the consequences of his success. They were still more obscure to others. Not only had Austria ceased to be the dominant Power in Germany. France had ceased to be the dominant Power in Europe. She could no longer play off one German power against the other. One Frenchman, slightly more farsighted, said: 'It is we who were beaten at Sadova.' But France would have been beaten even more decisively if Austria had won. France could dominate central Europe only so long as the conflict between Prussia and Austria was not resolved. The French politicians did not understand this. They insisted that France would receive the primacy of Europe if she received compensations for Prussia's gains. Napoleon was once more dragged reluctantly forward. Bismarck had often talked before the war of surrendering territory on the

Rhine in exchange for French support. Whether he meant this seriously we cannot know, for Napoleon had evaded the bargain. France had remained neutral, and, after Sadova, an unfriendly neutral. Bismarck refused to surrender any German territory. He turned the French demand to good purpose. He revealed it to the south German states; and they, lately the enemies of Prussia, concluded alliances with her, even agreeing to put their armies under Prussian command in time of war.[1] Bismarck remarked cynically: 'We shall need the national swindle later as protection against French demands.'

Though Napoleon did not know of these treaties, he drew back at the first sign of difficulties. Despite the warnings of his advisers, he had always wanted to be on friendly terms with national Germany, as he was with national Italy. In August the French envoy produced a proposal of a different nature. Napoleon would forget the gains of the past. Instead he offered an alliance, which should be a mutual-benefit society for the future. France should acquire Belgium; and Prussia should lay her hands on southern Germany. Bismarck had no objection in principle. He held that France should extend 'as far as French is spoken'. But he saw no reason to assist her, when he himself did not wish to move in south Germany and when Prussia certainly did not need French protection against either Austria or Russia. The negotiations ran away to nothing, leaving only a draft treaty which Bismarck was to use with devastating effect against France in 1870. But there was as yet no breach between France and Prussia. Napoleon thought that Prussia's aggrandisement and the division of Germany into three was a gain for France, despite the failure to get compensation; and Bismarck appreciated that Napoleon had

[1] It is often said that these alliances were a breach of the peace treaty with Austria, by which the south German states were to enjoy 'an international independent existence'. But this did not forbid their making alliances either with each other or with Prussia. Nor was Napoleon offended by the alliances when they were made public in 1867: he regarded them as primarily a guarantee against Austria, and he was more fearful of her than of Prussia in south Germany.

made things easy for him, despite occasional complaints.
Both were right. Bismarck had managed to defeat Austria
and remake northern Germany without offending either
France or Russia—a feat previously regarded as impossible. But he had done it only by a moderation in victory
which no other statesman has ever shown.

The victorious war also brought reconciliation at home.
A new Chamber had been elected on the very day of
Königgrätz; and Bismarck's opponents returned much
weakened. Even the most liberal regarded him as a national
hero—with some excuse. Bismarck came to meet them.
Even before the war he was putting all the blame for the
conflict on the king. He had needed the conflict with the
Chamber in order to keep a firm hold over William I and
to get his own way in foreign policy. Now the war was safely
past; and new difficulties on the way to building up a
strong national Germany were more likely to come from
William I than from the Prussian liberals. Bismarck was
quite ready to play the Chamber against the king. He said
publicly: 'Absolutism on the part of the Crown is just as
little defensible as absolutism on the part of parliamentary
majorities'; and, to the former opposition: '*In verbis simus
faciles.*'[1] He confessed that the expenditure of money
without parliamentary authorization had been illegal, and
asked for an indemnity. It was granted on 3 September by
230 votes to 75.

This vote is often described as the abdication of Prussian
liberalism; but it represented a genuine compromise and
even an assertion of constitutional legality. Perhaps Bismarck took the liberals prisoner, but he was also forced
into alliance with them. Some of his conservative associates
had been outraged by the war against Austria; the rest
were scandalized by the request for indemnity. Formerly
the Prussian reactionaries had cheered him on against the
liberals. Now the liberals helped him to ride over the
scruples of the reactionaries. He was not tied to either—
a lone hunter who followed no rules but his own. He had

[1] Kind words cost nothing.

set out to make Prussia the equal of Austria; and he had succeeded. Now his mind was turned to the north German confederation. The former advocate of great Prussia would soon be saying: 'Prussia needs Germanizing rather than Germany Borussianizing,' and he would describe Prussian particularism as 'the most powerful and dangerous enemy that we have to deal with'.

THE NORTH GERMAN CONFEDERATION

WHEN Bismarck took office in 1862 he found his policies
and his enemies ready-made. Austria and the Prussian
liberals did not need to be invented. They existed already;
and the assertion of Prussian equality in Germany was
the way to defeat both of them. Bismarck's policy had
been response to a challenge. His admirers have even
described it as defensive, though it certainly took an
aggressive form. There was no longer the same urgency
after the victorious war of 1866. Prussia still had enemies.
Francis Joseph might seek to undo the verdict of Sadova;
Napoleon III might be pushed by French opinion into
opposing any further advance towards the unification of
Germany. And there were domestic obstacles also to that
union. But the enemies were not active. Bismarck had
to take the initiative for the first time. The years between
Sadova and Sedan were for Bismarck years of transition
when he moved from defence to creation. He ceased to
be a Prussian and became a German. He almost became
a liberal. He did not admit this himself and marked
approvingly an article which described him as a revolutionary: 'Only chance decides whether conditions make
the same man a White or a Red.' In his case, chance
turned him into a moderate, holding back the extreme
current of events.

He had little idea of this when he returned to Berlin
from the Austrian campaign in September 1866. Indeed he
had no vision of future action; and it was as much this
as genuine nervous exhaustion which led to his retirement from affairs throughout the autumn. He buried
himself in the country, unable to read, hardly able to talk
coherently. Blue skies, green meadows brought him back

to life. By the end of October he was dictating to his wife scathing comments on his harassed colleagues. He returned to Berlin at the end of the year, seeking new worlds to conquer. He found this new world in the North German confederation. He had had no clear picture during the conflict with Austria of the Germany that would follow her defeat. Indeed, he had supposed that it would be much the same as before except that Austria and Prussia would somehow share the presidency and that Prussia would command the armed forces north of the Rhine. Now the old confederation had gone; and, though Prussia had annexed some of the north German states, there were enough left to make it necessary for her to organize a new one.

His first impulse was merely to perpetuate the old pattern: a federal diet of diplomatic representatives from the member states, with Prussia as the presiding power, and a parliament, elected by universal suffrage, to approve the legislation laid before it by the diet. Only gradually did he realize that times had changed, and he along with them. Previously he had been in opposition—fighting against Austria, against the Chamber, even against the king. No wonder that he wanted to cut down the power of others; it seemed the only way of preserving his own. Now he discovered that he was leading, and that the others were in opposition. He had to apply the spur, where previously he had put on the brake. A great national Germany led by Austria or even united by the liberals would have ruined Prussia—and Bismarck along with her. A national Germany made by Bismarck would bring him greater control of events. He had spoken contemptuously of German nationalism even after Sadova. By the beginning of 1867 he was talking as though he had taken out the patent for it. He got on well with the liberal politicians, who now appreciated his speeches and followed their arguments. He was impatient with the German princes and even with the King of Prussia. Of course, he did not capitulate to the liberals, though he made an alliance with them. His approach to politics was always that of a diplomat, balancing between the various forces and playing one off against another; and he aimed to be the dominant partner in any association. He never became identified with any cause, whether monarchy or German nationalism or, later, conservatism. This gave him freedom to manœuvre; but in the last resort the lack of any party of his own led to his fall.

When Bismarck returned to Berlin, the new federal constitution was still to be made. Immediately after the war, the member states had signed treaties with Prussia, agreeing that a new federation should come into existence. These little states would indeed have had to agree to anything that Prussia laid down; but Bismarck needed the appearance of a federal structure. Now in December 1866 he studied the Frankfurt constitution of 1849, and the constitution of the United States—the only important federal constitution then in being. Prussian experts made some early drafts. Then Bismarck tore them in pieces and produced a scheme which suited his plans. It was very much the old confederation except that the King of Prussia was firmly in control of the armed forces. The federal council, representing the princes, was to govern Germany and to initiate legislation; Prussia's representation gave her a veto on any changes of the constitution.[1] The parliament, elected by universal suffrage, was merely to approve the legislation which the Council laid before it.

Representatives of the states approved this draft early in 1867. It only seemed necessary for a constituent assembly to greet it with acclamation. But the liberal politicians felt the ground under their feet when it came to constitutional discussions. They held out firmly against political shams. There was an extraordinary and unexpected result. Having failed to trick the liberals, Bismarck went over to their side; and between February and April agreed with them on almost every decisive point. He accepted the secret ballot. He had intended to keep

[1] She got this by the simple device of adding to her former representation at the old diet the votes of the states just annexed.

universal suffrage a fraud, the peasants voting at the command of their landlords. The secret ballot ensured freedom for the political parties. In return Bismarck secured a concession which was in fact a blunder on his part. He refused to allow payment of members in order to avoid a class of professional politicians. He got something which he liked even less. Despite universal suffrage, parliament was long dominated by liberal intellectuals of independent means—the very class most alien to Bismarck. This was a relatively small issue. Greater concession soon followed over the army. In every state power rests with the armed forces; and whoever controls these forces controls, in the last resort, the state itself. Bismarck had fought the conflict of 1862–66 in order to ensure that the king, and not the Chamber, should determine the size of the Prussian army. Yet his victory turned out to be barren. For now, though the Prussian army continued to exist, it was merely the largest contingent in the federal army of North Germany; and whoever controlled that army would have the decisive power.

In his original draft Bismarck had written the federal army into the constitution: the annual intake of recruits was to be fixed on a percentage basis for good and all. The liberals held out more successfully than they had done in Prussia. There they had been tied by a constitution which gave the king much power, the constitution of 1850. Now the federal constitution could not come into being without their agreement. Bismarck tried to shake them with the argument, 'we cannot allow ourselves to fail'; but it was an argument that worked even more strongly against himself. After his repeated proposal of a German parliament and his repeated claim to represent Germany, he could not afford an open quarrel. Moreover he came gradually to see that concessions to the liberals would strengthen his own position, once he was in alliance with them. The states of southern Germany would join the federation sooner or later; and they would surrender their military autonomy more willingly to a German parliament than to the King

of Prussia. The German princes were now Bismarck's
opponents, parliament became his ally. In his own words:
'A parliament without liberal backing would not exercise
an effective pressure on the reluctant governments.' He
therefore compromised with the politicians, as previously
he had compromised with Austria, and put off the decisive
struggle. He persuaded parliament to authorize the army-
establishment for four years, that is, until 1871. No doubt
he hoped that by then something would turn up which
would enable him to avoid further surrender. Nothing did.
Instead imperial Germany turned up, and liberal confidence
was stronger than ever. Once more there was postponement
until 1874. Only then did he agree that the military
establishment must be authorized by parliament once every
seven years. This was much the solution which Oliver
Cromwell, Bismarck's prototype, laid down in his constitution of 1653.

No doubt it was a poor thing by the standards of modern
democracy in Great Britain or France, where the service
estimates have to be approved every year.[1] Yet, in the
last resort, it came to much the same. The interval—
whether one year, seven years, or (as later in Germany
after Bismarck's fall) five years—was less important
than the principle; and that had been established. The
German army could not exist permanently without
parliamentary approval; and power therefore rested,
though at a longer interval than usual, with a parliamentary
majority. Nor was this all. Bismarck had not originally
projected a federal budget. Once the parliament had
approved federal expenditure, the federal council would
call on the member-states to provide the money in agreed
proportions; and as ninety per cent. of this expenditure
was military, the parliament would give its approval
rarely. The politicians, however, insisted that they must
give their approval each year; and once more Bismarck

[1] Even democracy can manage to evade its own standards. Atomic power
was developed in Great Britain for some years without the authorization and
even without the knowledge of parliament.

gave way—it would strengthen his hand against the princes. A true budget came into existence, even though the federal parliament did not devise the taxes to meet it;[1] and the federal government could not keep going unless it somehow secured the agreement of a parliamentary majority.

This was a most unexpected consequence. Bismarck had not intended that there should be a federal government at all. The federal council was to be the organ of government, as it had been in the confederation of Frankfurt; and the Prussian agent who presided would receive his orders from the Prussian foreign minister, though he enjoyed the title of chancellor. But once the chancellor had to persuade parliament to authorize the budget and the army establishment, he became the keystone of power; and the liberals only underlined this when they insisted that the chancellor should accept 'responsibility'. Bismarck had to take the post. He refused to allow a federal ministry, at any rate in theory; he alone was 'responsible'. But the revolution had been made. Henceforth his relations with the Prussian chamber counted for nothing; his relations with the federal parliament were all-important. Bismarck so forgot Prussia that he did nothing to reform the three-class franchise, though he himself said that 'a crazier, more contemptible electoral law had never been thought of in any country'. The titles of Prussian prime minister and foreign minister were eclipsed; Bismarck held on to them solely to ensure that Prussia obeyed Germany's will. He lives in history as chancellor. Henceforth he spoke for Germany. Maybe the king had imposed Bismarck on parliament; but the support of parliament enabled Bismarck to impose his will on the king.

Bismarck often sought to disguise this. He liked to make

[1] The primary income of the confederation, as later of the Reich, came from indirect taxation, most of it fixed permanently on grounds of economic policy. But this was never adequate for federal needs; and the deficit was made up by 'matricular contributions' from the member-states. The Reich never imposed direct taxation itself until just before the outbreak of the first World war.

out that he depended on no one—neither on the king nor on the politicians. His very outward appearance symbolized his independence. In the days when he had been fighting the Prussian chamber for the sake of the army he always wore a civilian frockcoat. Now, when he had become a parliamentary statesman, he was never seen except in a military tunic. Only in old age did he explain, probably with some truth, that he had done it to save tailors' bills. An old uniform was respectable; a shabby tail-coat was not. But there was no escaping the reality. Bismarck may have intended 'to ruin parliamentarianism by parliamentarianism', as he himself boasted. In fact, he made Germany a constitutional country. Not only was the franchise the widest in Europe, with the only effective secret ballot. The parliament possessed every essential function. It was the seat of power. The King of Prussia, later called German emperor, directed the executive; but so did, and does, the president of the United States. And both president and emperor were closely bound by the terms of a written constitution. Bismarck was a parliamentary statesman exactly like Sir Robert Walpole or the younger Pitt, even though, like them, he depended on royal favour. A political party with a stable majority in parliament would have ruled Germany; and if no majority ever emerged the blame must lie as much with the politicians as with Bismarck.

The parallel with eighteenth-century England can be pushed further. Not only did the Hanoverian kings control the executive and appoint their own ministers. They commanded the army or handed it over to a commander-in-chief on their own volition. The British parliament of that age had only to authorize the military establishment and to find the money for it. When contemporary observers, Voltaire or Montesquieu, praised the classical constitution and called England a free country, they meant that there was the rule of law, not at all that parliament was supreme. Exactly the same was true of the Germany that Bismarck had created. Imperial Germany was a *Rechtstaat*, secure from arbitrary government. Bismarck spoke truthfully when he said during the constitutional debates: 'I too am convinced that it is the duty of any honest government always to strive for the greatest measure of popular and individual freedom which is compatible with the security and common welfare of the State.' He never claimed that the constitution of 1867 was perfect. It was simply the best they could do at the time; and only time would improve it. He hoped that it would grow 'as the British constitution has grown, not by the theoretical assertion of an ideal which must be aimed at without considering the obstacles in the way, but by organic development of what exists, taking every step forward that appears at the moment possible and harmless.' If the German politicians had known more English history and less political theory, if they had worked together more and criticized less, Bismarck's constitution would have opened the way to cabinet government and ultimately to parliamentary sovereignty. Perhaps 'organic development' was impossible by the middle of the nineteenth century. Everyone had become too conscious of the historical process, particularly in Germany. Bismarck, instead of ranking as a pioneer of constitutionalism, came later to be regarded as the precursor of a tyrannical demagogy which he of all men would have found abhorrent. All he had in common with Hitler was a determination to make his will prevail, but parliamentary statesmen, too, have not been free from this weakness—or strength. Certainly he meant to succeed as federal chancellor. It was his duty, he said, 'to develop the power of Germany and not that of a greater Prussia.'

We can imagine the difficulties that he would have made, if he had remained only Prussian prime minister and another had been chancellor. As it was, he brooked no opposition. His old Prussian friends dared to criticize him. He broke off relations with them and treated them as personal enemies. The Austrian war and its outcome turned the political situation upside down. Parties split

both on Left and Right. The majority of the liberals
formed the National Liberal party—still liberal in outlook,
but now willing to co-operate with the federal chancellor.
A minority of conservatives decided to follow Bismarck,
even if this meant swallowing liberal measures. Though
the Free Conservatives, as they called themselves, were
the more personal in their loyalty, this made them less
satisfactory as supporters: they never knew what they were
supposed to be advocating until Bismarck gave them the
signal. The National Liberals, on the other hand, had a
clear-cut legislative programme which happened to co-
incide with Bismarck's projects; and this gave a genuine
impression of co-operation between chancellor and parliament. They remained two independent authorities. Bismarck never became a member of the German parliament.
He sat aloof on the ministers' bench—the more aloof in
that he was for many years the sole German minister.
He never had social dealings with the politicians on their
own ground—in their clubs or homes, not even in the
smoking-room of the Reichstag. They had to come to him—
to the beer-evenings which he gave with the same conscious
condescension as is shown by a headmaster, entertaining
the senior boys. He never established relations of confidence
let alone of friendship, with any politician.

Still, Bismarck looked very like a liberal in the years
after Sadova. No doubt he sometimes lamented the past
days of feudal subordination, just as he had spoken
nostalgically of Metternich's system when he was moving
towards conflict with Austria. But he went to war with
Austria, despite his devotion to Metternich's principles;
and he became a reformer on a grand scale after 1866
despite his earlier conservatism. He claimed only to
understand foreign policy; and the post of president
of the chancellor's office was created for his technical
adviser, Delbrück. But Bismarck never relaxed his grasp
of responsibility; and perhaps his early training as a
Prussian administrator had left a deeper mark than he
liked to confess. He altered Delbrück's draft-laws to con-

form to a common pattern, and the new German *Rechtstaat* was largely of his making. In 1867 Germany did not exist except as a name on paper—her only common possession the commercial code which Bismarck had helped to carry through the federal diet. Now, under Bismarck's direction, Germany was given all the qualities of a great modern state. The civil and criminal codes were ready before the making of the Empire; a unified judicial system came into operation in 1873. In a curious, though trivial, gesture of decentralization, Bismarck allowed the High Court of Appeal to sit at Leipzig. Though he sometimes wearied of the legal technicalities, he enjoyed lecturing parliament on general principles. Perhaps he overreached himself when he argued that only those who believed in personal immortality could support capital punishment; this would seem to be a strong argument in favour of atheism. The new Germany was as much his work as modern France was the work of Napoleon; and Bismarck had to cajole more, could order less.

He never reconciled himself to the liberal demand for centralized administration. He paraded a countryman's distrust of bureaucrats—all the more from having been one himself; and used to claim that, unlike most of the deputies, he had been at the receiving end of government orders. He, as a landowner, was a taxpayer, belonging to the *misera contribuens plebs*; his liberal critics had 'no property, no trade, no industry'. In practice he did little to check the advancing march of bureaucracy. His economic ideas, too, were at this time little developed. He pushed on the establishment of a unified currency and of a unified financial system. Otherwise he accepted without much thought the Free Trade principles of his colleague, Delbrück. Yet he had qualms. He once proposed to subsidize the weavers of Silesia. When Delbrück answered that every industry would then ask for aid, and that therefore the state could do nothing, Bismarck commented: 'And therefore it is to help no one?—The state can do it!' As yet, no action followed.

In foreign affairs, even more than at home, Bismarck
had no clear aim after the victories of 1866. Previously
he had been determined to settle the problem of German
dualism. Now he asked only to be left alone; and his desire
seemed to challenge no one. He was content to leave the
south German states in their 'international independent
existence'. He said repeatedly: 'We have done enough
for our generation.' Austria was no doubt disgruntled; and
Francis Joseph showed his hope for revenge when he
appointed Beust, former prime minister of Saxony and
Bismarck's principal opponent among the German states,
as Austrian foreign minister. But the danger was remote.
The Austrian army was disorganized, her finances weak;
and every political force in the Habsburg monarchy pulled
against war. Bismarck understood this: 'The German
Austrians know that an Austrian victory would rob them
of their gains. The Hungarians know that a victorious
Austrian army would overthrow their constitution.' The
Prussian general staff never treated war against Austria
as a serious problem after the peace of Prague. The
German problem had been settled; and Bismarck now
counted that European controversies would arise elsewhere—at Rome or in the Near East—topics from which
Prussia and north Germany were profitably detached.

Of the other Powers, England was now moving towards
complete isolation from continental affairs. Bismarck foresaw in any case that she would soon elevate the new
Germany to the honorary position of 'natural ally' which
Austria had enjoyed since the congress of Vienna. Russia
and Prussia were on good terms, bound together not only
by family ties but also by common hostility to Polish
nationalism. Yet Bismarck recognized that they were not
as close as they had been. The course of events between
1848 and 1867 had moved Prussia spiritually westwards.
Before the revolutionary year Prussia had been an autocratic monarchy, dependent on Russian protection. Now
she had become the leader of a liberal confederation which
could protect itself. Much has been made of the French

claim to influence in southern Germany; but the Russian assumption of predominance at Berlin was much stronger. The tsar treated the King of Prussia as his satrap and showed resentment when he was disillusioned. Moreover, Bismarck was slowly coming to realize that, once Austria accepted Prussian hegemony in northern Germany, however unwillingly, she could claim the counterpart that Prussia had previously offered to her—a guarantee of her position against Italy and in the Near East. The Italian danger was no longer serious once Venetia had been lost; the Near East would become the central problem of Bismarck's diplomacy. He was as yet far from being willing to support Austria against Russia; but already he could not support Russia against Austria.

He wanted above all to avoid the choice. All his later diplomacy was devoted to this evasion. In 1867 an easy way of escape still seemed open to him. France and Prussia had no reason for conflict and much ground for agreement. If they came together, they could impose peace on Europe even in the Near East. Bismarck wrote in December 1866: 'I have always regarded this alliance as the natural expression of the lasting agreement of the interests of the two countries.' Napoleon III thought exactly the same. He welcomed the victory of the national principle in Germany, just as he had welcomed its victory in Italy; and he wanted to become the leader in an alliance of free national states, expressing in new form the civilization of western Europe. The obstacle came from the Bonapartist adventurers who demanded a revival of Imperial prestige. Bismarck diagnosed the problem: 'A king of Prussia can make mistakes, can suffer misfortune and even humiliation, but the old loyalty remains. The adventurer on the throne possesses no such heritage of confidence. He must always produce an effect. His safety depends on his personal prestige, and to enhance it sensations must follow each other in rapid succession. Napoleon III has recently lost more prestige than he can afford. To recover it he will start a dispute with us on some pretext or other. I do not believe he personally wishes war, indeed I think he wants to avoid it, but his insecurity will drive him on.'

Bismarck threshed around for some means of satisfying Napoleon's prestige without injuring German interests; and at the end of 1866 he thought he had found it. He had refused to cede any German territory—whether the Bavarian palatinate or even the 'frontiers of 1814' which would have given France the valley of the Saar. But there was a fragment left over from the old confederation which could not be fitted in to the new one. The grand duchy of Luxembourg was under the sovereignty of the King of Holland—the last remaining personal union. Its capital had been garrisoned by Prussian troops as a federal fortress. Here at last was a German 'Savoy'—territory which the French could acquire without offending against the national principle. The inhabitants did not regard themselves as Germans; the King of Holland would be glad to sell Luxembourg in order to pay his private debts; and, with the dissolution of the old confederation, the Prussian troops would in any case have to be withdrawn. Many writers, in the light of what followed, have accused Bismarck of setting a trap for France. This was not at all in keeping with his intentions in 1867, whatever it might have been three years later. For the moment, Bismarck wanted peace abroad so as to concentrate on making the new federal constitution at home; and the crisis over Luxembourg was most unwelcome to him. He cared nothing for Luxembourg itself: it had little value as a fortress, and its heavy industry was still undeveloped. Bismarck's anxiety, as usual, concerned the king. William I still lived in the atmosphere of the war of liberation against France in 1813. He would protest violently against the French acquiring Luxembourg. Therefore Bismarck wanted to take him by surprise: the French were to settle everything with the King of Holland and then present William I with a *fait accompli*.

The French procrastinated. They were perhaps a little

afraid of being tricked by Bismarck; but Napoleon III had never matured his conspiracies in a hurry. The King of Holland was not made ripe for cession until the end of March 1867. By then a North German parliament was in existence; and Bismarck needed to keep its favour in order to carry the constitution. He was caught for the first time by the national spirit that he evoked. Those who argue that he often disregarded public opinion fail to see that, whereas between 1862 and 1866 his political life depended on his being on bad terms with the liberals, now their support was essential for his political success. Nothing is free in this world; and the crisis over Luxembourg was the price which Bismarck paid for the North German confederation. He could perhaps have overruled the king. He could not disregard the liberal clamour against surrender of 'ancient Germanic lands'. Yet even so, he did not mean to give way to it. He sought, as so often, for a way out in which there should be 'neither victors nor vanquished'.

The Prussian generals, and some politicians also, were eager for war. Moltke wrote: 'Nothing could be more welcome to us than to have *now* the war that we must have.' Bismarck set his face against it. War, he held, should be fought only for essential interests, not for reasons of sentiment or prestige; and he did not regard Luxembourg as an essential interest for Germany. The experiences of the Austrian war had not left him unmoved. He was a civilian despite his military tunic and, what was more, a father with growing sons. He said on the battlefield of Sadova: 'It makes me sick at heart to think that Herbert may be lying like this some day'; and later: 'No one who has looked into the eyes of a man dying on the battlefield will again go lightly into war.' Bismarck allowed the German parliament to storm but he kept his hands free. Bennigsen, the National Liberal leader, demanded that Luxembourg should remain united with the rest of Germany, and that the Prussian garrison should not be withdrawn. Bismarck asked the deputies to have con-

fidence that he would defend Germany's national interests.
They did so. They were bewitched by his phrases and in
the outcome failed to notice that he had surrendered the
two points on which Bennigsen had insisted. Bismarck
settled the affair with the first of his many diplomatic
miracles—satisfying German public opinion and yet giving
the French all that they could reasonably claim.

In earlier years Bismarck had excluded the other Powers
from the German question when he had wanted to defeat
Austria. He called them in to the question of Luxembourg.
An international conference met on his initiative and
found a compromise which should have satisfied all parties.
Though Luxembourg remained an independent state, the
Prussian garrison was withdrawn; its fortifications were
razed, and its neutrality put under the collective guarantee of the Great Powers. All this was sheer gain for
France, yet achieved with German consent. Luxembourg
had long been called—with some exaggeration—'the
Gibraltar of the north'. Now this Gibraltar disappeared
and an ineffective guarantee took its place. Louis XIV
would have regarded this as a great triumph. The road
to invasion of Germany was more open than before to
the French if they cared to take it. The French generals
recognized this and, freed from the anxiety of a Prussian
force in Luxembourg, they planned more lightheartedly
the offensive strategy which, in fact, led them to disaster
in 1870. But French opinion wanted a symbolical triumph,
not a real one. Napoleon III was expected to show that
nothing could happen in Europe without gain for France.
Yet, one may ask, why should France acquire territory
merely because northern Germany had been united?
Unfortunately men do not reason in this way; and the
settlement of the Luxembourg question, though eminently
sensible, ruined good relations between France and Germany. Henceforth the French believed that they had been
tricked by Bismarck, and regarded every step forward
that he took as a step against them.

No one appreciated this at the time. Bismarck himself

feared the effect of the Luxembourg settlement on German, not on French opinion. His fears were not without foundation. One member of the North German parliament indeed protested against the compromise on grounds of national pride and appealed to the German people. This patriot was the Social Democrat, Bebel. War and an aggressive foreign policy were still the prerogative of the Left; love of peace still the most telling accusation that could be made against a man of the Right, and Bismarck showed his usual courage in facing the charge. His dealings with German liberalism were the exact counterpart to the implicit bargain which he had made with King William in 1862. Then he had defended the rights of the crown and had exacted the price in a foreign policy directed against Austria. Now he offered the Germans liberal institutions and imposed a pacific foreign policy in return. Many liberals would have liked to challenge France and to show that Germany had taken her place as *la grande nation*. Bismarck dreaded war with France, not from fear of defeat, but because of the consequences which victory would bring. He said during the Luxembourg crisis: 'I shall avoid this war as long as I can; for I know, that once started, it will never cease.' And later, to his friend Keyserling: 'Even if Prussia wins, where will it lead to? Even if we took Alsace, we should have to defend it, and in the end the French would find allies again, and then things could go badly!' The war against Austria had been fought for a practical purpose and with concrete aims; once these aims were achieved, peace could be made. War with France would be a test of strength without solid prizes; and the test would have to be repeated whenever the defeated party felt strong enough to challenge the verdict.

Bismarck knew that he could keep German feeling under restraint. He believed rightly that Napoleon III too was a man of peace; where he erred was in supposing that Napoleon controlled the French as firmly as he himself mastered the Germans. The second empire in France was slithering into decay; and Napoleon was constantly urged

to restore imperial prestige, if not for his own sake, then
for that of his son. Napoleon hated this line of policy.
He was a political conspirator, not a fighting man, by
nature and by experience. He disliked war and feared it;
he knew the gross defects of the French army; and he was
proud to have helped both Germany and Italy towards
national unification. Why should he regard the triumph
of his ideas as a blow against French prestige? When
Bismarck visited Paris in the summer of 1867, Napoleon
showed him all the old friendship of Biarritz. There
seemed no cloud between them. Only later did French
writers hit on the idea that Bismarck and Moltke had
come to Paris, not to see the great Exhibition, but to find
the best sites from which Paris could be bombarded. It
was not in regard to Prussia that the Paris exhibition
influenced international affairs. Alexander II and Gorchakov also came to Paris; and they hoped to revive the
entente with France which had been destroyed by the
quarrel over Poland in 1863. If they had succeeded, the
dynamic alliance of Bismarck's early years would have
been again in existence; and he might well have revived
the revolutionary plans which he had when he first took
office. The Habsburg empire might have been partitioned;
a greater Germany might have been created. Bismarck
was to win much credit from later observers for having
barred the way against greater Germany; but perhaps
the real credit should go to Alexander II and Napoleon III
for failing to hit it off during the exhibition.[1]

The Franco-Russian alliance seemed out of sight for
good. Some of Napoleon's advisers pushed him into a
futile search for some alternative combination. In August
1867 he and Francis Joseph met at Salzburg to demon-
strate an ineffective Franco-Austrian *entente*. Later they
attempted to negotiate a formal alliance, and in April

[1] The Paris exhibition had another, more trivial, influence on the future.
The Prussian crown prince was offended that his father, a mere king, took
second place behind the emperor of Russia; hence he became an enthusiastic
advocate of a revived German empire.

1869 Italy was drawn in as well. This grandiose Triple Alliance ended in empty talk. The new Austria-Hungary was concerned only to resist Russia in the Near East. Even Beust, Bismarck's old rival, admitted that the alliance could act in Germany only when it had showed its value in the eastern question. The Italians wanted to get the French out of Rome and knew that Prussian strength was their best guarantee against both Austria-Hungary and France. The French ministers wanted to push the two others against Prussia without going to war themselves; and Napoleon merely wanted to keep his name in the news. No negotiation was ever more barren or hopeless. Though Bismarck knew all about it, he never showed any anxiety. He called the talk of a Franco-Austrian alliance 'conjectural rubbish', and said of the Triple Alliance in 1869: 'I don't believe a word of it.' Some of his apologists have argued that the war of 1870 was launched by Bismarck to forestall a threatening alliance against Prussia. There is no contemporary evidence for this, and much against it. Bismarck did not fear this triple alliance; he did not favour preventive wars; besides he did not design the war of 1870—it took him by surprise and was most unwelcome to him. In later life he developed 'a nightmare of coalitions'. At this time he said: 'The day of permanent alliances is over. Alliances nowadays are made only for practical objects': and no power seemed to have a practical object for opposing Prussia.

Everything is relative in this world. Though Bismarck was later to display greater diplomatic activity than any other statesman in Europe, he was not a 'system-maker' in the sense that Metternich had been. Despite his conservatism, he was a man of the *laissez-faire* age, and was pushed into creative action against his will. Like all his contemporaries, he tended to assume that things would run themselves pretty well, once a few adjustments had been made. The political reformers, for example, in England as in Germany, always supposed that the spate of legislation would sooner or later come to an end when 'the liberal state' had been made; they never foresaw legislation as a continuous, endless process. Even the most radical Socialists, Marx and Engels themselves, imagined that politics would cease for ever once socialism had been created. Bismarck looked on foreign policy in much the same way. The international system had been unbalanced so long as Austria overshadowed Prussia in central Europe. Now this had been put right, and there was no more for Prussia to do. A natural order had been created, and it would maintain itself by its own weight. This was the liberal philosophy; and Bismarck shared it in his brief liberal period.

There were still, of course, practical problems in Europe, but Prussia was not concerned in them. The Polish question had been removed from the international stage after the failure of the revolt in 1863. The French claims for compensation from Prussia ceased with the Luxembourg crisis in 1867 and were never, in fact, renewed. Some French politicians planned to lay hands on Belgium. Bismarck had no objection to this, and it is silly to imagine that he encouraged these schemes in order to estrange England and France. Belgium was still an artificial state, not forty years old. If France had taken the French-speaking or Walloon districts of Belgium, Bismarck might have claimed the Flemish districts for Germany. Such a national division would have been in strict accord with his principles, as indeed with those of more liberal thinkers. It would have been a western equivalent to the partitions of Poland, on which the greatness of Prussia was based; and it might have cemented friendship between Prussia and France for a hundred years, just as the partitions of Poland cemented friendship between Prussia and Russia. It was not Bismarck's concern to overcome British objections—nor, however, to encourage them.

Apart from this, the only troublesome question in western Europe was Rome, still occupied by French troops, but claimed by Italy. Here again Bismarck's only aim was to keep out of the way. He would not join France

in guaranteeing papal sovereignty; still less would he help
the Italians to conquer Rome. The Eastern Question gave
him more anxiety, and he drew there a faint preliminary
sketch for his more elaborate diplomacy later on. During
the Crimean war he had wanted to take advantage of
Austria's difficulties; but Prussia could only lose by a
new eastern conflict now that she was satisfied in Germany.
His object was to keep Russia and Austria-Hungary at
peace so far as he had a foreign policy at all; and the task
was becoming more difficult. Russia was resuming her
interest in the Near East after her defeat in the Crimean
war; and the Austrians were turning to the Balkans
now that they had been excluded both politically and
economically from Germany. As early as 1868 Bismarck
laid down that Prussia could not allow either empire to
be again defeated; and he did something to ward off
incipient dangers. For instance in 1868, when Rumanian
irredentism disturbed Austria-Hungary, he prevailed on
the Hohenzollern ruler of Rumania to silence the campaign. Again in 1869, when a revolt in Crete threatened to
provoke war between Greece and Turkey and then to drag
in the Great Powers, Bismarck acted for the first time as
'honest broker' and arranged an acceptable compromise
in an international conference at Paris. These were isolated
episodes, dealing with occasional alarms. For most of the
time between 1867 and 1870, Bismarck—the greatest
master of diplomacy in modern history—had no foreign
policy except to be left alone.

Bismarck held the reins of power more loosely in his
hands after the Luxembourg crisis and the making of the
federal constitution. Indeed, he often talked of retiring
from political life altogether. Between 1862 and 1866
he had lived only for public affairs, except for his trips to
Biarritz with Kathi Orlov. Now he began to look after
himself, though he never saw Kathi again. Politics were
for him a duty, not a pleasure, at any rate consciously;
and he was always assuming that their claims on him
would one day come to an end. He never acquired a

home of his own in Berlin. In 1862 he moved into the house of the Prussian foreign minister in the Wilhelm-strasse, where Barberina—the platonic mistress of Frederick the Great—had once lived; and he stayed in these in-convenient old quarters for twenty-eight years, always giving visitors the impression that he was 'camping' there. His study gave directly off the entrance-hall. It was littered with books and bric-à-brac; a railway time-table, a Russian grammar, and costly presents from the tsar heaped up chaotically on tables and chairs. Paintings of crowned heads were piled against the walls—some of them remaining unhung for ten or twenty years. Upstairs some of the carpets were never laid. There were hardly any shelves for books and no separate library. The kitchen was inadequate for a public man; and the food had to be sent in from a restaurant on the one occasion in the year when Bismarck entertained the diplomatic corps to dinner. Only the cellars were properly stocked. When Bismarck left in 1890, 13,000 bottles of wine had to be cleared out in a couple of days. This is not surprising in view of his statement that he intended to consume 5,000 bottles of champagne in the course of his life—and this only as light refreshment after the table wines and brandy, to say nothing of beer. Bismarck built on a few office-rooms for his secretaries in the garden. Otherwise he made no attempt to provide the German chancellor with a suitable residence and met all expostulations with the remark: 'What does not belong to me does not interest me.'

In 1867, however, he got something to interest him. The grateful Prussian parliament voted him 400,000 thalers (say, £40,000) on his return from the Austrian war; and with them he bought the Junker estate of Varzin in Pomerania. This fulfilled all his youthful dreams. Though even Johanna found the house 'unbearably ugly', Bismarck was delighted. As he said: 'Whoever is interested in furnishing is not interested in food; the essential thing is to eat well.' He buried himself in Varzin for months at a time—five hours by slow train from Berlin, and then forty miles on bad roads. There were no visitors, and virtually no social life with the neighbouring gentry. The estate was covered with trees, indeed overburdened with them. It would have been sounder to clear the ground and cultivate it. But Bismarck said: 'If I wanted to see maize growing, I need not have left Schönhausen'; and he guarded every decaying tree as though his own life depended on it. There was something pathetic and yet absurd in this man of only fifty already identifying himself with an old weather-beaten oak. The sophisticated intellectual from Berlin was building up a legend even for his own benefit.

Not that Bismarck failed to turn Varzin into a money-making concern. He became an industrialist like many another Junker; he manufactured spirits for the market and ran a paper-factory, exploiting his political position to get favourable contracts from the Prussian and even from the Russian state. It was also characteristic that he got from William I a secret decree, exempting the entail of the property from stamp-duty. More than one Prussian official injured his career by claiming from Varzin the local rates for building schools or making roads. The old aristocratic politicians from the Duke of Newcastle to Metternich ruined themselves in the service of the state. Bismarck always saw to it that his accounts balanced, despite his ceaseless complaints of poverty. He lived at Varzin a patriarchal life, patronizing his peasants and even occasionally beating them. Yet the reality for which he lived was the daily arrival of the courier from Berlin. Nothing could be done without Bismarck. Internal affairs did not interest him, and he often delayed an answer for months at a time. But he poured out pencilled comments on foreign policy; and the North German confederation somehow kept going, though ambassadors complained that they never saw the man on whom policy depended.

Bismarck was already in search for new decisions. In 1866 he had grasped at what was within reach—the uni-

fication of Germany north of the Main. Now he was
intoxicated with his success in wielding the weapons of
liberalism; and he who had once sneered at the idea of
uniting Germany by public opinion and moral appeal
planned just this in regard to south Germany. The war of
1866 had dissolved the treaties of the Customs Union;
and when Bismarck renewed them he introduced a customs-
parliament, which was to be made by adding representatives of the southern German states to the existing federal
parliament. The south Germans would be elected by
universal suffrage, 'free from bureaucratic control'. In this
way an all-German parliament would come into existence
almost unperceived. The manœuvre was not a success.
The Roman Catholic peasants of south Germany used
their new franchise to bring a clericalist party, the Centre,
into existence. Bavaria returned 26 clericals out of 48
members; all Germany south of the Main returned 50
particularists against 35 supporters of unification; and when
the customs-parliament met in April 1868 the south
Germans took care that it never strayed from the narrow
path of tariffs. Bismarck preached patience: 'An arbitrary
interference in history brings only the gathering of unripe
fruit; and it is obvious to me that German unity is not a
ripe fruit at this moment.' He took the members of the
customs-parliament on a trip to Kiel, to see German war-
ships actually afloat, and to Hamburg, where they saw the
beginnings of Germany's world trade. There was a strange
symbolism in this echo of the Frankfurt parliament of 1848
with its abortive plans for a German navy; but it made
little appeal to the suspicious clericals from the south.

Thereafter Bismarck's hopes for German unity ran backwards. Later sessions of the customs-parliament proved
increasingly obstructive. The national enthusiasm of 1866
and 1867 began to die away. The southern states complained more and more against the burdens which their
military treaties with Prussia imposed upon them. The
Bavarians in particular would have liked to go over to a
militia on the Swiss model—a system which it would have

been impossible to amalgamate with the Prussian army in
time of war; and early in 1870 the Bavarian prime minister
Hohenlohe, who favoured co-operation with the North
German confederation, was overthrown by a particularist
and clerical majority. Bismarck continued patient: 'We
can put on our watches, but time doesn't go any faster
for it.' On the other hand, he saw approaching for the first
time the problem that was later to shape his policy again
and again. Parliamentary authorization for the federal
army would run out in 1871. Its renewal would be more
difficult now that the excitement of the Austrian war
lay far away. Bismarck needed to give Germany a new
'dose' of national enthusiasm. He thought early in 1870
of proclaiming the King of Prussia as German emperor;
but the plan came to nothing. He seemed at a loss for a
policy when he retired at Varzin in the spring of 1870 with
an attack of jaundice. No one could have supposed that
another great surge of German unification was just round
the corner.

Did he foresee it himself? Of all questions in Bismarck's
career this is the most difficult to answer. He was always
emphatic that he could not make events. He said once:
'Politics are not a science based on logic; they are the
capacity of always choosing at each instant, in constantly
changing situations, the least harmful, the most useful.'
And again, in more devout terms: 'A statesman cannot
create anything himself. He must wait and listen until he
hears the steps of God sounding through events; then leap
up and grasp the hem of his garment.' When someone
praised his direction of events between 1862 and 1871,
he pointed to many mistakes he had made and said: 'I
wanted it like this, and everything happened quite differently. I'm content when I see where the Lord wishes
to go and can stumble after Him.' Was this false modesty?
Did he in fact manœuvre the Lord's will just as he manœuvred William I? Perhaps he did, though not so much
as his enemies and later historians have alleged.

Certainly there is not a scrap of evidence that he worked

deliberately for a war with France, still less that he timed it precisely for the summer of 1870. He was always too impatient and highly-strung to let a crisis mature behind his back; and if he had really anticipated an explosion in July 1870, he would have remained in Berlin, controlling events. In fact he was at Varzin from April until 12 July, except for a few days at the end of May when he appeared in parliament and two days early in June when he and the king met Tsar Alexander II at Ems. At this meeting there was no hint of the coming war—no request for Russian support on the one side, no pledge of Russian support or even of neutrality on the other. Indeed, France was not mentioned—only Rumania and the affairs of south Germany. It is likely indeed that Bismarck planned some national stroke in south Germany quite soon to smooth the way for the military discussions in the federal parliament; and it is probable, too, that he anticipated protests from both France and Austria. But they would not necessarily lead to war. German-Austrian and Magyar opinion would oppose a war against Prussia; and together they dominated Habsburg councils. Napoleon III was becoming increasingly pacific; and 'the liberal empire' which he established early in 1870 was a further guarantee of peace.

Bismarck on his side had shown no sign of increasing hostility towards France. On the contrary, he made repeated gestures of friendship towards Napoleon. He pressed hard for a plebiscite in north Sleswig where the Danes were in a majority. This would please Napoleon's nationalist principles; and Bismarck favoured it also. He said: 'It is harmful that a hostile nationality should live in the same community with the Germans.' Opposition came from King William, who could not bring himself to renounce territory once he had conquered it. Bismarck even tried to get round the king's resistance by asking the Danes to invoke the assistance of the tsar—perhaps William would listen to him. The manœuvre was put into operation. Alexander II wrote to his uncle, reminding him of his promise for a plebiscite. William was furious, and Bismarck had hard work preventing an angry answer. The episode, though trivial, is a reminder that Bismarck had real difficulties with the king, which he could not always overcome; and he was not always responsible for German policy. At least the goodwill to improve relations with France was clear, though unsuccessful.

In May, 1870, there was a danger-signal from the French side. Napoleon quarrelled with his pacific foreign minister, Daru; and Gramont, the new man, was an extreme clerical who believed fervently in the Austrian alliance. He intended to humble Prussia at the first opportunity. Yet neither Gramont nor Bismarck foresaw the crisis that blew up in July 1870, when it suddenly became known that Prince Leopold of Hohenzollern was about to be elected King of Spain. This affair had a long and obscure history which has given rise to even more than the usual dogmatism always associated with 'war-origins'. In 1868 the dissolute Queen Isabella had been turned off the throne of Spain; and ever since the vacant throne had been hawked around Europe. The French were busy in Madrid, intriguing for one candidate after another, as though Spain was their private property; and early in 1869 Bismarck urged Prince Leopold to become a candidate also. Leopold was a Roman Catholic, but not a clerical; he was married to a daughter of the former King of Portugal and also closely related to the Bonapartist house of Murat; and his younger brother had become Prince of Rumania—on French nomination. It is impossible to decide with any confidence why Bismarck involved Germany in Spanish affairs; usually he tried to keep out of such remote questions. Perhaps he wanted the Hohenzollerns to think of themselves as rulers of a Great Power, and no longer obscure princes in north Germany. He may have had an eye on Spanish trade. There were two more practical motives. Firstly, Bismarck was not a Lutheran for nothing. He regarded Roman Catholicism as his enemy, particularly in the obscurantist form it was taking under the direction of Pius IX. The

clericals were already Bismarck's. principal opponents in
Germany, and the *Kulturkampf* against them was just
round the corner. It would be a great stroke against
clericalism, as well as against radical republicanism, if
Spain acquired a liberal Catholic king; and one highly
pleasing to Protestant German liberals.

There was also a motive in foreign policy. Leopold's
candidature was a precaution against the projected Franco-
Austrian alliance. Bismarck launched it in April 1869,
when the negotiations between Paris and Vienna were at
their height, and renewed it in May 1870, when Gramont,
the advocate of this alliance, became French foreign
minister. The alliance, if it had ever come to anything,
would not have operated in the first place against Prussia;
it would have operated against Russia in the Near East.
But Russia would then have turned to Prussia for support,
and this would have revived all the embarrassments of the
Crimean war. Spain under a German prince might deter
France from an active Eastern policy—at any rate it was
worth trying. Bismarck had no immediate plans so far as
southern Germany was concerned; but here, too, Leopold
would act as a brake on France. She would, he claimed,
have to keep two army-corps on the Spanish frontier, and
would therefore be unable to act on the Rhine. In short,
the Hohenzollern candidature, far from being designed to
provoke a war with France which would complete the
unification of Germany, was intended rather to make
German unification possible without a war.

Bismarck did not make much headway with Prince
Leopold for some time. The Spanish leaders were eager—
nothing could suit them better than a Catholic prince who
was not a clerical. Leopold was unwilling; he preferred a
quiet life. King William, too, was reluctant to consent—not
from fear of France, but from dislike of his family's being
involved in the turbulent politics of Spain. In May 1870
both at last gave way, William 'with a heavy, a very heavy
heart'. There followed a fantastic accident which changed
the course of world-history. On 19 June Salazar, the Spanish

representative in Berlin, telegraphed to Madrid that he would be back within a week with Leopold's consent in his pocket. The Spanish cortes was in session, and Leopold could be elected King before anyone knew what was happening. A cipher clerk at the Prussian legation in Madrid blundered; he passed on the message that Salazar would return in the middle of July. Prim, the Spanish dictator, dared not keep the Cortes hanging about; on 23 June he prorogued it until the autumn. When Salazar returned on 26 June he found Madrid deserted. Prim agreed to recall the Cortes, but he had to reveal why it was being summoned. On 2 July the news that Leopold was to be elected King of Spain reached Paris. This was Gramont's opportunity. He wanted to restore the prestige of the Napoleonic empire and to show that he was a more forceful foreign minister than his predecessors. Had he wished merely to bar Leopold from the Spanish throne, he should have protested in Madrid, and the Spaniards would have given way, as they did a fortnight later. But Gramont wanted to humiliate Prussia and to restore French primacy in Europe. He said on 6 July: 'We have unanimously agreed to march. We have carried the Chamber with us, we shall carry the nation also.'

Gramont had chosen his ground well. The Austrian ambassador in Paris said to him: 'You have seized the chance of either scoring a diplomatic success or of fighting a war on a subject where no German national feeling can oppose you.' And Gramont replied: 'You put it exactly.' The states of southern Germany resolved one after another not to be involved in the dynastic affairs of the house of Hohenzollern. But the Hohenzollern dynasty had no wish to be involved itself. Leopold was eager to give way, and King William encouraged him. On 12 July Leopold announced his withdrawal or, to be precise, his father announced it for him. The French success was complete. Bismarck had recognized the dangerous ground he was on from the first moment that Leopold's candidature had become known. Had he intended to provoke a war with

France, he would have hurried to join the king at Ems, just as he never quitted William's side during the crisis which preceded the war with Austria. Instead he remained buried at Varzin, even failing to answer the king's agonized requests for advice until too late. He was indignant when William listened to the French complaints; but he would have been equally angry if William had rejected them. His overriding consideration was not some high issue of foreign policy: it was to shift on to William the responsibility for any failure and yet to grasp for himself the credit for any success.

On 12 July Bismarck at last left Varzin. When he reached Berlin, he learnt of Leopold's withdrawal and of William's hope that the crisis was now over. Bismarck's first thought was to resign. He soon improved on this, and proposed to demand the summoning of the North German parliament, under threat of resignation if William refused. It was a beautiful combination. Bismarck would appear as the defender of German honour, either by resigning in protest or by delivering a flaming, though tardy defiance to France from the tribune of parliament: William would be discredited as the blundering spokesman of an outworn dynasticism. This policy showed little loyalty to the house of Hohenzollern, but Bismarck was often ready to risk the king's position when his own power or popularity were at stake. This time it turned out to be unnecessary. While Bismarck sat in Berlin intriguing against the king, Napoleon III and Gramont fired a new shot from Paris. They made further, more extreme demands—demands which would either display the humiliation of Prussia or force war upon her. William must endorse Leopold's withdrawal; he must apologize for the candidature and promise that it should never be renewed. If not, war would follow. These demands were presented to William I at Ems on 13 July. He still did not understand what was at stake. Though he rejected the new French demands, he repeated the announcement of Leopold's withdrawal and supposed that he had made a fine stroke for peace.

When William's report of these doings reached Berlin, Bismarck saw his chance at last. He cut out William's conciliatory phrases and emphasized the real issue. The French had made certain demands under threat of war; and William had refused them. This was no forgery; it was a clear statement of the facts. There is curious evidence of this, which is often overlooked. After Bismarck had issued his edited version of 'the Ems telegram', a second message from William reached Berlin. He had refused to see the French representative and had said: 'If what you have to say concerns the Spanish candidature, I have nothing to add.' Bismarck did not forge the king's message; he anticipated it. But, just as he had intended to blame William for any failure, now he would not allow him credit for any success. The edited 'Ems telegram' was to be presented henceforth as the cause of the war. What is more, Bismarck was now eager to snatch the initiative from the French. This is the key to all his subsequent explanations. He had neither planned the war nor even foreseen it. But he claimed it as his own once it became inevitable. He wished to present himself as the creator of Germany, not as a man who had been mastered by events. Moreover, attention had to be diverted from his carelessness in giving France an opportunity to humiliate Prussia and from his discreditable manœuvres to shift the responsibility for this on to the king. Therefore, against all his previous statements,[1] the war with France had to appear necessary and inevitable, long-planned by the master-statesman. Bucher, his closest associate, was soon calling Leopold's candidature 'a trap for France'; and Bismarck himself claimed to have provoked the war by the Ems telegram. Probably he came to believe his own story and spoke in all

[1] Bismarck betrayed his inner thoughts, when shortly after the outbreak of war he justified it by the example of Cavour who launched a European war to achieve the unification of Italy. But this is exactly what Cavour did not do. The Italian war against Austria in 1859 was the equivalent of Bismarck's war against her in 1866. In 1860 Cavour won southern Italy without an international war ; and no doubt Bismarck had planned to do the same with southern Germany.

sincerity on 30 July 1892, when he declared: 'We could not have set up the German *Reich* in the middle of Europe without having defeated France. . . . The war with France was a necessary conclusion.' Yet Germany had no reason for a war against France; and its gains proved a perpetual embarrassment. France had more reason for attempting to prevent German unification; and if the war had gone well for France, every French statesman would have been eager to take the credit for it. In truth, the French blundered into a war which was not unwelcome to them; and Bismarck, though taken by surprise, turned their blunder to his advantage. His contemporary verdict was far from his later claims to foresighted policy. On 15 July, when war was already certain, he underlined in his private book of devotion a sentence from Luther: 'In this affair no sword can advise or help, God alone must create here, without human thought and action.'

THE GERMAN EMPIRE IN THE DAYS OF LIBERALISM

THE war against France certainly achieved the unification of Germany, whether it was designed to do so or not. It was a very different affair from the war of 1866. That had been a Cabinet war, brought on by secret diplomacy and with no popular enthusiasm on either side—least of all in Prussia. The king had decided on war, however reluctantly; and the people of Prussia had to obey his orders. In 1870 William I was almost the last man to realize that war was about to break out. He still thought that he had handled things peacefully at Ems. Only when he read Bismarck's version of the Ems telegram, did he understand what had really happened; and soon he was complaining of the French insults which he had not noticed at the time. The feeling against France was irresistible throughout Germany. Even Bismarck's most radical opponents supported the war at any rate until the fall of Napoleon. The rulers of south Germany were driven to make common cause with Prussia much against their will. The Bavarian chamber voted for war against the advice of the government; and the King of Württemberg said farewell to the French envoy with tears in his eyes, still asserting his friendship with Napoleon III.

Bismarck did not, perhaps, appreciate fully the strength of feeling in southern Germany. At any rate, desire to whip up this feeling still further drove him to a fateful step. He announced that Germany would claim Strasbourg and Metz as security against a new French invasion. Strasbourg, of course, had been a radical demand in 1848; and the Romantic conservatives who dreamt of restoring the glories of the Holy Roman Empire also endorsed it.

The Prussian generals, too, were delighted that this time they would not win a war without taking territory from their defeated opponent. Bismarck did not usually sympathize with any of these emotions. His principle of sorting people out into their linguistic 'tribes' perhaps justified the claim to German-speaking Alsace; but Metz lay far in French-speaking territory, and even Alsace, with its Roman Catholic population, was unwelcome to him. Besides, it is a fundamental condition of good diplomacy not to lay down rigid conditions in advance; and the claim to Strasbourg and Metz caused Bismarck endless difficulties when he came to negotiate with the French. He was trapped by his own impetuosity, the prisoner of German public opinion, as he had been over Luxembourg in 1867. Later on he often lamented the blunder that he had made in taking Metz; but the blunder was of his own designing.

The difficulties that he had thus created soon became clear. The king, the generals, and public opinion might want to crush France for ever. Bismarck, as usual, wanted a quick victory and then a peace of reconciliation. The quick victory was achieved; the peace of reconciliation was beyond his reach. The French armies, which had planned to invade southern Germany, were beaten in the battles of the frontiers during August. On 2 September, Napoleon III and the bulk of the French army were surrounded and driven to capitulate at Sedan. Bismarck received the fallen Emperor in a peasant's cottage; it was a far cry from their last meeting at the Tuileries in 1867. The German press attacked Bismarck's courtesy to Napoleon. He answered German opinion in much the same terms as he had used to William I in 1866. 'The politician has to leave the punishment of princes and peoples for their offences against the moral law to Divine providence'; and again, with more worldly wisdom: 'The politician has not to revenge what has happened but to ensure that it does not happen again.' But Bismarck's politeness to Napoleon had no practical result. Napoleon, as a prisoner, refused to speak for France. On 4 September a provisional govern-

ment was set up in Paris; and Jules Favre, its foreign
minister, at once announced: 'We will not surrender an
inch of our territory or a stone of our fortresses.' A meeting
between Favre and Bismarck proved barren. Bismarck
had to demand Strasbourg and Metz, whether he would or
no; and Favre could not surrender them. Henceforth
France was fighting for her national integrity, not for
imperial prestige or for influence across the Rhine; and
the Germans were fighting a war of aggression and conquest. The war took on a new character—French partisans
on the one side, ruthless oppression (by the standards of the
time) on the other. Gambetta tried to inspire French
opinion and to create fresh armies; Bismarck sought to
make the French war-weary, and became war-weary
himself.

When Bismarck joined the king at military headquarters, he imagined that he would be back at Berlin
within a month. As it was, though the German armies
swept through northern France, they were held all winter
at the siege of Paris; and Bismarck, too, had to settle down
at Versailles, which he left only on 6 March 1871. It was a
strange system by which the sole responsible minister of a
great state remained for six months in a foreign town;
but Bismarck knew that he was powerful only so long as
he was in personal contact with the king, though even
then he was not always successful. At Versailles he had
three tasks—to influence the conduct of the war; to prevent
European intervention between France and Germany; and
to create the German *Reich*. Of the three, the first was
probably the most difficult, certainly the most exasperating
for him. The Prussian generals were determined not to
repeat their mistake of 1866, when Bismarck had snatched
the fruits of victory from them almost before the fighting
had started. This time they would allow no civilian, not
even Bismarck, to interfere with their war. Though Bismarck was now a major-general,[1] he was excluded from the

[1] He was made a full general on 18 January, 1871, the day when William I
became German Emperor.

councils of war; and he was reduced to learning the progress of the campaign from the Berlin newspapers. He replied by speaking contemptuously of 'the demi-gods' of the general staff and declared: 'None of them except the good old Moltke could stand up to critical scrutiny.' It was indeed fantastic that he should be kept ignorant of military developments; but, with perhaps less justification, he also wished to dictate them. Ever fearful of European intervention, he was impatient to force a French surrender and demanded that Paris be bombarded instead of being reduced by hunger. There may have been sound military reasons against this course. But Bismarck, as always, detected a 'conspiracy' against himself—perhaps by the crown prince, perhaps by his English wife, perhaps by Queen Augusta, in any case by someone. The demi-gods, he insisted, regarded Paris as the centre of modern civilization instead of as the modern Sodom. In the end he got his way and Paris was ineffectually bombarded, though it was hunger that brought surrender. The estrangement between Bismarck and the generals was never overcome; and nothing could be more false than to suppose that he favoured military rule in Germany. The only general he wished to see in power was General Count Bismarck.

The danger of European intervention was never serious. Neither Russia nor Great Britain regretted the defeat of France. Russia hoped for a freer hand in the Near East; Great Britain was relieved of her anxieties in regard to Belgium. Italy was content to have occupied Rome on 20 September and was already looking to Germany as her new patron. Only Austria-Hungary might have entered the war against Prussia and then only if France had won the first battles. She was saved from disaster by her usual policy of delay. By October Francis Joseph was saying to the Prussian ambassador: 'You cannot expect me to like what has happened. But I shall agree to anything; I shall do nothing.' The myth grew up later that Austria-Hungary had been kept out of the war by a threat of Russian intervention against her; and the Russians made great play with this myth during the great Eastern crisis of 1876–78. There was no truth in it. The Russians gave no promises to Prussia, made no threats to Austria-Hungary; more important, they made no military preparations. The Austrians kept out of the war solely from a well-founded reluctance not to tie themselves to a country that was already defeated. When Thiers, the veteran French statesman, toured Europe in an effort to provoke some intervention or at any rate mediation, he received only empty words. The British were busy building a 'league of neutrals', all pledged to stand aside. Beust said sadly to Thiers: 'I do not see Europe any more'; and the Russians told him that they would welcome an alliance with France —when the war was over. France had to do what she could on her own.

Bismarck had grown up when the Concert of Europe was a reality, and it was difficult for him to appreciate that it no longer existed. He was driven desperate by the fear of European intervention, while the demi-gods of the general staff fumbled on with the siege of Paris. He had a further alarm at the end of October when the Russians denounced the clauses of the treaty of Paris (1856), neutralizing the Black Sea. For, though Bismarck cared nothing about the Black Sea one way or the other, the clauses concerning it could only be undone by an international conference; and at this meeting the French might at last discover the Europe which had hitherto evaded him. Once more Bismarck acted as honest broker, as he had done over Crete in 1869, though this time to keep the other Powers out of his own war rather than at peace with each other. He persuaded the Russians to accept a conference on the understanding that it would free them in the Black Sea; and he persuaded the British to annul the clauses of the treaty of Paris on condition this was done by an international conference. In return both Powers gratefully accepted Bismarck's condition that the conference should limit itself strictly to the Black Sea and that the Franco-German war should not be mentioned.

Here again a myth grew up that Bismarck gave the
Russians what they wanted in the Black Sea in exchange
for their support against Austria-Hungary. In reality,
Bismarck was angry with the Russians for raising the
question at this time; and far from supporting them, he
balanced between Great Britain and Russia, as he was to
continue to do for the rest of his life. The Russians accused
him of being pro-British, the British of being pro-Russian.
He was neither. He considered only the interests of his
own country—always the worst offence that a statesman
can commit in the eyes of foreigners.

In much the same way, he was indifferent to the form of
government in France. What he wanted was to make
peace as soon as possible—of course, on his own terms.
If the provisional government in Paris had agreed to
surrender Strasbourg and Metz, he would have recognized
it without a qualm. When it tried to evoke a patriotic
revival, he developed constitutional scruples and announced that the Empire was still the legitimate government of France. But again all that mattered to him was a
quick peace. He negotiated with the Empress Eugenie,
who was in exile in London, and with Bazaine who held
out for a time in Metz; Napoleon III refused to exercise
any political activity while remaining a prisoner. None
of the Bonapartist spokesmen would agree to the surrender
of territory; and Bismarck soon dropped them, despite
his suggestion that an Empire, restored by German arms,
would be the most pacific form of French government in
the future. Certainly he talked of the social dangers which
would follow a long war; but the ghost was evoked to
frighten others, not himself. For the time being he failed
to shake French resolution, either among the Bonapartists
or in the provisional government; and he resigned himself
to the fact that no peace was possible until Paris had fallen.

During this long delay Bismarck feared that German
resolution would break down sooner than the French. The
unanimous enthusiasm of the first victories did not survive
Sedan. Some radicals and Social Democrats took the line

of high principle that Germany was now fighting a war of aggression; and anti-war agitators were imprisoned even in East Prussia. The princes and politicians of south Germany were more concerned to preserve their independence. On 23 September Lewis II of Bavaria, though still effervescing with German enthusiasm, said: 'But we are not going to enter the North German confederation, eh?' Even Bismarck had not intended any such thing when the war broke out. The military treaties had provided adequate unity on the battlefield; and he still had a deep Protestant distrust against organic unity with the Roman Catholics of south Germany. He wrote on 23 July, just after the outbreak of war: 'We shall let the measure of our mutual co-operation depend entirely on the free decision of our south German allies.' This was enough for the first victories; it would not last—or so he feared—for a long war. He pushed the south German states into the Reich not at all with a vision of a distant future, but solely to keep them in the war. They could make a separate peace so long as they remained independent states; they would have to hold on with north Germany once the empire was made. This anxiety explains the haste with which he drove the negotiations for unity forward. It explains the concessions which he made particularly to Bavaria.

Liberal critics later discovered in these concessions a deep and sinister design. Bismarck, it was said, kept the south German princes in existence in order to prevent Germany from becoming a democratic state. In fact, Bismarck thought always of the needs of the present, not of a speculative future; and the present need was to keep the south German states in the war. He welcomed the campaign of national propaganda which Lasker and other liberals conducted in south Germany; but he doubted whether popular feeling was enough to overcome the reluctance of the princes. He could, no doubt, have engineered disturbances and even revolts; but he could not afford a civil war in Germany with the German armies pinned down in front of Paris. Far from using the war in

order to promote unification, he sought unification in
order to continue the war. Besides, he always preferred
conciliation to force. When the crown prince said in his
National Liberal way: 'We have got them in our power!'
Bismarck replied: 'Your Royal Highness, a prince can
perhaps act in that way, a gentleman like me cannot.'

There was, too, a deeper calculation behind this high
sentiment. The force of public opinion might sweep away
the south German princes. It would not work with
William I, who was most reluctant to submerge the title
of King of Prussia in that of German Emperor. He was
even less ready to 'pick up a crown from the gutter' than
Frederick William IV had been in 1849. He would have
refused the imperial crown if it had been offered to him
by a German parliament; he accepted it grudgingly from
the princes. Bismarck needed these princes in order to
force William I on the path which it seemed necessary to
follow. Of course, he threatened that German unity would
be made against the princes if they held back; but he also
held out the prospect that they could be its makers. With
his usual adaptability, he first played national enthusiasm
against the princes and then played the King of Bavaria
against William I. The negotiations were more difficult
than those which preceded the North German federation in
1867. Then all the states had been trivial except Saxony;
and she had already agreed to federation as the penalty
for defeat in the war of 1866. Now, though only three
states had to be won over—Bavaria, Baden, Württemberg
—they had some real existence, two of them (Bavaria
and Württemberg) actually kingdoms.[1] The Grand Duke of
Baden was eager for unification, had indeed to be restrained
so as not to get out of step with the two others. The King
of Bavaria was obstinate for independence; the King of
Württemberg scarcely less so. Bismarck negotiated with

[1] Strictly there were three and a half states to be won. Hesse-Darmstadt
was a member of the North German federation for its territory north, and
independent for that south, of the Main. But clearly no new decision of
principle was needed here.

them separately, scaring each in turn with the story that the other two had given way.

He made some real concessions. Bavaria retained lighter duties on beer, her national industry; she issued her own postage-stamps, kept her own railways and even, in peace-time, her own army. A committee of the Imperial Council under Bavarian chairmanship was to consider German foreign policy. There would be full autonomy in domestic affairs. But the great cause was won. Germany became a united nation for foreign policy and for war. German power existed whatever the separate states might still claim. The south German princes and politicians did not foresee that the federal element in the Reich would be weakened with the passing of the years or that national sentiment would turn the states into empty symbols. Berlin would over-shadow Munich, Stuttgart, and Dresden. But Bismarck did not cheat them over this. He did not foresee it himself, and regretted it when it happened.

The treaties with the south German states were con-cluded in November. The greatest hurdle had still to be overcome—William I, the last independent German prince. Bismarck appealed to the romanticism of Lewis II and even evoked the time when the Bismarcks had been feudal vassals of the Wittelsbach house—a characteris-tically bizarre allusion, in that the estate for which they owed service was the one of which they had been deprived by the Hohenzollerns. Bismarck said: 'Such idiocies have their effect on the king.' It was probably more effective that he promised Lewis II a secret pension of some £20,000 a year out of the sequestered fortune of the deposed King of Hanover. Romantic flattery and bribery together did the trick. Lewis II wrote at Bismarck's dictation a letter offering the imperial crown to William I. The German people were also allowed their humble say. A deputation from the North German parliament requested William I to accept the crown when the princes offered it to him. The leader of the deputation had also headed the deputation from Frankfurt which made the offer to

Frederick William IV in 1849. This time Frederick William's condition was fulfilled—the effective offer was made by the German princes.

There were difficulties to the last moment. William I wished to be called 'Emperor of Germany'—a territorial title. Bismarck would only allow 'German Emperor'—a glorified presidency. He regarded this as trivial nonsense: *'Nescio quid mihi magis farcimentum esset'*[1], but he insisted as usual on getting his way. William felt more deeply about this question than about any of the great conflicts he had with Bismarck. He could forgive the making of peace with Austria in 1866 or later the alliance with her in 1879; he could not forgive being saddled with the wrong title. And this was natural. All men care most about the tools of their own trade; and kings are concerned with titles or orders just as a writer is offended by bad grammar or a cricketer by bad sportsmanship. Kings can determine the cut of a tunic or the precedence in a ballroom. They can do little to change the fate of the world—and they do not often try. Bismarck was impatient with the rigmarole. He wrote to his wife: 'The imperial delivery was a difficult one and kings—like women—have strange longings at such time, before they bring into the world what they cannot keep to themselves all the same.' The ceremony of acknowledging William I took place in the great gallery of the palace of Versailles on 18 January 1871. William I tried to cheat at the last moment. He told the Grand Duke of Baden to lead the cheers for 'the Emperor of Germany'. Bismarck intercepted the grand duke on his way upstairs, and suggested a safe compromise: cheers simply for 'Emperor William'. William was furious at the trick; and he ignored Bismarck's outstretched hand as he stepped off the Imperial dais.

Bismarck soon had other negotiations on his hands, this time with the French. Paris capitulated on 28 January; and an armistice followed, providing for a French national

[1] 'I don't know what could be a matter of more indifference to me'; or, in modern idiom, 'I couldn't care less.'

assembly, which should agree to the peace-terms. Bismarck now paid the penalty for his rashness at the beginning of the war. Though he was determined to claim Strasbourg, he wanted to give way about Metz: 'I don't like so many Frenchmen in our house, who do not want to be there.' He thought that the French would be resentful at their defeat in any case and wrote: 'This bitterness will be just as great even if they come out of the war without loss of territory.' But now it would have been a great stroke of conciliation if Metz had remained French after all the German talk. Bismarck failed to get his way. Moltke and the generals insisted in Metz; and after fierce debate William I supported them. Bismarck lamented that he would have done things very differently if he had had supreme power like Frederick the Great or Napoleon I. As it was, he had to set his hand to a peace which, he knew, would not be a peace of reconciliation. Still, he met the French on many points. He reduced the indemnity from six to five milliard francs,[1] and he allowed them to retain Belfort, despite Moltke's protests, discovering an easy compensation in a victory-march of the German army through the streets of Paris.

What was more important, he won the trust and even affection of Thiers, the principal French negotiator. Thiers had been prime minister of France when Bismarck was still a schoolboy; and Bismarck treated him with genuine respect. Once, finding the old man asleep in the ante-room, he covered him with his military cloak; and he did everything he could to make Thiers's task in governing France easier. When Bismarck in later years supported French republicanism, there was in this sentiment as well as policy—a sentiment of affection for the greatest French statesman of the day. The preliminary peace was concluded on 28 February. Bismarck marked in his devotional book the verse from Psalm 44: 'For they got not the land in possession by their own sword, neither did their own arm save them; but Thy right hand, and Thine arm, and

---

[1] This figure was calculated, on the basis of population, as the precise equivalent of the indemnity which Napoleon I imposed on Prussia in 1807.

the light of Thy countenance, because Thou hadst a favour
unto them'—a curious judgement on the Franco-German
war. The following day he took part in the march through
Paris. On 6 March he at last left Versailles, taking with him
the table from his lodgings on which the peace had been
signed. Apparently he did not pay for it or even ask his
landlady's permission.

Bismarck never saw France again, indeed never again
left German soil.[1] National hatreds affected the private
lives of statesmen for the first time in modern history.
He would not have been safe from insult in France. Perhaps
even Bismarck, too, was growing more nationalistic in
character, though he said sadly that the peace-treaty
should have contained a clause, authorizing him to visit
Biarritz each year. Perhaps the absence of Kathi Orlov
from Biarritz and her death a few years later deprived
foreign travel of its charm so far as Bismarck was concerned—all that remained of the romance was a god-child
at Biarritz, much persecuted during the Franco-German
war. But there were consolations, some of them valued by
Bismarck. On 28 March William I created him a prince
of the German empire. He was not impressed: 'I was a rich
Junker and I have become a poor prince.' He alleged that
his fellow-Junkers envied him, and he even attributed
their later opposition to this envy. Honours and decora-
tions never meant much to him. When William I gave
him the Grand Cross of the Hohenzollern Order in dia-
monds, he said: 'I'd sooner have had a horse or a barrel
of good Rhenish wine.' He received also a reward more to
his taste. William I granted him a princely domain at
Friedrichsruh in the duchy of Lauenberg—Prussia's first
acquisition under Bismarck's rule. This was an estate ten
times as big as Varzin, and Bismarck added to it by purchase.

Bismarck was now one of the greatest landowners in
Germany, particularly in timber. At Friedrichsruh he

[1] The phrase is deliberately chosen so as to cover his visits to Bad Gastein
and Vienna.

showed the same exaggerated love of old trees as at Varzin
and planted new ones as well. In 1887 he sent to Gladstone
the malicious message: 'Tell him that, while he is chopping
trees down, I am busy planting them.' He developed, too,
a love of animals and soon carried no weapon except a
pair of field-glasses. At Friedrichsruh and Varzin he wore
glasses so as to observe Nature. When asked why he did
not wear them in Berlin, he answered that he found
nothing to interest him there. This was not quite true.
He used to survey the Reichstag through an old-fashioned
lorgnette—perhaps, however, more to overawe the deputies
than to see what was going on. Bismarck took some time
to get used to Friedrichsruh. He visited it little in the first
decade when he was Imperial chancellor. Later, he settled
there more and more. It was more accessible, only two
hours by train from Berlin; and Hamburg lay near at hand.
The acquaintance with Hamburg which Bismarck made
from Friedrichsruh helped to develop his interest in
colonies; and the leading Hamburg newspaper became his
mouthpiece after his fall. The traditions of the Hanseatic
league came to mean something to him, as those of the
Holy Roman Empire never did.

The house at Friedrichsruh was even uglier than the one
at Varzin. The original mansion had long disappeared, and
its place had been taken by an hotel for week-enders from
Hamburg. Bismarck did not even trouble to remove the
numbers from the hotel-bedrooms. He did not instal
electric light, managing with oil-lamps to the day of his
death; and he stored in the cellar the countless books
which were given to him but which he did not read. He
knew nothing of contemporary literature, either German
or foreign. He condemned Sybel, his own official historian,
as one who muddied the waters of history. He never even
read Clausewitz, to whom he once referred as 'a distinguished general'. Ranke had always been his favourite
historian; and he made a revealing exception later for
Taine. He continued to soak himself in the Bible and
Shakespeare; and he developed a consuming passion for

the novels of Dumas. Otherwise his tastes remained those of his Romantic boyhood. He ignored altogether contemporary developments in philosophy, science, and economics; despised all artists; and dismissed Wagner, the greatest musician of the day, as 'a monkey'—perhaps because the wife of Schleinitz, his predecessor as foreign minister and now the confidential adviser of Queen Augusta, was a Wagnerian enthusiast. He attended the Opera in 1889 during the tsar's visit to Berlin; it was his first appearance there since he became chancellor. Indeed, though he now held the greatest position in Europe, he made no attempt to fulfil the representational side of his office. He never appeared at funerals, even at those of royal princes; and he ignored visiting foreign celebrities unless they had something interesting to say. He attended the court balls when he was first chancellor and danced with almost boyish zest. William I said that such dancing was too frivolous for an Imperial chancellor and forbade it; Bismarck did not appear at court balls again. He entertained the diplomatic corps once a year, otherwise hardly saw them. He never dined out. When the King of Saxony called at the Chancellery one morning, he was told by the porter to go away and make an appointment. A grand duke who was expected at 9 p.m. arrived a little late. He was greeted by Bismarck wearing an old coat and with the words: 'I had given up hoping for the honour of a visit from Your Royal Highness; it is 9.20.' Even the crown prince often failed to encounter Bismarck for months at a time.

Bismarck made an exception only for William I whom he saw every afternoon when they were both in Berlin. He established over the emperor an ascendancy that was great but never complete. The crown prince said shortly after the war of 1866: 'If Bismarck proposed an alliance with Garibaldi—well, he's at least a general. But if he proposed an alliance with Mazzini the king would at first walk up and down the room in distress and would exclaim: "Bismarck, Bismarck, what are you turning me into?" Then he would stop in the middle of the room and say: "But if you believe that it is absolutely necessary in the interests of the state, there's nothing more to be said".' Things did not really go as easily as this. For one thing, the old gentleman (whom Bismarck accused of always sleeping heavily) would complain of a restless night just when Bismarck meant to describe his own insomnia. He called the Emperor heartless and liked to repeat the saying: 'There are white men, there are black men, and there are monarchs.' Once, returning from an interview, he exclaimed: 'I cannot be the servant of princes.' William I lamented on his side: 'It is not easy to be emperor under such a chancellor.'

Bismarck suffered much ill-health during his first decade as Imperial chancellor. This was largely due to the nervous irritation which grew on him all the time. But he also smoked too many cigars (at one time fourteen a day) and ate and drank too much, worst of all a gigantic supper before going to bed. Then he would lie awake piling up grievances. He once announced: 'I have spent *the whole night hating*'; and when he had no immediate object for his hate he would go back over the injuries of twenty or thirty years before. 'I often forget, I never forgive;' only the second part of the statement was true. He suffered much also from toothache, but refused to see a dentist; and the pain brought on a nervous cramp of his cheeks. Between 1878 and 1883 this twitching became so bad that he grew a beard again to hide it. Though the twitch disappeared when the teeth were finally drawn, Bismarck never admitted the connexion—the blame had always to be put on his opponents or, still more, on his friends. Most of his ailments were probably imaginary, except for indigestion; but, of course, that did not make them any less painful. He looked and acted like an old man when he became Imperial chancellor—and a shaky old man at that. Yet he was only fifty-six with more than a quarter of a century of full activity before him. The one thing which really laid Bismarck low was boredom. He could always rise to an emergency and work with a penetration and efficiency that few men have shown. But he needed to live in a crisis all the time.

Like many men with deep family affections, he cared little or nothing for public causes in themselves. These were, as he once said frankly, 'luxuries'. What mattered to him was to make the instrument he controlled—first Prussia and then Germany—as strong as possible and therewith to increase his own power. He expounded this ruthlessly to the Reichstag in 1881: 'I have often acted hastily and without reflection, but when I had time to think I have always asked: what is useful, effective, right, for my fatherland, for my dynasty—so long as I was merely in Prussia—and now for the German nation? I have never been a doctrinaire. . . Liberal, reactionary, conservative— those I confess seem to me luxuries. . . . Give me a strong German state, and then ask me whether it should have more or less liberal furnishings, and you'll find that I answer: Yes, I've no fixed opinions, make proposals, and you won't meet any objections of principle from me. Many roads lead to Rome. Sometimes one must rule liberally, and sometimes dictatorially, there are no eternal rules. . . . My aim from the first moment of my public activity has been the creation and consolidation of Germany, and if you can show a single moment when I deviated from that magnetic needle, you may perhaps prove that I went wrong, but never that I lost sight of the national aim for a moment.' He cared as little for persons as for causes, and had few personal loyalties. He wrote once: 'The capacity of admiring men is only moderately developed in me, and it is rather a defect of my eye that it is sharper for weaknesses than good qualities.' He paraded an exception in favour of William I, but this exception operated only so long as the king agreed with him; and he gave his devotion free rein only when the emperor was safely dead.

Bismarck said to some politicians in 1874: 'I am bored; the great things are done. The German *Reich* is made.' So indeed it turned out. The period of making was over;

that of conserving had begun. Definitive peace between
France and Germany was signed at Frankfurt on 10 May,
1871—twenty years to the day since Bismarck first took
train to Frankfurt as Prussian representative at the
federal diet. There were no further wars between the
Great Powers in his lifetime; no frontier in Europe was
changed outside the Balkans; the German constitution
itself remained unaltered until 1918. These forty years of
stability became in retrospect 'Bismarck's system'; and
he was credited with profound foresight where there had
been only a quick instinctive response to events. Bismarck
had had a conscious plan when he became prime minister
in 1862, though he failed to operate it—the plan of a
revolutionary remodelling of Europe in co-operation with
France and Russia. He had intentions of a less definite
nature up to 1866: he wanted somehow to make Prussia
stronger in north Germany. He never meant to carry his
power south of the Main. All his political and religious
outlook was against it. Lutheranism was his deepest
principle. He regarded the south Germans as corrupted
by Roman Catholicism and French liberalism, moreover
beyond the reach of Prussian militarism. Schweinitz once
said to him: 'This expansion must cease where the supply
of Prussian officers gives out,' and he replied: 'I do not
say so, but it is the basis of my policy.' The military
treaties with the southern states were then all he wanted.
He was driven to go further first by the accident of the
war with France and then by its prolongation. He made
'little Germany' without ever intending to do so.

Could this 'little Germany' be permanent? Could
German nationalism be arrested at the Austrian frontier?
When the 'little German' programme was devised in 1848,
it was not proposed as an alternative to the 'greater
Germany' which should include the German-Austrians,
but as a practical first step made simply because the
greater programme was unattainable. Every 'little German' at that time expected 'greater Germany' sooner or
later. The only real alternative to greater Germany was

to divide Germany at the Main· with Austria; and this is what Bismarck had tried to do until 1866. The independence of the south German states was another, though inferior, version of the same idea. It had now broken down. The German *Reich* was unmistakably a national state, despite its federalism; and it was bound to exercise an increasing attraction on the Germans still outside it in the non-national Habsburg monarchy. Bismarck had not only done enough for his generation; he had done too much when, however inevitably, he overstepped the line of the Main.

He recognized this himself. No man was more convinced that Europe would never be settled until national reconstruction was complete or, as he put it, until the peoples were sorted out into their 'tribes'. Yet after 1871 he did everything to stave off the consequences of his own work. He tried to make out that his Germany was still an exclusively Protestant state with no interests in the valley of the Danube or in the Near East. There was no 'philosophy' behind this. Bismarck did not believe that his negations could be permanent; he merely shrank from further trouble and upheaval. 'When we have arrived in a good harbour, we should be content and cultivate and hold what we have won.' He constantly told the German-Austrians that they should lose their national character and develop loyalty to the Habsburgs; but the only reality he recognized in the Habsburg monarchy was the Hungarian gentry—the nearest equivalent in central Europe to the Prussian Junkers. Time often gives to things a sanctity which they did not possess at the start; and the frontier which Bismarck drew in 1871 between the Austrians and other Germans is now perhaps a genuine dividing-line. If this is so, Bismarck made 'little Germany' by accident; that he should have believed in it himself is to credit him with a foresight which he did not and could not possess.

It was the same in his relations with the other Powers. Metternich had perhaps planned a system of perpetual peace. Bismarck was content to avoid the troubles of the moment. He did not expect them to present much difficulty after the peace with France. She was too weak to challenge the settlement by herself; and no other Power was likely to aid her in doing so. He is often said to have aimed at the isolation of France. But this was unnecessary: the French did it for themselves. They too wished to avoid new troubles. Certainly Bismarck supported the republican form of government in France and even justified this by arguing that republicanism disqualified her as the ally of any monarchist Power. This was window-dressing for his emperor. His real concern was that a royalist or Bonapartist government in France—caring more for prestige and less for the French people—might turn to a grandiose foreign policy, as Gramont had done in 1870, and provoke a new war, disastrous for both France and Germany. Of course, the temptation might be irresistible even to the republicans if other Powers actively sought a French alliance. But they would do this only if they had themselves causes for quarrel with Germany; and these did not appear to exist. Bismarck had no colonial ambitions—it did not even occur to him to claim any French colony in 1871. Hence England and Germany were friends, if not 'natural allies', as England and Austria had been earlier. Austria-Hungary was reconciled to national Germany. Even Beust met Bismarck with every evidence of friendship in August 1871; and it was henceforth Bismarck's anxiety to avoid Austria-Hungary's alliance, not her enmity.

Nor did the rise of Germany seem to threaten a conflict with Russia. Bismarck, and indeed most Germans, remained hostile to Polish nationalism after 1871 as they had been before it. He repudiated any interest in the German 'Baltic barons', despite their ties of class with the Junkers. 'They have got into the ogre's cave, and we cannot help them. If I wanted to conduct a purely Machiavellian policy, I should even wish that they would be Russified as soon as possible; for as long as they remain German,

they form an element of strength and energy.' Germany
had no practical conflicts with any of the Powers. Therefore
he still assumed, as he had done between 1866 and 1870,
that she could follow a line of pacific detachment, friendly
to all, allied with none. He was never chary of kind words.
He emphasized to England their common character of
industrial progress and liberal monarchy; to France the
common need for a settled frontier. With Austria-Hungary
and Russia he revived the cause of monarchical solidarity,
and sometimes spoke as though it were his dearest wish
that the old Holy Alliance should return to life. He never
took this very seriously. He knew quite well that Francis
Joseph was no longer a despotic monarch and that even
Alexander II had to consider Russian opinion. When a
party of German officers visited St. Petersburg at the end
of 1871, the tsar said to one of them: 'You don't know
how I love you; I daren't even show it to you here.'

Bismarck himself was far from Metternich's position.
He was the chief minister of a constitutional state, ruling
in close co-operation with a great liberal party. Perhaps
he emphasized the conservative nature of his foreign
policy for that very reason. It is often said that home
and foreign policy should go hand in hand, each reflecting
the other. With Bismarck the opposite was the case. He
was always most revolutionary abroad when reactionary
at home; liberal at home when conservative abroad. He
had preached revolutionary nationalism between 1862
and 1866, when he was in conflict with the Prussian liberals;
he was pacific between 1867 and 1870, when making liberal
Germany. Later he abandoned the Holy Alliance just when
he broke with the liberal party in parliament. He liked to
make policy himself, not to have it dictated to him either
by politicians or by the emperor; and he practised in this
as in everything else a policy of balance—taking away
with one hand what he gave with the other. Though he
frightened the tsar and the Austrian emperor with talk
of 'the social peril', he did nothing against the Social
Democrats in Germany until after the Holy Alliance had

disappeared. Having one of Marx's friends among his own associates, he knew that the Marxist International was dying; yet he used its ghost as excuse for the League of the Three Emperors.

This League had nothing in common with Bismarck's later alliances. It was founded on sentiment, not on interests; and it had no precise terms. In 1872 the three emperors met in Berlin without making a written agreement of any kind. Later in the year Moltke drafted a convention with the Russian chief-of-staff, providing for military co-operation in time of war. Bismarck refused to confirm this convention, and it was never invoked later. In 1873, when Alexander II was in Vienna, Austria-Hungary and Russia at last got something down on paper. The essential clause was a promise that, if they quarrelled in the Near East, they would subordinate their differences there to the general interests of monarchical solidarity. Bismarck gave a vague approval to this agreement. He could hardly 'accede' to it in any real sense, having no stake of his own in the Near East. The League was not designed to isolate France—Bismarck had other means of doing this. Its object, so far as it had one, was to prevent a conflict between Austria-Hungary and Russia in the Eastern question—a conflict in which Germany could only lose. Like most associations based on sentiment from the Holy Alliance to the League of Nations, it turned out to be ineffective. It was a fair-weather system. The League of the Three Emperors was supposed to secure the peace of Europe. It survived only so long as the peace of Europe was secure. Monarchical solidarity was a luxury which was blown to the winds as soon as Russia and Austria-Hungary saw their eastern interests in danger.

Bismarck knew this from the start. No man had denounced alliances of sentiment more fiercely or more accurately. The League did no harm, though little good. It pleased William I, and, therefore, perhaps made it easier for Bismarck to continue the liberal line in home affairs which he had been following since 1867. His interest in foreign policy was at its lowest. He hardly troubled to do anything except record the successive payments of the French indemnity and, of course, to quarrel with his ambassadors. His legislative activity, on the other hand, was at its height, pushing through to a wider conclusion the liberal measures that had been prepared between 1867 and 1870. These measures were indistinguishable from those of Gladstone's contemporary ministry in England, except that they were more sweeping and more effective. The National Liberals regarded themselves as the government party. Bismarck consulted their leaders on the parliamentary work of the session; and their candidates were treated as Bismarck's men. Only a few conservatives supported Bismarck, and that grudgingly. A political conflict in 1872 showed how far Bismarck had travelled since the days when he was the Junker enemy of liberalism and the defender of Prussia against Germany. He brought forward in the Prussian parliament proposals for a modest element of self-government in local affairs—an attack on the Junker monopoly of local office. The liberals of the Prussian Chamber supported his proposals. The Upper House, on which he had once relied, rejected them; and William I had actually to create twenty-five peers to force the government measure through.

Nor was this all. Bismarck resigned his position as prime minister of Prussia, remaining only foreign minister and Imperial chancellor. It was not his affair, he said, to protect the interests of his former friends, and he was exhausted by contending with them. Even the Prussian ministers were too reactionary and timid for his taste. Roon, who had proposed Bismarck as prime minister ten years before, had now to repay the debt and become prime minister himself. The experiment was not a success. When Bismarck had planned the German constitution so that the chancellor was subordinate to the Prussian prime minister and the mouthpiece of the Prussian ministry, he was himself prime minister. Now he was furious to discover that the Prussian prime minister was not subordinate to the Imperial chancellor. Of course, neither Roon nor any other minister attempted to issue orders to the chancellor, as the Prussian ministry was entitled to do. But this was not enough. Bismarck insisted on issuing orders to them. He complained that legislative proposals were being made in Prussia without his knowledge. Prussia, he added, must now conform to a German pattern. Bismarck had resigned as being too liberal; Roon had taken his place as more conservative. But it soon turned out that Bismarck would not allow Roon to act on his conservative principles. His function, in Bismarck's eyes, was to exploit his reputation as a conservative in order to force through Bismarck's liberal measures with less fuss—above all with less nervous irritation for the great man. Roon would not play this part. He resigned within a few months, and Bismarck resumed the post of Prussian prime minister for the rest of his active life.

A further episode soon showed again how far Bismarck had moved from his original position of 1862. The German military establishment was still on a temporary basis. Parliament had authorized it in 1871 immediately after unification, for three years only. The general staff and the military cabinet of the emperor now tried to make it permanent. They submitted their proposal to the Reichstag without consulting Bismarck or asking his advice. The politicians resisted. They would authorize the establishment for the lifetime of a single parliament (three years) or, as a gesture of conciliation, for four years; they would not agree to the 'eternat'. Bismarck told the National Liberal leaders: 'The proposal is not my work. You can discuss it freely.' They took his hint and threw it out. William I announced that the conflict of 1862 had begun again and that he would fight it through once more. Bismarck, far from showing fight, first took to his bed and then offered to resign. The emperor gave way; and the politicians, threatened with a dissolution, gave way also. Bismarck imposed authorization for seven years—a compromise acceptable only to himself. The politicians did not get authorization by each Reichstag; the emperor did not get eternity. Bismarck had proved himself the master of both elements in the constitution, the agent of neither.

He often claimed to be educating Germany into parliamentary government. Nothing was more frequent than his call for a steady majority which should work hand-in-hand with the government of the day. He said in private: 'I am no absolutist. There should be only two parties, for and against the government. If the ministry is overthrown, the opposition party must be forced to form a new ministry.' He referred enviously to the example of England where there was 'a parliament with a strong majority, homogeneously organized, under a leadership such as was provided by the two Pitts or Canning, or even Palmerston, Peel.'[1] Such a parliament, he said, would soon reduce the king and the Upper House to a very little space and tie them down. He blamed the Germans for having 'eight or ten factions, with no constant majority, no united, recognized leadership'. And it was true that the Reichstag never knew a single majority-party. The National Liberals, even at their most powerful, could provide a majority only by associating themselves with the Bismarckian Conservatives on the one side or with the Progressives on the other; and they were themselves divided into a Left under Lasker and a centre under Bennigsen.

Yet it is difficult to put all the blame on the politicians. Though Bismarck called for a parliamentary majority, he disliked its consequences. His theories led him one way, his personality another. There is an exact analogy in his

[1] The existence of a two-party system in England ever since the Glorious Revolution was a received dogma of the time. If Bismarck had understood English history as we do now, he would have held up these statesmen as a warning, not an example. The elder Pitt never had any party support ; the younger Pitt had to juggle a number of groups, relying mainly on the support of the Crown. Canning was put in office by royal favour, against the will of the majority of the House of Commons. The Liberal party on which Palmerston relied was in fact a collection of differing factions. Only Peel had the support of a compact party—much to his discomfiture in 1846.

relations with William I. Bismarck said to Roon in 1872: 'I don't know why, I don't manage to please the king. As a gentleman and a soldier, I only want to obey him.' Roon, who knew his Bismarck, answered: 'Certainly you want to, but you don't do it.' It was the same with the Reichstag. He wanted a majority, but it had to be one which followed his lead unquestioningly. 'I have often spoken to English members of parliament, and they said to me in reference to some measure: I regard this measure as foolish, dangerous, and mistaken, but the minister who leads the party, the leader of the party wants it, he must accept the responsibility for it—I think he is making a mistake.' But what if instead the majority tried to impose its will upon Bismarck? He rejected the idea with violence. 'The crown prince wants me to obey the majority. That demands a suppleness of character and conviction that I do not possess.' And again: 'The foreign policy of a great country cannot be put at the disposal of a parliamentary majority without getting on to a false track.' Yet Bismarck can be defended by the English example to which he himself appealed. Sir Robert Peel was the first man to see that parliamentary government demanded a stable majority. He built up such a majority for the Conservative party and used it to force himself upon an unwilling queen in 1841. But when it came to the repeal of the Corn Laws, he repudiated his responsibility to the Conservative party and rejected its claims in words which Bismarck might have used: 'I am not under an obligation to any man or to any body of men. . . . I have served four Sovereigns and there was but one reward which I desired—namely, the simple acknowledgement, on their part, that I had been to them a loyal and faithful minister.'

It is surprising, indeed, that Bismarck co-operated with the National Liberals for so long or that he did not run earlier into a crisis such as brought Peel down. The breach was postponed by a great political struggle, in which Bismarck and the National Liberals seemed to be on the same side—the *Kulturkampf*, or conflict of civilizations between

national Germany and the Roman church. This conflict
had many deep causes. The Church itself was in combative
mood against every modern idea. In 1864 Pius IX denounced the mortal error that 'the Pope can and must
compromise and be reconciled with progress, liberalism,
and modern culture'; and in 1870 the Oecumenical council
at the Vatican proclaimed the Infallibility of the Pope
just when his territorial supremacy was being destroyed.
It is easy to see now that this infallibility was asserted only
in matters of doctrine. It seemed at the time that the
papacy was claiming again the right to excommunicate
and depose temporal rulers which it had tried to exercise
in the Middle Ages. The papacy had identified itself with
the defeated Powers in the war of 1866 and 1870. Antonelli,
the papal secretary of state, exclaimed on the news of
Sadova: 'the world is falling to pieces!', and Windthorst,
the Roman Catholic leader in Germany, said that the
Kulturkampf began on the day of Sadova. Similarly,
Napoleon III had been the protector of the papacy, and
Rome fell to the Italians as a direct consequence of Sedan.
Bismarck had some grounds for thinking that his work
could be undone only by a clericalist conspiracy, linking up
Paris, Vienna, and Rome. On the other hand, the decree
of infallibility seemed to · have opened a chink in the
clericalist armour. It was opposed by the leading German
theologians, and every German bishop at the Vatican
council voted against it.

The aggression was not all on one side. Bismarck and the
Reichstag were making liberal Germany; and the modern
liberal state came everywhere into conflict with the Church.
Education, for instance, could be a matter for compromise
so long as it was limited to a few. It was bound to cause
bitter dispute as soon as it became universal; and after
1871 universal elementary education was everywhere the
order of the day. Disputes over religious education dominated the politics of every European country in the last
thirty years of the nineteenth century—not merely Germany, but England, France, Belgium, and Austria-

Hungary, to name a few at random; and Germany, in fact, got by with a less fierce conflict than the others. What made the conflict seem sharper in Germany while it lasted was in part Bismarck's own ruthlessness of expression and still more the political associations of the Roman Catholics. Germany had been divided religiously for three hundred years, each state possessing a defined religious character of its own. In some states the Roman Catholics were a secure majority, in others a barely tolerated minority; and this made them infinitely adaptable. Prussia had long had peculiar difficulties. By tradition a purely Protestant state, she acquired a large Roman Catholic population on the Rhine in 1815; and there had been a full-dress rehearsal for the *Kulturkampf* (this time over mixed marriages) between 1836 and 1840, with priests and bishops in prison, churches standing empty, and the state impotent against a religious opposition. In 1840 the Romantic enthusiasm of Frederick William IV had led to a compromise, with the king actually attending celebrations at the Roman Catholic cathedral of Cologne in 1844. The conflict was postponed for a generation. Bismarck's victories renewed it in acuter form. The North German confederation was still predominantly Protestant; but the unification of 1871 created a state in which the Roman Catholics were a formidable minority.

Moreover, they were a minority clearly identified with the defeated cause. The clericals of Bavaria opposed unification to the last; and when the Roman Catholics created their own political party, the Centre, this won support from all those who disliked the Bismarckian *Reich*. The Poles and Alsatians who co-operated with the Centre were Roman Catholics; but Hanoverian separatists also voted solidly for it, though they were Protestants, just as on the other side Roman Catholic nationalists urged Bismarck on. It was, for instance, Hohenlohe, former prime minister of Bavaria and a Roman Catholic, who proposed the attack on the Jesuits in 1872. Bismarck emphasized the anti-national aspect of the conflict and even attributed it all to the Poles: 'I got involved in the struggle through the Polish side of the affair.' This was an exaggeration. The conflict would have happened even without Poland. The Centre was rather the rallying-point for those who, though German patriots, had a different German ideal—'greater Germany', a resurrection of the Holy Roman Empire, ruled perhaps from Vienna, perhaps from Frankfurt, but certainly not from Berlin. Bismarck expressed this when he called the Centrists *Reichsfeinde*, enemies of the empire. Windthorst answered: 'The prime minister is not the state and no minister has yet dared to call *his* opponents opponents of *the state*.' This was a telling reply: Bismarck easily identified himself with the state and did so increasingly as time went on. Yet the accusation was true. The Centrists were enemies of Bismarck's Germany, though not of Germany itself, and enemies above all of the state's claim to regulate all temporal affairs.

Bismarck was exasperated and driven forward against the Centre by his realization that he had himself put power into their hands. The Centre was the creation of universal suffrage and could not have existed without it. Bismarck, as so often, had got out of one difficulty only to find himself in a greater. He had carried universal suffrage in order to ruin the liberals, his opponents of the eighteen-sixties. His calculation proved correct. Middle-class liberalism had little appeal to a mass-electorate; and it fell to pieces in Germany as in every other country within a generation of the establishment of universal suffrage. But this did not strengthen Bismarck. Indeed, his parliamentary position would have been stronger if a compact liberal party had survived, and its backing would have enabled him to defy William II in 1890. When he introduced universal suffrage, he seems lightly to have assumed that the masses would vote dumbly for Conservatives and that these would give unquestioning, even unreasoning support to the Imperial chancellor. He had played the national appeal successfully against the king and against the liberal politicians; he supposed that he could play it just as easily against any rivals for the support of the masses. He did not realize that the free peasants of western Germany and the industrial workers had a very different character from the Prussian peasants whom alone he knew at first-hand. These masses had a national consciousness, but they expressed it by voting for democratic leaders, not for their landlords or their employers. Bismarck's Reich had two opponents—first the Centre, then the Social Democrats. Both owed their power, if not their existence, to Bismarck's own actions; and against them he had to rely on the National Liberals, whose decline he had irrevocably decreed.

The *Kulturkampf* was an effort to arrest this development at its start, to strangle the Centre in the cradle. And, of course, Bismarck always held that struggle against a common enemy was the simplest method for attaining political unity. It made it easier for him to carry the budget or the army-law when he could claim that he and the National Liberals were allies against the Roman church. The alliance was artificial. The National Liberals insisted that two philosophies of life were in conflict—clericalism against the modern spirit of secularism. Bismarck disliked both philosophies. He was defending the rights of the state, and he traced the struggle back to Agamemnon, contending with the priests at Aulis, or to the struggle between emperors and popes in the Middle Ages. He raised the old banner of Luther and declared: 'If I follow the pope, I shall lose my eternal salvation.' This Lutheran appeal, though it rested on genuine conviction, had also a political motive. Bismarck wished to escape from dependence on the National Liberals by enlisting the Conservatives, too, on his side. This manœuvre did not work. The Prussian conservatives, though Lutheran, disliked the attack on religion more than they liked the attack on Roman Catholicism. They acquiesced in 1872 when Bismarck proposed that all school inspectors should be appointed by the state; they jibbed when he added that henceforth they could be laymen. The rift grew wider in 1873. The Conservatives could swallow the 'May-laws', Bismarck's great engine against the Roman Catholics, by which the training and even the licensing of priests required state approval. They were outraged by civil marriage, an inevitable consequence of the struggle, but one which Bismarck had bitterly opposed in 1849. Even William I disliked the trend of policy: baptism, he thought, would go next.

Bismarck warned the Conservatives that they would be ruined if they went against him: 'You were elected under my name; if I withdraw my hand from you, you will not come back.' And so it proved. The Conservatives suffered disaster at the general election of 1874. But this did not help Bismarck. Gains went to the Left wing of the National Liberals and, much worse, to the Centre. It sprang from 61 to 95, and, allied with the Poles, the Alsatians, and the Danes (from north Sleswig) could command 120 votes— almost as many as the combined National Liberals. Repression, far from weakening the Centre, strengthened the Roman Catholic cause. It forced back on to the clericalist side nearly all those who had opposed the decree of infallibility in 1870. Priests and bishops were imprisoned; sees remained vacant; passions on both sides grew more bitter. On 13 July a young Roman Catholic attempted to assassinate Bismarck. He replied by saddling the Centre with responsibility for the attempt: 'Push the man away as much as you like. He still clings to your coat-tails.' From the Centrist benches came a cry of 'Pfui!'—one of the strongest German expressions. Onlookers expected Bismarck to strike the deputy or to reach in his pocket for a pistol. He stood at the tribune, rocked with rage; then mastered himself and said coldly: ' "Pfui" is an expression of loathing and contempt. Do not think that these feelings are far from me; I am only too polite to express them.' No public man knew better how to provoke others and how to control himself.

Though he could not control the Conservatives and quarrelled with his few remaining Junker friends, he could still control William I. When the emperor hinted his

doubts, Bismarck answered in December 1874 by offering
to resign. William I was contrite, even swallowed criticism
of his wife, and Bismarck swept tumultuously on his way.
He said in the Reichstag—if the pope triumphs, 'we
non-Catholics must either become Catholics or emigrate
or our property would be confiscated, as is usual with
heretics.' There was something old-world in this frenzy.
He tried to switch the conflict on to a field where he had
always been a master—foreign policy. From the beginning
his gravest charge against the Centre had been its international character. Yet he was prepared to exploit this
international loyalty. He tried repeatedly to negotiate with
the pope behind the backs of the Centre leaders, and
offered to drop the May-laws if the pope would order the
Centre to give him unquestioning support in the Reichstag
on everything else. A bargain of this kind ended the
Kulturkampf later. It was impossible so long as Pius IX
remained pope; and he survived until 1878. Since Bismarck could not dominate the Centre by its international
association, he tried to discredit them by the same means.
He accused them not merely of subservience to the pope,
but of collaboration with Roman bishops and clericalists
in other countries. Bismarck never found it easier to tolerate
criticism from abroad than at home. In 1874 he tried to
insist on a press-law against clerical writers in Belgium.
In the spring of 1875 he made the same move on a greater
scale and saw in France the heart of a great clericalist
conspiracy.

France had certainly recovered miraculously from the
defeat of 1871. Moreover, Thiers and the pacific republicans had been overthrown. The royalists had elected
Macmahon as temporary president, and they aspired to
increase their prestige by a challenging foreign policy.
Bismarck accepted their challenge. He even allowed his
associates to talk of a preventive war; and Moltke talked
of it also, without waiting for the chancellor's permission.
It is inconceivable that Bismarck meant this talk seriously.
A man cannot go against the habits of a lifetime, however

much he may change his ways of expressing them; and Bismarck never wavered in his dislike of war except as a last resort. Besides, he had always insisted that war must bring practical gains. What gain could victory over France have brought him in 1875? Only more discontented French voters, to strengthen the Centre in the *Reichstag*. But talk of war, or of the French danger, might discredit the Centre; it might even weaken the French clericals and bring a sensible republican government to power—or so Bismarck, in his bullying way, too easily assumed. On 5 April the *Kölnischer Zeitung* asked, 'Is war in sight?', perhaps not at Bismarck's instigation, but certainly with his encouragement. It was the signal for a crisis which did not work out to Bismarck's advantage.

Though the French government were alarmed, they did not respond, as Bismarck had hoped, with apologies or with a reduction of their armament-programme. Decazes, the French foreign minister, revealed the German talk of preventive war to *The Times*—a stroke as telling as Bismarck's publication of the French designs on Belgium in 1870; and he appealed to the European powers, this time more successfully than Thiers had done during the Franco-German war. Andrássy, the Austro-Hungarian foreign minister, alone did not respond. He was bidding for an alliance with Germany, not for the alliance with France which had escaped Beust even before the war of 1870. Indeed, Andrássy saw estrangement between Russia and Germany in the offing, and expressed his joy by three hand-stands on the table that had once been Metternich's. The British and Russian governments both expostulated seriously in Berlin—the British through their ambassador, the Russians personally on the occasion of a visit by Alexander II and Gorchakov. Bismarck gave way with the masterly grace which he knew how to use when necessary. The crisis turned out to be a false alarm, even helped to improve Franco-German relations. It left only a lasting estrangement between Bismarck and Gorchakov. Bismarck did not forgive the Russian interference and alleged that

Gorchakov had announced to his ambassadors: 'Peace is now assured'.[1] Gorchakov on his side was not sorry to humiliate the man who had once described himself as Gorchakov's admiring pupil; and he said in private: 'Bismarck is ill because he eats too much and drinks too much and works too much.' Though this was true, Gorchakov like others would have done well to remember that Bismarck, even when ill (or perhaps most when ill) was more formidable than most men when well.

The 'war-in-sight' crisis was a casual episode in Bismarck's policy, and it seemed to leave no mark on domestic affairs. The *Kulturkampf* was waged as fiercely as ever; Bismarck's alliance with the National Liberals grew closer. In February 1876 he openly denounced the *Kreuzzeitung*, the paper of the extreme right which he had helped to found in the bitter days of 1848. More than a hundred Junkers, including all the famous names of Prussia, answered with a declaration of loyalty to their paper and of defiance to Bismarck. He published the names in the official gazette and went over the offences of his former friends in many a sleepless night. Yet there were warning signs that his confidence in the National Liberals was on the wane. It left perhaps only a passing mark when in 1875 they defeated his attempt to smuggle into the criminal code provisions against stirring up class-hatred and civil disobedience which would have enabled him to prosecute the Social Democrats. It was more significant when Bismarck proposed later in the year the nationalization of the German railways—not in itself an illiberal measure, for Gladstone had favoured it in England, but an indication all the same that Bismarck was losing faith in Free Trade and *laissez-faire*. One of Bismarck's closest associates took the hint. In April 1876 Delbrück resigned. The most competent of officials and a convinced Free Trader, he would not follow Bismarck, yet shrank from conflict with

[1] The text of Gorchakov's message was in fact: 'The tsar leaves Berlin perfectly convinced of the conciliatory dispositions which reign there and which assure the maintenance of peace.'

him. At just the same time, Bismarck said of the National
Liberals: 'They always want to wash the fur without
making it wet and so always turn in shame from any
naked idea.'

Even Bismarck took some time to look facts in the face.
The German protective tariffs would expire on 1 January
1877. Thereafter Germany would become a Free Trade
country. In England Free Trade had been followed by
almost thirty years of uninterrupted prosperity. Germany
was going into Free Trade just when the boom after the
Franco-German war was ending and when trading conditions were becoming more difficult. Bismarck might have
told German industrialists to face these difficulties if Free
Trade had been an intrinsic part of his political thought,
and if industry alone had been threatened. But the
Prussian landowners were also encountering the competition of cheap Russian grain—first result of the new
Russian railways; and a prosperous agriculture was always
essential in Bismarck's outlook. It would be unfair to
ascribe his conversion solely, or even mainly, to his private
interest as a great landowner. He had allowed others to
introduce Free Trade, without much thought or leadership
of his own. There had always been a doubt beneath the
surface. Bismarck was never liberal in thought, though
sometimes in action. For him the state, not the individual,
was the mainspring of political action; and he did not
accept the 'night-watchman' theory of the state which
was common to all liberals. He held that the state could
lead in economic affairs, just as he had tried to take the
initiative in foreign policy and not wait upon events.

There was a second consideration. The *Reich* was not
financially self-supporting; it depended upon contributions
from the individual states for the bulk of its income. A
new tariff-system would both protect German industry
and give to the *Reich* a secure revenue of its own. No doubt
there were cruder political calculations. Tariffs might
win back the support of the Conservatives; they might
ruin the more doctrinaire National Liberals; in any case

they would supply a new national appeal to take the place of the *Kulturkampf*. The steps of God could again be heard sounding through history. It took Bismarck some time to grasp the hem of God's garment. He said as early as 1875: 'To give the German *Reich* a powerful, unshakable financial foundation, which provides it with a dominating position and brings it into organic union with every public interest in state, province, district, and commune—that would be a great and worthy task, which could tempt me to devote to it the last scrap of my failing strength.' But he added: 'The task is difficult. I am not an expert in this field, and my advisers have no creative ideas.' Bismarck might have found a target nearer home for the taunt which he discharged against Francis Joseph: 'The emperor of Austria has many ministers, but when he wants anything done he has to do it himself.' Bismarck was already Imperial chancellor, prime minister of Prussia, and foreign minister. When he turned to economics, he had to become also Prussian minister of trade; and he held all four posts until he left office in 1890.

His delays, his hesitation, his planlessness throughout 1876 were not surprising. He saw new tasks ahead, tasks for which he had no training or experience. His health grew worse. He had become enormously fat. His teeth were rotting. His list of ailments included jaundice, varicose veins, perforated stomach, gastric ulcers, gall-stones, shingles. He told his wife he was 'weary of life'. In March 1877 he again asked to resign. William I almost took him at his word, much to Bismarck's alarm. He withdrew his resignation and compromised on a prolonged leave of absence. On 15 April 1877 he retired to Friedrichsruh; in the summer to Varzin. He returned to Berlin only on 14 February 1878. During this absence he turned his ideas upside down. His return brought an upheaval in every aspect of economic, political and foreign affairs. The liberal Bismarck disappeared. A more universal Bismarck —more conservative but also more constructive—took his place.

THE CHANGE OF COURSE

BISMARCK claimed a consistency of policy and purpose. His speeches treated forty years of political activity as a single theme; and the memoirs which he wrote after his fall were designed to show that he had always pursued the same long-term aims. He boasted of being an opportunist only in the sense that his means and methods changed with the times. He said in 1887: 'What is an opportunist? He is a man who uses the most favourable opportunity to carry through what he regards as useful and appropriate.' And it is, of course, true that Bismarck remained unmistakably the same throughout his career always more concerned to get his own way than to lay down in advance what that way should be. He loved both combat and success. It was a sad contradiction to him that one excluded the other: by winning a combat, he also brought it to an end. He was devoted to his instruments—the Hohenzollern dynasty or the German nation—so long as they served his will; but ultimately it was the triumph of his will, a mastery of the external world, that mattered to him.

Yet, on a more practical plane, there were two occasions when he changed his outlook on life and public affairs so profoundly that we can speak of a real change of course, even of a change in himself. One man disappeared; and a different man took his place. No doubt the new man was equally determined to get his way, but the way went in quite a different direction. The first of these occasions was shortly after Bismarck went to Frankfurt in 1851; the second during his long absence from Berlin in 1877. When Bismarck went as Prussian representative to the Frankfurt diet, he was a 'reactionary', as he had been consistently since he entered serious politics in 1847. He wanted to suppress the revolution by force, indeed to resist every liberal idea. His foreign policy rested on a devout belief in the Holy Alliance; and he regarded it as his practical task to build up again Prussia's alliance with Austria. We cannot say what experience shook his faith in conservatism—perhaps it was no experience in particular. But within a few months, even a few weeks, of arriving in Frankfurt, he changed course. He abandoned resistance and went instead with 'the current of the times'—meaning no doubt to master and control it, but steering with events instead of against them all the same. He advocated conflict with Austria, sought alliance with revolutionary France, even with German nationalism.

Every step which Bismarck took for the next twenty-six years followed logically from this conversion of 1851. The champion of Olomouc co-operated with Hungarian revolutionaries, German radicals, and national Italy; the 'pure Prussian' unified Germany; the former reactionary gave her a liberal constitution, based on universal suffrage. The line did not change with the establishment of the Empire. Far from defending the old order, Bismarck took the modern ideas of others and gave them practical form— in codes of laws or in economic and social policy. Germany under his guidance became a *Rechtstaat*, fought the Roman Catholic church, and went over to Free Trade. He was too great, too domineering, too skilful, to be controlled by a parliamentary majority; but it began to look as though a liberal majority would control the government when he went. *Laissez-faire* ruled in foreign affairs as at home. Bismarck made alliances solely as the prelude to wars; and he made wars to settle immediate practical dangers. He assumed until 1878 that the balance would work itself once it had been set right by his wars against Austria and France; and he relied, like any liberal statesman, on the natural community of interests between states to give Germany peace and security. Bismarck's foreign policy between 1871 and 1878 was indistinguishable from Gladstone's between 1868 and 1874. Both avoided alliances and kept their hands free; giving offence to none, they both assumed that no one would give offence to them.

It was difficult to say between 1871 and 1877 whether Bismarck or the National Liberals determined the character of German policy. Certainly the Liberals owed part of their strength to the fact that Bismarck favoured them. But equally Bismarck got his way because they supported him. At the beginning of 1877 this alliance still seemed secure. A general election returned the National Liberals in undiminished number. The Centre was unshaken, and there were a few more Social Democrats; but the National Liberals and the loyal Conservatives still provided a secure Bismarckian majority. The campaign against the Roman Church was still being pursued; Free Trade had been reached; Bismarck made no attempt to go over to an active foreign policy despite the growing clouds in the Near East. His alliance with the National Liberals seemed to be on the point of growing even closer. He invited Bennigsen, the National Liberal leader, to Varzin and offered him the post of Prussian minister of the interior. This would have been a dramatic step—the first time that a parliamentarian had joined the government. Bennigsen was willing. He only stipulated that two other National Liberals should join the Prussian government at the same time. Bismarck raised no objection. He foresaw difficulties from the emperor, but expected as usual to overcome them. The two men met again in December. Bennigsen repeated his condition; Bismarck left it unanswered. The National Liberal leaders began to practise their manners as Prussian ministers.

The negotiations ended with explosive violence when the Reichstag met in February 1878. Camphausen, the Prussian minister of finance, proposed a tax on tobacco, but added that this was not the prelude to a tobacco-monopoly, which the National Liberals opposed on general economic principles. Bismarck rose from the chancellor's seat and announced: 'I am working for the monopoly and accept the proposal in this sense as a first step.' It was the moment of decision. Bennigsen broke off the negotiations with Bismarck, and the National Liberals ceased to co-operate with the government. What had happened? The tobacco-monopoly was a symbol, though no trivial one—it was the weapon of centralized governments both in Austria and in France. Bismarck described it as 'the feather which suddenly turns the scales'; and the scales certainly turned against liberalism, towards a wider, more constructive conservatism than any known before. Even the negotiations with Bennigsen may have been a preparation for this. Bennigsen certainly intended to make Bismarck the prisoner of parliamentary government; perhaps Bismarck intended to make Bennigsen a prisoner of a different sort. He often suggested that parties should take the helm in order to carry out the policy which they opposed and held up the example, which he claimed with some exaggeration to have found in England: 'If reactionary measures are to be carried, the Liberal party takes the rudder, from the correct assumption that it will not overstep the necessary limits; if liberal measures are to be carried, the Conservative party takes office in its turn from the same consideration.'

It would be foolish to suggest that Bismarck's breach with the National Liberals was a personal whim. Old-fashioned liberalism was dying everywhere. It ended in Italy in 1876, in Austria in 1879. Gladstone was so conscious of its being played out that he resigned from the leadership of the British Liberal party after the general election of 1874. Legal and administrative reform was exhausted; social improvement would take its place. Bismarck declared: 'Political parties and groups based on high policy and political programmes are finished. The parties will be compelled to concern themselves with economic questions and to follow a policy of interests. . . . They will melt like ice and snow. Voters with the same interests will co-operate and will prefer to be represented

by people of their own instead of believing that the best
orators are also the most skilful and most loyal representatives of their interests.' In the same spirit he told the
Prussian ministers that he wanted to see 'moderate
Conservatives who would offer the people material benefits
in place of those who thought only of formal guarantees.'
No doubt he wished to defend his independent power from
the encroachment of the National Liberal party; no doubt
he was alarmed at the rise of the Social Democrats; and
no doubt the effects of Free Trade heightened his general
turn against *Laissez-faire*. But his concern for social welfare
was genuine and of long standing. He had defended
Silesian weavers against their employers in 1865; he always
avowed his belief in 'the right to work'—the most revolutionary demand of 1848; and he wrote as early as 1871:
'The action of the state is the only means of arresting the
Socialist movement. We must carry out what seems justified in the Socialist programme and can be realized within
the present framework of state and society.' He apologized
in 1872 to an academic advocate of social welfare: 'I too
am a Socialist, but I cannot fight two campaigns at the
same time.' There was nothing surprising or unprincipled
in his breach with the National Liberals. The surprise was
rather that it had been so long delayed.

There were other factors, some of a more temporary
nature. He had already proposed an exceptional law against
Social Democratic propagandists in 1875; he was anxious
to renew this proposal in the Reichstag session of 1878,
and knew that he must quarrel with the National Liberals
over this, if over nothing else. There seems to have been
no urgent cause for his anxiety. Indeed the 'social peril' was
rather a spectre which Bismarck raised against the
National Liberals than one which disturbed his own sleep—
but of course he always took care to experience genuine
alarm at the ghosts with which he frightened others. One
of his greatest gifts was to believe in his own spooks and
legends so long as these suited his purpose. On the other
hand, he cared less about the conflict with the Roman

church. It had been going on too long; and Bismarck no more favoured siege-operations against the Roman Catholics than against Paris in 1870. Quick victories, followed by reconciliation, were always his ideal; and, as a first step, he was already propagating the legend that the *Kulturkampf* was none of his doing. It was a bit of luck for this legend that he had been temporarily out of office as Prussian prime minister just when the 'May-laws' were passed in 1873; and he impudently claimed that he had been too busy to read them. Roon was indignant at this excuse; and even Bismarck contradicted it in private: 'I carried on the struggle against the papal claims more energetically than any of my colleagues, including Falk [the minister actually responsible for the May-laws].' The legend did as a starting-point when a prospect of agreement showed itself. And this happened in 1878. Pius IX died. Leo XIII, his conciliatory and worldly-wise successor, was elected two days before Bismarck took the tobacco-monopoly under his wing in the Reichstag. Though he could not foresee all Leo's moderation and diplomatic skill, he already had in his pocket a letter to William I from the new pope, hoping for an improvement in relations. It would make it easier for Bismarck to end the *Kulturkampf* if he quarrelled with the National Liberals and posed as a Conservative. And, to put it the other way round, he could shake himself free of the National Liberals if he ended the *Kulturkampf*. Apart from these tactical considerations, the Centre, as the party of the small man, favoured social welfare; it was, in fact, a perfect 'interest-group' such as Bismarck now advocated. And as the champion of dogmatic Christianity, it might also favour legal measures against the Marxists—at any rate it had no objections of liberal principle.

Bismarck always loved to balance. He never committed himself irrevocably to any course. In foreign policy his alliances often led to wars; and his wars were the prelude to alliances. Alliance with Austria in 1864 led to war against her in 1866; and that war produced in time the

alliance with Austria-Hungary in 1879. That alliance in
its turn might have been broken if he had remained
longer in power. The near-alliance with France of 1866
was followed by the war of 1870; and it was not Bismarck's
fault that the war did not lead to a renewed alliance in 1877
or later between 1883 and 1885—with again a new period of
hostility in 1886. Italy was the only ally with whom he did
not go to war; and that was merely from lack of opportunity—his phrases were often hostile enough. It was the
same in home affairs. Bismarck straddled between king
and parliament, later between emperor and Reichstag,
and played them off against each other. He was always
ready to tell the Reichstag that his only responsibility was
to the emperor—'my only constituent'; and he warned
the politicians that they could not even cut his salary—
it was guaranteed by the constitution, and he would go to
law for it. Things were very different when he went to
court. Then he insisted that the emperor must agree to the
Reichstag's wishes, whatever Bismarck interpreted them
to be.

Bismarck had an easy time with the Reichstag between
1871 and 1878, a difficult time with the emperor. The old
gentleman did not like the successive doses of liberalism,
and still less the measures against the Roman church.
Bismarck spoke of William with increasing contempt.
'The emperor does not smoke, reads no newspapers, only
documents and dispatches; it would be more useful if he
played patience.' He described William to the palace
gardener as 'an officer who does his duty, well-mannered
with ladies'; and on another occasion said that William
was 'cold, hard as a stone'. He made no secret of his feelings: 'I took office with a great fund of royalist sentiments,
and veneration for the king; to my sorrow I find this fund
more and more depleted.' His special grievance was that
William listened to the empress when his back was turned,
and that she always opposed him: 'Either marriage or
monarchy; both together are impossible!' His weapon
against the emperor was the threat to resign; and he used

it repeatedly in these years—in 1869, twice in 1874, in May 1875, in April 1877. Though his excuse on each occasion was the state of his health—once he even threatened to go mad like Frederick William IV—the real reason was always that William I had criticized or opposed him. It is significant that at this time he never threatened the Reichstag. Each Reichstag ran its full course; and there were regular elections in 1871, 1874, 1877.

Now he decided to play things the other way. There was only one more threat of resignation—in September 1879, and that was for a special purpose. Its object was to force on William I the alliance with Austria-Hungary, not some legislative programme. After September 1879, the threat was never repeated. On the other hand the Reichstag was ceaselessly bludgeoned. There were forced elections in 1878 and 1886. Bismarck considered more extreme measures. In 1878 he proposed 'a legal *coup d'état*'. The princes, who had made the empire, should be summoned and should suspend parliamentary government. In 1881 on the eve of a general election, he again proposed that the Reichstag should be abolished; and in 1884, at the next general election, he wanted to return to open voting. His swing to conservatism made it easier for him to get on with the emperor, though it would be an exaggeration to say that their relations were ever perfect or that Augusta ever ceased to criticize him. There was a more important consideration. William I was now over eighty—he had been born in 1796. He could not last much longer. His successor, the Crown Prince Frederick, was liberal in outlook, though not always in practice. Bismarck had needed a liberal Reichstag so long as he was faced with a conservative emperor. He began to prepare a Reichstag of conservatives and clericals when a liberal emperor was in the offing. Still, this was not urgent. In 1877 William seemed as fit as ever. Bismarck got the final push to his change of course from the two attempts to assassinate William in 1878—the second of which he seemed unlikely to survive. Perhaps Bismarck would have remained longer

on the liberal side if he could have foreseen that the
emperor would live another ten years.

It is impossible to say which of these factors was decisive.
Even Bismarck did not pretend to know which feather
turned the scale. He often gave the impression that personal resentments determined his actions; but they did
so only when they fitted in with the needs of more general
policy. He would have swallowed his dislike of the National
Liberals and his apprehensions of the crown prince, if
Pius IX had remained as pope; he would not have been
reconciled with the Centre, if he had not wanted to carry
protective tariffs; he would have postponed social welfare,
if he had not been alarmed at the increase of the Socialist
vote; and he felt this alarm principally because he wanted
a rallying cry at a new general election. Accidents, such as
the election of Leo XIII or the attempted assassination
of William I, were simply the signal for Bismarck to do
what he had long decided to do; yet he might not have
done it without them. He would certainly have done these
things at some time, though perhaps not in that order.
He was again bored, as he had confessed to being in 1874.
It was a contradiction of his nature that he aimed always
at peace and security and then was discontented when he
got them. He said in 1877: 'I have been hunting since day-
break; it is late, I am tired, and I will leave it to others to
shoot at hares and partridges. But if you have seen the
slot of a wild boar, that is another story.' The wild boar in
Bismarck's life could only be the chance to turn upside
down everything which he had accomplished and to set
out on new tasks.

A piece is missing in this jigsaw puzzle, though the fact
that it completes the picture does not necessarily make it
more important than the others. An upheaval in foreign
policy as well as in home affairs followed Bismarck's return
to Berlin in February 1878; and probably one could not
have happened without the other. The upheaval in this
case was certainly not of Bismarck's making. In his great
formative years he had welcomed quarrels between other

Powers, so that Prussia could herself make easy gains. He had wanted to exploit the Crimean war; he had reaped enormous advantage from Austria's difficulties in Italy; and it had been a great misfortune for him that the Eastern question had remained obstinately quiet before 1866. But once Germany was satisfied, he wanted every other Power to be peaceful too. The nearest he came to activity in foreign policy after 1871 was to keep Russia and Austria-Hungary on friendly terms. But he could not dictate to the subjects of Turkey in the Balkans. There was a rising in Bosnia in 1875; and a worse rising in 1876 which provoked the Turks to the Bulgarian horrors. Russian opinion was outraged by the sufferings of the fellow-Slavs; the Habsburg monarchy was concerned to preserve another 'ramshackle empire'. Bismarck cared nothing for the Eastern question one way or the other. When Gorchakov urged that this was not a German or a Russian, but a European question, he replied: 'I have always found the word Europe on the lips of those politicians who wanted something from other Powers which they dared not demand in their own names.' Of course, he added, 'as Christians we ought to have sympathy for suffering humanity everywhere and especially for suffering Christians in foreign lands.' But this sympathy did not oblige him to risk 'Germany's power, her peace and her European relations'.

In December 1876 Bismarck first used a famous phrase that he often repeated later. Germany, he said, had no interest in the Eastern question 'that was worth the healthy bones of a Pomeranian musketeer'.[1] The phrase was more revealing than he perhaps intended. In his more expansive moments, he would show sympathy for Austria's 'German mission' down the Danube and in south-eastern Europe, just as he once called Trieste (an Austrian port) 'Germany's outlet on the southern seas'. But when he wanted to define Germany, it was Pomerania on the Baltic, not the Rhine-

[1] The more familiar grenadier took the musketeer's place in a speech of 1888.

land, Bavaria, or Austria which came into his mind. And
certainly, Pomerania was remote from the Eastern question,
however much this affected the German communities of
Transylvania, Constantinople, or Salonica. The other
Great Powers had vital interests in the Near East. Bismarck's Germany stood aloof, as though in a different
continent.

Bismarck tried, therefore, to adopt an attitude of ami-
cable detachment during the discussions which went on
between Russia and Austria-Hungary. He despised the
Turks with a true Lutheran contempt; and he believed,
as in other cases, that a partition of the Balkans on
national lines would be the safest and most sensible solution. But since his two friends could not agree on this, he
joined with them in advocating futile programmes of
reform. He welcomed Andrássy's initiative in recommend-
ing reforms for the Ottoman empire in December 1875;
and when these failed, he invited Andrássy and Gorchakov
to Berlin in May 1876 for a further effort. England and
France were excluded from the Berlin meeting but not
from malice or monarchical prejudice. Bismarck took
trouble over Russia and Austria-Hungary solely because
they seemed the two likely to quarrel. Nor did he insist
on being a party to their agreements so long as they
agreed. In July 1876 Gorchakov and Andrássy met at
Reichstadt and agreed, or so they thought, on what they
would tolerate in the Balkans, if the Ottoman empire
collapsed. Unfortunately it failed to do so. Quite the
reverse, the Turks suppressed the risings and defeated the
semi-independent Slav state of Serbia. Pan-Slav enthusiasm
in Russia could no longer be restrained. The tsar was cap-
tured by it and resolved on war against Turkey. But the
example of the Crimean war made him hesitate. Gorchakov
was always insisting that Russia must not fall again into
the isolation that had then led to disaster.

. Alexander II, free at Livadia from Gorchakov's control,
thought that he would pull off a great stroke on his own. He
would invoke the traditional friendship between Russia and

Prussia and would ask William I to keep Austria-Hungary neutral by threats as he now genuinely imagined that Russia had done in 1870. It was a typical bit of old-style diplomacy between crowned heads that might have once worked. Now Bismarck stood in the way, even though Gorchakov might be evaded. Alexander II made his inquiry of William I in October 1876. The old German emperor had long lost all independence of action in foreign affairs. Bismarck snatched the question out of the monarchs' hands. He replied to Gorchakov, not to Alexander: Germany was friendly to both Russia and Austria-Hungary, and she could not allow 'any of the factors on which she counted in the Balance of Power to fall out of it'. There was nothing new in this answer—it was no different from the line that Prussia had taken during the Crimean war, though then to brush off Austrian, not Russian, demands for support. It was not an 'option' for Austria-Hungary; it was a refusal to take sides, a hope that the balance would still work of itself. Gorchakov was not surprised or offended; more probably, he welcomed the snub to Alexander II's amateur diplomacy. He knew that Russia could not go to war against Turkey without the permission of Austria-Hungary; and he obtained this permission in a convention negotiated at Budapest in January 1877.

One new question was raised in Bismarck's answer, though not with much serious purpose. He suggested that Germany might support Russia if she received in return a Russian guarantee of Alsace and Lorraine. A little later he took a similar line with the British government, which was preparing to resist Russia for the sake of the Ottoman empire; an Anglo-German alliance against Russia was possible only if it was also directed against France. Bismarck knew perfectly well that neither Russia nor Great Britain would commit themselves in this way. Both courted France—the Russians to prevent 'the Crimean coalition', the British to resurrect it. Nor did Bismarck want their support—war against France was far from his thoughts, and he could not bind the future. Gorchakov said truly:

'This guarantee would be of little use to you, treaties have very little value nowadays.' Bismarck's answer was a friendly evasion, no more, and was so accepted by all parties. A myth grew up later, encouraged by Bismarck, that in October 1876 he had offered to go with Russia 'through thick and thin' and that decisive estrangement followed Russia's refusal. In fact, Bismarck had simply kept out of the Eastern question, as his predecessors had done before him. Russia bought Austria-Hungary's neutrality; went to war with Turkey in April 1877; and was bitterly engaged throughout the year. Bismarck at Varzin and Friedrichsruh ignored foreign affairs and brooded on his domestic problems.

The Eastern question took a new turn in February 1878. The Russians had defeated Turkey; their troops were at the gates of Constantinople. The British government determined to preserve the remains of the Ottoman empire. The British fleet passed the Straits. War between Russia and Great Britain seemed imminent—a war in which Austria-Hungary was likely to be involved. Bismarck decided that he could no longer stand aside. He was indifferent to the fate of the Balkans; he could not be indifferent to the Balance of Power. Germany had nothing to gain from a general war, and much to lose; therefore she must act as peace-maker. On 19 February Bismarck announced in the Reichstag that Germany came forward not as arbitrator but 'as an honest broker'. Bleichroeder, Bismarck's man of business, commented: 'There are no honest brokers.' But in this case Bismarck was really concerned to settle the affair, not to earn a percentage. His action, far from being hostile to Russia, helped to save her from a disastrous war. The Russians imposed the treaty of San Stefano on the Turkish empire in March. Then, urged on partly by Bismarck's mediation but more by their own fear and weakness, they agreed to submit the treaty to a European congress. Bismarck tried to dodge further responsibility. He suggested that the congress should meet in Paris; and when this was rejected, offered the chairmanship of the congress to Waddington, the French representative. Bismarck's efforts were in vain. He had made Berlin the capital of Germany, and Germany the centre of Europe. Now he had to pay the price for his success.

By the spring of 1878 Bismarck had cast off from his old moorings. He was not yet running with full sails before a fresh wind. Doubtful of the old course, he could not yet see the new. The first storm signals of February 1878 were followed by some months of calm. At home, the alarm over the tobacco-monopoly was forgotten—the monopoly never in fact achieved. The National Liberals continued to assume that they were Bismarck's allies, even though he had not admitted them to the government. At most they thought to make him more amenable by a little harmless obstruction. Bismarck, on his side, found reconciliation with the Roman Catholic Centre more difficult than he had at first supposed on the death of Pius IX. Leo XIII was a match even for Bismarck. Though he wanted a settlement, he was prepared to wait for it. In April he demanded the repeal of the May-laws and the restoration of the legal privileges which the Roman church had enjoyed in Germany, before he would advise the Centre to compromise itself politically. These were terms of unconditional surrender; and Bismarck would not 'go to Canossa' even for the sake of protective tariffs and social welfare. He broke off negotiations with Leo XIII and waited in his turn. In foreign affairs equally, Bismarck did not admit that a new era had begun. The approaching congress was a nuisance; but he still imagined that it would settle the differences between the Great Powers and that the natural order of peace and security would then reassert itself. He had some thought of a grandiose initiative, proposing a partition of the Ottoman empire—Egypt to England, Bulgaria to Russia, Bosnia to Austria-Hungary, Tunis or Syria to France. But even this was far from a policy of permanent alliances. Foreign affairs in his eyes were something that could be dealt with and finished, a book to be closed. In April he retired again to Friedrichsruh.

Two unforeseeable accidents pushed him again into action. On 11 May a crazy youth attempted, ineffectively, to assassinate the emperor. Bismarck at once answered by laying before the Reichstag the 'exceptional law' against the Social Democrats which he had failed to carry in 1875. He was not concerned with public order—the police themselves did not want the law. His object was to ruin the National Liberals. They still had liberal principles, though they supported Bismarck's legislative programme; and some of them at any rate would oppose exceptional measures against the Socialists. On the other hand, refusal to take an anti-Socialist line would estrange their respectable voters. When it came to a vote in the Reichstag, the National Liberal party stuck unitedly to liberalism. Indeed, every party except the Conservatives voted against the exceptional law on 24 May. Bismarck, who had remained quietly at Friedrichsruh, affected to treat the bill as solely the work of his ministerial colleagues; and merely remarked that they were unfortunate in their dealings with the Reichstag.

Then came a further accident, so providential for Bismarck that he might almost have arranged it. On 2 June another crazy anarchist shot at William I, and this time wounded him severely. When the news reached Bismarck, he exclaimed: 'Now we'll dissolve the Reichstag!' He did not stop to inquire whether the criminal was a Social Democrat. He almost forgot to ask about the Emperor's condition. He saw decision and victory before him, as he had seen it on 13 July 1870, when his pencil remodelled the telegram from Ems. By a curious irony, William I not only survived the attempted assassination, but benefited from it. The shock acted as a stimulus to his aged frame and freed him from the fainting fits which previously afflicted him. He often said truly in the following years: 'Nobiling [the assassin] was the best physician I ever had!'

Bismarck often emphasized in later years that 2 June 1878 had marked for him the beginning of a new course, though he was less frank about its meaning. He said in

1882: 'I thought in 1877 that I was entitled to resign. But after I had seen my lord and king lying in his blood, I felt that I could never desert this lord, who had sacrificed body and life for his duty to God and men, against his will.' The picture is less moving when one reflects that Bismarck did not see 'his lord and king' for nearly a week after the attempt. By then William was out of danger, and the political consequences were well in train. Bismarck gave a rather different version in private. 'Now I've got the scoundrels!'—'Your Highness means the Social Democrats?'—'No, the National Liberals'—and it was a matter of indifference to him that most National Liberals, after the second attempted assassination, supported the exceptional law. The Reichstag was dissolved without being given a chance to reverse its previous decision. The important thing for Bismarck was not to pass the exceptional law, but to impress the electors. Previously he had waited for the results of general elections and then made the best of them; now he tried to dominate the electoral campaign.

He did this in a curious way—by his absence. Western democracies expect the political leader, whether president or prime minister, to be the centre of public agitation. General elections are themselves a form of running debate. But Bismarck never argued or took part in the cut-and-thrust of debate. He rhapsodized in the Reichstag, standing ostensibly above the parties; and he would slip into his speeches some general philosophic reflection from which the voters were expected to divine the correct party-moral. Once an election began, he alone of all Germans was condemned to silence. Every politician had a platform, literally and metaphorically. Bismarck had none. He never identified himself with a party or laid down a precise programme; he never addressed a public meeting until after his fall. A tongue-tied leader of a country with universal suffrage seems strange, though not so strange then as now. In every constitutional country, but particularly in Germany, the deputies were supposed to be 'independent' of the government, both in policy and in origin. Even British

members of parliament made out that they followed the
dictates of the party-whip purely by accident. The electors
also were expected to reason things out for themselves.
Bribery had ended; mob oratory by respectable politicians
had not begun. No British prime minister, or even former
prime minister, addressed a public meeting until Gladstone
broke the ban over 'the Bulgarian horrors'. Bismarck was
not likely to follow this example. He knew that he could be
talked down, and therefore appealed from words to facts.
From 1878 onwards he always started the election campaign
with some explosion which, he hoped, would muffle the
oratory of the politicians. 'The social peril' which he invoked after the attempted assassination of the Emperor
on 2 June was his first experiment in this method. It was
meant to ensure that the voters would lose their heads and
hence the use of their ears.

Bismarck used one weapon to influence public opinion
which brought down on him much high-minded disapproval. He issued directives to the press and employed
his own men, Busch and Bucher, to write leading articles
which were then widely distributed. More than this, he
drew on the sequestered funds of the ex-King of Hanover
to bribe the press directly. This was the 'reptile fund'
which received as much notoriety in Bismarckian Germany
as the secret service fund had done in eighteenth-century
England. The parallel supplies a useful warning. Our
historians now regard the secret service fund as more of a
myth than a reality; and the 'reptile fund' was much the
same. Newspapers with a wide circulation, solidly but-
tressed by advertisements, did not need subsidies, as *The
Times* was the first to discover. Newspapers with a small
circulation needed financial support either from private
persons or from the government; and most German papers
were still in this condition. Why should Bismarck alone
be without a journalistic voice? As a matter of fact, the
'reptile fund' was used mainly as the secret service money
had been—to do things that were better not talked about.
Elderly servants of the state were saved from penury; the

indiscreet from the penalty of their mistakes. Of course, Bismarck—like Walpole or the Duke of Newcastle—expected loyalty in return for his financial assistance; but, like them, he was often disappointed.

The Reichstag was dissolved on 11 June, much against the will of Crown Prince Frederick, who was acting as his father's representative[1] and who foresaw the ruin of his liberal friends. Bismarck sent out instructions to all government officials, much after the fashion of eighteenth-century England: the object of the election was to split the National Liberal party, and it was to be fought with the two cries of the social peril and tariff reform. Once this circular had been dispatched, there was little more that Bismarck could do. A general election was for him a time of leisure, not of political activity; and he conveniently fitted the congress of Berlin in before the poll on 30 July. The congress was a grandiose episode in Bismarck's life rather than a vital event in his policy. It still sprang from the hope that all international rivalries between the Powers could be finally settled and that foreign affairs would then look after themselves. It was the last great effort of *laissez-faire* in foreign politics, not the prelude to a more conscious system. Indeed, it was mainly significant, so far as Bismarck was concerned, for what it left out, not for what it discussed or settled. Statesmen of the earlier nineteenth century, or even Napoleon III, would have been astonished at a European congress where the questions of Poland, Germany, and Italy were not mentioned. All these questions had received an answer in previous years, largely according to Bismarck's wishes, but without any intervention by the Concert of Europe. The Congress of Berlin dealt only with the Eastern question, and even with that in a limited sense —the French made their attendance conditional on the exclusion of Syria, Egypt, and North Africa from the

---

[1] In 1857 Bismarck had urged Prince William to revolt against being merely his brother's representative and to insist on becoming regent. In 1878 Bismarck silenced the crown prince's claim to the regency by an imperial Order which the emperor had been too weak to sign.

agenda, and Bismarck seconded them. The European order which Bismarck had created did not receive even formal approval. It rested, and continued to rest, on German strength, not on the agreement of the Great Powers.

The congress of Berlin confined itself to the settlement of the Balkans and its task was little more than to register the private agreements which had already been reached between Russia and England and between Russia and Austria-Hungary. In fact, Bismarck regarded the congress as a device for saving the face of the Russians. They could make to European opinion the concessions which would seem humiliating if made to British and Austro-Hungarian threats. Bismarck tried to win Russian favour by taking their side over the details which remained in dispute. But this did not satisfy them. He hoped to please the Russians by mitigating the effects of their defeat; they thought that he ought to have prevented the defeat itself. Their grievance was justified. It would have been small consolation to Bismarck in 1866 or 1870 if the Great Powers had intervened to impose a settlement and if Russia had then thrown to Prussia a few trivial concessions. He had settled with Austria and France in isolation; and this is what the Russians had wanted to do with Turkey. No polite phrases could conceal the fact that they had failed to repeat Bismarck's success, though more from their own blunders than from any maliciousness of his.

The congress was a show-piece for Bismarck's personality. It was the only international gathering over which he presided; and no one ever presided in the same manner. He gave the great statesmen of Europe a taste of the rough jovial manner with which he entertained German politicians at his 'beer-evenings'. He even appeared at the early sessions in a beard, and shaved it off only for the composite portrait which concluded the congress. The exuberant joy with which he disregarded aristocratic conventions revealed his nature—half-country squire, half-revolutionary. He bustled through the formal sessions, commenting audibly if the Turkish delegate or even Lord Salisbury dared to raise a new point, and scribbling during Gorchakov's opening speech: 'pompos, pompo, pomp, po'. Protocol was ignored; everything subordinated to punctual and enormous meals. Bismarck was to be seen, stuffing shrimps into his mouth with one hand, cherries with the other, and insisting—not surprisingly—that he must leave soon for a cure at Kissingen. Any real difficulty was settled by Bismarck privately behind the scenes, and to great effect. Gorchakov, who could remember the congresses of Ljubljana and Verona, was horrified at this brusque procedure. But the congress was a model for all time in its way of doing business and reaching results, even if less in the results themselves. Bismarck was not interested in these or in the fate of 'the people down there'. 'We are not here to consider the happiness of the Bulgarians but to secure the peace of Europe.' He wanted to get everything settled and to start getting his weight down at Kissingen.

Bismarck had often met Gorchakov and Andrássy before. He was now on cold terms with Gorchakov, whom he found vain and senile; and he did not care for Andrássy's grand Magyar ways. Nor, despite political courtesy, did he find any common ground with Waddington, the French delegate—a man distinguished as the only prime minister (French or British) to row in the university boat-race. Bismarck at this time disliked Salisbury, the second British delegate, whom he described as 'a lay preacher' and as 'wood painted to look like iron'. Perhaps Bismarck sensed that Salisbury had gone one better than himself and that he could combine equal cynicism in policy with a genuine moral earnestness. Bismarck estranged the ethically-minded politicians of the time when he appealed to 'blood and iron'. Salisbury could rest his policy on 'the right of conquest because it is the simplest and most effective' and yet retain the admiration of English Nonconformists—even of Gladstone.

The real hit of the congress was the personal tie between Bismarck and Beaconsfield. No doubt Bismarck flattered 'the old Jew' in order to extract concessions for Russia's benefit. But the mutual affection was genuine. The two men recognized their common qualities. When they had last met in 1862, Disraeli was the struggling leader of the Conservative opposition, Bismarck merely Prussian minister at Paris. Now both had arrived. Bismarck was a prince, Disraeli was Lord Beaconsfield and soon to receive the Garter. Each admired the actor in the other, and characteristically each noted the beauty of the other's voice. Both had the brooding melancholy of the Romantic movement in its Byronic phase; both had broken into the charmed circle of privilege—Bismarck as a boorish Junker, Disraeli as a Jew; both had a profound contempt for political moralizing. Was it Disraeli or Bismarck who said of himself: 'My temperament is dreamy and sentimental. People who paint me all make the mistake of giving me a violent expression'? Was it Disraeli or Bismarck who said on becoming prime minister: 'Well, I've climbed to the top of the greasy pole'? In politics both men had used universal suffrage to ruin liberalism or, in the English phrase, 'to dish the Whigs'. Both genuinely advocated social reform; Disraeli had once defended protective tariffs. Both used foreign success to strengthen their position at home. When Bismarck was told of the British occupation of Cyprus, he exclaimed: 'This is progress! It will be popular: a nation loves progress!' Beaconsfield was annoyed at having the words taken out of his mouth and commented sourly: 'His idea of progress obviously consists in taking something from somebody else'—an idea which Beaconsfield had made the basis of Tory policy. When they dined together Bismarck played for sympathy in his usual manner by abusing others and told Beaconsfield: 'Don't imagine that my illness is the result of the French war; its cause is the horrible conduct of my king.' Beaconsfield was a match for him: 'I have not seen any of this two-facedness in the monarch whom I serve; she is frank and upright, and all her ministers love her.' At least this is the reply which he recorded for the benefit of Queen Victoria. The conversation has an added piquancy from its date. It took place on 17 June, barely a fortnight after Bismarck had seen William I weltering in his blood (at any rate in imagination) and when the German election campaign was ringing with the cry of monarchical loyalty.

The congress ended on 13 July, settling the Eastern crisis, though not the Eastern question. Bismarck went off to Kissingen, where the waters failed to counteract the effects of his gluttony. He had there a further failure. He met the papal nuncio from Munich and tried again to strike a bargain. The pope should order the Centre to support Bismarck; then the Imperial government would gradually cease to apply the May-laws. Leo XIII, though conciliatory, was still obdurate: he insisted on the ending of the *Kulturkampf* before he would intervene in German politics. After this Bismarck could not be altogether content with the results of the general election on 30 July. The National Liberals were certainly weakened, losing some thirty seats; and their successful candidates were all pledged to support the anti-Socialist law. The two Conservative groups (one loyal to Bismarck, one more independent) took the place of the National Liberals as the strongest single party. But the *Reichsfeinde*, the enemies of the Empire, were unshaken: the Social Democrats lost only three out of twelve seats, the Centre came back stronger than before. Bismarck's impulsiveness had, as so often, rebounded against himself. Disillusioned with liberal policy, perhaps irritated at the liberal claims to office, he had set out to ruin the National Liberal party; and he had succeeded—the party was weakened and soon split. But this success did Bismarck little good. The mass-electorate turned against liberalism, as Bismarck told them to, but they did not turn towards conservatism. They voted in increasing numbers for the two mass-parties, the Socialists and the clericals. Bismarck realized too late that liberalism was a barrier against the two causes that he feared, though also a barrier against himself.

Bismarck resurrected his alliance with the National

Liberals when the Reichstag met in the autumn, if only as a
temporary expedient. He described the National Liberals
and the two Conservative factions as 'regiments of one and
the same garrison'; and this garrison gave him his anti-
Socialist law—though on National Liberal insistence only
for three years. The renewal of the law at triennial intervals
gave Bismarck a further problem to add to the septennial
crisis over the army-law—and the problem finally brought
about his downfall in 1890. He was angry at this compromise which had been forced upon him and again determined to escape from National Liberal control or interference. Tactics might force him on to their side; funda-
mentally he hated a party which rested, however feebly, on
principle instead of on material interest. He gave a sign
that the breach with them would soon be renewed. The
National Liberals were still hoping for a parliamentary
ministry. Bismarck now promoted a law, by which the
Imperial secretaries of state (hitherto merely administrative subordinates) could act as 'substitutes' for the
chancellor. The secretaries were made Prussian ministers
without portfolio and were thus qualified as the Prussian
representatives at the Imperial Council. But the chancellor
remained the sole 'responsible' minister for Germany.
Bismarck continued to insist that cabinet or committee
government was impossible in Germany. He never gave
any reason; and indeed the only reason was that he could
not stomach colleagues. Imperial Germany continued to
be ruled by one man—a man who was sometimes restrained
or obstructed, but never controlled, by parliament. There
was another curious point. Though there were now secretaries of state for foreign affairs, for the navy, for justice,
for finance, later for the colonies, there was no secretary
for the army. That remained the exclusive concern of the
emperor and of the chief-of-staff—an arrangement which
Bismarck, considering his open hostility to the generals,
tolerated rather than welcomed.

The last step in Bismarck's change of course came during
the winter of 1878–79. It was a masterstroke of improvisa-

tion. His projected time-table since the death of Pius IX
had clearly been, first to end the *Kulturkampf*, then to
carry protective tariffs with the support of the Centre.
This had not worked out: the *Kulturkampf* had not been
ended. But in October 1878 the Centre came out in favour
of protective tariffs. At once Bismarck reversed his order
of tactics. He would first propose fiscal reform and thus
compel the Centre to support him, even before the *Kulturkampf* had been brought to an end. The new economic
order in Germany was Bismarck's own work as much as the
legal and constitutional order had been. He studied political
economy, saying: 'I am ashamed to understand so little of
this subject', and drafted all the principal tariffs. Having
once abandoned Free Trade, he now wanted thorough-
going Protection, and stirred the sectional interests to bid
against each other. The Conservative agrarians, for
instance—most of them aristocrats—agreed to the tariff
on iron and steel only in exchange for a high tariff on grain.
As in every auction, Bismarck the auctioneer collected his
percentage. The groups were all tied to him, though hostile
to each other.

This fiscal revolution produced its political effect. Bismarck's anticipations were realized. On 3 May 1879,
Windthorst, the leader of the Centre, appeared at Bismarck's beer-evening, and remarked as he left: '*extra
centrum nulla salus*'—'no salvation without the Centre'.
Bismarck responded by attacking in the Reichstag the
intellectual politicians of the National Liberal party, 'who
neither sow nor reap, weave nor spin . . . these gentlemen
whom our sun does not warm, whom our rain does not
make wet, unless they happen to go out without an
umbrella!' Bismarck always made great play with his
practical activity as a cultivator of the soil. But he had
gained his estates by being the most intellectual politician
of his time and was no more a farmer than our present-day
company directors who go in for agriculture to offset their
liability to surtax. Joseph Chamberlain, the English
radical, turned the same phrase—'they toil not neither do

they spin'—to a more appropriate use a few years later, when he fired it against the great landed aristocracy, the class to which Bismarck now belonged. On each occasion the phrase infuriated the other side. The alliance between Bismarck and the National Liberals, which had lasted twelve years, tumbled down in a few weeks. Falk, the leading fighter of the *Kulturkampf*, resigned in July; Bennigsen soon withdrew altogether from politics; the National Liberals dissolved into fragments—one group merging with the Progressives who had opposed Bismarck since 1862; another constituting itself the mouthpiece of heavy industry; and a third drifting disconsolately in the hope that a liberal Bismarck would one day re-appear.

The Centre was caught, as Bismarck had expected: its social basis made it support protective tariffs even though the May-laws were still on the statute book. But the Centre claimed a price, though of a different sort. Bismarck had two objects in mind when he introduced tariff reform: one was to protect German industry, the other was to end the dependence of the *Reich* on the matricular contributions from the separate states. Most of the National Liberals were ready to swallow tariffs for the second reason, if not for the first; but they insisted on voting these tariffs annually, so as to strengthen the budgetary control of the Reichstag. The Centre were prepared to vote for permanent tariffs, but not for the profit of the central authority. They insisted in their turn that the yield from customs-dues, above a limited amount, should be shared out among the member-states in the same proportions as their matricular contributions. In this curious way an artificial deficit was created in the Imperial budget, which the states would be called upon to fill. Bismarck could make his choice between parliamentary liberalism and federalism. He did not hesitate a moment. Though he had often urged the Reichstag to develop its authority and had dismissed the states as contemptibly unreal, he chose the concession to federalism —perhaps for this very reason.

This financial jugglery between the *Reich* and the states completed the ruin of German liberalism. Bismarck had insisted, when the federal constitution was made, that the central authority should levy only indirect taxes—customs and excise. Direct taxation remained the prerogative of the member-states. This was perhaps reasonable so long as the new *Reich* was not expected to be any more powerful or effective than the old German confederation. It soon appeared that Bismarck's *Reich* was the real centre of power; and the National Liberals claimed that a *Reich*, which maintained the greatest army in Europe and challenged the Roman church, should also raise its own direct taxes. Protection defeated this claim. What is more, by providing further revenue for the member-states, it actually lessened their direct taxation also. The political and social consequences were profound. Indirect taxation falls equally on all members of the community, rich and poor; indeed, when a tariff on grain is included, it falls more heavily on the poor than on the rich. Direct taxation, even when not progressive, is proportioned to the means of the taxpayer; and when it is made progressively heavier, it becomes of itself an engine of social revolution. Gladstonian finance was the decisive step towards making England a social democracy, or something like it. Bismarckian finance, as it operated after 1879, made the rich richer, even if the economic expansion of Germany prevented the poor from becoming poorer. In England the rich paid the taxes and therefore worked to keep them down; in Germany the rich profited from the expenditure of the *Reich* and therefore worked to increase it. So far as men of liberal principle still existed, they entered politics in the separate states, where alone direct taxation was possible. The politicians of the *Reich* promoted the economic interests of sectional groups, and their own into the bargain. High principle disappeared; horse-trading took its place. The German Junkers were saved just when the English landowners were ruined, though they had to take the great industrialists into partnership. Bismarck had been more concerned to ruin

liberalism than to save the Junkers; but he saved them all
the same.

By the summer of 1879 Bismarck's change of course in
home affairs was virtually complete. Protection had been
established; the anti-Socialist law was in operation; he
was only waiting for a favourable opportunity to compromise over the *Kulturkampf*; and social welfare was just
round the corner. In September 1879 he took an equally
decisive step in foreign affairs by making a defensive
alliance with Austria-Hungary. The policy of detached
friendships ended; and a complicated system of alliances
took its place. It is hard to establish a formal, let alone a
conscious, connexion between the changes in home and
foreign affairs. Of course, agrarian protection in Germany
was directed principally against Russian grain and therefore, perhaps, weakened the traditional sympathy between
Prussian and Russian landowners. But men did not act on
such simple economic motives even in the nineteenth
century; and there were still many factors, from class-
solidarity to anti-Polish feeling, which held Prussian and
Russian nobles together. It is more to the point that
abandoning Free Trade meant a shift of emphasis from the
Hanseatic towns, Hamburg and Bremen, with their essentially maritime and 'little German' attitude, to the heavy
industry of the Rhineland, where the traditions of the
Holy Roman Empire were still strong, and where the
Habsburg monarchy was still regarded as German.

The real connexion lay deeper. The changes in home and
foreign affairs both sprang from Bismarck's abandonment
of the liberal belief that all things would work together for
good if only they were left alone. He ceased to believe that
peace and prosperity were natural; he took thought for
the morrow and secured them by conscious effort. Protection, as the name implied, involved the deliberate fostering
of German industry and agriculture against the dictates of
'economic law'; just as the anti-Socialist laws were an
attempt to direct men's thoughts. Bismarck's alliances
were also a form of protection, imposing a conscious design

on international relations instead of waiting upon events. He was not alone in this change of outlook. At the very moment when Bismarck was concluding an alliance with Austria-Hungary, Gladstone—greatest of liberals—left his old line of moral detachment and preached in the Midlothian speeches a creative foreign policy, based on the Concert of Europe. Bismarck and Gladstone reached no doubt very different conclusions, but they both started from the same point—the loss of faith in *laissez-faire*.

It would be easier to explain Bismarck's new foreign policy if he had not explained it so much himself. His explanations were not made for the benefit of posterity, a subject which never interested him. They were advocacy, directed to the person with whom he was arguing. William I had to be frightened by the story that Germany was in danger of immediate attack from Russia or even—being a very old man—by echoes from the Seven Years' war. More hard-headed diplomatists had to be told that Bismarck wished to revive the 'organic union' of all Germans which he had destroyed in 1866. The French were assured that his object was to prevent the dismemberment of the Habsburg monarchy—a cause in which they also were deeply interested. The British were told that the alliance would create an unbreakable barrier against Russia; the Russians that it would sever Austria-Hungary from Great Britain— 'I wanted to dig a ditch between her and the western Powers.' No doubt there was some truth in all these stories. It was part of Bismarck's strength that he always believed what he said, at any rate while he was saying it. Only one story was pure legend, created in after years. In 1870 Bismarck was taken by surprise and improvised a war at the last moment. It suited him better later on to make out that he had planned the war against France for many years. Exactly the opposite was true in 1879. He deliberately planned the alliance with Austria-Hungary; but when its consequences appeared inconvenient for him, he made out that he had been bustled into it by events. Yet even in this there is a fragment of truth. His nervous illness and his

toothache were at their worst; and he might not have acted
so swiftly and decisively if he had been in better control
of himself.

The alliance was caused by the diplomatic events which
followed the congress of Berlin rather than by the congress
itself. Bismarck had hoped that the congress would really
end the eastern crisis: it would enshrine a reasonable
compromise and save Russia from humiliation. It did this
at first so far as Russia was concerned. Her strength was
exhausted; the Russians, like most liberators, were on bad
terms with the people whom they had liberated; and they
asked only to be rid of their Balkan worries. The discontent
was on the other side. The Austro-Hungarian, and still
more the British, government now regretted the opportunity of defeating Russia of which Bismarck seemed to
have deprived them; and they tried to make up for lost
time. Their representatives in the Balkans sought not a
settlement, but to eject Russia altogether. Russia, it
seemed, would be pressed to the wall; and she would respond by the most violent expedients of diplomacy, as she
had done after the Crimean war. Then she had offered her
friendship to any Power who would help her to overthrow
the treaty-settlement, and she had made a 'revisionist'
alliance with France—an alliance which Bismarck, in his
revolutionary days, had been eager to join. Now he was
conservative, anxious to preserve the European order that
he had created. The dangers which he feared were perhaps
imaginary. Russian ambitions were turning to central Asia
and away from the Near East; the republic in France, now
consolidated, was resolutely pacific; and the statesmen at
Vienna had abandoned any hope of recovering the old
Habsburg position in Germany. But even the greatest men
cannot foresee the future; they can only expect it to repeat
the pattern of the past, and Bismarck was now warding
off the dangers that had followed the congress of Paris,
not the dangers of 1879. He had argued long ago that
Prussia should not remain isolated, should not miss her
chance: she should join the revolutionary alliance of France

and Russia. His own position being now reversed, he reversed the conclusion also and insisted on a conservative alliance with Austria-Hungary. He was determined not to repeat the former mistake. There could be no more dangerous course: what was mistaken twenty years before is often the wisest policy in the present. Great disasters are caused by trying to learn from history and to correct past mistakes. Men being what they are, it is probably better to think about the present, not about the past—or the future. As Bismarck said to Napoleon at Biarritz: 'One must not make events; one must wait for them to happen.'

Now, for whatever reason, he was determined to guard against future dangers, not present ones. The great improviser built a system against the improvisation of others. Early in 1879 he resolved on alliance with Austria-Hungary. There was no obstacle on the Austrian side. Beust had proposed an alliance as early as August 1871; Andrássy had sought German backing throughout the eastern crisis. The difficulty came from William I, as it had often done before. His aged mind was choked with sentimental attachments; and he had to be jockeyed into alliance with Austria-Hungary, as he had once been jockeyed into war against her. Russia had to be provoked; and her response seemed to justify Bismarck's precautions. The German representatives on the Balkan commissions opposed Russia instead of supporting her; irritating restrictions were put on her trade with Germany; the new tariffs played a useful part. Most provocative of all, Bismarck published an agreement by which Austria-Hungary released him from the obligation, incurred in the treaty of Prague, to hold a plebiscite in northern Sleswig.[1] The honest broker seemed to have collected his percentage after all. Alexander II was bewildered by this unaccustomed German hostility. He supposed that there must be some misunderstanding, and

[1] Actually the agreement was made on 13 April 1878, before the congress of Berlin, when Austria–Hungary was still in difficulties and had to acquiesce in any German demand. Now Bismarck antedated it only to 11 October 1878. It therefore looked like an Austrian payment for services rendered, whereas it was in fact more like buying off a blackmailer.

he tried to remove it by writing privately to William I on 15 August. Being a tsar, he expressed himself in arrogant terms, and Bismarck professed to see in the letter a threat of war. William I saw nothing of the kind. He was as bewildered as Alexander II, and bustled off to see him at Alexandrovo on 3 September. He returned, confident that all difficulties had been removed. Bismarck behaved very differently. He proposed a meeting with Andrássy even before Alexander II dispatched his letter; negotiated with Andrássy before the meeting at Alexandrovo; and went on to Vienna, where he signed a treaty against William I's express instructions.

There followed a battle to extract approval from the old emperor—the last of many battles between him and Bismarck. William I brought out all Bismarck's old arguments—the traditional friendship with Russia on which Hohenzollern success had been based; the danger of driving Russia into the arms of France; the repeated warnings against 'alliances which bind our hands'. Once more he threatened to abdicate. Bismarck answered with a torrent of arguments on his side, but his real weapon was a threat to resign and to carry the whole Prussian ministry with him. The pledge never to desert his noble master had not lasted long. William I confessed: 'Bismarck is more necessary than I am.' Besides, the threat to abdicate was pointless; William knew that the crown prince would favour alliance with Austria-Hungary, however much he differed from Bismarck in other questions. On 3 October William I gave way: 'My whole moral strength is broken.' This was true, and not only in regard to the Austro-German alliance. William I never opposed Bismarck again or tried to influence policy.

The alliance was ratified on 5 October. Formally it contained nothing which had not been said a dozen times before. Each ally would aid the other, if attacked by Russia; in any other war, in which one ally was involved, the other would remain neutral. During the negotiations Bismarck tried to get a pledge of Austro-Hungarian aid

against France, but he gave way readily. Andrássy des-
cribes how he said threateningly: 'You must accept my
terms. If not——,' and he rose dramatically from the table:
'——then I must accept yours.' In fact, Bismarck made the
demand only to please his emperor. He was quite content
with Austro-Hungarian neutrality, and even made out
that it would undo the verdict of 1866 if a Habsburg army
again mounted guard on the Rhine. The essential part of the
treaty was Germany's pledge to support Austria-Hungary
against Russia. Bismarck had already warned Russia in
October 1876 that he would not allow an attack against
Austria-Hungary; but it was one thing to warn Russia,
quite another to give a pledge to Austria-Hungary. The
alliance did not increase German security in the least.
On the contrary it brought her nearer to war; for there
was no danger of a Russian attack on Germany except as a
consequence of the pledge to Austria-Hungary. The alliance
was a liability for Germany, not an asset. Bismarck never
explained why he thought it a necessary liability.

Bismarck rushed into the Austro-German alliance without considering the remote consequences. He was always
impulsive; and the alliance seemed a quick way of ending
the tension in the Balkans. Austria-Hungary would feel
secure; she would no longer co-operate with Great Britain;
and Russia, therefore, would escape further humiliation.
Frederick William IV had made an alliance with Austria
(against Bismarck's advice) for much the same reasons at
the outbreak of the Crimean war. Probably Bismarck
assumed that this alliance would fade away as his earlier
alliances had done. But there was a fundamental difference.
The alliance with Austria in 1864 or with Italy in 1866 had
been alliances for more or less immediate war. They ended
when the war was fought and won. The alliance of 1879 was
an alliance to prevent war and therefore endured as long as
peace lasted. Whoever tries to secure peace becomes a
system-maker, and Bismarck did not escape this despised
fate. Henceforth he was, like Metternich, a philosophic
statesman. He had to make out that the dismemberment

of the Habsburg monarchy would make Russia too powerful; or that the national principle, which he advocated
elsewhere, would not produce a stable order in eastern
Europe. These were merely rationalizations. The truth was
simpler. He had come to desire peace for its own sake. In
earlier days he would have faced the reconstruction of
eastern Europe, as he had faced the reconstruction of the
west. Now he shrank from the turmoil that this reconstruction would involve. Security and tranquillity had
become his watchwords. He had done enough reconstruct-
ing. All he wanted was a quiet life.

Once he had been ready to stake everything on fortune's
wheel. Now he tried to stop it from spinning. How contemptuous he had been of the old Prussian statesmen who
had helped to prop up 'Metternich's system'. How strenu-
ously he had warned against tying Prussia's trim, seaworthy frigate to Austria's worm-eaten galleon. Now he
did everything that he had condemned in his predecessors.
Prussia's frigate had become the great German man-of-
war: Austria's galleon was more worm-eaten by twenty-five
years. Yet Bismarck tied them together for the rest of their
existence. The alliance of 1879 only recognized existing
facts; but, by recognizing, it sought to perpetuate them.
In 1866 Bismarck failed to carry through the thorough-
going national reconstruction of Europe which he had
advocated earlier. He allowed the Habsburg monarchy to
survive. Now he went further and committed Germany to
its survival. No more events must be allowed to happen.
The keeper of the Elbe dike had resumed his old employment.

No sooner had he taken this decisive step than he tried
to belittle it. He always reacted violently against arguments
that were put before him. One of his colleagues said:
'Beware of opposing Bismarck immediately if you disagree
with him. If you do, he—being so excitable—finds such
crushing arguments for his opinion and becomes so obstinate that no power on earth can move him from it.'
William's opposition during the negotiations had made

Bismarck behave as though the alliance was the be-all and end-all of German policy. Once he had got his way, he reacted against his own tumultuous arguments; and soon became as distrustful of the Austro-Hungarian alliance as he had once been enthusiastic, until at the end of his life he was almost its only critic and opponent in Germany. The alliance was to last only for five years, though then automatically renewed unless denounced. Bismarck always refused to make it permanent and left obscure hints to his successors that they should shake it off as he had shaken off the earlier alliance with Austria in 1866. During the negotiations he had put the Pomeranian grenadier on half-pay and had declared in romantic terms: 'According to a thousand-year-old tradition the German fatherland is also to be found on the Danube, in Styria, and in Tyrol.' Once the alliance was signed, he claimed that the most important thing in it was what it left out; it asserted by a significant silence that Germany would not support Austria-Hungary in the Balkans. She would be supported against a direct Russian attack. If she wanted to pursue Balkan ambitions, she must find other allies.

What is more, he did his best to ensure that she should not find these allies. The Austrians had been opposing Russia in Bulgaria with the help of Great Britain; and they hoped to add Germany to this combination. Even Bismarck approached the British government during his negotiations with Andrássy and talked of an Anglo-German alliance. He broke off abruptly as soon as the Austro-German alliance was made; and the Austrians were soon complaining that the principal effect of the alliance, so far as they were concerned, was to thwart their Balkan policy. As early as September 1879 Bismarck was assuring a Russian emissary that Austria-Hungary was now safely under control and that Russia would meet with no further obstacles in the Near East: 'The Crimean coalition is dissolved.' He decked this out with much talk of monarchical solidarity against the 'socialist' countries of western Europe; but this was window-dressing—Bismarck could always discover sentimental ties with any country whom he happened to favour. His real aim was to perform a gigantic conjuring-trick. He would satisfy Russia by concessions in the Near East and compel Austria-Hungary to acquiesce by insisting that her security depended on the alliance with Germany, not on Balkan predominance or gains.

This might have worked if he had limited himself in 1879 to a simple declaration of policy, as he had done in October 1876 or on many previous occasions. As it was, he became the prisoner of his own act. The treaty with Austria-Hungary was the first formal alliance between two Great Powers concluded in peace-time since the outbreak of the French revolution and the end of the *ancien régime*. The Powers might have sentimental attachments, such as the so-called 'Holy Alliance'. They signed treaties of alliance only before a war or on its outbreak; and these alliances ended when the war was over. So it had been with the Anglo-French alliance of the Crimean war; the Austro-Prussian alliance in 1864; and the alliance between Prussia and Italy which preceded the war of 1866. The written alliance with Austria-Hungary which Bismarck now made set a rigid pattern which shaped international relations until the first World war. Bismarck might say that every treaty contained an unwritten clause, *rebus sic stantibus*.[1] The solemn recital of full powers and the seals ponderously affixed were among the things that remained the same. Though no treaty can bind the future, a formal treaty influences the future by its very existence. Bismarck never gave the slightest hint why he had recorded Austro-German friendship in this formal way. His haste and dogmatic insistence almost justify the conclusion that he genuinely believed in the danger of attack from Russia in August 1879. But there were surely limits even to what Bismarck could make himself believe. The explanation is presumably to be found, as on many earlier occasions, in the effect on William I. Only a formal alliance would convince the Austrians that William I had really turned

[1] 'So long as things remain the same.'

against Russia; and William could be turned only by talk of immediate war.

Whatever the explanation, the effect was unmistakable. The alliance with Austria-Hungary overshadowed Germany's foreign policy; and in time it even came to be felt that countries could not be on friendly terms unless they had a written alliance. Bismarck sometimes argued that formal alliances were made necessary by democracy and the growth of public opinion. The masses could not understand diplomatic gestures; they had to be tied by precise words. But the statesmen were tied as much as the masses. The signature of the Austro-German alliance, though not its terms, was announced at once; and German national feeling was enthusiastic. 'Greater Germany' seemed to have been achieved in a roundabout way. Bennigsen said truly: 'For the first time the Chancellor has made an act of foreign policy, to which all interests, all parties, yes all Germany, joyfully agree.' Bismarck was embarrassed by this enthusiasm, but he could not repudiate it just when he was preaching the 'national' cause in economics and social welfare. He had prepared a strange fate for himself. He, the greatest and most successful enemy of the Habsburg monarchy, the man who had destroyed its predominance in Germany and ended it in Italy, became henceforth its guarantor and protector. He did not relish the part; and every subsequent step in his foreign policy aimed at escaping the inevitable consequences of what he had done in October 1879.

THE CONSERVATIVE CHANCELLOR

THE end of the year 1879 opened a new epoch in Bismarck's life. Gone were the days when he had unified Germany on the basis of universal suffrage and given her modern institutions with the help of a great liberal party; gone the days when he welcomed conflicts between the other Great Powers and profited from them. Now he echoed Metternich and became 'a rock of order'. The change has given him another cycle of posthumous fame. Fifty years ago Bismarck was admired as the great nationalist and revolutionary; now he is held up as the man who sought to preserve Europe's traditional civilization. Both pictures are true, though of different times. All revolutionaries become conservative once they are in power; and Bismarck had always longed for tranquillity even when he was a revolutionary.

Personally, Bismarck enjoyed more absolute power than ever before. The old emperor became a figurehead; even Augusta ceased to criticize, especially when the *Kulturkampf* was relaxed. His only fear now was of what would happen when the crown prince came to the throne; and Bismarck pursued with destructive hatred any political figure who he imagined might be the head of a so-called 'Gladstone ministry'. This was a spook of his own creation. The crown prince was too weary and too ineffective to have any clear plans. It was characteristic of Bismarck that whereas he had constantly expressed weariness of office when he was regarded as indispensable he now clung to it with frenzied determination. He said in 1888: 'I shall refuse to sign any letter of resignation. I shall cling to my chair and not go even if they try to throw me out.' Previously he had had colleagues of some independence and ability. Now he had underlings to carry out his orders. He distrusted even them and felt secure only in 1885 when he made his son Herbert secretary of state. He meant to found a Bismarck-dynasty and remarked complacently: 'Louis XIV said, *L'état, c'est moi*. I say, *Moi, je suis l'état.*' He cared for his son more than for any ruler or any public cause; yet he crushed this son with all his ruthless energy at the first sign of independence. Herbert fell in love with a divorced princess and proposed to marry her. Divorce was no handicap in Lutheran Germany—a few years later Bülow became chancellor, though married to a divorced woman, when this would have debarred him from the lowest ministerial post in England. But Herbert's lady was related to Schleinitz, Bismarck's old enemy. Bismarck used every weapon. He threatened to dismiss Herbert from the public service; announced that he would kill himself if the marriage took place; and got William I to exclude from the entail on Friedrichsruh and Varzin anyone who married a divorced woman. Herbert gave way and worked off on others the impatient brutality that had been no match for his father.

Bismarck did not reveal his thoughts even to Herbert, but he trusted him to execute orders. He trusted no one else. Suspicion grew with power; and he broke ministers and ambassadors who showed any sign of independence. He still pursued with unrelaxed hatred supposed opponents who had been dead for many years. His old friend Keyserling was amazed to discover in 1891 that Bismarck remembered petty slights which he had suffered during their student-days. When Lasker, the National Liberal politician, died during a visit to the United States, Bismarck forbade the Reichstag to accept a message of condolence from Congress. Lasker had given invaluable aid in 1870 in winning south Germany for unification; but, according to Bismarck, he had prevented Bennigsen from becoming a minister in 1878. The charge was quite untrue—Bennigsen was capable of making up his own mind; and Lasker's real offence was to have kept his independence of judgement. Bismarck's hostility was not confined to politicians. Though he could flatter foreigners, such as Jules Ferry or Salisbury, when it suited his purpose, it maddened him that they were out of his reach. His greatest contempt was reserved for 'professor' Gladstone, perhaps because he recognized there his only equal.

This irritability and petty spite could earlier be excused by Bismarck's nervous temperament and his constant ill-health. It had less excuse in his last decade of power. He no longer needed to worry about his tenure of office; he was secure for William I's lifetime and could retire to Friedrichs-ruh or Varzin without risk of intrigue against him at court. In 1883 a startling change took place in his health. A new medical attendant, Schweninger, at last imposed modera-tion on the genius who had imposed it on others, but never on himself. At their first meeting, Bismarck said roughly: 'I don't like being asked questions.' Schweninger replied: 'Then get a vet. He doesn't question his patients.' The battle was won in a single round. Bismarck ate and drank less, kept more regular hours. When Schweninger was present, he even kept his temper. He underwent a slimming diet, which consisted exclusively of herrings. However curious this seems by contemporary standards, it did the trick. Bismarck's weight went down from eighteen to fourteen stone; he slept long and peacefully; his eyes became clear, his skin fresh and almost youthful. The full beard came off in 1884, not to reappear again until extreme old age. He took up horse-riding after a ten-year interval; and recovered a capacity for steady, sustained work which he had not known since his days at Frankfurt. He still sobbed easily; but there was no more nervous collapse even at the time of his fall. Schweninger got his reward. He had been guilty years before of a moral offence,[1] all the graver, says one of Bismarck's biographers, from being committed in a churchyard. Bismarck compelled the university of Berlin to make Schweninger a professor, despite the out-raged protests of the medical faculty. An appropriate ex-

---

[1] Rape? sodomy? bestiality? It is more interesting not to inquire.

change: Bismarck got fifteen years of life, Schweninger a university chair.

Every observer noted the change in Bismarck; and it can be seen in his photographs. In 1877 he is bloated, choleric, bursting at the seams; in 1883, before Schweninger took over, a bearded old man, bewildered at life and hardly able to control his twitchings long enough to face the camera. In 1885 he is fresh, clean-shaven, chin upright, face finely drawn, master of himself, seventy years old no doubt, but a man with long life before him. His talk and writing gave further evidence of renewed health. It was more serene, relaxed and patient, though still full of cunning, always with a calculated effect. Bismarck was never spontaneous, even with himself. His speeches and instructions now had an air of inner communing, which only the old can have, as though he were more interested in eternity than in events. It was a hard task to be one of Bismarck's ambassadors. He never learnt to give precise instructions, just as he never learnt at Frankfurt to write accurate reports. He would always explore remote aspects of a topic and turned easily aside to by-ways of historical allusion of personal reminiscence. The wise ambassadors kept quiet; when they acted on their instructions, they usually acted wrongly. For instance, in May 1884 Bismarck wrote to Münster, his ambassador in London, that the British government must be more sympathetic to German needs if they wanted to keep German backing in the Egyptian question, and in particular they should consider ceding Heligoland; he also remarked, in a casual aside, that Great Britain should show consideration for German trading interests in Africa. But Münster was only told to raise the question of Heligoland. He had long advocated Anglo-German co-operation and was delighted; he began to ask for Heligoland at once. A fortnight later Bismarck told him to drop the question. The following year Bismarck rebuked Münster in a Reichstag speech for not complaining about British obstruction over colonies—a question that Münster had never been told to raise; and the British government were also attacked for ignoring complaints that had never been made. Münster was lucky to escape only with the penalty of being moved to Paris. His offence was to have carried out instructions that he had received and for failing to carry out instructions that he had not.

Bismarck's speeches in the Reichstag also took on this character of grandiose obscurity. He spoke often—indeed, since he did nearly all the work of government, more often than ever before. When he had something to promote in the Reichstag—whether the army-law or social insurance—he attended every day and spoke to every amendment. But he no longer tried to identify himself with a party, as he had identified himself with National Liberal policy between 1867 and 1877. He seemed to stand aloof from the Reichstag and above its members, meditating aloud, sometimes striking out a dramatic phrase, more often wrestling for words exactly in the manner of Oliver Cromwell. He would wander from his notes, remain silent for a minute on end, and then break off to drink brandy-and-water—an observer once counted eighteen tumblerfuls in a single speech. The members would cough, laugh, and talk among themselves, until Bismarck, beside himself with rage, would shake his fist or stare them down through his lorgnette. His final resort was to exclaim: 'I am no orator . . . I am a minister, a diplomat, a statesman and I should be offended to be called an orator.' His speeches are among the greatest literary compositions in the German language, despite their repetitions and their clumsy, fragmentary phrases. But their historical allusions to the revolutions of 1848, to Metternich, or even to the Frankfurt diet, must have seemed remote to members who could hardly remember the founding of the North German confederation, let alone the Crimean war. Yet in the end Bismarck's personality forced itself through; and he usually got his way even in a Reichstag composed mainly of his opponents.

The basic argument of Bismarck's speeches in this last decade was always that he alone spoke for the nation, for Germany. This Germany existed only in his imagination.

He knew little or nothing of contemporary German life. He read no new books, knew none of the leading thinkers, never went out even in Berlin. Though he boasted that, unlike the intellectual politicians, he knew the German people, his knowledge stopped forty years before. The only men of the people with whom he exchanged a word were the labourers on his estates, where an antiquated social order was kept artificially alive. When he spoke of industrial conditions, his illustrations were drawn from the Silesian textile industry—the centre of eighteenth-century industrialism—not from the Ruhr. He never saw a coalmine in his life, was never in the Ruhr, and did not visit the Rhineland between 1871 and 1892. Even his attitude to Marxism was old-fashioned. Marx died in 1883, his best work done twenty years before; and Bismarck knew nothing of trade-union development nor of the practical points in the Socialist programme. For him the Social Democrats were always 'the red revolutionaries' of 1848, just as he still saw the Roman Catholics with the eyes of Luther.

Bismarck complained that the Reichstag was a chaos of factions, but this chaos was largely of his own making. He had forced a split in both the Conservative and the National Liberal parties; and, still worse, by launching universal suffrage, he had cleared the way for parties which were not 'upholders of the state' at all in his sense. To defeat the middle-class politicians by universal suffrage turned out to be itself a middle-class idea. Bismarck reacted by denouncing others, not by confessing his mistake. In the first years after 1867 he had almost ignored the Prussian diet. Later he praised it as a truer expression of the national will, and in 1885 actually sought a vote of confidence from it when he had been defeated in the Reichstag over his Polish policy. Again, he had found no words strong enough with which to criticize the German princes—their lack of any national feeling, to say nothing of the trouble that they caused him. In the eighteen-eighties he turned round and exalted their patriotism above that of the politicians. He even included in his *Reminiscences* a passage, contemptuous of German nationalism, where he asserted that the dynasties were the only effective bond of union. This was to fly wilfully in the face of the facts; and Bismarck knew it. He did not value the princes nor respect them; he merely wanted to repay in kind the exasperation which the politicians had caused him. He claimed to serve 'the State', almost to worship it. Yet he criticized the Prussian bureaucracy, complaining that it was as 'intellectual' as the politicians—'there is no difference between the man at the green desk and the man at the orator's tribune'. The State was, in fact, a name for that 'heroic will' which Keyserling had seen long ago as Bismarck's dominating characteristic. When Bismarck said that the state should be served, he meant that he ought always to get his own way.

Bismarck owed his difficulties with the Reichstag to his own success. He had constantly preached that interest-groups should be substituted for parties based on national principle; the voters and even the party-leaders took his advice. The Old Conservatives of the eighteen-seventies became spokesmen of the Junker estates in the eighteen-eighties; the National Liberals became spokesmen of heavy industry. But now Bismarck told the electors and the deputies that they should consider only the national good. Was not this a principle like any other? In practice he had usually to promote the national good by concessions to the interest-groups, a horse-trading that grew ever more elaborate. A small section of Conservatives, called the Empire party, and a small section of the National Liberals tried to turn support of Bismarck into a principle, accepting his identification of himself with the nation; but this adherence to principle ruined them, as Bismarck had foretold. The two parties outside the national fold, the Centre and the Social Democrats, were abhorrent to him both because of their principles and because he disliked their practical interests. Yet he often had to play for their support so as not to be taken prisoner by one of the respectable parties. He jeered at the Reichstag for being unable to provide a stable government-majority and asked: what sort of a government would it be, where Windthorst of the Centre, Bebel the Socialist, and Richter the Progressive, sat side by side? As a matter of fact, this was exactly the coalition which sustained the Weimar republic; and it would have given Germany a secure parliamentary system if it had not been for the 'national' parties which Bismarck had patronized.

Bismarck's jugglery with the Reichstag in the eighteen-eighties rested on a simple calculation. The Conservatives supported him firmly once they were won over by agrarian protection; but he needed further votes to secure a majority. The National Liberals supported the *Kulturkampf*, but opposed protective tariffs and authoritarian government; the Centre opposed the *Kulturkampf*, but supported protective tariffs and perhaps would not mind authoritarian government if it were not applied against themselves. In 1879 Bismarck thought that he had out-manœuvred the Centre by promoting tariffs, without relaxing the *Kulturkampf*. The manœuvre did not work: the Centre went back to opposition as soon as the tariffs were passed. In 1880 he had a further, graver disappointment. Leo XIII was anxious to compromise. He disliked the head-on conflict with the modern state and in any case regarded the German Reich as the least of his enemies; if he could settle with Germany, he could play her against France or against his most dangerous opponent, national Italy. In February 1880 Leo XIII, not Bismarck, went to Canossa. He accepted Bismarck's principle that the age-long conflict could not be fought out: church and state should find a workable compromise. As a first gesture he agreed that Roman priests should henceforth register with the state-authorities; in return the May-laws would be more laxly applied. Bismarck and Leo XIII had reckoned without the Centre leaders. They refused to settle for anything less than repeal of the May-laws. Windthorst ex-claimed: 'Shot in the field! shot in the back!' He thought at first of retiring from politics; then decided, despite Leo XIII's prompting, to oppose all Bismarck's measures.

Bismarck swung back. He renewed his friendly relations with the National Liberal leaders almost for the last time; and in the summer of 1880 a liberal-conservative coalition carried the first renewal of the septennial army-law. Fortunately for Bismarck his diplomacy had promoted a peaceful Europe; and he asked only for renewal, not for increase, of the military establishment. He now embarked on a bolder manœuvre still. Since he could not shake the Centre, he would win over the Social Democrats—not certainly by appealing to their leaders, whom he was persecuting and sending to prison, but by a constructive social programme, which he hoped would detach the working-class voters from the Social Democratic party. It would be unfair to say that Bismarck took up social welfare solely to weaken the Social Democrats; he had had it in mind for a long time, and believed in it deeply. But as usual he acted on his beliefs at the exact moment when they served a practical need. Challenge drove him forward. He first avowed his social programme when Bebel taunted him with his old friendship with Lassalle. He answered by calling himself a Socialist, indeed a more practical Socialist than the Social Democrats; and he provocatively rejoiced in echoing Frederick the Great's wish to be *le roi des gueux*, king of the poor. Richter, the Progressive leader, called Bismarck's proposals 'not Socialistic, but Communistic'. The proposal was merely that part of the cost of Social Insurance should be borne by the state; and nowadays Bismarck seems the progressive, Richter the unenlightened reactionary.

The system of Social Insurance which Bismarck inaugurated in 1881 and completed in 1889 just before his fall would be enough to establish his reputation as a constructive statesman even if he had done nothing else. He recognized this and wanted to put into William I's mouth the words that 'it would be the finest work of our government which has been so clearly blessed by God'. William objected that unification ranked higher and struck the words out. Yet unification had been achieved by other countries. German social insurance was the first in the world, and has served as a model for every other civilized country. The great conservative became the greatest of innovators. Earlier it had been Bismarck's weakness that he did not share the basic principles of liberalism even when he worked with the National Liberals; now it was his strength. His very lack of principles gave him a clearer vision into the future. Of course, Bismarck did not promote social reform out of love for the German workers. Sympathy and affection had never been his strong points. His object was to make the workers less discontented or, to use a harsher phrase, more subservient. He said in 1881: 'Whoever has a pension for his old age is far more content and far easier to handle than one who has no such prospect. Look at the difference between a private servant and a servant in the chancellery or at court; the latter will put up with much more, because he has a pension to look forward to.' Social security has certainly made the masses less independent everywhere; yet even the most fanatic apostle of independence would hesitate to dismantle the system which Bismarck invented and which all other democratic countries have copied.

Bismarck's policy revealed the contradictions of his social outlook. He had always fought for his independence—from parties, from princes, from foreign countries. He believed that life was a ceaseless battle: 'Struggle is everywhere, without struggle no life, and if we want to go on living, we must be ready for further struggles.' Yet he wanted to combine this fighting independence with security, always seeking a verdict from the referee before he would enter the ring. His foreign policy was packed with insurances and reinsurances; and he kept away from war simply because victory could never be guaranteed. In his private life he was always beating down others, yet demanded security for himself. He hoarded money and estates, worrying endlessly about the old age that he did not expect to survive into. He would not tolerate any interference in his own concerns as landowner or industrialist and even

stormed at having to pay rates on the chancellery buildings. Yet his sensitive imagination was racked by the
thought of the worker who had no protection against
accident or old age. He preached rigour at one moment,
security at the next. He would not tolerate factory
inspection or any legal limitation of hours; the factory
owner must be 'master in his own house'. But he proposed
to insure every German worker against accident, sickness,
and old age. At the end he talked of 'the right to work'
and thought of insurance against unemployment—the
final step to the welfare state of the twentieth century.

These ideas were too novel for Bismarck's contemporaries. Most resisted them on the basis of liberal economics.
Even the Social Democrats were more interested in the
conquest of political power than in social reform. Even
when social insurance was carried, the Reichstag defeated
Bismarck on one essential point. It struck out the contribution from the state, and left insurance as a direct levy on
worker and employer. The politicians acted wisely from
their point of view. Bismarck wanted to make the workers
feel more dependent on the state, and therefore on him.
Ultimately he wanted to put the politicians out of business.
He talked of ending the representation of individual voters
and of substituting for it 'corporative associations', based
on the insurance system. The idea carried further his
emphasis on interest-groups instead of high principle. The
phrase and the device were to be picked up again by the
twentieth-century exponents of Fascism. But Bismarck
was not being a prophet. He was merely repeating the
medieval fantasies with which Frederick William IV had
long ago surrounded the first steps towards parliamentarianism in Prussia. Here was another illustration—
curious, rather than important—of the way in which Bismarck reverted to the outlook which he had despised in
his early years. He followed Metternich in foreign policy;
echoed Frederick William IV at home. The 'mad Junker'
of the rebellious eighteen-forties would have hard and
contemptuous words for such nostalgic regression.

Though social insurance helped to swell Bismarck's reputation in history, it was not a success as a move in practical politics; and this was what Bismarck cared about above all else. He put his proposals before the Reichstag in February 1881; the date was no accident—Bismarck was acutely conscious that the term of the Reichstag was running out, and he needed a new fighting cry for the approaching election. There was no chance that the emperor would be shot at again. There was no crisis in foreign affairs. Bismarck therefore must be made to appear as the sole champion of social welfare. The manœuvre was a failure. Certainly the Reichstag played into his hands. It reduced the employer's contribution and struck out the contribution of the state altogether—the liberals from individualism, the Centre in defence of federalism. Bismarck responded by getting the Imperial Council to reject the amended law. Then he dissolved the Reichstag. The electorate failed to respond, or rather it responded in an unwelcome and surprising way. Voters, even of the working-class, turned to the anti-Bismarckian liberals, who now over-topped the Centre as the largest single party. Add together these progressives, the Centre, the Social Democrats, and the various protesting fragments (Poles, Alsatians, Danes from north Sleswig, Guelfs from Hanover); and the German Reichstag had for the first time a majority consciously opposed to Bismarck, though agreed on nothing else.

Bismarck owed his defeat to his contempt for mankind. He always slipped readily into the mistake of underrating the power of ideas, particularly the great revolutionary ideas of freedom and equality; hence the admiration which disillusioned idealists profess for him nowadays. He was quick to assert his own claim to equality, and tolerated no encroachment on his own freedom. He never understood that others might feel the same. He was impatient enough with educated people who worried about principles and the rule of law; but he shrugged this off as an ineradicable effect of their education. What took him by surprise was that the uneducated cared just as deeply, or perhaps even more so. The Social Democratic party had been little more than a sect until the passing of the anti-Socialist law; then every working man regarded himself as persecuted and was not to be bought off by insurance against accidents. In 1881 the Social Democratic party was sufficiently hampered by illegality to lose some of its votes; but these votes, and many more, went to the parties which would oppose Bismarck on whatever ground. Many observers drew the conclusion at the time, and it was valid enough: the prospect of security cannot induce men to sacrifice their freedom. Yet Bismarck had perhaps anticipated the future, though he was wrong in the present. The men of the nineteenth century, even the most uneducated men of the lowest class, had the ideas of the French revolution in their bones. Freedom seemed essential to them. Three-quarters of a century later even educated men put security before freedom. Bismarck's dream has been accomplished. Men can be transformed into contented animals so long as they are secure and well-fed. Few care for great abstract principles at home or abroad; they ask only for a quiet life. This is exactly what Bismarck projected. But there is a difference between Bismarck and our present-day statesmen. He would at least have fulfilled his promise and provided the quiet life; our rulers find even this too difficult for them.

It was no consolation to Bismarck that his ideas would triumph fifty years after his death. He had to face the opposition which dominated the Reichstag between 1881 and 1887. Fortunately no septennial military-law fell in this period; and there was little damage for the opposition to do. As usual, Bismarck retreated when a gesture of violence had failed to achieve its end. He echoed, though with a wryer face, his threat to Andrássy in 1879: 'Accept my policy, if not . . . I must accept yours.' Before the election Bismarck had insisted that social insurance was worthless unless carried through according to his dictate. After the election he swallowed the Reichstag's amendments: 'You have rejected the contribution from the state, and I have bowed to this necessity in order to achieve something.' The state paid nothing; the levy on the worker was increased. With these changes health insurance was established in 1883; accident insurance in 1884. Bismarck lost interest in them once they ceased to be useful as weapons of political struggle. He did not devote a single sentence to social welfare in his *Reminiscences*. Admittedly the *Reminiscences* were designed for political effect, not as a contribution to history; still, it is strange that Bismarck forgot so completely what is now regarded as his most individual claim to fame. In the Reichstag of 1881–84 Bismarck attacked the opposing forces from a different side. Since he could not shake the Progressives and social welfare had miscarried, only concessions to the Centre remained. In 1882 Bismarck renewed German diplomatic representation at the Vatican after a lapse of ten years; and he weakened the obligation of priests to register with the state. But Leo XIII would not again risk the snub from the Centre which he had received in 1880. Rome remained silent; and the Centre, though less virulent, was not won over. Its votes were cast in favour of a renewal of the anti-Socialist law in 1884, but against Bismarck's old favourite, the tobacco-monopoly. Bismarck fell back on his final resort—a *coup d'état*. He talked of making the chancellor a pure figurehead, who should preside over the Imperial Council and no more. Then the Reichstag would find no responsible minister whom it could attack and would be reduced to impotence. The representatives of the states insisted that it was impossible thus to dismantle German unity; and he put the idea unwillingly aside. Yet he was determined to remain in power and to enforce his will. As he said in the Prussian diet a little later: 'I regard the minister as a wretched coward who does not risk his honour and his head to save his country even against the will of majorities.' These were brave words. All they meant in practice was that Bismarck intended to be the only permanent feature in the German political scene. He had always to be right even though this made everyone else wrong.

An English analogy again comes to mind. The years between 1881 and 1887 in Germany, when the groups in the Reichstag were strong enough to oppose the chancellor but were divided against each other, had much in common with the years of political confusion and instability in England which followed the Seven Years' war. There was restlessness and faction, but no uniting principle. In England a young king with weak ministers made the confusion worse. But suppose the old king, George II, had lived another ten years and suppose the political genius, William Pitt, had remained in full health, we might have seen a Bismarckian decade, with Pitt defying the House of Commons and refusing to bow to its temporary majorities. Even the younger Pitt, a lesser man, adopted much this attitude twenty years later. Maybe such analogies do not take us very far. But if we are to make them at all, they are better made for Germany at this time with an England that was still strongly monarchical and where the House of Commons had only the function of opposition than with the contemporary England which had two generations of full parliamentarianism behind her.

Bismarck's claim to be the indispensable man seems more justified when foreign affairs are brought into the picture. Here his uncanny sensitivity and his inexhaustible expedients had always made him a worker of miracles; and in the eighteen-eighties he developed a diplomatic mastery without parallel. He was the Napoleon of alliances; and, unlike Napoleon, he never met his Moscow or his Waterloo. He often used his domestic policy to strengthen his position in foreign affairs; and, with less excuse, he sometimes played tricks in diplomacy in order to influence affairs at home. The principal object of the alliance which he made with Austria-Hungary in 1879 was undoubtedly to make Austrian policy less anxious and aggressive; but he also paraded it in Germany as a national, even a nationalist, gesture—the diplomatic counterpart to protective tariffs

and social welfare. This emotional coating which he had
laid on the alliance, caused him difficulties later when he
wanted to treat Vienna more coolly. The Austrians could
always turn on him and claim that their alliance, unlike
any other, was an affair of the heart as well as of the head.
Bismarck disliked this: he had made the alliance in order
to prevent a Balkan conflict, not to support the German
cause on the Danube. His interpretation prevailed in the
first years after the alliance was made. The Austrians
wanted to oppose Russia in Bulgaria and at Constantinople.
Bismarck insisted that they had no quarrel with Russia
now that they had the security of the German alliance;
and the Austrians were dragged reluctantly in his wake,
particularly when the victory of the English liberals under
Gladstone deprived them in 1880 of any hope of an alliance
with England.

A surprising result followed—surprising, that is, to all
except Bismarck. The Austro-German alliance of 1879 had
been made against Russia. Less than two years later it
produced a reconciliation with Russia, the so-called League
of the Three Emperors. This was not, despite its name, a
sentimental association of conservative monarchs; it was
a hard-headed practical agreement, welcome to Russia,
forced on Austria-Hungary by Bismarck. The three partners promised to remain neutral if one of their number
were engaged in war with a fourth power. Since the only
war Austria-Hungary would fight would be against Russia,
this meant in practice a Russian promise of neutrality in
case of a German war against France and an Austro-
German promise of neutrality in case of a Russian war
against England—this latter promise given most reluctantly by Austria-Hungary. Only a war against Turkey
was excluded—for that Russia must first get the permission
of her two partners. This was no real concession: it sprang
from the nature of things and had always been true, in the
Crimean war as in 1877. Germany got security; Russia got
a firm promise that Austria-Hungary and Germany would
give her diplomatic support against England in any dispute

over Bulgaria or at the Straits; Austria-Hungary got nothing except the German alliance which she had already.

The League of the Three Emperors, signed in June 1881, represented the triumph of Bismarck's deepest wishes. It gave him what he wanted—escape from having to choose between Russia and Austria-Hungary. Russia's friendship was recovered at the expense of Austro-Hungarian and British interests in the Near East. Bismarck cared nothing for the first and was quite pleased to injure the second. The security of Germany's rambling eastern frontier was worth a high price, particularly when paid by others. Bismarck always held that it was more important for Germany to stand well with Russia than with any other Power. He took this line from beginning to .end of his career. He said in 1863 when first in power: 'The secret of politics? Make a good treaty with Russia.' Almost his last public utterance in 1896 was to present himself, in contrast with his successors, as the man of the Russian alliance. Germans of a later age who advocated good relations with Russia could rightly claim to be 'Bismarckian'. Yet Russo-German friendship had a grave, indeed a fatal flaw for Bismarck, as for his heirs: it was intensely disliked by the overwhelming majority of Germans. The nation, divided in all else, was united in hostility to Russia. This was shown both at the outbreak of the first World war and in June 1941. It was equally clear in Bismarck's time. Only the old emperor, with his fading memories, agreed with Bismarck. All other Germans looked on Russia as their enemy, though the Russians asked nothing except to be left alone.

The liberals regarded Russia as reactionary and backward; the Centre disliked her oppression of the Roman Catholic Poles; the Social Democrats inherited hatred of Russia from the radicals of 1848; the conservatives had an agrarian jealousy of Russian grain; the generals, including even Moltke, eagerly planned war against Russia, the only power that they had not fought; the younger generation wanted to assert the German cause everywhere—on the Danube and in the Near East more than anywhere else.

Bismarck would have had a united nation behind him if he had gone against Russia; and he could have it in no other way. Instead he made friendship with Russia the keystone of his foreign policy. Social conservatism perhaps counted for something with him, fear of a revived Poland for more. Most deeply he feared that war against Russia would be a war to the death. Wars with other Powers could be fought, as he had fought them, for limited objects. War with Russia must end in the destruction of one or other combatant, as Napoleon had found and as Hitler was to find later on. Now Bismarck wanted a quiet life, however revolutionary he had been earlier. His greatest, and most admirable, quality was to be content with limited success; and this was the one thing which war against Russia could never give.

He was alone in his view. William I and a few elderly courtiers also wanted friendship with Russia, but on grounds of monarchical conservatism. Bismarck exploited their prejudices. The League of the Three Emperors was a conspiracy between Bismarck and William I against the German people. William I and Bismarck were also partners against the Reichstag between 1881 and 1887. But at least there were in the Reichstag some deputies who agreed with Bismarck over home affairs. No German politician would have applauded his foreign policy if it had been made known. Hence it remained a rigid secret. Bismarck boasted of the Austro-German alliance from the day that it was made; later, when Italy was added, he boasted of the Triple Alliance; later still, he boasted of his association with England. He never mentioned the League of the Three Emperors; and it remained an obscure mystery until thirty years after his death. In the same way, later German statesmen—whether Stresemann, Hitler or those of the present—have had to treat friendship with Russia as a guilty secret. German emotion has always been against it. Even when the second World war had made clear the full penalty of conflict with Russia, a German liberal writer could condemn Bismarck for seeking the friendship of

Russia instead of making an alliance with England, though this must inevitably have led to European war.

In 1881 Bismarck could ignore the German people; he could not ignore his Austrian allies, and they complained ceaselessly against the League of the Three Emperors. Bismarck did something to quieten them. He would not underwrite Austro-Hungarian interests in the Balkans. Instead, in May 1882, he brought Italy into the Austro-German partnership. The essential clause of this Triple Alliance was Italy's promise to remain neutral in a war between Russia and Austria-Hungary. The promise, Bismarck claimed, 'was worth four army corps'—the troops which otherwise Austria-Hungary would have to keep on her Italian frontier. The price for this bargain was paid by Germany: she, but not Austria-Hungary, undertook to support Italy in a war against France. This was a strange outcome. Bismarck despised Italy, who had, he said, 'a large appetite and very poor teeth'; and he did not rank her among the Great Powers—for him they remained five, not six. When Italy demanded territorial gains at the congress of Berlin, he asked: 'What, has she lost another battle?' Devotion to monarchy, even if it weighed with him, could hardly extend to the Italian royal house—at best, the Triple Alliance gave a convenient excuse for evading a revival of the temporal power of the papacy. His claim that the Holy Roman Empire had been restored and that 'the great powerful area of all central Europe had finally come together again after being torn apart by strokes of destiny and fierce struggles' was mere window-dressing to please German opinion. The Triple Alliance showed Bismarck's determination, almost his obsession, to keep the Pomeranian grenadier out of the Balkans. He would do anything rather than support Austria-Hungary there; he would even risk a war for Italy's sake against France.

The risk was not great. Bismarck used his alliance with Italy to prevent a war against France, just as he used his alliance with Austria-Hungary to prevent a war against Russia. As soon as he got allies, he took them under his control. He insisted that they must do what he wanted; and what he wanted was peace. The alliances had a further value: they fixed the limits of his concessions to France and Russia. After 1879 he was willing to do anything the Russians wanted short of sacrificing Austria-Hungary; after 1882 he would do anything to please the French short of sacrificing Italy. The parallel was not exact. He felt less committed to Italy despite the terms of the Triple Alliance. In 1879 he really came to believe, for whatever reason, that the integrity of Austria-Hungary was essential to the security of Germany, at any rate to the security of his Germany. Italy did not mean so much to him. Perhaps he feared obscurely that the Habsburgs might renew their claims in Germany if they recovered their predominance in Italy—and men in Vienna still talked of reconquering Venetia and Lombardy. But he jettisoned Italy's Mediterranean interests for the sake of French friendship; and he might even have let the Italian monarchy disintegrate if he could have won both France and the pope completely to his side. As it was, both, like Russia, remained too independent. They would not accept his control. Austria-Hungary and Italy had for Bismarck the attraction that they were the weaker and therefore the more subservient Powers. In foreign affairs, as in private life, men do not like equals; they like dependents—Bismarck more than most men.

Nevertheless he went on from the Italian alliance to an attempted reconciliation with France, just as he went on from the Austro-Hungarian alliance to a reconciliation with Russia. The reconciliation with Russia succeeded, at any rate for some years; that with France did not and has therefore attracted less notice. Yet it was the core of his policy from 1882 until 1885 and the most grandiose task that he ever attempted. For Germany would really be secure if France were reconciled. The Eastern question would lose its terrors; and Berlin would be the centre of a new European order. Alsace and Lorraine stood in the way, as Bismarck knew; and he attempted to win over the French

by insisting rather clumsily that the two provinces would
never have been annexed if it had depended on him. This
was tawdry stuff. His more serious effort was to support
France 'everywhere in the world except at that little
corner on the Rhine'. He said to the French ambassador:
'I have had *one* aim in regard to France for the last fourteen
years, since the making of peace: to get her to forget the
war . . . I want you to forgive Sedan as you have forgiven
Waterloo.'

The aim seemed more plausible in 1884 than it does now
after half a century dominated by Franco-German antagonism. All the Great Powers had fought each other at some
time, but resentment had died away. France had made it
up with England after Waterloo; Russia had made it up
with France after the Crimean war; Austria-Hungary,
defeated in 1866, was now the ally of Germany. There
seemed no reason why the Franco-German war should be
any different in the long run. Bismarck was not alone in
hoping for better relations. Gambetta, the great apostle
of resistance in 1870 after Sedan, shared this hope and was
actually planning to meet Bismarck at the time of his early
death. Though Gambetta certainly did not forget the lost
provinces, he believed that they would be recovered by
friendship with Germany, not by a new war against her.
He pinned his faith to 'immanent justice'. Jules Ferry,
prime minister of France from 1882 to 1885, had the same
outlook. Though he, too, had an honourable record in 1870,
he put Alsace and Lorraine in the background and sought
to build a colonial empire for France, preferably with
German backing. Tunis, Indo-China, Egypt, and central
Africa were prizes which made patience over the lost
provinces worth-while. Though the initiative came from
Bismarck, the French were eager to accept his proffered
hand.

Bismarck's diplomacy led inevitably to the isolation of
England. Austria-Hungary and Italy were the two Powers
on whom England counted—the one to resist Russia at the
Straits, the other to resist France in the Mediterranean.

Alliance with Germany snatched them away from England's side, though it could not turn them into her enemies.[1] The League of the Three Emperors was implicitly an anti-British combination. By reconciling Russia and Austria-Hungary, still more by giving Russia security at the Straits, it cleared the way for a Russian advance in central Asia, which implicitly threatened the British empire in India. In exactly the same way, good relations between France and Germany left France free to press her colonial ambitions in rivalry with the British. Nor was she alone. In 1884 Bismarck, too, entered the colonial field. His reasons for this are obscure. Hitherto he had kept his gaze riveted to Europe and had insisted that Germany had enough to do in protecting her security and in developing her resources. He had rejoiced to be free from the rivalries which caused conflicts among others. He said repeatedly: 'I am no man for colonies.' Now he created a great colonial empire, each unit of it seemingly designed to exasperate British feeling. The first, which grew into German South-West Africa, was at the backdoor of Cape Colony. The Cameroons broke into an area where the British had monopolized trade for many years. German East Africa threatened the British control of Zanzibar. And finally, German New Guinea encroached on the British colonies in Australia.

There were, of course, domestic motives for Bismarck's colonial policy. Hamburg was on the point of entering the German customs-union at last; and colonial markets were perhaps held out to the Hamburg merchants as some compensation for the loss of their Free Trade privileges. There were wider grounds, too. Men everywhere—not only in France and England, but in Italy and even in little Belgium—were talking about 'the age of imperialism', and the Germans were anxious not to be left out. Colonies provided a new 'national' cause, which drove a further wedge between the Progressives, who opposed them, and the

---

[1] Italy insisted on adding to the Triple Alliance a declaration that it could never be directed against England.

remaining National Liberals, who still supported Bismarck. Moreover, Bismarck welcomed conflict with England for its own sake. He was always angered by British aloofness and independence, particularly when 'professor' Gladstone was prime minister. Still more important, the colonial disputes were a blow at 'the Gladstone ministry' in Germany which Bismarck always professed to fear. The crown prince would be crippled when he came to the throne if Germany and England were on bad terms. Herbert Bismarck later gave this as the essential motive: 'When we started colonies, we had to face a long reign by the crown prince . . . and therefore had to launch a colonial policy in order to be able to provoke conflicts with England at any moment.' It was not the first time that Bismarck had sought to discredit his supposed opponents by accusing them of favouring Germany's enemies. Once he had accused the conservatives of friendship with Austria; then he had condemned the south German states for their friendship with France; now the crown prince was to be smeared with English liberalism.

As usual, one hand washed the other. Probably Bismarck would not have developed colonial ambitions in order to win French friendship, if this had not suited his plans at home; but equally he would not have exploited German enthusiasm for colonies, if he had not seen the opening for a Franco-German *entente*. Whenever Bismarck advocated something, every argument went in the same direction—foreign policy, the balance in the Reichstag, dynastic calculations, all gave the same answer to the sum. It seemed inconceivable that there could be any other course. Yet he could change his mind overnight, and then every argument pointed just as decisively in the reverse direction. Only one thing remained constant: Bismarck was always right. Right when he was against colonies; right when he acquired them. Right when he went to war; right when he kept the peace. Loyal when he agreed with William I; loyal also when he disagreed with him. In other countries a change of policy needed a change of government. Bismarck made his own changes, ruthlessly attacking his own arguments of yesterday. Like a great man of our own day, he was a coalition in himself.

Bismarck's foreign policy brought him in the summer of 1884 unrivalled success. Serene in temper, recovered in health, he became, for a brief moment, the pivot of Europe. In September the three emperors—Francis Joseph, Alexander III, and William I—met at Skierniwice in Poland. It was the most open display of their League and seemed to be more—a revival of the Holy Alliance. Bismarck dominated the meeting, and the emperors hung on his words. Each of them could have said, as Nicholas I of Russia once said to Metternich: 'I come to sit at your feet, as the pupil at the feet of his master.' Scarce back from Skierniwice, Bismarck told the French ambassador that they should build up a maritime league, an Armed Neutrality, to resist British control of the seas. Bismarck's old friend Keyserling commented: 'Curious that Bismarck is being led in this way to a Continental System *à la Napoléon I* and that he has practically all Europe together for it.' Bismarck surpassed his prototype. The great Napoleon had had to fight many wars in order to impose his Continental System. Bismarck had done it by magic. There lay the weakness. The differences between the Great Powers had not been settled. They were conjured away, and they reappeared as soon as Bismarck's back was turned. Content himself, he had nothing to give the peoples and rulers of Europe except lassitude. They should forget their hopes, their ambitions, their enthusiasms, and should accept what life, or rather Bismarck, had to offer them. Bismarck wanted peace; therefore everyone else must want it too. He offered nothing positive, nothing creative, nothing which could make men square their shoulders and look hopefully forward. He should have lived in the despairing twentieth century, not in an age when men still believed in a progress without limits.

The colonial disputes gave a Bismarck a cry for the general election in the autumn of 1884—effective, but not effective enough. The Progressives lost a third of their

seats; the Conservatives gained. But the Centre was un-
affected despite its opposition to colonies; its roots were in
south Germany, remote from the sea. More dangerous still,
the Social Democrats doubled their representation. 'Imperialism' was never a cause which appealed to the masses,
despite all the arguments proving that it should do so.
It was a creation of middle-class radicals trying to be
popular, not of the masses themselves; and politicians
everywhere—not only Bismarck, but Jules Ferry in France
and later Joseph Chamberlain in England—were disappointed when they tried to capture the votes of the
masses with the Imperialist cry. In 1884 the German
Social Democrats became a serious force in the Reichstag
for the first time. The European economy was experiencing
its first depression since the great industrial expansion;
and social discontent was everywhere increasing. The
Social Democrats would make a formidable opposition if
they combined with the Centre. Bismarck sought to prevent this coalition by relaxing the *Kulturkampf*. Some
of the May-laws were repealed; and later in 1885 Bismarck
even invoked Leo XIII as arbitrator in a colonial dispute
with Spain over the Carolinian Islands. Leo XIII responded
by hailing Bismarck as 'the great chancellor'; Windthorst
was not won over so easily.

Bismarck did not discard his colonial claims and his disputes with England, even though they had failed of their
domestic purpose—proof perhaps that this had been a
secondary consideration all along. Reconciliation with
France was reward enough in itself; and this seemed to
grow stronger during the winter of 1884–85. An international conference met at Berlin to settle the future of the
Congo basin; and France and Germany made common
cause against the British. In the spring of 1885 Bismarck
launched a new colonial dispute over New Guinea. In
April the continental league made its most open demonstration. Russian forces were threatening Afghanistan. Great
Britain and Russia seemed on the brink of war; and the
British planned to attack Russia by passing the Straits

and entering the Black Sea. Not only the powers of the Triple Alliance, but France, too, warned the Sultan to keep the Straits closed against the British. Bismarck piously asserted that he had done nothing to promote the Anglo-Russian conflict 'on general Christian principles'. Herbert Bismarck was not so high-minded. He remarked to a friend: 'If England and Russia quarrel, I can only say, bad luck for every blow that misses.' Christian principles apart, a war between England and Russia would give Germany the effortless mastery of Europe; and Bismarck was not the man to overlook it.

The happy situation was too good to last. Bismarck's continental system tumbled down almost overnight. Russia and England failed to go to war; instead they settled the Afghan affair by negotiation. On 30 March Jules Ferry was overthrown in France. A trivial defeat of French forces at Langson in Indo-China brought him down. If his friendship with Germany had been known, he would have fallen all the sooner. Freycinet, Ferry's successor, took a more cautious line. At the end of May, Bismarck was complaining that the French would not play 'the great game'—the game of a continental league against England; and he warned them that he would win in a competition for English friendship. As usual, he did not confess that he had been wrong in his policy. He professed to believe that the old emperor was dying; then the crown prince would come to the throne with a pro-British policy. 'We are in for an era of Coburgs'; and tears ran down his cheeks for the benefit of the French ambassador. The tears were genuine enough—Bismarck had been sobbing for years whenever it crossed his mind that William I was mortal. But he did not intend either to change his policy or to lose his position merely because Frederick III was on the throne instead of William I. In any case, it was all a false alarm—William lived woodenly on for another three years.

The continental league was not really destroyed either by ministerial changes in France or by the failing health of William I. The Eastern question was always its most

vulnerable point, as in every continental league from that
between Alexander I and Napoleon in 1807 to that between
Hitler and Stalin in 1939. Russia would never allow
Austria-Hungary to dominate the Balkans; Austria-
Hungary would never trust Russia nor renounce co-
operation with Great Britain. The two could be held
together only so long as the Balkans remained quiet; and
Bismarck's miracle really depended on 'the sheep-stealers'
whom he so much despised. In September 1885 the Balkan
settlement of the congress of Berlin broke up and threatened to break up the European order along with it. Eastern
Roumelia, which had been made merely autonomous in
1878, revolted and joined Bulgaria. The Russians had
once sought a great Bulgaria; they opposed it now that
Bulgaria had broken loose from their influence. As a last
gesture of loyalty to the League of the Three Emperors, the
Austrians joined with Russia in demanding a new partition
of Bulgaria. The scheme was wrecked by the western
Powers, France and England, and by the Bulgarians themselves. In the summer of 1886 the Russians scored a last
success: they dethroned the Prince of Bulgaria, Alexander
of Battenberg—much to Bismarck's pleasure. However
unlikely it seems, he had detected in Alexander a possible
head of the 'Gladstone ministry' in Germany. The success
did Russia no good. The Bulgarians continued to take an
independent line; and a new crisis seemed to be approaching in the Near East, with Russia seeking to reconquer
control of Bulgaria, and England and Austria-Hungary
defending Bulgarian independence.

Bismarck was determined not to be drawn in. He cared
nothing for Bulgaria, though much for the integrity of
Austria-Hungary. 'We are completely indifferent who rules
in Bulgaria and what becomes of it. . . . We shall let no one
put a noose round our necks because of this question in
order to drag us into conflict with Russia.' The new crisis
in the Near East, together with the fall of Ferry in France,
had one important effect on Bismarck's policy: it led him
to drop his colonial ambitions, so as to make it easier for

Austria-Hungary and Great Britain to draw together. As early as September 1885 he was explaining to a British visitor that he had only developed colonial interests in order to please France and that he was now disillusioned. A little later he said to a German explorer of Africa: 'Here is Russia and here is France, with Germany in the middle. That is my map of Africa.' Bismarck made no further colonial claims after the summer of 1885. He had an occasional tiff with the British over Zanzibar just to keep his hand in, but usually he spoke of colonies with his old contempt. Germany had acquired a vast African empire which Bismarck did nothing to develop. Indeed, in 1889, he tried to give German South-West Africa away to the British. It was, he said, a burden and an expense, and he would like to saddle someone else with it. Not till the twentieth century did Germany draw profit from her colonies, and then only from the Cameroons.

Bismarck's estrangement from France had more important results. It provided him with a strong excuse for refusing aid to Austria-Hungary. Germany, he claimed, was in immediate danger of attack from France and could spare no troops for a war against Russia. The excuse had some reality. A French nationalist revival had certainly followed the fall of Ferry. The tinsel hero, General Boulanger, achieved an easy popularity by talk of 'revenge'. Bismarck deliberately exaggerated the danger. As he confessed afterwards: 'I could not invent Boulanger, but he happened very conveniently for me.' He ignored the opinion of the German general staff that a French attack was out of the question. He suppressed reports from Münster in Paris that French feeling was overwhelmingly peaceful. He whipped himself, and all Germany, into a state of anxiety and panic.

The Boulangist alarm did not merely serve the needs of Bismarck's foreign policy. It was even more effective in giving him his greatest victory in home affairs. The Reichstag elected in 1884 proved the most difficult that Bismarck had to encounter. The Centre was always threatening to boat into an alliance with the Social Democrats and the Progressives. It would only agree, for example, to renew the anti-socialist law for two years—clear indication that it was keeping the door open for a change of course. Later in 1885 the coalition of *Reichsfeinde*, as Bismarck called his opponents, actually came into being. Bismarck had launched a campaign against the Poles—partly to offset the concessions he had made to them as Roman Catholics, more as a gesture of friendship to Russia. Poles without German nationality were expelled from the eastern provinces—30,000 of them, an unexampled number for those days. Bismarck followed this up by a compulsory expropriation of Polish landowners. He always regarded Polish nationalism as an upper-class affair and said contemptuously: 'It can't matter to us whether the labourers speak Polish or German.' Bismarck declared that this was a domestic question which only concerned the Prussian diet. The Reichstag insisted on discussing and condemning it. Bismarck was the more enraged because in his view this interfered with his foreign policy of good relations with Russia. As a matter of fact, his calculation was all at sea. The Russian government, looking forward to war against Austria-Hungary, were anxious to conciliate the Poles and were irritated by Bismarck's revival of the old anti-Polish front.

Now, in the autumn of 1886, Bismarck believed that he had found the winning card. Tariffs, the social peril, colonies, had all failed of their 'national' appeal. The cry of 'the *Reich* in danger' would do the trick; and what was more, Germany could evade foreign commitments while she was torn by political controversy. In November 1886 Bismarck presented a new army-law to the Reichstag, though the old one had two years to run. The Centre and the Progressives saw their danger. They tried to avert it by offering to vote 'every penny and every man' if Bismarck would compromise on three or even five years instead of seven. This would have been reasonable if the immediate danger of war had been the real motive for increasing the army. But it was not. Bismarck wanted a political victory, not greater armaments; and he wanted to drag out the conflict so as to turn his back on his allies. When the pope offered to influence the Centre in favour of the law, Bismarck brushed him off: 'Rejection would give the government a different and perhaps much more favourable basis for operations.' The military experts, half-convinced of the danger, made concessions to the Reichstag; Bismarck repudiated them as he had done in 1863.

Determined to provoke a decisive conflict, he remained quietly at Friedrichsruh until the majority against the army-law had consolidated itself. Then on 11 January, 1887, he appeared in the Reichstag and delivered his most powerful speech since the days of 'blood and iron'. It was a conjuring trick of the highest class. On the one hand Bismarck had to justify the increase of the army and therefore to display a Germany in imminent danger of attack; at the same time he had to claim that Germany was on good terms with all the Powers thanks to his unique diplomatic gifts. It is impossible for the reader, and must have been still more impossible for the listeners, to discover Bismarck's firm opinion, the summing-up of probabilities on which he acted. Was he really afraid of attack from France and not afraid of war with Russia? Did he inflate the French danger in order to glide over his greater anxieties in the Eastern question? Or were the dangers on both frontiers exaggerated for the purposes of home policy? At any rate, he was carried away, as often happened with him, by the excitement of his peroration, and let slip his real object: he wanted an army-law that would last for ever, not merely for seven years. 'The Germany army is an institution which cannot be dependent on changing majorities in the Reichstag. It is an absolute impossibility that the fixing of military strength should depend on the casual constellation and opinion of the Reichstag. Do not strive for such fantastical ideas, gentlemen!'

It was the old issue of a parliamentary or royal army, the

issue which had first brought Bismarck to power in 1862.
Now it worked better for him. The limited Prussian
electorate of 1862 had stuck to its principles; in 1887 the
masses responded to the national appeal. On 14 January
the Reichstag limited the army-law to three years by 186
votes to 154. Centre and Progressives had combined to
defeat Bismarck. The Social Democrats abstained—
ostensibly because they were unwilling to vote for the army
at all, secretly because they were unwilling to vote against
an army that might one day be used against Russia. The
Reichstag was at once dissolved. Bismarck's opponents
were massacred at the polls. The Social Democrats lost
12 seats (half their number), the Progressives 50. The
Centre held its own as always (it lost one seat); but its
moral strength, too, was broken when Bismarck published
a letter from the pope, condemning its vote against the
army-law. The National Liberals became the largest single
party in the Reichstag—for the last time; and they
joined the Conservatives in a 'cartel', sole basis of which
was unconditional support for Bismarck. He had at last
manufactured a subservient majority for himself after
twenty-five years of failure or half-success.

The army-law passed the new Reichstag for its full
seven-year term by an overwhelming majority—223 to 40.
Bismarck enjoyed his triumph in silence and did not go
near the tribune. Seven members of the Centre obeyed the
pope's instructions and voted for the law; the other
eighty-three, including Windthorst, abstained. Leo XIII
got his reward. Most of the May-laws were repealed in
March 1887, Bismarck personally inspecting the vote in
the Prussian diet to ensure that it went the right way. The
religious orders were allowed to return, the Roman church
recovered control of its seminaries. Bismarck said airily:
'What do I care whether the appointment of a Catholic
priest is notified to the state or not—Germany must be
at one!' Once he had used the argument of national unity
to justify the *Kulturkampf*; now he used the same argument to justify its end. Whatever his faults, he certainly

did not lack resource. He showed the same opportunism over the cry of 'the *Reich* in danger' which had just won him the general election. For, as soon as the election was over, it turned out that the *Reich* was in no danger at all. A dispute over a French frontier official, Schnaebele, wrongfully arrested by the Germans, was amicably settled. Münster in Paris, poor old gentleman, was rebuked for sending reports on Boulanger, where earlier he had been rebuked for not sending them; and in May a resolute French government pricked the Boulanger bubble. It had all been a false alarm, very convenient for Bismarck, whether he was ever taken in by it or not.

The alarm in the Near East was less false. Bismarck did not invent the crisis over Bulgaria nor even exploit it. He kept control of Europe by the most elaborate diplomatic devices—dancing among eggs, one observer called it, juggling with five balls at once, said William I. Yet the basic principle of his diplomacy was clear and simple: maintenance of Austria-Hungary as a Great Power, but no support for her ambitions in the Balkans. It was a sort of 'Locarno' between Russia and Austria-Hungary; keeping the friendship of both and offering an additional premium to whichever followed the more peaceful course. Bismarck had followed this policy steadily since 1879; only its execution became more elaborate and difficult. His most immediate problem was the Triple Alliance. It had been made in 1882 for five years and was due for renewal in May 1887. Originally it had served to bring Austria-Hungary and Italy under German control. Now a flamboyant renewal would seem to capture Germany for an Austro-Hungarian drive against Russia and an Italian drive against France. Bismarck hesitated; and his hesitation pushed England forward. Great Britain had refused to back either Austria-Hungary or Italy so long as Gladstone was in power—hence in part the original Triple Alliance. Now, with Salisbury at the foreign office, British policy returned, more or less, to the line of 1878.

In February 1887 Salisbury made a secret agreement

with Italy to support the *status quo* in the Mediterranean, an agreement which Austria-Hungary soon joined. This first 'Mediterranean agreement', as it came to be called, was a mere declaration of policy, not a binding alliance. But it was firm enough to lessen the dangers of the Triple Alliance for Bismarck. Henceforth, if Austria-Hungary or Italy appealed for his assistance, he could reply that they should invoke British aid first. He made no further difficulties in renewing the Triple Alliance. Indeed, by a separate treaty, he gave Italy more binding promises against France than before. Since he was now confident that French policy was peaceful, these promises involved little risk. As always, Bismarck made them so as not to have to carry them out.

Russia was a more difficult affair. The Russians had never liked the League of the Three Emperors and the friendship with Austria-Hungary that this implied. They wanted a straight promise of German neutrality, which would leave them free to attack Austria-Hungary or at any rate to threaten such an attack if she interfered with them in the Balkans. Bismarck had refused to give this promise in 1876 and during the crisis before the congress of Berlin. It was still more out of the question now that he was bound by the Austro-German alliance. Always frank when it suited him, he showed the text of this alliance to the Russian ambassador. But he offered mutual neutrality of a limited kind. Germany would remain neutral unless Russia attacked Austria-Hungary; Russia, to make things equal, would remain neutral unless Germany attacked France. This was the basis of the Reinsurance treaty, which Bismarck concluded with Russia on 18 June 1887. In theory Germany was still exposed to the risk of war on two fronts; and Bismarck was wrong when he claimed later to have warded off this risk. Indeed the Franco-Russian alliance, as made in 1894, was strictly compatible with the Reinsurance treaty; for by it the Russians did no more than promise to aid France against a German attack. But war on two fronts was not the pressing danger in 1887. The

danger which Bismarck feared was of a Balkan war between Russia and Austria-Hungary; and the Reinsurance
treaty did something to lessen it. A secret protocol
promised Germany's diplomatic aid to Russia in Bulgaria
and at the Straits. Bismarck could not prevent Russia's
going to war; but the temptation for her to do so was less
if the tsar believed that he could get his way by diplomacy.

The Reinsurance treaty was Bismarck's last great stroke.
It has often been described as dishonest and immoral.
Dishonest against whom? Whom did it deceive? Bismarck
had told the Austrians from the beginning that he would not
support them in the Balkans; he had always told the
British that, in his view, the *status quo* implied the closing
of the Straits even against their fleet; and he had always
told the Russians that he would not allow Austria-Hungary
to be destroyed. The Reinsurance treaty did no more than
repeat these statements. When two Powers or groups of
Powers are contending, it always seems immoral to them
that another Power should try to remain friendly with both
sides. Prussia had come in for the same accusations of
'shiftiness' and unreliability during the Crimean war; Bismarck had been condemned both by the Russians and by
the Austrians and the British for acting as honest broker
in 1878. It all depends on the point of view. Germany was
in the middle of Europe. She had to keep in with both
sides, unless indeed she took the lead one way or the
other and became after a great war (if she won it) the
dominating Power in Europe. This had perhaps appealed
to Bismarck in his young revolutionary days at Frankfurt.
Now he was elderly, resigned, without ambitions for the
future—except to keep things as they were. His only object
was to maintain the peace of Europe. Those who admire this
call it operating the Balance of Power; those who do not,
condemn it as dishonest jugglery.

This is not to say that Bismarck's diplomacy alone pre-
served peace. Like all successful diplomacy it contained a
double bluff. He made the Austrians believe that he would
not support them; he made the Russians fear that he would.

But suppose either side called his bluff, what could he do
then? It was no good saying that he would go against
whichever was the aggressor. This was a moral conception
of the sort that Bismarck always insisted had no relevance
in international affairs: 'I have never judged international
disputes by the standards which prevail at a student's
duel.' Bismarck would have had to go to the rescue of
Austria-Hungary, however aggressively she had behaved,
if her existence was endangered. He managed to put over
the bluff by the force of his personality; those who came
after him were less successful. Bismarck did not make any
exaggerated claims for the Reinsurance treaty at the time,
whatever he said in bitter resentment later. All he claimed
was that it made Alexander III feel more secure and therefore made it easier for him to resist his bellicose advisers.
This is the most that diplomacy can ever do. It cannot
prevent war; it can merely make peace more attractive.

So events worked out now. Most Russians were weary of
the Near East and were only anxious to leave it alone if
it would leave them alone. In the summer of 1887 the
Bulgarians elected a new prince in defiance of Russia; and
she did nothing. It was the sign that there would be no
war in the Balkans. But men took some time to read it.
The Russians were angry at their humiliation in Bulgaria,
even though they would do nothing to remedy it; and on
the other side the Austrians wanted to launch a preventive
war against Russia in Galicia. Bismarck repeated his
diplomacy of the spring in more elaborate form. He conjured up for the Austrians a tighter, more extensive
'Mediterranean agreement' with Great Britain and Italy;
and he explained frankly to Salisbury the principles of his
policy. 'We shall avoid a Russian war so long as that is
compatible with our interest and security . . . but German
policy will always be obliged to enter the struggle if the
independence of Austria-Hungary is menaced by a Russian
aggression.' On the other hand, he brushed the Austrians
off with a sharp rebuke when they tried to lure the German
generals into staff-talks preparatory to a Russian war; and

he did his best to keep on good terms with the Russians, even coming out of his retirement at Friedrichsruh to meet Alexander III at Berlin in November. The interview was not very successful. Alexander III was sulky and resentful, using friendly phrases only to the French ambassador; and Bismarck talked to his intimates of a war against Russia for the resurrection of Poland—only to add that Russo-German friendship would be restored by a new partition of Poland afterwards.

This was a desperate remedy, and not much more than thinking aloud. His actual remedies were desperate enough. On 3 February 1888 he published the text of the Austro-German treaty without waiting for permission from Vienna. This is often described as a gesture against Russia. On the contrary it was a stroke against Austria-Hungary. The Russians had already learnt the terms of the alliance from Bismarck the previous year. Publishing them stressed the defensive nature of the treaty; it was a warning that German strength would not be used, as Bismarck put it, 'for Hungarian or Catholic ambitions in the Balkans'. He made one concession. He suppressed the final clause which limited the alliance to five years (though with automatic renewal), and thus unwillingly admitted its permanence. Three days later, on 6 February, he introduced a new army-law in the Reichstag, raising the age-limit of the reserve from 32 to 39 years, and spoke on foreign policy for the last time. Germany, he insisted, would defend her interests; she would not follow a policy of power or of prestige. Though she did not fear Russia, she would not be dragged by Austria-Hungary into a policy of Balkan adventure. Implicitly he repudiated the value of all alliances, and declared that Germany must rely on her own strength. 'The pike in the European carp-pond prevent us from becoming carp.' His last sentence rounded off a career that had begun with 'blood and iron': 'We Germans fear God and nothing else in the world.' It was a strange peroration for a lifetime of apprehensions, where God had often seemed to be the only thing that Bismarck did not fear.

Less than a month later, on 3 March, he appeared at the tribune to announce the death of William I. Tears choked his voice. He wept not only for a beloved master whom he had always claimed to serve though rarely obeyed. He wept still more for the end of his own mastery in Germany.

THE FALL FROM POWER

BISMARCK made one of his rare public appearances at the funeral of William I. Afterwards in the evening he sat with his family, lost in thought, speaking softly and almost to himself of the ruler whom he had served for so long. An occasional tear ran down his cheek. Suddenly he pulled himself up, straightened his back and exclaimed in a rough, harsh voice: 'And now forward!' Forward to what? To further struggle which became more and more personal. Contemptuous of the new emperor, careless of public opinion, Bismarck meant to remain in power till he died. He believed that only he could rule Germany, indeed that he alone was Germany. Everyone else was factious, particularist, or a *Reichsfeind*. For more than twenty years he had played off Reichstag and emperor against each other. A parliamentary majority could not overthrow him as long as he possessed the emperor's confidence; indeed, every parliamentary attack strengthened William I's conviction that Bismarck was the only barrier against democracy. On the other hand he could always get his way with the emperor by threatening to resign and so open the gates to the democratic flood. Now Frederick III was on the throne—an emperor long critical of Bismarck's opposition to liberalism and long friendly to the National Liberal politicians.

Bismarck had been taking precautions against this catastrophe for many years. He had surrounded Frederick and his wife with his own creatures; he had broken the National Liberal party; and now he had a majority in the Reichstag pledged to his support. As a matter of fact, the precautions were largely unnecessary. Frederick was a National Liberal, not a democrat. Despite his occasional

disagreements, he belonged to the generation which had
been enthusiastic for Bismarck's great achievements. The
outstanding men of the National Liberal party supported
the cartel of 1887. Bennigsen resumed his political life
solely to advocate it; Miquel, once an associate of Karl
Marx, was for the moment Bismarck's follower. The new
emperor, too, would stand with the cartel and with Bismarck's policy. A few years earlier Bismarck told Frederick
that he would be prepared to remain in office on two conditions: no parliamentary government and no foreign
influences on policy. Frederick agreed to these conditions.
By March 1888 he was ready to agree to anything. He was
a dying man, cancer of the throat far advanced. He had
already lost his voice and had only three months to live.

Bismarck remained master of the situation. There was no
change of policy. But he wanted a public demonstration of
his power. He had been ready enough to invoke Russian
influence on William I when this suited him. Now he was
determined to show that English influence counted for
nothing, even though the new empress was a daughter of
Queen Victoria. He soon found an excuse for conflict.
Frederick's daughter had been in love for some time with
Alexander of Battenberg, formerly Prince of Bulgaria. Bismarck had opposed the marriage as an offence to the tsar,
with whom Alexander was on bad terms; and the old
emperor had supported his objection. Now Alexander had
abdicated the Bulgarian throne and was living a retired
life in Germany. The political difficulties seemed to have
disappeared, and Frederick wanted to do something for his
daughter in the remaining few weeks of his life. He gave his
consent to the marriage. Bismarck was up in arms. He made
out that the marriage remained offensive to the tsar and
would therefore ruin his foreign policy. Perhaps he himself
still had some genuine resentment against one whom he had
detected years ago as head of a 'Gladstone ministry'. Most
of the fuss was pretence or imagination. The tsar cared
nothing about the marriage one way or the other; Alexander of Battenberg had neither talent nor ambition for

politics. Bismarck merely wished to show that his will was law. He threatened to resign (the first such threat since 1879) and he appealed to public opinion by giving the news to the press. Queen Victoria came to Berlin in order to sustain her dying son-in-law. Bismarck was a match even for this. He bewitched Victoria as he had once bewitched Napoleon III. She found him 'very charming, very reasonable' and joined her urgings against 'Sandro'. The wretched emperor gave way. Alexander was repudiated, the marriage forbidden.

Bismarck was radiant with success. He became more jovial and irresponsible as the shadow emperor sank into the grave. His last act in Frederick's reign was little more than a schoolboy prank. The cartel majority had just prolonged the life of future Reichstags from three to five years. This did not need Imperial assent.[1] The Prussian diet followed suit with a similar law. Frederick assented unwillingly. At the last minute Bismarck went to him and said: 'Show for once that you are king and care neither for ministry nor for chamber. If you'd rather, forbid the publication of the law.' Was he mocking the dying man? Teasing his Prussian colleagues? Or merely rejoicing in his power? At any rate, Frederick did not respond to the prompting. A fortnight later, on 15 June, he was dead. His last act was to press his wife's hand into Bismarck's as a gesture of farewell and reconciliation. Bismarck was not affected by such gestures. He carried his battles beyond the grave. Three months after Frederick's death a German periodical published excerpts from the diary which he had kept during the war against France. The passages, though harmless enough, revealed something of Bismarck's manœuvres with the German princes and his rejection of the crown prince's advice to appeal to the German people. Bismarck was enraged. First he denounced the diary as a forgery; then he tried in vain to prosecute the editor for treason. Only Bismarck, it seemed, was allowed to reveal

[1] Prussian assent to Imperial laws was given by the delegates to the *Bundesrat*. The emperor, as president of the confederation, did not assent to laws.

secrets of state. An observer commented: 'Bismarck re-gards the glory of creating the German empire as an enormous cheese which is his sole property; anyone who cuts off a slice is a thief.'

With the death of Frederick III, Bismarck seemed to have come into undisputed possession of this property. He had had to allow William I some grudging share of historical glory, if only as his assistant (*Handlanger*); and despite his intellectual superiority he had always been a little afraid of the old emperor. Though he got his way in the end, he had to fight for it; and William I expected everything to be explained to him. Perhaps there would have been harder fights if Frederick III had reigned longer and been in good health. But Bismarck did not foresee any trouble with Frederick's son, William II. The new emperor was not yet thirty—impulsive, vain, untrained. Bismarck supposed that he would be happy playing at emperor—dressing up in fine uniforms, inspecting troops, making a speech on some formal occasion. It did not occur to him that a mere boy—born when Bismarck was already am-bassador at St. Petersburg—might have ideas on policy, still less want his own way. When Bismarck first became prime minister, he never left William I's side until he had established his personal ascendancy. He went to the palace every afternoon or wrote long letters every day when William I was absent from Berlin. He took no such trouble with William II. He spoke to him casually at Frederick III's funeral; then left Berlin and did not return for eight months. He conducted foreign policy without reference to the emperor, never explaining what he was doing. If William II made a suggestion, Bismarck would write back a few contemptuous lines, pointing out how dangerous and silly his suggestions were. Then he would go back to serious business.

Bismarck did not neglect William II altogether. He as-sumed that Herbert Bismarck, who was running foreign affairs as secretary of state, would keep an eye on him. Bismarck adored Herbert; and it did not cross his mind that others might not share this emotion. William II certainly feared the elder Bismarck when he came to the throne; and he was perhaps impressed by Herbert's arrogance and knowledge. But there was never a tie of affection between them; and William II soon found other confidential advisers. Herbert was ill-suited to the part for which his father had cast him. He was forceful, assertive, even rude; and he had the technical training to run an office. But he lacked the charm which his father could use; and he had no understanding of men. Bismarck would have seen danger blowing up if he had been constantly in Berlin; Herbert noticed nothing until the last moment, and then it was too late. The starting-point was not any difference over policy. It was William II's desire, which many a young ruler has had, to be his own master. In William II's case, it was reinforced by impressions of an unhappy childhood and by resentment against physical disability. His parents had disliked him; and he had a stunted left arm. His behaviour in power could have been foreseen by any psychologist—ought to have been foreseen by Bismarck. William II said a few weeks after ascending the throne: 'I shall let the old man snuffle on for six months, then I shall rule myself.'

William II was mistaken over his timing. Bismarck's last bout of power lasted not six months, but a year and a half. It was the happiest period of his life. He was without a care in the world and looked serenely into the future. He was in splendid health—'I feel better than for many years past', as he insisted at the moment of his fall. The emperor was a figurehead; the cartel provided a subservient majority in the Reichstag; Herbert's succession was secure when he himself began to fail. He had at last managed to combine his contradictory wishes—supreme power and life in the country. He left Berlin in July 1888 and returned only the following January. He left again in May and only re-appeared for an occasional day until the crisis of January 1890. English people complained of Queen Victoria's long absences at Osborne or Balmoral. What would they have said if it had been the prime minister, not the queen, who lived like this? Bismarck was not merely Imperial chancellor—the only 'responsible' minister whom the Reichstag could criticize or question. He was also foreign minister—needing to see foreign ambassadors, one might suppose, to say nothing of German representatives abroad. He was prime minister of Prussia, expected to preside at the Prussian council of ministers and to co-ordinate its policy. And he was Prussian minister of trade, conducting all economic policy. He had to wind up the remnants of the *Kulturkampf*; to introduce further measures of social welfare if there were to be any; and to hold together the parties of the cartel.

He could do none of these things when he was absent from Berlin. But he would allow them to be done by no one else. The Reichstag was ignored; and the cartel was always threatening to fall to pieces—the Conservatives moving towards a coalition with the Centre, the National Liberals looking wistfully towards the Progressives. A favoured ambassador was occasionally invited to Friedrichsruh; the others were sent brusquely packing by Herbert. The Prussian ministers met under their vice-president, but never to any purpose; they were not allowed to initiate legislation or to strike out on a new line. The minister of Finances collected the taxes; the minister of the interior directed the police. In everything else there was silence, stagnation. Meanwhile Bismarck, in the American phrase, was living the life of Reilly at Varzin or Friedrichsruh. He would get up late, swallow two raw eggs, and then ride or walk out into the fields and woods. In his long black coat and black cowboy hat, he looked like an elderly clergyman. And, in fact, he spent most of his solitary excursions in meditation. He would watch the birds and wild animals; examine the growing crops or admire the timber. Then he would dream for hours at a time; embroider in imagination his past triumphs, recall dead friends—Motley or Kathi Orlov; look with resigned melancholy towards death, with less resignation to Germany's future dangers.

He would come in wet, tired, but exuberant in the late afternoon; and eat, under Schweninger's watchful eye, a meal less enormous than formerly but still enough for two normal men. He would talk in his soft melodious voice— always recollections of the past, never a reference to the present; and these recollections improved at each telling. His first quarrels at the Frankfurt diet; his appointment as prime minister of Prussia; the disputes with William I over the peace terms with Austria; the manipulation of the Ems telegram; these were set-pieces of which he and his family never wearied. In these magical evenings he was more Henry Irving or Walter Scott than a practical statesman. At last, as night fell, he would work—scribbling pencilled comments in the margin of documents, throwing aside what did not interest him, and occasionally composing a literary masterpiece of diplomacy. And so on to another idyllic day, imagining that Germany, the emperor, the world would lie always under his spell. He wanted everything to remain unchanged, the balance of foreign powers and of German parties to produce a perfect equilibrium. His sons and his younger associates thought that he was losing his force with old age. But in truth he had always disliked steady routine work. He was only great in a crisis, driving himself then to exhaustion. He let things slide easily when he was not faced with some immediate challenge; and now none presented itself. He no longer wanted to create; he wanted to preserve, and this soon turns into negation. A negative foreign policy means international peace; and, therefore, Bismarck seemed to keep his grasp of diplomacy to the last. In home affairs negation is barren; and Bismarck seemed here to have nothing to offer. In reality his attitude was all of a piece at home and abroad. He had once condemned those who put the clock forward. Now he tried to make it stop.

His mastery of foreign affairs was most complete just before it fell to pieces. Though the great alarm of 1887 had blown over harmlessly, there was still great tension in the Near East. The Austrians could not believe that

Russia would remain quiet, and they pressed harder than ever for joint military action against her. William II and the young men round him were anxious to respond. Support for Austria-Hungary would have been overwhelmingly popular. It was the 'German' cause; and it would have shown that Germany no longer feared anyone in the world. Besides, on a more practical level, the new generation of Germans were no longer Pomeranian grenadiers. They were financiers and railway-promoters with a deep stake in Turkey. If they fought Russia at Constantinople, it would be for German interests, not for those of Austria-Hungary or Great Britain. Bismarck would have none of this. He disliked the Austro-Hungarian alliance more than ever and talked wistfully of ending it. He remained firmly indifferent to the affairs of the Ottoman empire, even though he had to tolerate a visit by William II to Constantinople in October 1889—safely, as he supposed, under Herbert's control. When the Austrians asked for German backing, he referred them to London: they should make an alliance with Great Britain if they wanted to fight a Balkan war.

Bismarck did something to help the Austrians. Relations between Germany and England were never closer than in his last two years of power. He repudiated all interest in colonies and even proposed to hand over the existing German colonies to the British. In January 1889 he proposed to Salisbury a formal defensive alliance between the two countries, and in March sent Herbert to London to promote it. Salisbury saw through Bismarck's game. The alliance was to operate only against France. If a crisis arose in the Balkans, Germany would remain neutral, and Bismarck would argue that, with French intervention ruled out, England could safely take the lead against Russia. Salisbury did not need an alliance against France; rather he hoped to win her back to the side of 'the Crimean coalition'. And he certainly did not mean to be manœuvred into carrying alone the burden of Austria-Hungary. Bismarck's proposal was politely declined with the safe excuse of parliamentary difficulties. Salisbury and Bismarck remained on good terms, each admiring the other's skill; but England was not caught for the Bismarckian system.

The 'natural alliance' with England was popular in Germany except among colonial enthusiasts. Bismarck talked of it openly and did not resent Salisbury's doing the same. But he never intended to commit himself wholly to the British side even against France and still less against Russia. If the written alliance had come off, he would have insisted on its defensive nature and treated Anglo-French quarrels much as he treated the disputes between Russia and Austria-Hungary—remote luxuries which were not Germany's affair. His essential object was to keep all these quarrels under control so that Germany should not be involved in a general war, from which in his belief she could gain nothing. He kept on good terms with France and what was more important, with Russia. This was the most difficult part of his policy—not from technical reasons of diplomacy, but from the current of German opinion. The Germans had no strong feelings against France; they were ready to be friendly so long as this did not involve any concession over Alsace and Lorraine. But German estrangement from Russia mounted apace; and William II reflected it. Bismarck alone adhered to the line of the Reinsurance treaty; and he had to do it in deep secrecy.

Tsar Alexander III was no fool. He knew that only Bismarck stood in the way of an anti-Russian policy; and it was this belief, not the failure in itself to renew the Reinsurance treaty, which made Bismarck's fall the prelude to the Franco-Russian alliance. Bismarck usually achieved what he set out to do; and his last great success in diplomacy was to retain the confidence of the sulky, suspicious tsar. When Alexander III visited Berlin in October 1889, Bismarck actually left his country retirement to meet him. The tsar asked him to sit down, while remaining standing himself; and Bismarck accompanied him to the opera, a tremendous gesture. It was his only appearance there since he became chancellor. He saw *Rheingold*, but made no

comment; it cannot have been much to his taste, which
stopped with Chopin. The meeting raised one cloud. Though
Alexander III expressed full confidence in Bismarck, he
asked: 'Are you sure that you will remain chancellor?'
Bismarck was taken aback. He muttered that he hoped to
enjoy many years of good health and that he would remain chancellor as long as he lived. It had not yet occurred
to him that William II might have different ideas. The
tsar's instinct was sounder.

Bismarck was not worrying about William II. His
thoughts in the autumn of 1889 were on the next general
election for the Reichstag which must come in February
1890.[1] He had made poor use of the cartel which he had
successfully manufactured three years before. He had
carried the army-law in 1887 and the increase of the
reserve in 1888. Otherwise there had been nothing.
Previously he had complained that the opposition parties
in the Reichstag prevented his legislative activity; now
he did no better in a Reichstag almost of his own choosing.
The session of 1888 was made entirely barren by the deaths
of the two emperors, William I and Frederick III. Bismarck did a little better in 1889. He took up the policy of
social welfare, which he had neglected since 1884, and
rounded it off with a scheme for contributory old-age
pensions. On 18 May 1889 he made his last speech in the
Reichstag, arguing that welfare was the true conservatism.
He spoke from genuine conviction. Yet there were tactical
motives also behind his policy. He had sensed something
of William II's craving for popularity and wished to ensure
that chancellor, not emperor, should get the credit for
social welfare. More than that, he was already planning to
use the social peril once more as the slogan for the elections
of 1890. Old-age pensions and a renewal of the anti-socialist
law (due to lapse just before the election) were the two
complementary parts of this policy.

His tactics always followed the same simple pattern. He

[1] The extension of the Reichstag's life to five years applied only to future
Reichstags, not to that elected in 1887.

translated the world of Grimm's fairy tales into political
terms. Ogres and witches were waiting to chop Germany
into bits, and Bismarck alone could defeat their spells.
He acted from fear himself and expected it to work with
others. He was always on the look-out for danger—
liberalism, Roman Catholicism, red revolution. Even his
constructive policy warded off perils—*defensive* alliances,
economic *protection*, social *insurance*. First he raised the
ghost; then he laid it. Security was what he wanted from
life, and he supposed that everyone else wanted it too.
He was often right, particularly with the Germans—an
apprehensive, spook-ridden people. The danger of liberalism made William I Bismarck's prisoner from 1862 until
the day of his death. Similarly, with the electorate, Bismarck always played on the alternative perils of revolution
at home and enemies abroad. Foreign danger had the more
effective appeal. It gave Bismarck the leadership of Germany in 1870 and again, more artificially, in 1887. But it
was a clumsy weapon, causing too much stir in the world
and reflecting adversely on Bismarck's diplomatic skill.
It could certainly not be used two elections running.

Revolution was the other, though less decisive, card.
The Roman Catholics had once provided an effective alarm
in 1874. Now the *Kulturkampf* was over, and Bismarck
was planning to recruit the Centre for his coalition. Only
the Socialist peril remained. The danger from them had
worked in 1878, though it miscarried in 1881 and 1884.
Bismarck still took it seriously. For him the Social Democrats remained the barricade-fighters of 1848. He believed
their threat of a general strike against war and said: 'If
the *Socis* strike, then the war is lost before it starts.' He
was alone in this belief. Most Germans knew that the
Social Democrats had become respectable conservative
trade-unionists. Bismarck had cut down his own flag. He
had made the Germans feel secure; and they swung round
from apprehension to an opposite extreme of confident
arrogance. It was clear before the election of 1890 that the
Socialist danger would not give Bismarck a majority in

the Reichstag. This did not perturb him. He had talked
often enough of tearing up the constitution and abolishing
universal suffrage. William I had been reluctant to face
new turmoil. Now, with a young emperor on the throne,
Bismarck might do it. This would not only be a stroke
against democracy and revolution; it would also be a stroke
against the emperor. William II would become his prisoner
as William I had been; Bismarck would be again the indispensable man, 'the chancellor of conflict'. Just at this
time he hummed to the French ambassador the old song:

> 'Et l'on revient toujours
> A ses premiers amours',

and added: 'Perhaps that will happen with me.' The great
days of 1862 would come again. Maybe he would revenge
the humiliations of 1848. Alternatively, he might switch
the blame for repressive measures on the emperor and
become again 'the republican and democrat' that he had
been at the beginning. William II would be accused of
seeking to destroy universal suffrage, and Bismarck would
save it. At any rate, he would provoke a crisis of some sort.
Then St. George would again slay a dragon.

Bismarck was in a gay mood when he left Friedrichsruh
for Berlin on 24 January 1890. He had skilfully arranged to
wreck the renewal of the anti-socialist law, much as he
wrecked the renewal of the army-law in 1886. The National
Liberals would support the law only if the clause were left
out which allowed the police to expel Social Democrats
from their home-towns; the Conservatives would accept
this weakening only if Bismarck told them to. He remained
silent. The National Liberals insisted on their amendment;
and the bill was then defeated, only the National Liberals
voting in its favour. Bismarck rubbed his hands: 'The
waves will mount ever higher.' He looked forward con-
fidently to industrial disturbances, strikes, civil war. Then
'blood and iron' would rule again. But when the Prussian
council of ministers met, he discovered that his calculations

had gone wrong. He had assumed that William II would be content to echo the policy of William I in 1862. The emperor would be the advocate of repression, Bismarck of conciliation. William II refused to play the part for which Bismarck had cast him. He refused to start his reign by shooting on Germans. Stealing Bismarck's own phrase, he said that he wanted to be *roi des gueux*, protector of the poor. Instead of fighting the Socialists, he would win them over by factory inspection, limitation of hours, guaranteed wages—all things-which Bismarck had been resisting for twenty years. Worse still, the Prussian ministers backed William II, not Bismarck. He glowered at them silently, and they avoided his gaze. William II drafted his own programme of social reforms, and it appeared on 4 February without Bismarck's signature—the first imperial act since the founding of the Empire not to be countersigned by the chancellor.

On the other side, the Social Democrats, too, refused to play Bismarck's game. They had nothing to gain from violence. They were going to win the election. As Engels pointed out from his exile in London, the Socialists now had the law on their side; it was the reactionaries who appealed to force. Bismarck's family expected him to strike back at once. When he remained passive, his son Bill complained: 'My father can no longer wield the sledge-hammer.' But this had never been Bismarck's way. He was far more a diplomat than a fighter, despite his fierce appearance. He cajoled men, played on them, and gave a sharp bark only when he had got them safely into the pen. Now he appeared to retreat. He said of William II's social programme: 'I think we must go along with it'; he resigned the Prussian ministry of commerce; and he even talked of giving up everything except control of foreign affairs. He was really waiting for the results of the election on 20 February. These, he calculated, would be so disastrous that William II and every respectable German would be driven back into his arms.

The election certainly came up to his expectations. The

National Liberals and the Bismarckian conservatives each lost more than half their seats. The Social Democrats polled more than any other single party.[1] The three anti-Bismarckian parties taken together—Social Democrats, Centre, Progressives—held nearly two-thirds of the seats in the Reichstag. Now surely the time had come for a *coup d'état*. Bismarck assured William II that there could be no renewal of the anti-Socialist law and no new army-law with the existing Reichstag, or indeed with any other returned by universal suffrage. The princes who had made the German *Reich* in 1871 should now come together and dissolve it. This was a piece of constitutional nonsense, on a level with the famous 'hole' in the Prussian constitution which Bismarck had discovered in 1862. The *Reich* had been made by agreement between the German states, not by the arbitrary act of absolute princes; and Bismarck, who drew up the treaties of union, knew this perfectly well. But the theory served his turn. It would give him a fighting cause. William II was swept away for a moment. He grasped Bismarck's hand and exclaimed: 'No surrender'.

The emperor's mood soon changed. He was not by nature a man of violence, despite the theatrical utterances which subsequently made him a byword in Europe. As Bismarck said, he was more Coburg than Hohenzollern—conciliatory, anxious for popularity, and above all, high-minded. Unlike his grandfather, he had read the imperial constitution and understood it. He would not start his reign with illegality and bloodshed. Rather he would abandon the anti-socialist law, postpone even the increase of the armed forces, and seek to conciliate the working-classes by labour legislation. On 4 March Bismarck learnt that the emperor had again changed his mind and was opposing a repressive policy. According to the imperial constitution, the chancellor should resign if he lost the emperor's confidence. But

[1] The Social Democrats did not receive representation according to these numbers owing to the system of a second ballot where no candidate received an absolute majority at the first poll. At these second ballots all parties combined against the Social Democrats. They had therefore only 35 deputies, the Centre—with fewer votes—108. But the moral effect was the same.

Bismarck had threatened to resign only when he knew that his resignation would not be accepted. Even now, he was misled by the memories of his old successes against William I. He did not understand that there was an essential difference. William I always retained confidence in Bismarck, even when he opposed his policy. William II had no confidence in Bismarck and wished to be rid of him.

Bismarck would not believe that a mere boy could overthrow him. He tried to mobilize the forces which he had resisted and despised for nearly thirty years—public opinion, Prussian ministers, the parties. The news soon leaked out that Bismarck was threatening to resign. It made no stir. National feeling had been behind Bismarck in the *Kulturkampf*; it had responded to the cry of foreign dangers; it had even agreed with him over such a family affair as the Battenberg marriage in 1888. The social peril failed to work in March 1890, just as it had failed to work in the elections three weeks earlier. How could Bismarck claim to have public opinion behind him when the majority of the electorate had voted for the parties hostile to him? Even the propertied classes—the Conservatives and the National Liberals—did not really believe in the Socialist danger. They had acquiesced in the anti-socialist law because Bismarck insisted on it; they did not regard it as necessary. They certainly did not want the imperial constitution destroyed merely to keep Bismarck in power. Bismarck failed to grasp that, though he was still admired, this was as a historic figure, not as a leader of the present. The generation of Germans that had grown to maturity in the *Reich* were impatient with Bismarck's caution and restraint. They wanted great new achievements, not a quiet life. William II, not Bismarck, represented German feeling.

It was the same with the Prussian ministers. They had long groaned under Bismarck's control; but they had put up with it so long as he was 'the indispensable man'. Now he seemed to be provoking civil war simply to keep in power. The ministers sat silent when Bismarck developed his plans for civil conflict; and Boetticher, the Prussian vice-president, ostentatiously accepted from William II the Order of the Black Eagle. Deserted by the ministers, Bismarck tried to silence them. He dug out of obscurity a royal order of 1852 that ministers could advise the Crown only with the knowledge and consent of the prime minister. Ironically enough, Frederick William IV had issued the order to strengthen the then prime minister, Manteuffel, against ambitious underlings of whom Bismarck was one. It had never been operated in the long years when Bismarck was far away at Varzin and Friedrichsruh. William II exposed its absurdity by asking: 'How can I rule without discussing things with the ministers, if you spend a large part of the year at Friedrichsruh?' Bismarck refused to annul the order. The breaking-point had come.

Bismarck's expedients were not exhausted. In despair he turned to the parties in the Reichstag. If he could only build up a majority, then he could impose himself on the emperor as a constitutional chancellor—the very thing that he had resisted since the founding of the *Reich*. He planned this new majority as a coalition between the Centre and the Conservatives, and even imagined that the Centre would bring over also his bitterest enemies, the 'separatists'—Poles, Danes and Alsatians. It was a wonder that he did not appeal to the Socialists; perhaps he would have done if they had had more deputies. On 12 March, Bleichroeder, Bismarck's man of business, brought Windthorst to the chancellery. It was the first friendly meeting between Windthorst and Bismarck since the attempted reconciliation of 1879. The interview was not a success. Windthorst demanded complete surrender: the Roman church should be restored to the privileged position that it had enjoyed in Prussia before 1872. He said as he left: 'I come from the political deathbed of a great man.' In any case, the Conservatives would not join in the game. Their leader refused to see Bismarck and told William II that his party would go into opposition if the government made a deal with the Centre. In resisting Bismarck, William

II was not only defending his personal power; he was reflecting opinion in the Reichstag and making it possible for the government to work with it.

Early on the morning of 15 March, William II came to the foreign ministry to have things out with his chancellor. His note, making the appointment, had miscarried. Bismarck was still abed. By the time he had dressed and come across to the foreign ministry, both men were in a bad temper. William told Bismarck that he ought not to have seen Windthorst. Bismarck replied that he must be free to meet the party leaders. 'Even if your sovereign forbids it?'—'The power of my sovereign ceases at the door of my wife's drawing-room.' Bismarck's self-control seemed to desert him. He flung his dispatch case furiously on the ground. For a moment William II thought that an inkpot would come flying at his head. But Bismarck had a better trick. He fumbled at his case as he picked it up, appearing to conceal papers that he had in fact brought for the purpose. William demanded to see them. Bismarck pretended to refuse. William snatched the papers from Bismarck's hands and read that Alexander III had said of him: 'C'est un garçon mal élevé et de mauvaise foi'. Bismarck certainly remained true to his maxim: 'à corsaire corsaire et demi.' Though defeated, he had humiliated the man who defeated him. There was no more to be said. William stalked down to his carriage; and Bismarck accompanied him with every gesture of loyal subservience.

Bismarck's long reign was over. It was only left for him to resign. When Gladstone left power and political life under somewhat similar circumstances four years later, his only thought was to conceal the difficulties that he had had with Queen Victoria and to make things easy for the colleagues who had thwarted him. The truth became known only long afterwards. Bismarck had no scruples of this kind. He must have realized, in his calmer moments, that return to office was impossible for him after his quarrel with William II; and he ought to have hushed things up for the sake of the *Reich* which he had created. Bismarck did not want a stable or quiet Germany, but revenge. He intended to discredit William II and hoped that Germany would become unmanageable. He laboured for three days over his letter of resignation, coolly assuming that William II would allow him to publish it. The letter was a manifesto, not a statement of real differences, still less a testament of political advice. It would not do to mention the anti-Socialist law or his plans for overthrowing the constitution. Though these had been the practical occasion for conflict, they found no place in Bismarck's letter. They were quietly rubbed out of existence, and rediscovered to everyone's surprise only when the Bismarckian *Reich* had perished. Bismarck now laid all his emphasis on the royal order of 1852, which had come late into the dispute, and presented himself as the defender of orderly constitutional government against the arbitrary whims of the emperor.

Even this was rather thin as an excuse for resignation. If Bismarck and William II were really in agreement, then everything could be settled by Bismarck's spending more of his time in Berlin. On 16 March, while still composing his letter, he had a stroke of luck. Reports came in from the German consul at Kiev, describing some Russian troop-movements. William II, overwrought and highly-strung, saw an imaginary danger of war. He insisted that measures of precaution be taken and that the Austrians be informed. At the very same moment, the Russian ambassador called on Bismarck to propose the renewal of the Re-insurance treaty which was due to expire in June. Bismarck redrafted his letter of resignation and added a new climax, in which he appeared as the peacemaker of Europe, William II as the firebrand who would lead Germany into a disastrous war. In reality foreign affairs had played no part in the immediate conflict between Bismarck and the emperor. Domestic questions, and in particular policy towards the Reichstag, had been the only issue. Even now, though Bismarck's fall proved a turning-point in relations between Germany and Russia, this was accidental. The Russians would have been prepared to renew the Reinsurance treaty with his successors, despite his allegations to the contrary; and William II at first intended to renew it. The new office-holders seized on the Reinsurance treaty as an excuse for marking their breach with Bismarck's 'system'. Its rejection gave them some better ground for a quarrel than if they had stood on merely personal jealousy. But this was unpremeditated and certainly far from being the motive behind Bismarck's overthrow.

Bismarck's letter of resignation gave a false picture of what happened in March 1890. But it represented, in however perverted a form, the underlying issues at stake. Bismarck wanted to stand still; William II and the men round him wanted to go forward. The appeal to the royal order of 1852 was not merely a bid by Bismarck for personal authority; it implied essentially that the emperor should be kept under control. If Bismarck had wanted to act, he would still have had to get the emperor's approval. It was because he wanted not to do things, and to prevent others from doing them, that he brought out the royal order. Nor was the dispute settled by Bismarck's fall. Later chancellors went on trying to control William II; and in 1908 Bülow succeeded. During the *Daily Telegraph* affair William II promised 'to respect constitutional responsibilities'—whatever that might mean; and Bülow imagined for a few months that he had won the battle where Bismarck had been defeated. He was soon disappointed; and his fall again showed what Bismarck had realized in his last fumbling negotiations with Windthorst—that the chancellor could control the emperor only if he had a majority in the Reichstag behind him. The order of 1852 was a poor substitute for genuine constitutional government.

In the same way, the course of German foreign policy was not settled once and for all by Bismarck's overthrow. Bismarck's and William II's foreign policy, or to speak more truly, a cautious and a forward policy, went on contending until the outbreak of war in 1914. Good relations with Russia implied abstention in the Near East and a pacific policy at any rate in Europe; and though the Reinsurance treaty was never renewed, there were long periods when it existed in all but name. Wholehearted support for Austria-Hungary was practised for two or three years after 1890; and the enthusiasts for German nationalism were preaching *Mitteleuropa* for a generation before the word was invented. But they had little influence over official policy. The statesmen at Vienna got firm German backing only at the time of the Bosnian crisis in 1909; and this was an aberration. The decision to break with Bismarck's policy of restraint was effectively taken only on 6 July 1914, when William II and the then chancellor, Bethmann Hollweg, committed themselves and Germany to Austria-Hungary's attack on Serbia. Even then Bismarckianism was not dead. Between the world wars cautious German diplomatists still clung to the line of the Reinsurance treaty—a line not altogether discarded even at the present day. Bismarck in short dramatized in personal terms a conflict of wider meaning; and even in his letter of resignation asserted that he was the only conservative, the one 'indispensable man'.

His letter was ready on 18 March. He refused to deliver it personally, alleging that he was too unwell to leave the house. No sooner was it gone than he called for his horse and rode leisurely through the streets and the neighbouring park. It was a last futile attempt to provoke a demonstration in his favour. The passers-by hardly acknowledged him. After his rare visits to Berlin, he seemed like a ghost from a great epoch of history that was already past. William II tried to keep up appearances once he had won the struggle. Not surprisingly, he refused to allow Bismarck's letter of resignation to be published, and gave out that Bismarck was resigning for reasons of health. Bismarck was implacable: 'I am better than I have been for years past.' William II created him Duke of Lauenberg and offered him a grant of money. Bismarck refused the money, comparing it to a Christmas box given to the postman. Though he could not escape the title, he announced: 'I hope everyone will continue to address me as Bismarck; I shall use the title only when travelling incognito.' His last official dealing with the state which he had served so long was to receive a demand for the repayment of his salary for the period between 20 March and 31 March, when he was already drawing his pension. He commented contemptuously: 'By such means the Prussian state has become great.'

Bismarck spent his last days in Berlin strengthening his legend for the future. He was reconciled to his old enemy the Empress Victoria, widow of Frederick III, and said to her: 'All I want is a little sympathy.' The sentiment was not altogether sham. William II could have saved himself much trouble if he had occasionally sobbed during his arguments with Bismarck; though even this would hardly have prevented the final break. On 27 March Bismarck went ostentatiously out to Charlottenburg and laid three roses on the grave of William I, saying: 'I have been to bid farewell to my old master.' The flowers came to him on the cheap: he had chosen them hastily and at random from the tributes sent to him by admirers. On his return from Charlottenburg, he took Holy Communion in his drawing-room. The pastor announced a sermon on the text 'love your enemies'. Johanna bade him be silent and turned him out of the room. Bismarck, lying on the sofa, reviewed his life: 'I am seventy-five, my wife is still with me, I have not lost any of my children. I always believed I should die in service. I have been at my post for twenty-eight years, in sickness and in health, and have discharged my duties. I really do not know what I shall do now, for I feel in better health than for years past.' A very characteristic utterance. No human beings existed for him except his wife and children; there was no thought of his great achievements, no hint of policy for the future; the German *Reich*, it seems, had been brought into existence solely to save Bismarck from boredom—and now it could fall to pieces.

Bismarck did his best to create confusion for the future.

He refused to advise his successors, saying: 'Only Herbert knows my secrets.' William II made some attempt to persuade Herbert to stay on. Bismarck claimed not to influence him: 'My son is of age.' But he warned Herbert not to remain with a ship that was running on to the rocks; and Herbert resigned with a resentment even more bitter than his father's. No father and son were ever bound together by a deeper mutual affection. Yet the father had first ruined his son's private happiness and now destroyed his public career. Meanwhile Bismarck was packing his papers and planning future revelations. Knowing how he would have behaved to another under similar circumstances, he feared that his papers would be seized—they were after all official state-documents. He went through the files at random with Busch, his former press jackal; and the two old men grabbed at the most telling documents, Busch smuggling them out of the house at night and concealing them. These precautions were unnecessary. Neither William II nor Caprivi, the new chancellor, made any inquiry. The remaining papers were crammed into some three hundred packing-cases. Along with them went thirteen thousand bottles of wine and all the accumulated bric-à-brac of twenty-eight years, hideous little mementoes from every statesman and crowned head in Europe. Bismarck made it a great grievance that he was turned out of his house at a day's notice and even alleged, untruly, that he had heard the axe already being laid to his favourite trees. In fact he was given nine days' grace; and the chancellery was after all an official residence. It was not the fault of the *Reich* that Bismarck had no house in Berlin of his own.

Bismarck gave a dinner to the Prussian ministers, all of whom (save one) were remaining in office. It was an uneasy occasion. Bismarck would not offer his hand to Boetticher, and burst out towards the end of dinner: 'I see only smiling faces among you; it is your fault that I am no longer chancellor.' The ministers invited him to a dinner in return, but he refused to go. He did not exchange a single word of affection or regret either with his colleagues or with officials. The only man to whom he gave a parting present (extracted from one of the packing-cases) was the old messenger who had carried dispatches for twenty years between chancellery and palace. On 29 March Bismarck left Berlin. Crowds lined the streets. A guard of honour, and all the great dignitaries of the Empire—but not the emperor—were at the station. As the train drew out, the military band struck up a slow march. Bismarck leant back in the carriage and said: 'A state-funeral with full honours.'

INTO THE GRAVE—AND BEYOND IT

WHEN Metternich returned home on 13 March 1848 after being dismissed, he said to his wife: *'Oui, nous sommes tous morts.'*[1] Bismarck would not give up so easily. He was free to lead the life of an independent country gentleman. But forty years in the service of the state, twenty-eight years in supreme power, had spoilt him for retirement. He had always been easily bored; now he was bored all the time. 'I was turned out at 75, but I feel young, far too young to do nothing. I was used to politics; now I miss them.' He dreamt at first of an early recall, and said before leaving Berlin: *'Le roi me reverra.'* When the public and the politicians ignored him, he came to feel that he was already dead, and he aimed instead at a revenge from beyond the grave. He would appeal from the present to the future. 'What the newspapers write about me is so much dust which I brush off. I only care what history will say about me later.' Herbert dashed off a bitter, spiteful account of his father's dismissal, which Bismarck approved,[2] and took as his example. He would write a grandiose survey of his entire career in the same spirit, exalting his achievements and scoring off all his enemies past and present. Schweninger encouraged the project in order to give Bismarck something to do. Cotta, the publisher, agreed to take six volumes and to pay the fabulous sum of £5,000 a volume. Here was work which would last Bismarck's lifetime.

Bucher settled at Varzin to organize the material and to write at Bismarck's dictation. The work made slow pro-

---

[1] 'Yes, we are dead all right.'
[2] It ultimately appeared as the 'suppressed' third volume of Bismarck's *Reminiscences*.

gress. Bismarck had never been a systematic worker. Now he was more erratic than ever. He would dictate the dramatic episodes of his career to Bucher again and again, adding new and less likely details at every sitting; but he could not put his thoughts into order, and he was impatient when reminded of the facts. Bucher was shocked at his disregard for the truth. For instance, he denied all initiative in the affair of the candidature for the Spanish throne, though Bucher had been to Spain on his instruction and now showed him a letter to Prim, the Spanish dictator, in his own handwriting. He lost interest once he had dictated his favourite stories, and he would lie for hours on a sofa, flicking over the newspapers that he claimed not to care about, while Bucher sat silent and disapproving, waiting in vain for the dictation to begin. Bucher got down a good deal, which he arranged in some sort of chronological system and padded out with documents from Bismarck's vast store. After a few months he fell ill, and in 1892 he died. There was no one else to keep the work going. Cotta set up the fragments, and Bismarck made a few verbal changes in the proof. He dictated no more; and the presses were still standing when he died.

Bucher had done enough to fill two volumes instead of the six originally projected. The great set-pieces showed Bismarck's literary genius in all its grandeur, though he had often told the same stories better at the dinner-table. But there was little sense of history or of philosophic detachment. Men and women long dead were pursued with the same relentless hatred. Judgements were inserted not for their historic truth, but for their effect on the present— jibes against the parties, attacks on Austria-Hungary, hits at William II. There was little explanation of Bismarck's motives. This was not surprising. He had never understood the secret of his career, and had been driven on by unconscious forces which mastered him before he mastered others. He was not interested in winning over posterity; but even if he had been, he would have found it beyond him.

Bismarck soon neglected the idea of a posthumous victory. He resolved to rise from the grave and to achieve victory even now. Like John Gabriel Borkman, he still expected to be recalled to life, and talked of those whom he would dismiss when he returned to power. No one associated with court or government was admitted to Varzin. The emperor's health was drunk on his birthday in disapproving silence; and laudatory references were allowed only to William I. Bismarck carried his dislike so far that he always laid out the coins from his pocket with the imperial eagle uppermost, in order—as he told Herbert —'not to see that false face'. He would not have minded, or so he said, if William II had told him frankly that he was not wanted; but he resented intrigue—forgetting the similar intrigues by which he had got rid of ministers throughout his career. Sometimes he emphasized his own moderation in contrast to that of his wife and sons: 'I am the only monarchist in this house. All the rest are republicans.' Occasionally he spoke with less restraint. He said to Sir Charles Dilke: 'Were it all to come over again I would be republican and democrat; the rule of kings is the rule of women; the bad women are bad and the good are worse.' A strange saying. No woman had a hand in his fall. But Bismarck did not forget his feud with Augusta even in his stronger dislike of William II.

The war was not kept within the family circle or carried on only for the benefit of visitors. Bismarck talked with equal freedom to journalists, even supplying a separatist journal in southern Germany with an attack on the Hohenzollerns. Soon he established a regular connexion with a daily newspaper in Hamburg, for which he dictated leading articles, unsigned but recognizable in every line. Here, of course, he appeared to rise above personal feeling. His theme was always the blunders and inexperience of his successors. Though he wanted rest and retirement, he could not stand silently by and watch his work being destroyed. He wrote mainly on foreign policy, and especially on relations with Russia. He hinted very early that he had been the only one who knew how to get on with the Russians, though it was not until 1896 that he broke all the rules by telling the story of the Reinsurance treaty and of the failure to renew it in 1890. No doubt he would have railed just as fiercely if his fall had been followed by cooler relations with England. As a matter of fact, Caprivi, the new chancellor, did not change much in Bismarck's line after the first dramatic months. Though he talked more about Austro-German solidarity for the sake of public opinion, he kept on good terms with St. Petersburg and was soon repeating Bismarck's refusal to back Austria-Hungary in the Balkans. William II got over his anti-Russian fever in a year or two, and after 1894 was far more intimate with Tsar Nicholas II than his grandfather had been with Alexander II, let alone Alexander III. Germany did not seem to need the wand of the magician—at any rate until well on in the twentieth century.

It was the same in home affairs. Caprivi turned out a sensible, efficient administrator—no genius indeed, but capable of one feat that had been beyond Bismarck. He kept on good terms with a Reichstag where the Centre, the Progressives, and the Socialists (Bismarck's *Reichsfeinde*) had a majority, and in 1893 even carried an increased army grant, a stroke which Bismarck had declared impossible with any Reichstag elected by universal suffrage. One National Liberal, anxious to support the imperial government and yet still devoted to Bismarck, journeyed specially to Varzin in order to be instructed in Bismarck's objections. He returned unenlightened and told his friends: 'I couldn't help saying to myself that Bismarck did or would have done many of the things for which he blames the present government.' In the last resort Bismarck had a very simple message. He had founded the Empire with some assistance from William I, his *Handlanger*. William II would destroy it.

There were those who tempted Bismarck to come yet more into the open. In 1891 a Hanoverian constituency elected him to the Reichstag at a by-election on the National Liberal list—an odd combination after Bismarck's attacks on Hanoverian separatism. A constituency in Pomerania or East Prussia would have seemed more appropriate; but none presented itself, and Bismarck was, in fact, more popular with middle-class German liberals in the west than with the Junkers whom he is supposed to have saved. Despite his desire to protest and to assert his greatness, he never took his seat in the Reichstag. He explained that he had no house in Berlin and was too old to go to an hotel. Again, it would be improper for him to criticize his successor over details. He would wait for some great crisis; and none came. In earlier years, he had never found it difficult to create a crisis when it suited him. Now he had lost the gift; or perhaps, after all, feared to exercise it. Despite his railings against the seclusion of Varzin, he shrank from the harsh world outside. The Reichstag had not been a docile audience even when he spoke with the prestige of a chancellor. Would it listen to him at all as a detached individual? Or would he be humiliated by some despised 'orator'—Bebel or Richter?

Though Bismarck enjoyed the reputation of a fighter and looked like one, he never fought on equal terms. He always insisted on being in a unique position—the only Junker with brains, the only politician with noble blood, the only imperial minister, in short 'the indispensable man'. His greatest gift was in packing the cards, not in playing the hand. He confessed this frankly to Dilke: 'Cavour, Crispi, even Kruger, were greater than myself. I had the State and the army behind me; these men had nothing.' Open debate in the Reichstag had no attraction for him. He dreamt of returning to power, not by winning over public opinion, but as the result of an appeal from the emperor. There would be a dramatic reconciliation; then Bismarck and William II would once more defy the world. Hence his exasperation when William II remained coldly aloof. He was indignant with the emperor, yet would not burn his boats by openly denouncing him. He had gained

power by court-intrigue, and never learnt a better
trick.

Nevertheless he made some approach to public opinion
if only from force of circumstances. Crowds collected when
he went on his yearly visit to Kissingen. Universities
presented him with addresses. Societies elected him to
honorary membership. He had to make some formal reply
and, once begun, he could rarely break off without an
attack on the present rulers of Germany. He developed,
too, an affecting passage where he would look to the past
and break into sobs before he could pronounce the words,
'my old master, Emperor William I'. In 1892 he went to
Vienna to attend Herbert's wedding. He had meant it as a
purely private visit, for, after all, his family was always
more important to him than any political affair. Caprivi
foolishly instructed the German ambassador to ignore
Bismarck; William II, even more foolishly, followed suit
with a private letter to Francis Joseph. Excluded from
official circles, Bismarck had to play the popular hero
whether he would or no. He stopped on the return journey
at a number of German towns, ending with a speech in the
market-place of Jena. William II's coldness brought Bismarck out as a liberal. 'Perhaps my dutiful behaviour has
been the cause of the deplorable lack of backbone in Germany.' He urged his hearers to be more critical of the
government, more independent in their views. Absolutism
was bad, bureaucracy worse. 'It is a dangerous experiment
to strive for absolutism nowadays . . . I was never an
absolutist and shall certainly not become one in my old
age.' The Reichstag was not powerful enough. 'I want a
stable majority in parliament . . . I am anxious for the
future of our national institutions unless the Reichstag can
effectively criticize, check, warn, under certain circumstances direct the government.'

This was not new doctrine for Bismarck. Though he had
always opposed parliamentary sovereignty, he had often,
in his more restrained moments, preached the virtues of a
balanced constitution, just as he had always upheld the

Balance of Power in foreign affairs. He knew his own love of power too well to trust unchecked power to anyone else. He did not invent constitutional principles merely because he was out of office; but he had failed to apply his own principles when he was in. He confessed as much in his speech at Jena: 'Perhaps I myself contributed unconsciously to depressing the influence of parliament to its present level'—a sentence in which only the word 'unconsciously' stirs a query. There was a deeper flaw in Bismarck's argument. Even now the stable majority that he desired was to be composed only of the parties 'that upheld the state'—'the old cartel' of Conservatives and National Liberals. This cartel had perished. Even if it were restored, it could not win a majority under universal suffrage. A German statesman who wanted to make the constitution a reality would have to win the parties of the masses for constructive ends—the Centre and the Social Democrats. Bismarck had always treated them as *Reichsfeinde*; and he established a tradition which made it impossible for these two parties to become supporters of the government until after the fall of the Empire.

In private Bismarck often foretold the victory of his old enemies. 'Perhaps God will send Germany a second era of decay, followed by a new period of glory—that will certainly be upon a republican basis.' The class war, he insisted, must be fought to a finish: 'When the final victory comes, it will be the victory of labour.' He was not the sort of conservative who admires existing institutions for their own sake and defends them for their intrinsic value. He was a despairing conservative, staving off a dreaded, though inevitable, future, clinging to the present for fear of something worse. Real conservatism is rooted in pride of class. Bismarck had no feeling for the Junkers from whom he sprung. In taste and outlook he was nearest to the rich merchants of Hamburg. It was no accident that he wrote for a Hamburg newspaper and died virtually in a Hamburg suburb. Here was his spiritual home. Merchant-princes are civilized, restrained, balanced, but essentially uncreative and without hope for the future. Bismarck resembled them. A gifted young observer, Harry Kessler, visited Bismarck with a party of students in 1891. He was impressed with Bismarck as a historic character, 'his white cravat in the style of 1848', but he was disappointed that the creator of the *Reich* had no vision for the new generation. 'He offered us young Germans as object in life the political existence of a rentier, the defence and enjoyment of what had been won; our creative urge was ignored . . . He was no beginning, but an end, a grandiose final chord —a fulfiller, not a prophet.' We might be at home with the Buddenbrooks.

Bismarck could always command an audience, but it was one that counted for nothing in the world of affairs. No German politician visited him until Tirpitz came in 1897. Even when a foreigner appeared, it was Dilke—a man excluded from political life in his own country. The enthusiasts for Bismarck were either those for whom life had not begun or those for whom it had ended—students or fellow-visitors at a watering-place. The university students were always ready to put on their corps-uniform, while Bismarck, also absurdly decked in a corps-cap, harangued in their midst. But they forgot his words when they became state servants, just as English students forget the rhetoric which delighted them at their university Union. The old gentlemen at Kissingen would cheer Bismarck as he walked across for his daily glass of thermal water; but rheumatism, not the future of Germany, was their real concern. Despite his explosions of rage and impatience, Bismarck could not step out of his grave.

For most of the time, he did not even attempt it. He was alone at Varzin for months on end—alone and bored. Johanna could offer him no real companionship. She had never had any intellectual or political interests, and was now failing fast. Herbert made his home at Varzin and continued to do so after his marriage. But Bismarck could only train him for a revenge that would never come. Bismarck needed friends. Where were they to be found? He had none in his own class. Motley had died in 1877.

Keyserling had not met him since 1868. On Johanna's promptings, Keyserling left his Baltic home in 1891; and the two old men spent some happy weeks together. When Keyserling left, Johanna implored him to return; and he did so. But apart from friendship, Keyserling had little to offer Bismarck. He advised Bismarck to cultivate 'a harmonious personality'. Bismarck replied fiercely: 'What have I to be harmonious about?' The two talked about religion. Bismarck confessed that 'during the struggles of the last decades he had moved further from God.' Some have seen in this a doubt as to the morality of his political actions. Nothing could be more mistaken. Bismarck's religion was pietistic, not ethical. It was active life in itself, not particular acts, which had taken him further from God. He gave Keyserling a more curious explanation. He had moved away from God, he said, as his erotic passions declined. That has the true Bismarckian ring. He had called in God to keep him away from pretty girls and to make him a respectable married man. When his desires faded—perhaps when Kathi Orlov died—he needed God no longer and had dismissed Him. On another occasion he expressed doubt of an omnipotent God directly controlling the universe. It seemed to him more likely that there were subordinate principles of Good and Evil in endless conflict; a Balance of Power, in fact, in the unseen world as in the world of states. His old rebelliousness blazed out still more clearly at the end of his life. 'I repeat the prayer "Thy will be done". I try to understand it, but I don't always succeed.'

Keyserling did not come again after 1891, and there was no one to take his place. In Bismarck's diaries the monotonous entries increased: 'bored'; 'tired'; 'bored and tired'. Though he still went out in the woods, he could not walk for long. After 1892 he could not ride. By 1894 he was condemned to a carriage, and soon to a wheeled chair. In November 1894 there was a worse catastrophe. Johanna died. Just before her death Bismarck took Holy Communion at her bedside—for the last time in his life. He

turned even his wife's death into an excuse for resentment.
'If I were still in office, I should now work hard. That would
be the best help; but this comfort is denied me.' In
December 1894 Bismarck moved from Varzin to Friedrichsruh. He never saw Varzin again. At Friedrichsruh he was
nearer the bustle of Hamburg and could hope to see more
people, despite his growing weakness.

William II had already made it up with him. The open
estrangement was humiliating for the emperor; there was
no danger in ending it when Bismarck had so obviously
lost all real influence. In January 1894, after much diplomacy, Bismarck was invited to visit William II in Berlin.
He went still hoping to be consulted on great affairs; and
some of the men in office expected to be turned out. Yet
at the same time he felt that he was venturing into the
enemy camp; and he did not go unattended. He leant on
Herbert's arm as he mounted the steps of the imperial
palace. Herbert and Bill, his younger son, sat near him at
the formal dinner in the evening. But nothing dramatic
happened one way or the other. William II kept the talk
firmly to polite trivialities. No serious advice was sought or
given; no insults were exchanged. Bismarck was treated
as a visiting royalty, not as the great chancellor. He
realized fully for the first time that he had indeed passed
beyond the grave.

It was much the same with the celebrations which
marked his eightieth birthday on 1 April 1895. Every
German prince and city, all the great public corporations,
sent greetings. The universities joined in a common
demonstration, the rectors glorious in their robes and
golden chains, the students in their corps-uniforms. But
they were celebrating the past, not acting in the present.
They honoured the maker of German unity, not the living
statesman. William II said ruthlessly: 'We honour to-day
the officer, not the statesman'; and Bismarck accepted the
distinction. He appeared for the last time in military uniform, complete with helmet, and played his old mas-
querade: 'The best in me and my actions has always been

the Prussian officer.' There was one discordant note. When a motion to congratulate Bismarck came before the Reichstag, Progressives, Centrists, Social Democrats and Separatists combined to defeat it—Bismarck's old *Reichsfeinde* paid him the compliment of acting as though he were still alive. He had always hated more than he had loved; and no doubt it pleased him that there were still some who returned his hate.

There was little stir at Friedrichsruh after April 1895. Bismarck still spoke contemptuously of Germany's present rulers, even though he was supposed to be on good terms with Hohenlohe, who had followed Caprivi as chancellor in 1894. True to his rural affectation, he urged the Farmers' League against 'the drones who govern us' in June 1895. But the deputations, and even the individual visitors, dwindled. Bismarck's energy dwindled on the other side. In December 1897 William II came to Friedrichsruh for the last time, 'to see how long the old man will last.' Bismarck was by now confined to a wheeled chair; yet he played the host with the formal graces of the society that had perished in 1848. He tried to lead the conversation to serious themes. William II kept to the tone of worldly frivolity which he had learnt from his uncle Edward VII. Bismarck got in a last stroke. He told how he had advised Napoleon III to stick to personal government so long as he could count on the imperial guard; otherwise ministerial responsibility was the safer course. Then, speaking directly to William II, he concluded: 'Your Majesty, so long as you have your present corps of officers, you can do what you like; but if not, things will be very different.' He accompanied William II to the door in his wheeled chair. Later he said: 'Jena came twenty years after the death of Frederick the Great; the crash will come twenty years after my departure if things go on like this'—a prophecy fulfilled almost to the month.

Bismarck's last political visitor was Tirpitz, drumming round for a great German navy. Bismarck was enthusiastic for naval power; applauded torpedo-boats and coastal defences; but he could not be caught for an aggressive battle-fleet. 'Germany should keep within her frontiers.' It was his last political judgement, and an appropriate one. He had been as ruthless and unscrupulous as any other politician. What had distinguished him had been his moderation. In Goethe's words, which everyone quotes: *In der Begrenzung zeigt sich der Meister*.[1] He had reined in his political passions, and those of others; given to no one the victory; preached moderation and often practised it. He wanted Germany to remain content with the frontiers that he had drawn for her. Perhaps then she would have kept them. As it is, only Germany's frontier with Austria remains as Bismarck made it; and few would give much for its permanence.

In 1898 Bismarck fell into his last decline. He still harboured resentment, but now against his own weakness: 'There will be only one happy day for me: that is the day when I wake no more.' His mind remained fresh and alert, following political events even on his deathbed. Towards the end he lay sometimes talking, sometimes singing softly to himself. The only book by his bedside was a volume of Schiller's poems. Once, opening his eyes, he asked his daughter why she was so sad. 'Because you are so ill, Papa.' Bismarck smiled and whistled quite clearly, '*La donna è mobile*'—touching, though inappropriate. Six hours before his death, he raised his hand sharply and called out: 'That is impossible on grounds of general public policy! [*raison d'état*].' The great artist knew his lines to the last. It was not, however, his final word. Just before he died, he was offered refreshment from a spoon. He pushed the spoon aside, exclaimed 'forward', grasped the glass, and drank its contents unaided. This was even better than his prepared speech. He died on 30 July 1898, shortly before eleven o'clock in the evening.

William II was cruising in the North Sea when the news of Bismarck's death reached him. He hurried back for the funeral. It was an uneasy occasion. Bismarck had refused

[1] Genius is knowing where to stop.

a state-funeral. He was buried at Friedrichsruh, separated from his house by a railway-line—a modern note such as had often appeared incongruously in his career. William II and his glittering courtiers stood on one side of the grave; Herbert and the family, glowering with renewed hate, on the other. There was no gesture of reconciliation. William did not even enter the house. This was hardly surprising. The first shots in Bismarck's posthumous campaign had already been fired. On the day after Bismarck's death Busch released to the press the letter of resignation which had been drafted with such care in March 1890. Cotta was eager to publish the fragmentary recollections which Bismarck had left. Herbert jibbed at the narrative of Bismarck's fall which, in fact, he had drafted. The Bismarck family, he insisted unctuously, could do nothing to weaken the emperor's prestige; and it must wait until William II's death. Perhaps he feared prosecution, and with some reason. Perhaps he feared that William II would make a telling reply. Here, too, he was justified. Cotta regarded himself as freed from the restriction by the fall of the Empire in 1918 and published the so-called 'third' volume despite the protests of Bismarck's heirs. William II had the leisure in exile to tell his side of the story, and did so effectively. No one now would take the version of Bismarck and Herbert at its face value.

The *Reflections and Recollections*[1] which came out later in 1898 were more powerful without the bitter conclusion. Bismarck appeared detached, aloof, an Olympian statesman; and his praise of William I pointed the contrast with the present emperor sharply enough. As a further gesture his tomb, on his own instructions, bore the words: 'A true German servant of Emperor William I.' Herbert tried to

[1] The publisher Cotta put the words of the title in this order. Bismarck had intended them in the singular and the other way round, *Memory and Thought*. This was a truer description of the book, where Bismarck was stirred by memory into reflecting on the past. It was also typical of this great man of action that he should find thought more important than events when he came to describe his life. The original title was restored in the Friedrichsruh edition of Bismarck's collected works.

carry on the fight against William II in more practical
ways. He entered the Reichstag and spoke often on foreign
policy, criticizing the estrangement from Russia and the
emperor's supposed friendship with England. To wreck
this friendship, Herbert became a virulent pro-Boer. His
criticism carried little weight. Even those Germans who
were hostile to England did not wish to return to Bismarck's moderation and balance; they proposed to challenge both Russia and England at once. No Bismarckian
party grew up in the Reichstag. Herbert fell ill, withdrew
from the Reichstag, and died in 1904. His death passed
unnoticed. The younger members of the family became
unassuming state servants, and the name of Bismarck
ceased to count in German affairs.

Yet there were Bismarckians, though there was no
Bismarckian party. Bismarck became the hero of all those
for whom the unification of 1871 was a great, but also final,
step. The Junkers cared nothing for Bismarck. They disliked German nationalism and were now concerned only
to defend their agrarian interests. The new generation of
diplomatists ignored Bismarck's tradition. They had to
make a 'world-policy', and his caution seemed irrelevant
to them. The German masses wanted social reform and a
greater Germany which would bring in the Germans of
Austria-Hungary. The only Bismarckians were the former
National Liberals, few in numbers but strong in intellectual
influence. They were judges, university professors, solid
bankers, steady men of affairs, the real *bourgeoisie*. In
France this class had followed Thiers, one of the few statesmen whom Bismarck admired; and the France of Louis
Philippe was their true ideal, as it was Bismarck's. They
wanted a national state, constitutional monarchy, and the
rule of law; and they admired Bismarck because he had
given them these things without revolution or without
forcing them into an alliance with the radicals. One of their
number, Meinecke, who survived until after the second
World war, confessed their error in extreme old age. They
believed that they could have the rule of law without

democracy. In Germany no Gambetta need follow Thiers; Gladstone, the follower of Peel, need not become 'the People's William'. The monarchy, the army, established authority, could go unchallenged; yet all that was meant by liberal civilization would be secure.

This was the theme for all the work on Bismarck between his death and the outbreak of the first world War. The great historians who wrote about him—Erich Marcks, Max Lenz, Erich Brandenburg—all concentrated on the period of unification. They were contemptuous of the Prussian radicals with their absurd moral scruples and insisted that liberal ends could be achieved, had been achieved, by unscrupulous methods. The wise liberal did not stick to his principles; he accepted the results of *Realpolitik* and rejoiced at doing so. If Bismarck had failed or if he had merely defended absolutism, they and their class would have remained fighting liberals. But the German *Rechtstaat* was in being. What sensible liberal could ask for more? They passed by Bismarck's social policy with uneasy embarrassment; and they neglected his later foreign policy. There was as yet little material for its study. Besides, this would have raised awkward contrasts with the present conduct of foreign affairs; and they had learnt from Bismarck not to criticize 'authority'. They did not approve the threats to France, the great navy, or the Baghdad railway; but they did not foresee disaster. The Bismarckian Reich, they believed, would always remain essentialy conservative and pacific.

The first World war belied their belief. It sprang from Germany's 'world-policy', from her determination to challenge both Russia and Great Britain as world powers. But it was presented to the German people as a war of defence, especially against Russian aggression. This case was accepted by the Social Democrats, and by the Bismarckians also. The great industrialists might dream of annexing Belgium and north-eastern France; the generals might claim all western Russia; the imperialist projectors might foresee a *Mitteleuropa* stretching from Hamburg to Baghdad. The sober German citizen of the middle or working class thought only of defending the *Reich* of 1871; and Bismarck was their common symbol. The centenary of his birth in 1915 saw him more truly a national hero than he had ever been. It was ironical that these celebrations were held in support of a war that was being directed, ostensibly at any rate, by William II.

The defeat of Germany and the fall of the monarchy in 1918 threw the admirers of Bismarck into confusion. What had perished—the Hohenzollern dynasty or Bismarck's work? A few former Bismarckians answered firmly: only the dynasty. Thomas Mann, for instance, had been Bismarckian to the core. Sprung from a line of Hanseatic merchants, he had drawn a proud contrast during the war between German culture and the decadent democracies of England and France. Now he urged that the high German *bourgeoisie*, his own class, should work with the Social Democrats to consolidate the republic. He was met with jeers and hisses when he preached this doctrine at Berlin university in 1923. Soon he left Germany and became an alien not only in place but in spirit. The great majority of the Bismarckians, with the university professors at their head, remained faithful to the dead monarchy. They wore their reservist uniforms with pride, as Bismarck had done; and they used his name as a stick with which to beat the republic.

The German universities became schools of nationalism. The professors condemned the policy of fulfilment and appeasement. They denounced Locarno and the attempts at reconciliation with France. Germany, they taught, could rise again only when she was freed from 'the shackles of Versailles'. They applauded secret rearmament, had no word of blame for the political assassinations. They still prized the *Rechtstaat*, the rule of law; but they supposed that it would survive the overthrow of the republic. The great event in Bismarck's career at this time was the Friedrichsruh edition of his works: nineteen stately volumes, presented with an opulence of type and paper which recalled a vanished greatness. Bismarck's despatches, speeches and letters were brought together; every scrap of talk was recorded; the text of his *Recollections* was edited with meticulous scholarship. Thimme, the principal editor, surpassed his pre-war colleagues. They had argued that Bismarck had done wicked things, but that all had turned out for the best. Thimme sought to show that Bismarck had not behaved wickedly at all. Far from planning the wars against Denmark, Austria and France, he had acted in a purely defensive spirit. They had been the aggressors; Bismarck had merely happened to get his blow in first. The Danes had aimed to eliminate the Germans of Sleswig and Holstein; Austria planned to destroy Prussia; France was intending to dismember Germany and to annex the Rhineland. Bismarck had been forced into war much against his will.

Thimme was also the leading spirit in publishing the records of the German foreign office between 1871 and 1914. Here, too, he built up the case for Bismarck's pacific policy —a case which it was indeed easy to make. But there was a more doubtful implication. Not only was Bismarck's policy peaceful and defensive; his method was the only one by which peace could be secured. Hence Bismarck's legacy was *Realpolitik*. Away with the League of Nations; back to practical diplomacy. This lesson was drawn not only by German professors. The most profound and scholarly survey of Bismarck's diplomacy after 1871 was written by the American professor, W. L. Langer; and *Realpolitik* was taught to a generation of students who were to deter- mine American policy after the second world war—not the least of Bismarck's victories. Many causes combined to win sympathy for Germany in England and the United States. Sentimental regrets at victory counted most; the complaints of economists against reparations for something. But the name of Bismarck counted too. Previously Anglo- Saxons had regarded him as the type of German power. Now they began to believe that *Realpolitik* was right after all and that the doctrines of Gladstone—or their modern version, the doctrines of Wilson—were wrong.

The Bismarckians got their way. The republic was overthrown by Hitler in 1933. The shackles of Versailles were broken off: reparations ended, a great German army restored. Then the Bismarckians discovered to their horror that, while they had got everything they wanted, they had also lost everything that they prized. The *Rechtstaat*, the rule of law, had vanished. The Nazi barbarians ruled. The Bismarckians were helpless. They had never known how to oppose. Now they could not even protest. They clung to their official positions, trying to limit the evil, acquiescing in much of it, falling one after another by the wayside. They lost the army, the foreign office, the administration, even the universities and the learned world. Meinecke, for instance, was turned out of the editorship of the *Historische Zeitschrift* in 1936 for refusing to include a section of anti-Semitic history. A few, such as Rauschnigg and Hans Rothfels, left Germany for a new spiritual home in America, much as the defeated radicals had done after 1848. Most of them lay low. Bismarck had set them the example of acquiescence—wearing a revolutionary rosette in 1848, conforming to the prejudices of William I, talking the language of liberalism to please the Reichstag. The only method they knew was intrigue, not opposition. They hoped vaguely to manœuvre Hitler on to a saner, more moderate course, as Bismarck had drawn William I along unwelcome paths.

But Hitler was not an elderly gentleman of simple mind and political innocence. He was the greatest of demagogues, confident of his powers, marching somnambulistically to world-conquest. Instead of the Bismarckians manœuvring Hitler, he manœuvred them. They were his instruments; and he launched Germany into the second world war, despite the Bismarckians pulling at his coat-tails. Once more, as in 1914, the respectable Germans of all classes tried to present the war as one of defence, and they clung desperately to the hope that the *Rechtstaat* would be restored when the war was over. They continued to serve Hitler though they disagreed with him, just as Bismarck

had continued to serve Frederick William IV and Manteuffel between 1851 and 1858; and this grumbling service
would have gone on to the end if Hitler had continued to
succeed. Allegiance to Bismarck was their gesture of self-
respect, a sign that they were serving another Germany
than Hitler's. A. O. Meyer, for instance, who completed his
life of Bismarck in 1943, described it as 'my contribution
to national service during the war.'

By a strange turn of the wheel, Bismarck had now
become the symbol of opposition—no longer against a
foreign treaty, but against a German government. He was
the rallying point for all those Germans who were too
respectable to resist Hitler, yet also too decent to acquiesce
in his system. Meinecke records how a Danish historian
said to him during the war: 'You know that I cannot love
Bismarck; but now I recognize that he belonged to our
world.' It was this world of Bismarckians who made up
the silent German opposition, inactive, helpless, yet disapproving. In 1944 Hitler's failure, not his policy, drove
them to resistance. This was tardy, incompetent, in-
effectual. Yet the heirs of Bismarck attempted something
against Hitler, however late in the day. The outside world
puzzled over the objects of this German 'resistance'. The
answer is simple: they wanted the Bismarckian Reich.
They had no contact with the German people, no faith in
democracy. They still wished to combine militarism and
the rule of law, to find somehow an 'authority' that would
be moderate from its own decency.

The terror which followed the abortive rising of 20 July
1944 fell principally on the Bismarckians. Few survived the
end of the war. The Bismarckian tradition was itself in
tatters—Friedrichsruh ruined, Varzin in Russian occupation, Berlin no longer the capital. In the German universities the name of Bismarck was challenged for the first time.
A few unrepentant Bismarckians still praised *Realpolitik*
and even contended that there would have been nothing
wrong with Hitler if he had left the Christian churches alone
and not persecuted the Jews. But most professors had

doubts. They hinted that the academic world had been seduced by Bismarck's success. Perhaps it should have admired ethical values more, and worldly power less. Perhaps Gilbert Murray, not Treitschke, was the true example for a university professor. Yet was this more than a reflection of Germany's passing weakness? Did it not judge Bismarck by his own standards and condemn him solely because in the long run his work had failed?

Bismarck seemed to have nothing to offer the Germany that followed the defeat of 1945. The Roman Catholics and the Social Democrats dominated western Germany; the Communists had an artificial monopoly of power in the east. All alike were Bismarck's *Reichsfeinde*. And how could the Bismarckian tradition be applied in foreign affairs? No doubt Bismarck would have striven to liberate and to reunite Germany. But in what way? By co-operating with one world-antagonist against the other? Or by seeking to stand aside from their quarrels, as he had advocated neutrality in the Crimean war? Winston Churchill called Dr. Adenauer 'the greatest chancellor since Bismarck'— so completely had Bismarck's name become a word of praise even for non-Germans. But there was little parallel. Adenauer was a Roman Catholic from the Rhineland, for whom the unity of western Europe came first. The few German conservatives who tried to reunite Germany by negotiating with the Russians were perhaps nearer Bismarck's line—certainly they thought so themselves. But the essential conditions for a Bismarckian policy were lacking. He had counted on a strong Prussian army as the starting-point from which he made Germany the centre of Europe. Now Germany could not be a 'third force' so long as she was disarmed. Perhaps the days of German greatness have vanished for good. Even an independent Germany may still be overshadowed by the two world Powers, Soviet Russia and the United States, and may find herself much on the level of any other European country. But perhaps not. A new Bismarck may yet arise to exploit the antagonism of Germany's neighbours and to make her again 'the tongue in the balance'. At all events, Bismarck would be content that his name is still a symbol of policy and he himself a subject of controversy.

BIBLIOGRAPHY

THERE is an immense literature on Bismarck. A full list will be found in the latest edition of Dahlmann-Waitz, *Quellenkunde der deutschen Geschichte*. G. P. Gooch discusses 'the Study of Bismarck' with a survey of the outstanding books in *Studies in German History* (1948).

1. BISMARCK'S WRITINGS

Die gesammelten Werke, 19 vols. (1924–35). *Politische Schriften*: Vol. 1: to 1854. Vol. 2: 1 Jan. 1855 to 1 March 1859. Vol. 3: March 1859 to September 1862. Vol. 4: September 1862 to 1864. Vol. 5: 1864 to June 1866. Vol. 6: June 1866 to July 1867. Vol. 6a: Aug. 1867 to 1869. Vol. 6b: 1869 to 1871. Vol. 6c: 1871 to 1890.

Gespräche: Vol. 7: to the founding of the German Reich. Vol. 8: to Bismarck's dismissal. Vol. 9: to Bismarck's death.

Speeches: Vol. 10: 1847–69. Vol. 11: 1869–78. Vol. 12: 1878–85. Vol. 13: 1885–97.

Letters: Vol. 14/I: 1822–61. Vol. 14/II: 1862–98.

Erinnerung und Gedanke: The original text of *Gedanken und Erinnerungen* (first published in 1898).

The title of the collected works is misleading. Though collected, Bismarck's works are not complete. His writings on foreign policy after 1871, for instance, have to be sought in *Die grosse Politik der europäischen Kabinette*, Vols. 1–6 (1922). His speeches can be found in full only in the 14 volumes, edited by Hans Kohl (1892–95). There are many collections of his letters. For example: to his wife (1900); to William I (1903); to his sister Malvine von Arnim (1915); to Kleist-Retzow (1919); to his son Bill (1922); to Ludwig von Gerlach (1896); to Schleinitz (1905).

2. RECOLLECTIONS OF BISMARCK

M. Busch: *Bismarck: Secret Passages from his Life*, 3 vols. (1898).
H. Hofmann: *Fürst Bismarck 1890–1898*. 3 vols. (1913).

R. von Keudell: *Fürst und Fürstin Bismarck* (1901).

Lucius von Ballhausen: *Bismarck-Erinnerungen* (1920).

H. von Poschinger: *Bismarck und die Parlamentarier*, 3 vols. (1894–96).

C. von Tiedemann: *Aus sieben Jahrzehnten*. Vol. 2: *Sechs Jahre Chef der Reichskanzlei under dem Fürsten Bismarck* (1909).

3. ANTHOLOGIES

H. Ameling: *Bismarck-Worte* (1918).

R. Ingrim: *Bismarck selbst.* (1950).

Tim Klein: *Der Kanzler* (1943).

Hans Rothfels: *Bismarck und der Staat* (1954).

A. Stolberg-Wernigerode: *Bismarck-Lexicon* (1936).

4. LIVES

Erich Eyck: *Bismarck. Leben und Werk*, 3 vols. (1941–44).
    Bismarck and the German Empire (1948).

J. W. Headlam: *Bismarck* (1898).

Max Lenz: *Geschichte Bismarcks* (1913).

Erich Marcks: *Bismarck. Eine Biographie 1815–1851* (1940).

Paul Matter: *Bismarck et son Temps.* 3 vols. (1907–09).

A. O. Meyer: *Bismarck. Der Mensch und der Staatsmann* (1944).

C. Grant-Robertson: *Bismarck* (1919).

5. BOOKS ON SPECIAL TOPICS

G. Anschütz: *Bismarck und die Reichsverfassung* (1899).

Otto Baumgarten: *Bismarcks Religion* (1922).

C. W. Clark: *Franz Joseph and Bismarck* (1934).

W. H. Dawson: *Bismarck and State Socialism* (1891).

Georg von Eppstein: *Bismarcks Staatsrecht* (1923).
    Fürst Bismarcks Entlassung (1920).

Maria Fehling: *Bismarcks Geschichtskenntnis* (1922).

E. Franz: *Der Entscheidungskampf um die wirtschaft-politische Führung Deutschlands 1856–67* (1933).

H. Goldschmidt: *Das Reich und Preussen im Kampf um die Führung* (1931).

H. Kessler: *Gesichter und Zeiten I* (1935).

G. Mayer: *Bismarck und Lassalle* (1927).

A. O. Meyer: *Bismarcks Kampf mit Österreich am Bundestag zu Frankfurt* (1927).

Bismarcks Friedenspolitik (1930).

Bismarcks Glaube (1933).

W. Mommsen: *Bismarcks Stürz und die Parteien* (1924).

B. Nolde: *Die Petersburgen Mission Bismarcks 1859–62* (1936).

N. Orloff: *Bismarck und Katherina Orloff* (1936).

A. Richter: *Bismarck und die Arbeiterfrage* (1935).

Gerhard Ritter: *Die preussischen Konservativen und Bismarcks deutsche Politik 1858 bis 1876* (1913).

Hans Rothfels: *Bismarck und der Osten* (1934).

K. von Schlözer: *Petersburger Briefe* (1921).

Carl Schweitzer: *Bismarcks Stellung zum christlichen Staat* (1923).

E. Schweninger: *Dem Andenken Bismarcks* (1899).

Helene von Taube: *Alexander Keyserling* (1921).

A. J. P. Taylor: *Germany's First Bid for Colonies* (1938).

Walter Vogel: *Bismarcks Arbeiterversicherung* (1951).

W. Windelband: *Bismarck und die europäischen Grossmächte 1879–1885* (1940).

E. Zechlin: *Staatsstreichpläne Bismarcks und Wilhelms II* (1929).

INDEX

INDEX

A(LAN) J(OHN) P(ERCIVAL) TAYLOR, Fellow of Magdalen College, Oxford, was born in 1906 at Southport, Lancashire. Educated at Oxford and at Vienna University, he was from 1930 to 1938 a Lecturer in History at Manchester University. While he was at Manchester, Professor Taylor published *The Italian Problem in European Diplomacy, 1847–49* and *Germany's First Bid for Colonies, 1884–85*. Both these books deal with problems in his special field of interest, recent international history. In 1938 he became a Fellow of Magdalen College. He was Ford's Lecturer in English History at Oxford in 1956, Leslie Stephen Lecturer at Cambridge in 1961, and is a Fellow of the British Academy. *The Habsburg Monarchy, 1809–1918*, the work for which Professor Taylor is best known, was published in 1948. He is also the author of *The Course of German History; From Napoleon to Stalin; Rumours of War; The Struggle for Mastery in Europe, 1848–1918; Politics in Wartime, and Other Essays;* and *Origins of the Second World War*. He is a regular contributor to the *New Statesman* and the *Manchester Guardian*.

"Your sister thinks you should marry…"

Bethany's face grew hot. "Husbands don't exactly grow on trees in New Covenant."

"Anyone you chose would be getting a fine wife."

She looked up to study Michael's reflection in the glass, but it wasn't clear enough to let her see what he was thinking. "Are you making me an offer?"

"You would be getting a very poor bargain if I was."

She turned around so she could look into his eyes. "Why do you say that?"

"Because it's the truth."

There was so much pain in his voice and deep in his eyes that she wanted to hold him and promise to make everything better.

She couldn't. "What's wrong, Michael?"

"Nothing that you can fix."

"How do I know that if you can't tell me what troubles you?"

"Trust me. You don't want to know." He turned and walked down the hall and out the back door.

He was so wrong.

Bethany wanted to know everything about Michael Shetler.

After thirty-five years as a nurse, **Patricia Davids** hung up her stethoscope to become a full-time writer. She enjoys spending her free time visiting her grandchildren, doing some long-overdue yard work and traveling to research her story locations. She resides in Wichita, Kansas. Patricia always enjoys hearing from her readers. You can visit her online at patriciadavids.com.

Books by Patricia Davids

Love Inspired

North Country Amish

An Amish Wife for Christmas

The Amish Bachelors

An Amish Harvest
An Amish Noel
His Amish Teacher
Their Pretend Amish Courtship
Amish Christmas Twins
An Unexpected Amish Romance
His New Amish Family

Brides of Amish Country

Plain Admirer
Amish Christmas Joy
The Shepherd's Bride
The Amish Nanny
An Amish Family Christmas: A Plain Holiday
An Amish Christmas Journey
Amish Redemption

Visit the Author Profile page at Harlequin.com for more titles.

An Amish Wife
for Christmas

Patricia Davids

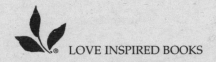

LOVE INSPIRED BOOKS

Recycling programs
for this product may
not exist in your area.

ISBN-13: 978-1-335-50982-6

An Amish Wife for Christmas

www.Harlequin.com

Printed in U.S.A.

That he would grant you, according to the riches of his glory, to be strengthened with might by his Spirit in the inner man; That Christ may dwell in your hearts by faith; that ye, being rooted and grounded in love, May be able to comprehend with all saints what is the breadth, and length, and depth, and height; And to know the love of Christ, which passeth knowledge, that ye might be filled with all the fullness of God.

—*Ephesians* 3:16–19

This book is dedicated with great admiration to my longtime and dare I say long-suffering editor, Emily Rodmell. I'm sure I have tried your endless patience far more often than any other author, but you have never failed to help me get back on track. During the bleak moments of my personal life and in some weird and crazy times you have remained confident in my talent and pushed me to write a better book even when I wasn't sure I wanted to go there. Thanks for your faith in me. Here's hoping it isn't misplaced. Onward and upward.

Chapter One

"Your brother's behavior reflects badly on you, Bethany, and on our community. Something must be done."

Bethany Martin sat across from Bishop Elmer Schultz at her kitchen table with her head bowed and her hands clasped tightly together in her lap. Her dear friend Gemma Lapp sat beside her. Bethany was grateful for Gemma's moral support.

"We Amish are newcomers here," he continued. "We can't afford to stir ill will among our *Englisch* neighbors. Don't you agree?"

Bethany glanced up and met his intense gaze. She nodded slightly. An imposing man in his midfifties, the bishop had a shaggy gray-and-black beard that reached to the middle of his chest. A potato farmer and owner of a shed building business, he was known for his long and often rambling sermons, but he was a fair man and well liked in their small Amish community. Bethany didn't take his visit lightly. She prepared to defend her brother.

"Ivan isn't a bad boy. It's just that he misses his grandfather. He's angry that God took Elijah from us and he feels guilty. The two of them were very close." Her heart ached for her troubled brother.

"Time will heal this," Gemma added.

The bishop sighed. "Your grandfather Elijah was a fine man, Bethany. I have no doubt that he kept the boy's high spirits in check, but Ivan has quickly put one foot on the slippery slope that leads to serious trouble. He needs a firm hand to guide him and mold him into an upstanding and righteous man."

"I can do that," Bethany assured him. "I've raised Ivan from the time he was five and our sister, Jenny, wasn't much more than a newborn babe." She might be their sister, but she was also the only mother they had ever known. Both mother and father to them after the man who bore that title left his family for the fourth and final time. Bethany's anger surged to the surface but she quickly brought it under control. At least her mother had been spared knowing about his final betrayal. She had been positive he would return to care for his children after she was gone. He hadn't. Bethany brought her attention back to the matter at hand.

Gemma waved one hand. "Ivan is almost fourteen. Boys that age get into mischief."

It was a weak argument and Bethany knew it. Her brother's recent behavior was more than mischief, but she didn't know what to do about it. He seemed to be done listening to her.

The bishop's expression softened. "Bethany, your grandfather was concerned that you have sacrificed your chance to have a family of your own in order to care for your siblings."

She drew herself up straight. "I don't feel that way. Ivan and Jenny *are* my family."

The bishop laced his fingers together on the table. "I am the spiritual leader of this community and as such I have a duty to oversee the welfare of all my flock. Normally I would leave the discipline of children to their parents. In this case I feel duty bound to step in. Elijah was my dear friend. It was his vision that founded our new community here. It was his desire to see it grow. For that we need the goodwill of our *Englisch* neighbors."

"I'm aware of that. I spent many months helping him search for the best place to settle. New Covenant is as much my dream as it was his." She didn't like the direction the bishop seemed to be going.

"Then you agree that we can't let the reckless actions of one boy ruin what has been created."

"He isn't trying to spoil anything." Bethany was compelled to defend Ivan, but the truth was she didn't know what was wrong with him. Was he acting out because of his grief or was something else going on?

His schoolwork had suffered in the past weeks. His teacher had complained of behavior issues in class. He had been in several scuffles with non-Amish boys earlier in the year but they weren't anything serious. It was his recent secrecy and withdrawal that bothered Bethany the most. How could she help him if she didn't understand what was amiss?

She lifted her chin. "There is no proof that he damaged Greg Janson's tractor or that he is responsible for letting Robert Morris's cattle loose."

Bishop Schultz leveled a stern look at her. "He was seen near both farms at the time and he'd been in fights with both the Janson and Morris boys."

"That's not proof," she insisted.

The bishop pushed back from the table. "I have written to your uncle in Bird-in-Hand."

She frowned. "To Onkel Harvey? Why?"

"Elijah mentioned that Harvey and his family plan to visit you this Christmas."

"That's true. We are expecting them to stay a week as they were unable to come to the funeral."

The bishop rose to his feet. "I have asked your uncle to take Ivan with him when the family returns to Pennsylvania."

Bethany's mouth dropped open. "*Nee*, you can't send Ivan away. This isn't right."

"It was not an easy decision. I know your intentions are *goot* but the boy needs the firm guidance of a man. You are too easy on him."

"Because he's still a little boy." The situation was quickly slipping out of her control. They couldn't take her brother from her. Fear sent her pulse pounding in her temples. "Please, Bishop, you must reconsider."

"I will not."

Bethany pressed both hands to her heart. "I promised my mother before she died that I would keep the family together. I promised her. Don't do this."

The bishop's expression didn't change. Her plea had fallen on deaf ears. Men were the decision makers in her Amish community. The bishop had the last word even in this family matter.

He took his coat and hat from the pegs by the door and put them on. "Bethany, if you were married I wouldn't have to take this course of action. Your husband would be the one to make such decisions and discipline the boy. With Elijah gone, I see no other choice. I must think of what is best for all, not just for one."

He nodded to her and left. Bethany wanted to cry, to shout at him, to run after him and beg him to change his mind, but she knew it wouldn't do any good.

"I'm sorry." Gemma laid a hand on Bethany's shoulder.

"What am I going to do? There has to be a way to change the bishop's mind."

"Why don't I make us some toast and a cup of coffee. Then we'll put our heads together and come up with a plan."

"We're out of bread and I don't want any coffee."

"What Amish woman runs out of bread?"

"This one. There has been so much to do since Daadi's passing I haven't had time to bake. If Ivan straightens up and starts behaving, if he apologizes to the bishop maybe he'll be allowed to stay. It's five weeks until Christmas. That's enough time to prove he has changed."

"Or you can get married. That will fix everything."

Bethany gave her friend an exasperated look. Gemma knew Bethany's feeling about marriage. It wasn't for her. "It's unlikely that I could find someone to wed me before Christmas, Gemma."

"If you weren't so particular, maybe not. Jesse Crump holds you in high regard."

Bethany wrinkled her nose. "Having a conversation with Jesse is like pulling teeth. He's a nice enough fellow, but he never has anything to say."

"Ack, you're too fussy by far."

"You marry him."

Both Gemma's eyebrows shot up. "Me? Not a chance. Besides, it isn't my brother that is being sent away."

Bethany battled her rising panic. "I wish Daadi were still here. I don't know what to do."

Gemma slipped an arm around Bethany's shoulders and gave her a hug. "If your grandfather was still alive we wouldn't be having this conversation."

"I know."

Ivan's troubling behavior had started when their grandfather became ill early in the fall but it had gotten much worse since his death. Her gaze moved to the closed door leading to her grandfather's workroom. Their grandfather had happily spent hours repairing clocks and antique watches during the long winter months in his tiny shop. With the door open she used to hear him humming or muttering depending on how a particular project was progressing.

The workshop hadn't been opened since Ivan found Elijah slumped over his desk barely breathing. The boy ran to find help but by the time it arrived Elijah was gone.

She should have mailed his unfinished works back to their owners before now but she couldn't bear to enter the room. The grief she tried so hard to control would come pouring out when she did.

Tears stung the backs of her eyelids, but she quickly blinked them away. The quiet strength and unquestioning love of her grandfather had seen Bethany through the worst times in her life. It was still hard to accept that she could never turn to him for guidance again.

She drew a deep breath and squared her shoulders. He would tell her prayer and hard work solved problems. Worry and regret never did. There had to be a way to keep her family together and she would find it. Perhaps her uncle would side with her. She would write her own letter to him and plead her case.

She slipped into her coat. "Thank you for coming today, Gemma, but I'd best get the rest of my chores done."

Gemma followed her to the door. "I don't know how you'll manage this farm without Elijah and Ivan."

"One day at a time and with the help of our neighbors if I need it."

"I've never known you to ask for help." Gemma moved to put on her black bonnet and coat.

"I asked you to sit with me when the bishop came today, didn't I?"

Gemma rolled her eyes. "Okay, you have asked for help one time. I wish I knew what to say but I think it is all up to Ivan. I'm surprised he wasn't here this morning."

"He's at school. I didn't want to take him out of class."

The New Covenant Amish community was too small yet to have their own school. The five Amish children in their church, including her brother and sister, attended the nearest public school. It was far from ideal but the teachers and school board had taken great pains to accommodate the needs and customs of the new Amish pupils.

The two women walked outside together. Gemma pulled on her gloves. "Do you want me to come over this evening when you talk to him?"

Bethany shook her head. "*Danki*, but I think it's best I speak to him alone."

"All right. I'll stop by tomorrow and you can tell me all about it." The two women exchanged a hug. Gemma climbed into her buggy and drove away.

Bethany's breath rose as puffs of white mist in the chilly mid-November morning as she crossed the snow-covered yard to the newly completed red barn. It was the latest building to be added to the new community. The bulk of the structure had been raised in a single day with the help of an Amish community from upstate New York. Thirty men had traveled all night by bus and worked feverishly to complete the barn before taking the long bus ride home again that night. Someday the people of New Covenant would return the favor.

Her grandfather had had plans for half a dozen additional structures to attract more Amish families to New Covenant. It had been his dream to form a thriving Amish district in Maine, far from the tourist centers in Pennsylvania. To him, fewer tourists meant less money but more time to spend close to God and family without worldly influences. If only he could have lived to see his dream grow and thrive.

Bethany fed and watered the chickens, gathered the eggs and then fed and watered the geese before heading to the barn. Her mind wasn't on her chores. Her conversation with the bishop replayed in her head as she fed and watered their two horses. Outside the milk cow's stall, Bethany paused and leaned on her pitchfork. "I've got trouble, Clarabelle."

The cow didn't answer her. Bethany pitched a forkful of hay to the family's placid brown-and-white Guernsey and then leaned on the stall door. "The bishop has decided to send Ivan to Bird-in-Hand to live with Onkel Harvey. It's not right. It's not fair. I can't bear the idea of sending my little brother away. It will break his heart and Jenny's, to say nothing of mine. We belong together."

Clarabelle munched a mouthful of hay as she regarded Bethany with soulful deep brown eyes. The bell around her neck clanked softly as she tilted her head to allow Bethany to scratch behind her left ear. Bethany complied. As a confidant, Clarabelle was unassuming and easy to talk to, but she was short on advice.

"Advice is what I need, Clarabelle. The bishop said Ivan could stay if I had a husband. Someone to discipline and guide the boy. I don't believe for a minute that is the solution but I'm getting desperate. Any idea where I can get a husband before Christmas? And please don't suggest Jesse Crump. Jedidiah Zook might be a possibility if he smiled more. Maybe he just needs a wife to make him happier. What do you think?"

"I doubt your cow has the answers you seek but if she does I have a few questions for her about my own problems," a man said in an amused drawl.

Bethany spun around. A stranger stood in the open barn door. He wore a black Amish hat pulled low on his forehead and a dark blue woolen coat with the collar turned up against the cold. He carried a duffel bag over one shoulder and he leaned on a black cane.

The mirth sparkling in his eyes sent a flush of heat to her cheeks. How humiliating. To be caught talking to a cow about matrimonial prospects made her look ridiculous.

She struggled to hide her embarrassment. After looking the man up and down, she stabbed the pitchfork into the hay again and dumped it into Clarabelle's stall. "It's rude to eavesdrop on a private conversation."

"I'm not sure talking to a cow qualifies as a private conversation but I am sorry to intrude." The man put down his duffel bag.

He didn't look sorry. He looked like he was struggling not to laugh at her. At least he was a stranger. Maybe this mortifying episode wouldn't become known in the community. She cringed at the thought of Jedidiah Zook hearing the story. "How can I help you?"

"Mind if I sit here for a minute?" He pointed to a stack of straw bales beside the barn door.

She wanted him to go away but her Amish upbringing prevented her from suggesting it. Any stranger in need deserved her help.

He didn't wait for her reply but limped to the closest bale and sat down with a weary sigh. "The bus driver who dropped me off said New Covenant was a little way along on this road. His idea of a little way does not match mine."

"It's less than half a mile to the highway from my lane."

He rubbed his leg. "That's the farthest I've walked in six months. How much farther do I have to go?"

"You have arrived at the south end of our community."

He tipped his head slightly. "I thought New Covenant was a town."

"It's more a collection of houses strung out on either side of the road right now, but it will be a thriving village one day." She prayed she spoke the truth.

"Glad to hear it. I'm Michael Shetler, by the way." He took off his hat and raked his fingers through his thick dark brown hair.

She considered not giving him her name. The less he knew to repeat the better.

He noticed her hesitation and cleared his throat. "It's rude not to introduce yourself in return."

She arched one eyebrow. "I'm being rude? That's the pot calling the kettle black. I am Bethany Martin," she admitted, hoping she wasn't making a mistake.

"Nice to meet you, Bethany. Once I've had a rest I'll step outside if you want to finish your private conversation." He winked. One corner of his mouth twitched, revealing a dimple in his cheek.

Something about the sparkle in his blue eyes invited her to smile back at him but she firmly resisted the urge. She stabbed the pitchfork into the remaining hay and left it standing upright. "I'm glad I could supply you with some amusement today."

"It's been a long time since I've had something to smile about."

The clatter of hooves outside caught her attention as a horse and wagon pulled up beside the barn and stopped. She caught a glimpse of the driver through the open door. He stood and faced the barn. "Ivan Martin, are you in there? It's Jedidiah Zook. I want to speak to you!"

Her gaze shot to Michael. His grin widened. Her heart sank as he chuckled. "I may not have given Clarabelle enough credit. It seems your preferred beau has arrived. It was Jedidiah Zook you hoped would come courting, right?"

She glared and shook a finger at him. "Don't you dare repeat one word of what you heard in here."

Michael couldn't help teasing her. The high color in her cheeks and the fire in her eyes told him she was no meek Amish maid. He wagged his eyebrows. "Do you need a go-between? Shall I speak on your behalf? I'll be happy to help any way I can."

"If you say anything, I'll…I'll…" She clamped her lips closed. The sheen of unshed tears gathered in her eyes, but she quickly blinked them back and raised her chin.

Teasing was one thing. Upsetting her was another. He held up one hand. "Relax. Your secret is safe with me. If the cow spills the beans, that is not my fault."

"Stay here." Bethany rushed past him out the wide double doors. "*Guder mariye*, Jedidiah. Ivan isn't in here. He's at school. Can I be of any help?"

"Your brother has gone too far this time."

The man's angry voice brought Michael closer to the

open door to watch. Bethany faced Jedidiah defiantly with her head up and her hands on her hips. "What has he done?"

"Two thirty-pound bags of potatoes and a ten-pound bag of dried beans are missing from my cellar."

"What makes you think Ivan took them?"

"Because he sold a bag of potatoes to the general store owner just this morning."

She folded her arms in front of her. "That's not proof he took them. Maybe it was one of our sacks that he sold."

"Was it?"

"I'm not sure."

"You tell him I came by and that I'm on my way to report this theft to the bishop. This has gone beyond what can be ignored. It must stop. If you can't control the boy someone else will have to." He lifted the reins, turned the wagon around and headed down the lane.

Michael limped out to stand beside her. "Not a very jolly fellow. Are you sure he's the one?"

She shot him a sour look. "In spite of what you think you heard earlier, I am not in the market for a husband."

Why wasn't she married already? She was certainly attractive enough. Not that he was in the market for a relationship. He wasn't. He might never be. He sobered at the thought. The men who shot him and robbed the store he had worked may have robbed him of a family, too. He had no idea if his PTSD would get better living in the isolation of northern Maine, but it was his last option.

Bethany brushed past him into the barn, a fierce scowl marring her pretty features. "I need to speak to my brother and get to the bottom of this. You are welcome to rest here."

He was glad he wasn't the brother in question. She went down the aisle and opened the stall door of a black mare with a white blaze. She led the mare out, tied the horse to a hitching post and began to harness her.

"Let me do that for you." He took a step closer.

"I can manage," she snapped.

He took a step back and held one hand up. She didn't need or want his help. In short order she had the harness on and then led the animal outside, where she backed the mare in between the shafts of the buggy parked in a lean-to at the side of the building.

"May I?" he asked, pointing to the buggy. She nodded. He finished securing the traces on one side while she did the other. He buckled the crupper, the loop that went around the mare's tail to keep the harness from sliding forward on the animal, as Bethany finished her side and came to check his work.

"Danki."

She thanked him like it was a chore. Bethany Martin was clearly used to doing things by herself.

Michael realized that he hadn't looked over his shoulder once since hearing Bethany's voice. That had to be some kind of record. He glanced around out of habit but there was nothing sinister in the farmstead and empty snow-covered fields that backed up to wooded hills on either side of the wide valley. All throughout his trip to New Covenant he'd been on edge, expecting danger from every stranger that came close to him. He'd spent most of the bus ride from Philadelphia with sweating palms and tense muscles, expecting another attack or a flashback to overtake him at any second. They never came when he was expecting them.

He rubbed a hand across the back of his neck. For the first time in weeks the knots in his neck and shoulders were missing. Maybe he was getting better. Maybe this move was the right thing, after all. He prayed it was. Nothing here reminded him of the Philadelphia street or the shop where his life had changed so drastically.

Here the air was fresh and clean. The next house was several hundred yards up the road. Nothing crowded him. He could start over here. No one would look at him with pity or worse. He had a job waiting for him in New Covenant and a place to live all thanks to the generosity of a man he'd never met. He needed to get going, but he was reluctant to leave Bethany's company for some reason. Her no-nonsense attitude was comforting. He pushed the thought aside. "I should be on my way. Can you give me directions to Elijah Troyer's farm?"

She shot him a startled look and then glanced away. "This was his farm," she said softly with a quiver in her voice.

"Was? He sold it?" Michael waited impatiently for her to speak.

She kept her gaze averted. "I'm sorry but Elijah Troyer passed away three weeks ago."

Michael drew back with a sharp intake of breath. "He's dead? That can't be."

He fought against the onrush of panic. What about the job? What about the place to live? Were his hopes for a new life dead, too?

Chapter Two

Bethany watched as Michael limped away and sat down on the hay bale inside the barn door. He rubbed his face with both hands. She could see he was deeply affected by the news of her grandfather's death. Sympathy made her soften her tone. "I'm sorry to give you the sad news. Did you know my grandfather well?"

Michael shook his head. "I never met him."

If he didn't know her grandfather, why was he so shaken by his passing? As much as she wanted to stay and find out Michael's connection to Elijah, she had to speak to Ivan as soon as possible. If he had stolen the potatoes and beans as Jedidiah claimed, the items would have to be returned at once, but there had to be some mistake. Her brother wasn't a thief.

Please let it be a mistake, Lord.

The bishop would never reconsider sending Ivan to live with Onkel Harvey if Jedidiah's claim was true.

She slipped the reins through the slot under the winter windshield of the buggy. "I'm sorry you didn't have a chance to meet my grandfather. He was a wonderful man."

"He offered me a job working for him. Is that job still available?"

"I know nothing about such an offer. Are you sure it was my grandfather who promised you work?"

"Elijah Troyer, in New Covenant, Maine. That's what the letter said. Is there another Elijah Troyer in the community?"

"There is not. I don't know what my grandfather had in mind, but I can't afford to hire someone right now."

"I was also told I would have a place to stay. I reckon if there's no job there's no lodging, either?"

Was he talking about the small cabin that sat at the back of her property? Her grandfather had mentioned readying it for a tenant before he became ill, but she didn't know if he had finished the repairs. Besides, she wasn't ready to host a lodger. Nor did she want to leave Michael Shetler like this. He appeared dazed and lost. Her heart went out to him.

"You should speak to our bishop, Elmer Schultz. I'm sure he can help. He won't be at home this time of day, but I can give you a ride to his place of business."

"It seems I don't have much choice. *Danki.*"

Michael slowly climbed into the passenger seat. Bethany walked around the back and got in on the driver's side. She picked up the reins. "The school is about three miles from here."

"I thought we were going to the bishop's place of business."

"We are but I must stop at the school first. I hope you don't mind."

"As long as I don't have to walk three miles I don't mind."

From the corner of her eye Bethany noticed him rubbing his leg frequently. It must pain him a great deal.

This close to him she noticed the dark circles under his eyes, as if he hadn't slept well. He was pale, too. She sat silent for the first half mile of their trip but her curiosity about Michael got the better of her. "Where are you from?"

"My family lives in Holmes County, Ohio. My father and brother have a construction business in Sugarcreek."

"Did you work in construction with them?"

"Nee." He didn't elaborate.

"I've heard that's a large Amish community. Do you have a lot of tourists who visit there?"

"We do."

"Like where I am from. Bird-in-Hand, Pennsylvania. My grandfather wanted to start a community that wasn't dependent on tourism. Don't get me wrong, he knew how important the industry is to many Amish who can't make a living farming, but it wasn't the lifestyle he wanted to live."

Michael pulled his coat tighter. "There had to be warmer places to settle."

She chuckled as she looked out over the snow-covered fields that flanked the road. "The coldest part of the winter has yet to come."

"So why here?"

"The price of land and the ability to purchase farms large enough to support big families were more of a consideration than the weather. Plus, we were warmly welcomed by the people here. Many local families have been here for generations. They like the idea that we want to be here and farm for generations, too. A lot of the elders in the community remember farming with horses when they were children. Folks are very independent minded in Maine. They know what hard work is.

When someone has to sell farmland they would rather sell it to the Amish because we will live on it and farm it as their grandparents did. They consider it preferable to selling to a large farming corporation intent on grabbing up as much land as possible."

"What do you grow here besides snowdrifts?"

She smiled. "Potatoes. Maine is the third-largest producer of potatoes in the United States. Broccoli grows well in the cool climate as do many other vegetables."

"As long as you don't get an early freeze."

"That's true of farming in Ohio or almost anywhere."

"I guess you're right about that."

The main highway followed the curve of the river and after another mile Fort Craig came into view. Bethany turned off the highway into a residential area at the outskirts of town. The elementary school was located in a cul-de-sac at the end of the street.

As she drew the horse to a stop in front of the school she noticed several of the classes were out at recess. She stepped down from the buggy and caught sight of her sister, Jenny, playing with several other girls on the swings. Jenny spotted her and ran over. "Sister, what are you doing here?"

"I've come to speak to Ivan. Did he get on the bus with you this morning?"

Jenny shook her head. "*Nee*, he said Jeffrey's mom was going to bring him to school."

"And did she?"

"I don't know. Sister, I have *wunderbar goot* news."

Bethany crouched to meet Jenny's gaze. "Have you seen Ivan today?"

Jenny screwed up her face as she concentrated. "I don't think so. You should ask his teacher."

Bethany stood upright. "That's exactly what I plan to do."

"Don't you want to hear my news?"

"In a minute."

Jenny's happy expression faded. Michael got out of the buggy. He took several stiff steps. "I just need to stretch my legs a little."

"Who is that?" Jenny asked in a loud whisper.

Bethany was inpatient to find Ivan but she made the introduction. "This is Michael Shetler. He's a newcomer. This is my sister, Jenny."

He nodded toward her. "I'm pleased to meet you, Jenny. I'd love to hear your news."

"You would?" Jenny asked hopefully.

"Sure. It must be important. You look ready to burst."

Jenny smiled from ear to ear. "I got picked to be in the community Christmas play. I'm going to be the aerator."

Bethany looked at Michael. He returned her questioning gaze and shook his head slightly. Jenny was bouncing up and down with happiness.

Bethany smiled at her. "That is *wunderbar*. What does the aerator do?"

"I get to tell everyone the Christmas story in English and in Pennsylvania Dutch while the other kids act out the scenes. Ivan is going to sing a song by himself."

From the corner of her eye, Bethany saw Michael rub a hand across his mouth to hide a grin. Bethany was afraid she'd start laughing if she looked at him again. Learning English as a second language was difficult for many Amish children who spoke only Pennsylvania Dutch until they started school. "I'm sure you will make a *goot* narrator if you practice hard."

"I'll practice lots and lots if you help me."

"You know I will."

"I need to have an angel costume, too. I'm going to be an angel aerator."

"Angel *narrator*," Michael corrected her in a gentle tone.

"Narrator," Jenny replied slowly. He nodded and she grinned at him.

Bethany patted her sister's head. "We'll talk about it when you come home from school this evening."

"Okay." Jenny took off to rejoin her friends.

"Cute kid," Michael said, still grinning. "How many siblings do you have?"

"Just Jenny and Ivan. Excuse me while I check on him." Bethany headed through the front doors of the school. She found the eighth-grade room and looked in through the open door. Ivan wasn't in his seat. His best friend, Jeffrey, was missing, too.

A bell sounded in the empty hall, startling her. The boys and girls in the room filed to the back to gather their coats, mittens and hats from hooks before rushing past her to get outside. After the last child exited the room Bethany stepped inside. "Ms. Kenworthy, may I have a word with you?"

The teacher looked up from her desk. "Miss Martin, of course. Do come in. I was just getting ready to write a note to you."

"About Ivan?"

"Yes. I hope he is feeling better. He's missed almost an entire week of school. I have a list of homework assignments for him to complete and hand in when he returns."

Bethany's heart sank. "My brother is not sick at home."

"I see." Ms. Kenworthy opened a desk drawer and

pulled out a sheet of notebook paper. "Then I assume you did not write this note?"

Bethany removed her gloves, took the note and quickly scanned it. It informed Ms. Kenworthy that Ivan would be out of school for a week due to his illness. It was signed with her name. Bethany sighed heavily and handed the letter back. "I did not write this. It is not my signature."

Ms. Kenworthy took the letter and replaced it in the drawer. "I thought it was odd that Jeffrey was the one who delivered it to me and not your sister. Do you know what Ivan has been doing instead of coming to school?"

"I wish I did. He doesn't confide in me these days."

"He was close to his grandfather, wasn't he?"

The understanding in the teacher's eyes allowed Bethany to unburden herself. "They were very close. Since Elijah's death Ivan has refused to talk to me about what's troubling him. He's changed so much. I was hoping he might have confided in you."

"I am deeply sorry for your loss. Elijah was well liked in this community."

"Thank you."

"Your brother's grades were not the best before your grandfather passed away. Since that time, he has earned nothing but Fs for incomplete work. Even when he is here he seems withdrawn until someone speaks to him. Then he's ready to start a fight over nothing. Unless he does extra-credit work and turns in his missing assignments, I'm afraid he is going to flunk the semester. I know that according to your religion this is his last year of education, but I still have to follow state guidelines. That puts me between a rock and a hard place. If he flunks the semester, he'll have to attend summer school."

Bethany shook her head. "Ivan will be needed on the

farm this summer. I don't see how we could spare him even a few hours a day."

"In that case he will have to repeat this grade next year. Talk to him. Try to make him see what's at stake." She removed a folder from another drawer. "Give these assignments to him. Hopefully he can finish most of them over the weekend."

"I will. Thank you." Bethany was angry with Ivan for his deceit, but she was more disappointed in herself. Where had she gone wrong? How had she failed him? She tried to be a parent to her siblings but without her grandfather's help she didn't know how to reach Ivan. Maybe letting him return to Pennsylvania would be for the best.

Except that it didn't feel like the right solution. She loved her brother. She couldn't imagine life without his annoying habits, constant teasing and his hearty laugh. She had to make him see that his actions were tearing the family apart.

But she needed to find him first. Clearly Jeffrey was in on whatever Ivan was up to. His parents lived a mile farther up into the woods from her home.

Bethany left the school building and saw Michael sitting on the buggy step. She'd forgotten him. A thin yellow hound lay a few feet away from him. The dog wagged its tail tentatively as it watched him. Michael pulled his gloves off and took something from his pocket. He held it toward the dog. The animal crept a few inches closer.

"Good girl," Michael said, tossing the item at the dog's feet. She snapped it up. At the sound of Bethany approaching, the dog darted for cover between two nearby parked cars.

Bethany stopped beside Michael. The dog grew bold

enough to peek out from between the cars but didn't approach. "I see you made a new friend."

He rose to his feet. "She was sniffing at the trash cans and trying to get them open. I could see she was looking for a meal. I had a little leftover jerky I picked up on the bus ride here. She appears to need it more than I do. Is your brother at school?"

"*Nee*, but that doesn't prove he stole provisions from Jedidiah."

"You're still giving him the benefit of the doubt?"

"Of course. He's my brother."

"I hope your confidence isn't misplaced."

"I pray it's not but I will admit I'm at my wit's end. His teacher says he hasn't been to school all week. His friend gave the teacher a note that was signed with my name that said he was sick at home. I have to find out what's going on. He's left each morning to catch the school bus with his sister and he's walked home with her each evening, yet he hasn't been in school."

"Don't think too badly of him. Boys his age are sometimes impatient to grow up and live their own adventures. Then they make foolish mistakes because they aren't as smart as they think they are."

"Are you speaking from experience?"

"I am. My own."

"How many forged notes did you send to your teacher?"

A wry grin curved his lips. "My teacher happened to be my mother's youngest sister, so none."

"I'm afraid of what the bishop will say when Jedidiah tells his side of the story."

"If the bishop is a reasonable man he'll listen to your side of the story, as well."

She was grateful for his reassurance, but he didn't know how serious the situation was becoming. She held on to the hope that her uncle could be persuaded to let Ivan remain with her. "I will take you to see the bishop now."

"I appreciate that." He moved to open the buggy door for her and took her hand to help her in.

His grip was firm but his hand was soft. His skin lacked the calloused roughness of a man who made his living farming the land or woodworking. It wasn't the hand of a laborer, yet she found his gentle strength oddly comforting.

Perhaps he was a shopkeeper. Her grandfather had had plans to open a small grocery in New Covenant. Maybe that was the job he had promised Michael. It didn't matter. Her grandfather was gone, and she wasn't in a position to continue his work. At least not yet.

She looked up and met Michael's gaze as he continued to hold her hand longer than necessary. There was a profound sadness in the depth of his eyes that she didn't understand. What troubled him? What was he thinking?

Michael stared into Bethany's light blue eyes as the warmth of her touch went all the way to the center of his chest and warmed a place that had been cold for a long time. He studied her face, trying to find out why she triggered such a strong reaction in him.

Her pale blond hair was parted in the middle and worn under a white prayer covering. Her skin was fair with a scattering of freckles across her dainty nose. She was an attractive woman, too attractive for his peace of mind.

He let go of her hand, stepped away and limped around the back of the buggy, letting the pain in his leg remind him of why he had no business thinking about how perfectly her small hand had nestled in his. If things had been different, if he wasn't so damaged he would have enjoyed getting to know her better, but things weren't different. He had to accept that.

He also had more serious things to think about. He needed a job and he needed somewhere to live. Preferably a good distance away from other people in this remote community. His neighbors wouldn't appreciate being awakened in the middle of the night by the screams that sometimes accompanied his nightmares.

Thoughts of his dreams filled him with apprehension as his pulse shot up. He quickly scanned his surroundings. A car drove past the school, the tires crunching on the snow. Children were playing on the playground. He could hear their laughter and shouting. Someone stood at the corner of the school building. He thought it was a woman but he couldn't be sure. The person was bundled in a parka with the hood up. Perhaps a teacher watching the children. He struggled to convince himself that there was nothing sinister here but he couldn't shake the feeling that something bad would happen at any second. His heart began to pound as tightness gripped his chest.

The dog ventured out and came to stand in front of him. He focused on her unusual golden eyes. She looked to be part yellow Labrador retriever and part pointer. Her white-tipped tail wagged slowly. He held out his hand and she sniffed it. It was a shame he didn't have more to feed her. She retreated again and he got in Bethany's buggy.

Inside the small space he started to relax. No one could get behind him now. He glanced at Bethany. She was watching him intently. Could she see how anxious he was? He needed to divert her attention. "Are you waiting for something?"

"Nee." She turned the horse and headed back up the

street. The clip-clop of the mare's hooves was muffled by the snow that covered the road. It was the only sound other than the creaking of the buggy. He discovered he would rather hear Bethany's voice.

"What kind of business does the bishop own?"

"Our bishop builds and sells storage sheds as well as farming, but he's thinking of branching out into tiny homes."

"Then he is a progressive fellow?"

"In his business, but our church is a conservative one."

"I noticed a propane tank at your home."

"Our Ordnung allows us to use propane to power business machinery, our refrigerators, washing machines and hot water heaters. We also have running water and indoor bathrooms. We aren't that conservative but our cookstoves and furnaces must use wood or coal."

He glanced out over the dense tree-covered hillsides and the snowcapped mountains in the distance. "It doesn't look like you'll run out of fuel anytime soon as long as you have a strong fellow to chop and haul it."

"My brother does that for me." Her voice was strained. Worry marked her brow with frown lines.

"How old is he?"

"Almost fourteen. Our mother died when Jenny was born. Our father was gone soon afterward." The undertone of bitterness in her voice surprised him.

"So you were raised by your grandparents."

"My grandfather took us in. He was a widower."

"It must've been hard to be both mother and sister to your younger siblings." He found it easier to talk to Bethany than anyone he'd spoken to since the attack. Maybe it was because she talked to cows. He smiled at the memory.

"I never saw caring for my siblings as a burden." She turned the horse off the street into the parking lot surrounded by various sizes of storage sheds.

A tall, muscular Amish fellow stepped away from a half-finished shed and slipped his hammer into a tool belt that hung on his hips. He didn't sport a beard, so Michael knew he wasn't married. His clothes were tattered and sweat-stained, but his smile was friendly as he greeted them. "*Guder mariye*, Bethany. Need a new shed, do you?"

Bethany opened her door but didn't step out. "Good morning, Jesse. Is Bishop Schultz about?"

"*Nee*, he isn't. He's gone to Unity. Their bishop is laid up with pneumonia, and Elmer has gone to do the preaching for their service this Sunday and perform a wedding on Tuesday. He won't be back until Wednesday night."

"Have you seen Ivan today?"

"*Nee*, I've not. Who is that with you?"

"Jesse, this is Michael Shetler. He is a newcomer. He came expecting to work for my grandfather. He hadn't heard about Elijah's passing. I thought perhaps the bishop would know of some work and could find a place for him to stay."

Jesse hooked his thumbs under his suspenders. "There is work aplenty here. You're welcome to bunk on my couch until you can find a place, but you'll have to suffer through my cooking. I'm no hand with a skillet."

Michael got out of the buggy and grabbed his duffel bag. He would rather stay somewhere alone, but he didn't have much choice. He forced a smile and a lighthearted reply. "Your cooking can't be worse than mine. You have yourself a boarder until I can find a place of my own. We can work out the rent later."

"No need for that." Jesse moved to take Michael's bag. "Let me get this for you."

Michael handed it over. Jesse nodded toward the building he had been working on. "If you don't mind, I'd like to finish this shed before taking you out to my place."

"I don't mind. I'll give you a hand with it."

Looking at Michael's cane, Jesse raised one eyebrow. "Are you sure?"

"I can still swing a hammer."

"Then your help will be welcome. I'll see you get paid for the work you do."

"Danki."

Michael turned to Bethany. "Looks like your brother has been granted a reprieve if Jedidiah wasn't able to speak to the bishop."

Bethany's eyes brightened. "That's right."

"Oh, Jedidiah was here and spoke to Elmer before he left," Jesse said cheerfully.

Michael watched the hope fade in her eyes and wished there was something he could do to console her.

Chapter Three

Michael watched Bethany drive away with a sharp unexpected sense of loss. She was a lovely woman, but he sensed she was much more than a pretty face. It was obvious that she cared about her family. Anyone who asked a cow for advice had to have a good sense of humor.

He smiled then quickly pushed thoughts of her out of his head. As much as she intrigued him, he was better off not seeing her.

Forming a relationship with Bethany would mean letting her get close. He couldn't risk that. He had jumped at the chance to come to this part of Maine because it was remote and thinly populated but it held an Amish community. He had left his Amish upbringing once with devastating consequences. After the attack he had returned home hopeful that rejoining his faith and family would repair his shattered life. It hadn't worked out that way. He didn't know what more God needed from him.

Michael's plan for his new life was simple. Live and work alone while coming into contact with as few people as possible. He wasn't a loner by nature. He had become a recluse out of necessity. Avoiding people was the only way he felt safe. The only way he could keep his affliction hidden. Staying with Jesse was risky, but he had nowhere else to go. He could only pray he didn't have an episode in front of him.

A doctor in Philadelphia had called it PTSD. Posttraumatic stress disorder, the result of a robbery gone wrong at the jewelry store where he had worked. What it meant was that his life was no longer his own. He lived in near constant fear. When a full-blown flashback hit he relived every detail as his coworkers, his friends, were killed in front of his eyes. The gunshots, the screams, the sirens—he saw it, heard it, felt it all again just as if it were happening to him the first time.

He never knew when a flashback would happen, making it impossible for him to return to work. Even a walk down a city street left him hearing the footsteps of someone following him, waiting to feel the cold, hard barrel of a gun jammed in his back.

He was the one who had let them in. He was the only one who came out alive. Sometimes he felt he should have died with the others, but he couldn't dwell on that thought. God had other plans for him. He just didn't know what they were.

The heavy thudding of his heart and the sweat on his brow warned him that thinking about it was the last thing he should be doing. He took a deep breath. Concentrate on something else. Think about Bethany asking her cow for advice and the shocked look on her face when she realized he'd heard her conversation. He visualized her in detail as his pulse slowed to a more normal speed.

From the corner of his eye he caught sight of the yellow dog trotting along the edge of the highway in his direction. Did she belong to someone or was she a stray surviving as best she could? Her thin ribs proved she wasn't being cared for if someone did own her. Her chances of surviving the rest of the winter on her own didn't look good. She approached as close as the drive leading into the parking lot. After pacing back and forth a few times she sat down and stared at him.

He turned to Jesse. "Do you know who that dog belongs to?"

Jesse glanced at her and shook his head. "I've seen her around. I think she's a stray."

"Would you happen to have anything I can feed her?"

Jesse laughed. "Are you a softhearted fellow?"

"Is there anything wrong with that if I am?"

"*Nee*, I like animals, too. Maybe more than most people, but I think I'm going to like you, Michael Shetler." Jesse clapped him on the back with his massive hand, almost knocking Michael over. "There's a couple of ham sandwiches in the refrigerator inside the office. You are welcome to them. For you or for the dog. Your choice."

"Danki." Michael walked into a small building with Office in a hand-lettered sign over the door. Inside he found a small refrigerator with a coffeepot sitting on top of it. He took out two of the sandwiches, happy to see they contained thick slices of ham and cheese. After taking a couple of bites from one, he walked out with the rest in his hand. The dog was still sitting in the driveway.

He walked to within a few feet of her and laid the sandwich on the ground. As soon as he moved away she jumped up and gulped down the food. Looking up, she wagged her tail, clearly wanting more.

"Sorry, that's all there is. We are two of a kind, it seems. You needed a handout and so did I. We have Jesse over there to thank for sharing his lunch." Michael chuckled. He had teased Bethany about talking to her cow but here he was talking to a dog. It was too bad Bethany wasn't here to share the joke.

What surprised him was how much he wanted to see her again.

Jeffrey Morgan's home was a little more than a mile farther up the road from Bethany's house. As she pulled in she saw Jeffrey's mother getting out of her car. When she caught sight of Bethany she approached the buggy hesitantly.

"Good afternoon, Mrs. Morgan." Bethany stepped down from the buggy unsure of what to say.

"You are Ivan's mother, aren't you?" The woman remained a few feet away.

"I'm his older sister. Our mother passed away some years ago."

"That's right. Jeffrey told me that. I'm sorry about your grandfather. Jeffrey was fond of him."

"Thank you. Is Jeffrey here?"

"No. He's at school."

"I'm afraid he isn't. I just came from the school. Neither he nor my brother showed up for class today."

Mrs. Morgan looked around fearfully and moved closer to Bethany. "Are you saying that the boys played hooky today?"

"I don't know that word."

"*Hooky?* It means they skipped school without permission."

"Then *ja*, they played hooky."

Mrs. Morgan looked toward the house at the sound of the front door opening. Mr. Morgan stepped out.

Jeffrey's mother leaned closer. "Don't tell my husband about this. I will speak to Jeffrey."

Puzzled by her fearful reaction, Bethany nodded. "Please send Ivan home if you see him."

"I will."

Bethany waved to Mr. Morgan. He didn't return the gesture. She got in her buggy and left. Where were those boys and what were they up to?

Bethany arrived home just after noon. She parked the buggy by the barn and stabled her horse. She wasn't any closer to finding her brother or figuring out what he was up to. As she came out of the barn, a car horn sounded. She glanced toward the county road that ran past her lane. Frank Pearson's long white passenger van turned off the blacktop and into her drive. Frank was the pastor of a Mennonite congregation a few miles away. He and her grandfather had become good friends. Frank used to visit weekly for a game of chess and to swap fishing stories.

Frank pulled up beside her and rolled down his window. "Good day, Bethany."

"Hello, Frank. Would you like to come in for some coffee?"

"I'm afraid I don't have time today. I have my bereavement support group meeting in twenty minutes. I just stopped in to see how you're getting along and to invite you and your family to attend one of our meetings when you are ready. It doesn't matter what faith you belong to or even if you are a nonbeliever. We all grieve when we lose loved ones."

"*Danki*, Frank. I don't think it's for me."

"If you change your mind, you're always welcome to join us. Please let me know if you need help with anything. I miss Elijah, but I know my grief is nothing compared to yours. I promised him I'd check in on you."

"Our congregation here is small, but we have been well looked after."

"I'm glad to hear it. I'll stop by again in a few days and stay awhile."

Maybe Frank could reach Ivan. "Why don't you come to dinner on Sunday? I know Ivan and Jenny would enjoy seeing you again. Maybe you can interest Ivan in learning to play chess."

"You know, I believe I will. Your cooking is too good to resist. Thanks for the invite."

"You are always welcome here."

After Frank drove away, Bethany headed for her front door. The smell of warm yeasty dough rising greeted her as she entered the house. Gemma was busy kneading dough at the table. Bethany pulled off her coat and straightened her prayer *kapp*. "What are you doing here again so soon? I thought you said tomorrow?"

"What does it look like I'm doing?"

"It looks like you are making a mess in my kitchen."

Gemma giggled as she surveyed the stack of bowls, pans and the flour-covered table. "It does, doesn't it?" She punched down the dough in a second bowl and dumped it onto a floured tabletop.

"Why are you baking bread in my kitchen?"

"Because you didn't have any. I realized on my way home this morning that the least I could do for a friend was to remedy that."

"I appreciate the gesture but why not bake it at your home and bring the loaves here."

"I didn't want to mess up my kitchen. I just finished washing the floor." Gemma looked at her and winked. "Where have you been, anyway?"

Should she confide in Gemma about Ivan's recent actions and Jedidiah's accusations? Once more Bethany wished her grandfather were still alive. He would know what to do with the boy. She hung her coat on one of the pegs by the kitchen door. "It's a long story."

Gemma looked up. "Oh?"

Bethany went to the far cabinet and pulled out a cup and saucer. She felt the need of some bracing hot tea. "Jedidiah came by earlier. He accused Ivan of stealing two bags of potatoes and a bag of beans from his cellar."

Gemma spun around, outrage written across her face. "He did what?"

"He said Ivan stole those items and he had proof because Ivan sold some of the potatoes to the grocer this morning."

"I don't believe it. I know Ivan has been difficult at times, but he is not a thief."

Bethany filled her cup with hot water from the teakettle on the back of the stove. "That's what I said. I went to the school to hear Ivan's side of the story."

"And?"

"And he wasn't at school. He hasn't been to school all week. He forged a letter from me telling the teacher that he is out sick." Bethany opened a tea bag, added it to her cup and carried it to the kitchen table, where she sat down.

After a long moment of stunned silence, Gemma came to sit across from her. "You poor thing. Still, that doesn't mean he stole from Jedidiah."

"It doesn't prove he didn't. And it certainly doesn't speak well of his character. Jedidiah went straight to Bishop Schultz with the story. I had hoped to speak with the bishop, too, but he is gone to Unity until Wednesday. I don't know how I'll ever convince him to let Ivan remain with us now. What is wrong with my brother? How have I failed him?"

Had Ivan inherited his father's restlessness and his refusal to shoulder his responsibilities? She prayed that wasn't the case.

Gemma reached across the table and laid a comforting hand on Bethany's arm. "I'm so sorry. I had no idea things had progressed to this degree of seriousness. He's always been a little willful, but this is unacceptable behavior and it is his own doing. Bethany, you did not fail him."

"Danki." Bethany appreciated Gemma's attempt to comfort her.

Gemma returned to the other end of the table and began dividing the dough into bread pans. "You'll simply have to talk to the boy and tell him what the bishop has planned. Perhaps that will convince him to mend his ways."

"I hope you are right. Christmas is only five weeks away. I don't know if a change in Ivan's behavior now will be enough to convince Onkel Harvey and the bishop that he should stay with us. Stealing is a serious offense."

Bethany had lost so many people in her family. She couldn't bear the thought of sending her brother away. She had promised to look after her brother and sister and to keep the family together. It felt like she was breaking that promise and it was tearing her heart to pieces.

"You still have the option to marry. I think Jesse would jump at the chance if you gave him any encouragement."

"I saw him this morning and he didn't appear lovestruck to me."

Gemma laughed. "Did you honestly go see him with marriage in mind?"

"Of course not. I took a stranger to see the bishop at his workplace. The bishop wasn't there but Jesse was."

"What stranger?" Gemma looked intrigued.

"His name is Michael Shetler. He claims my grandfather offered him a job and a place to stay."

"Did he?"

Bethany shrugged. "I never heard Grandfather mention it."

"What's he like? Is he single?"

"He's rude."

"What does that mean? What did he say to you?" Gemma left the bread dough to rise again and returned to her seat, her eyes alight with eagerness. "Tell me."

Bethany blushed at the memory of Michael listening to her conversation with Clarabelle. That was the last time she would speak to any of the farm animals. "He wasn't actually rude. He simply caught me off guard."

"And?"

"When I told him about Elijah's passing he was very upset. I thought the bishop would be the best person to help him find work, so I gave him a ride to the shed factory. Jesse said he would put him to work."

"You took a stranger up in your buggy? Is he old? Is he cute?"

"He walks with a cane."

"So he's old."

"*Nee.* I'd guess he's twenty-five or so. I had the impression it was a recent injury to his leg."

"So he's young. That's *goot*, but is he nice looking?"

Bethany considered the question. "Michael isn't bad looking. He has a rugged attractiveness."

"Michael?" Gemma tipped her head to the side. "He must be single. Is he someone you'd like to know better?"

"I have too much on my mind to spend time thinking about finding a man."

"That's not much of an answer."

"It's the only answer you are going to get. You'll have the chance to see Mr. Shetler for yourself at the church service next Sunday."

"All right. I won't tease you."

Gemma walked over and put on her coat. "Ivan is a good boy at heart. You know that."

Bethany nodded. "I do. Something is wrong, but I don't know what."

"You'll figure it out. You always do. I'm leaving you with a bit of a mess but all you have to do is put the bread in the oven when it's done rising."

"*Danki*, Gemma. I'm blessed to have you as a friend."

"You would do the same for me. Mamm is planning a big Thanksgiving dinner next Thursday. You and the children are invited of course."

"Tell your mother we'd love to come."

"Invite Michael when you see him again."

"I doubt I'll see him before Sunday next and by then it will be too late."

"My *daed* mentioned the other day he needs a bigger garden shed. Maybe I'll go with him to look at the ones the bishop makes. You aren't going to claim you saw Michael first if I decide I like him, are you?"

Bethany shook her head as she smiled at her friend. "He's all yours."

Bethany was waiting at the kitchen table when both children came home. Ivan sniffed the air appreciatively. "Smells good. Can I have a piece of bread with peanut butter? I'm starved."

Bethany clutched her hands together and laid them on the table. "After I have finished speaking to you."

"Told you," Jenny said as she took off her coat and boots.

"Talk about what?" Ivan tried to look innocent. Bethany knew him too well. She wasn't fooled.

"Why don't you start by telling me what you did wrong and why." Bethany was pleased that she sounded calm and in control.

"I don't know what you are talking about." He couldn't meet her gaze.

"You do so," Jenny muttered.

"Stay out of this," Ivan snapped.

"I went to school today. I'm not in trouble," Jenny shot back.

"I'm waiting for an explanation, Ivan." Bethany hoped he would own up to his behavior.

"Okay, I skipped school today. It's no big deal. I can make up the work." His defiant tone made her bristle.

"You will make up the work for today, and Thursday and Wednesday and Tuesday. You will also write a letter of apology to your teacher for your deliberate deception. Is there something else you want to tell me?"

He stared at his shoes. "Like what?"

Bethany shook her head. "Ivan, how could you? Skipping school is bad enough. Forging a letter to your teacher is worse yet, but stealing from our neighbors is terrible. I can't believe you would do such a thing. What has gotten into you?"

"Nothing."

"That is not an answer. Why did you steal beans and potatoes from Jedidiah?"

Ivan shrugged. "He has plenty. The Amish are supposed to share what they have with the less fortunate."

"What makes you less fortunate?"

When he didn't answer Bethany drew a deep breath. "Your behavior has shamed us. Worse than that, your actions have been reported to the bishop."

"So? What does the bishop have to do with this?"

"The bishop is responsible for this community," Bethany said. "Because you have behaved in ways contrary to our teachings, the bishop has decided you need more discipline and guidance than I can give you."

"What does that mean?"

"When Onkel Harvey and his family come to visit for Christmas, you will return to Bird-in-Hand with them."

"What? I don't want to live with Onkel Harvey."

"You should've thought about the consequences before getting into so much trouble."

Jenny, who had been standing quietly beside Ivan, suddenly spoke up. "You're sending him away? Sister, you promised we would all stay together." She looked ready to cry. "You promised."

"This is out of my hands. The bishop and your uncle have decided what Ivan needs. They feel I have insufficient control over you, Ivan. I'm afraid they are right. Bishop Schultz believes you need the firm guidance of a man. If your grandfather was still alive or if I was married, things would be different."

"That's stupid," Ivan said, glaring at Bethany. "I didn't do anything bad enough to be sent away. It isn't fair."

"None of us wants this. You have time before Christmas to change your behavior and convince them to let you stay. You will return the items you've taken from Jedidiah. He knows that you sold one of the bags of potatoes you took. You must give the money you received for them to Jedidiah. You will have to catch up on all your missed schoolwork and behave politely to Jedidiah and to the bishop. We will pray that your improvement is enough to convince Bishop and Onkel Harvey to let you remain with us."

Ivan glared at her. "Jedidiah Zook is a creep. He's never nice to me, so why should I be nice to him?"

Bethany planted her hands on her hips. "That attitude is exactly what got you into this mess."

Jenny wrapped her arms around her brother's waist. "I don't want you to go away. I'll tell the bishop you'll be good."

"They don't care what we think because we're just kids and we don't count."

"That's enough, Ivan. You and I will go now to speak to Jedidiah and return his belongings this evening."

"I can't."

"What do you mean that you can't?"

He shrugged. "I don't have the stuff or the money anymore. I gave it away."

"Who did you give it to?" Bethany asked.

"I don't have to tell you." He pushed Jenny away and rushed through the house and out the back door. Bethany followed, shouting after him, but he ran into the woods at the back of the property and disappeared from her view.

Jenny began crying. Bethany picked her up to console her. Jenny buried her face in the curve of Bethany's neck. "You can't send him away. You can't. Do something, sister."

"I will try, Jenny. I promise I will try."

Ivan returned an hour later. Not knowing what else to do, Bethany sent him to bed without supper. Jenny barely touched her meal. Bethany didn't have an appetite, either. She wrote out a check to Jedidiah for the value of the stolen items and put it in an envelope with a brief letter of apology. She couldn't face him in person.

After both children were in bed, Bethany stood in front of the door to her grandfather's workshop. He wouldn't be in there but she hoped that she could draw comfort from the things he loved. She pushed open the door.

Moonlight reflecting off the snow outside cast a large rectangle of light through the window. It fell across his desk and empty chair. She walked to the chair and laid her hands on the back of it. The wood was cold beneath her fingers. She closed her eyes and drew a deep breath. The smell of the oils he used, the old leather chair and the cleaning rag that was still lying on the desk brought his beloved face into sharp focus. Tears slipped from beneath her closed eyelids and ran down her cheeks. She wiped them away with both hands.

"I miss you, Daadi. We all miss you. I know you are happy with our Lord in heaven and with Mammi and Mamm. That gives me comfort, but I still miss you." Her voice sounded odd in the empty room.

Opening her eyes, she sat in his chair and lit the lamp. The pieces of a watch lay on the white felt-covered board he worked on. His tiny screwdrivers and tools were lined up neatly in their case. Everything was just as it had been the last time he sat in this chair. The cleaning rag was the only thing out of place. She picked it up to return it to the proper drawer and saw an envelope lying beneath it. It was unopened. The name on the return address caught her attention. It was from Michael Shetler of Sugarcreek, Ohio.

Chapter Four

"Why didn't you tell me that you repair watches?"

Michael looked up from Jesse's table saw. Bethany stood in the workshop's doorway he had left open to take advantage of the unusually warm afternoon. She stood with her hands on her hips and a scowl on her pretty face.

The mutt, lying in the rectangle of sunlight, had already alerted him that someone was coming with a soft woof. She shot outside and around the corner of the building. The sight of Bethany made Michael want to smile. She was every bit as appealing as he remembered, even with a slight frown marring her face.

He pushed away his interest. Jesse had filled in a lot of details about the family last night. Bethany was trying to keep her family together. Jesse said without her grandfather and her brother to work the farm she could lose it. A handsome woman in need of help was trouble and Michael had enough trouble. He positioned the two-by-four length of pine board and made the cut. As the saw blade quit spinning he took the board and added it to the stack on his right. He kept his face carefully blank when he met her gaze. "I didn't think it would make a difference."

"It certainly would have."

"How so? Your grandfather is gone. You said you couldn't afford to hire help."

"You neglected to tell me you had sent the first and last months' rent on the cabin."

He picked up another board and settled it in the slot he had created for the correct length so he didn't have to measure and mark each piece of wood. Bishop Schultz used a diesel generator to supply electricity inside his carpentry shop. The smell of fresh sawdust mixed with diesel fumes that drifted through the open door. Michael squeezed the trigger on the saw and lowered the blade. It sliced through the pine board in two seconds, spewing more sawdust on the growing pile beneath the table.

He tossed the cut wood on the stack and reached for another two-by-four. Bethany crossed the room and took hold of the board before he could position it. "Why didn't you tell me you had already paid the rent?"

"I figured you would mention it if you knew about it. Since you didn't say anything and you already had a crisis to deal with, I thought it could wait for a better time."

"That was very considerate of you. A better time is right now. My grandfather never deposited your check. In fact, he never read your last letter. I only found it yesterday evening."

She let go of his board and reached into a small bag she carried over her arm. "I have the check here. I've been unable to bring myself to clean out his workshop. For that reason, his agreement with you went undiscovered." She held out the check. He didn't take it.

"Do you know the rest of your grandfather's offer?" He kept his gaze averted.

"Your letter said you agreed to work with him for six months. Was there more?"

"If he considered me skillful enough after that time he would make me a fifty-fifty partner in the business." He looked at her. "I can show you his offer in writing if you want to see it."

"There's no need. I believe you. Are you still willing to do that?"

"How can I be a partner now that he is gone?"

"The business belongs to me but I can't repair watches, so it is worthless except for his tools. I had planned to sell them unless Ivan showed an interest in learning the trade."

"Has he?"

"Not yet."

"How is the boy?" he asked softly.

A wry smile lifted the corner of her mouth. "I wish I knew. Right now he seems mad at the world."

"Boys grow up. He'll come around."

"I pray you are right. I have a proposition for you, Mr. Shetler."

"Call me Michael."

She smiled and nodded once. "Michael. It's similar to the one my grandfather offered you. Work for me for six months. You keep two-thirds of everything you earn during that time. I will keep one-third as rent on the shop, for the use of Grandfather's client list and his tools. If at the end of that time I am satisfied with your skill I will sell you the business or we can continue as partners."

"Who is to decide if my skills are adequate?"

"My grandfather did the majority of his work for a

man named George Meyers in Philadelphia. He owns a jewelry shop and watch repair business. If Mr. Meyers is satisfied with the quality of work you do, then that is all the assurance I need."

Michael smiled inwardly. One part of the puzzle had finally been solved. George had started this whole thing. It was certainly like George, to go out of his way for someone who didn't deserve the kindness. Michael wondered how much, if anything, George had shared about his condition with Bethany's grandfather. "I wondered how your grandfather got my name. Now I know."

"I'm afraid I don't follow you."

"I used to work for George Meyers." Up until the night he had let two armed criminals into the business George owned.

"Why did you quit? Is that when you got hurt?"

His heart started pounding like a hammer inside his chest as the onset of a panic attack began. In another minute he would be on the ground gasping for air. He wasn't about to recount the horrors he saw that night to Bethany. He had to get outside. "I don't like to talk about it."

He grabbed an armful of cut wood and pushed past Bethany. "Jesse is going to wonder what's keeping me."

She followed him outside. "I'm sorry if it seemed that I was prying. If you don't want to work for me, I understand, but the cabin is still yours for two months."

"I'll think about the job, but I'll take the cabin." He kept walking. It wasn't that he wanted to be rude but he needed her to leave. His anxiety was rising rapidly.

"The cabin is yours whenever you want."

The yellow dog came around the side of the building and launched herself at him. He sidestepped to keep from being hit with her muddy paws. One of the boards slid out of his arms. "Down."

She dropped to her belly and barked once, then rolled over, inviting him to scratch her muddy stomach.

"I see you still have your friend," Bethany said, humor bubbling beneath her words.

He looked from her to the dog. "I don't have anything to feed you, mutt, unless you eat two-by-fours."

The dog jumped to her feet, picked up the board he had dropped and took off with it in her mouth.

"Hey, bring that back!"

The dog made a sweeping turn and raced back, splashing through puddles of melted snow. She came to a stop and sat in front of him, holding the four-foot length of wood like a prized bone.

"Goot hund." He reached for the board but the dog took off before he touched it. She made a wild run between the sheds lined up at the edge of the property where the snow was still deep.

Bethany burst out laughing. "Good dog, indeed."

He liked the sound of her laughter. The heaviness in his chest dissipated and he grinned. "It seems her previous owner didn't spend much time training her."

"I can see that. She is friendlier since she's had a few meals. She seems to have a lot of puppy in her yet. In a way she reminds me of my brother."

"How so?"

"A lot of potential, but very little focus."

"I'd like to meet this kid."

"I'm sure you will since you'll be living just out our back door."

He frowned. "The cabin is close to your house?"

"Fifty yards, maybe less."

"I assumed it was more secluded."

"It is set back in the woods. We won't bother you if that's what you are worried about."

"I like my privacy." He couldn't very well explain he was worried she'd hear him yelling in the middle of the night.

The dog came trotting back and sat down between them, still holding her trophy. Michael bent to grab the board as Bethany did the same. They smacked heads. His hat flipped off and landed in the snow. The dog dropped the wood, snatched up the hat and took off with it.

Michael held his head and glanced at Bethany. "Are you okay?"

Bethany rubbed her smarting forehead. Maybe it was a sign that she needed some sense knocked into her. She had come to give Michael his money back and had ended up offering him a job instead. The thump on her skull had come too late. "I'm fine."

"Are you sure? Do you want some ice?"

"*Nee*, it won't leave a mark. Will it?" She pulled her hand away.

He bent closer. "I think you're going to have a bump."

"Great."

"I am sorry." He looked down at the dog, now standing a few feet away, still holding his hat. "See what you did to Bethany."

The dog whined and lay down, the picture of dejection. Bethany crouched and offered her hand to the animal. "Don't scold the poor thing. It wasn't her fault. Are you going to keep her?"

"I can't walk away and leave her to fend for herself. Besides, her goofy behavior leaves me smiling more often than not. *Ja*, I will keep her. She seems to have decided she belongs with me."

Bethany knew she should leave but found herself reluctant to go. There was something intriguing about the man. One minute they were discussing his job and the next second he went pale as a sheet and couldn't get away from her fast enough. A few minutes later they were both laughing at the antics of a stray dog. The truth was she liked him. A lot. But she had to find a way to keep her family together. She couldn't allow a distraction to interfere with that.

She took the hat from the dog and handed it to Michael. "I should get going."

"Right." He nodded but didn't move.

She took a few steps toward her buggy but something made her turn around. He was still watching her. "Michael, do you play chess?"

"I enjoy the game. Why?"

"Would you do me a favor?"

"If I can."

"I have a friend of my grandfather coming to supper on Sunday evening. He and Daadi used to play chess every week. I know he misses Daadi and their games. I don't play. If you aren't doing anything, would you like to join us for supper and give Pastor Frank a game or two?"

Hadn't she just decided she didn't need a distraction? Maybe he would say no. "Don't feel obligated just because I asked."

"I need to get moved in. I'm not sure I'll find the time."

"You have to eat."

"Another time maybe."

"Of course." She turned away, more disappointed than she cared to admit.

"Bethany?"

"Ja?" She spun around hopefully.

"I appreciate the job offer. I'll give it some serious thought. Do I get the key to the cabin from you?"

"It isn't locked. You'll find the key hanging on a nail just inside the door. When you come to my place you'll see a wooded ridge behind the house. The cabin is up there. Just follow the lane. Do you have transportation? I can send Ivan to pick you up."

"Jesse has offered me the loan of a pony and cart until I can send for my horses. Is there someone locally who sells buggies?"

"There's a carriage maker in Unity. I've heard he is reasonable."

"I'll look into it."

"If you change your mind about having supper with us tomorrow night, just show up. There will be plenty to eat."

"Are you a *goot* cook?"

She grinned. "Do you expect a modest Amish woman to brag on herself?"

"I expect a modest Amish woman to tell the truth."

She bobbed her head once. "I could tell you that I'm a very good cook, but I suggest you come to supper and decide for yourself."

After stepping up into her buggy, she looked back and saw he was still watching her. A tingle of pleasure at his interest lifted her spirits. Just as quickly, she dismissed her feeling as foolishness. Her mother's unhappy life spent loving the wrong kind of man had driven home to Bethany just how cruel romantic love could be. She was determined not to suffer the same way. If she married it would be a beneficial arrangement based on sound judgment. Not love. She waved and then drove away. Would Michael come or wouldn't he? She would have to wait an entire day to find out.

Jesse walked past Michael with a load of boards in his arms. "Have you decided to hang on to her or are you going to ignore her and hope she goes away?"

Michael scowled at him. "What does that mean?"

Jesse stopped and gave Michael a funny look. "I was just wondering if you are planning to keep the dog. What did you think I meant?"

Relieved that he wasn't referring to Bethany, Michael decided to share the joke. "Bethany Martin was just here."

Jesse chuckled. "I wouldn't tell a fella to ignore Bethany and hope she goes away, but the same can't be said for some other single women in this community."

Although Jesse hadn't made Bethany's wish list when she had been talking to the cow about walking out with someone, Michael liked the man and thought he would make a decent husband. "Do you have your eye on one maid in particular?"

"Me? *Nee*, I'm not ready to get into harness with any female. They talk too much, and they expect you to talk back to them. I don't have that much to say. I can't imagine a lifetime of staring at a woman who is waiting for me to utter something interesting. If you are looking to go courting, Bethany Martin is a fine woman. You wouldn't be stepping on anyone's toes."

"I'm not interested in courting, but I did wonder why she isn't already married."

"Her grandfather told me that she wants to get her

brother and sister raised before she looks to start another family."

"Did you know Elijah well?"

"He was a fine friend. Everyone loved him. He was always laughing, quick with a joke, always ready to lend a helping hand. It didn't matter if you were Amish or not. There are only twenty adult members in this church, six *youngees* and five *kinder.* We know each other well."

Youngees were unmarried teens in their running around time or *rumspringa.* The potential marriage pool in the community was small indeed. Bethany would have to look for a marriage partner farther afield if Jesse or Jedidiah didn't work out.

Michael couldn't seem to curb his curiosity about her and her family. "What's the story with her brother?"

Jesse was silent for a long moment. "I'm not one to speak ill of another."

"I'm sorry. I wasn't looking for gossip. I can form my own opinion of the family. You don't have to say anything."

"It's not that. We are newcomers to this area. Bethany and her family have been here the longest. Two years now. I came sixteen months ago. Jedidiah and the other families came after I did. We get along with the *Englisch* and for the most part they get along with us. There are a few exceptions. People who would like to see us leave. When something goes wrong, those few are quick to point to the Amish and say it must be our fault. Ivan has been a mischief maker for as long as I've known him, but I don't believe all that is said against him these days."

"You think he is getting blamed for what someone else is doing?"

Jesse stared into the distance for a long minute, and then he looked Michael in the eye. "I think he makes an easy target."

Michael considered Jesse's carefully worded reply. "What does the bishop think?"

"He hasn't confided in me. I should get back to work. I don't want him to think I slack off when he's gone. Oh, and I meant to tell you I've got some extra nylon webbing if you want to fashion a collar for your mutt. What did Bethany want, anyway?"

Michael followed Jesse to the skeleton of the shed he was putting up. "She discovered her grandfather did rent a cabin to me. She found my rent check last night. She came to give me a choice of getting my money back or staying on the property."

"So, am I losing you as a roommate already?"

"You are. I'll leave tomorrow."

"*Goot.* That makes you the best kind of houseguest."

Michael glanced his way. "What kind is that?"

"One who leaves before he has worn out his welcome." Jesse grinned and clapped Michael on the back then pulled his hammer from his tool belt and went to work.

Michael relaxed. He laid down the boards he'd cut and walked back to the workshop. He thought getting a few answers about Bethany would appease his curiosity but he had been mistaken. It seemed it wasn't so easy to put her out of his mind.

Maybe he'd made a mistake telling her he still wanted to rent the cabin. How was he going to stop thinking about her if he lived fifty yards from her home? If he took the job she was going to be his boss.

He would have to discourage her from visiting the workshop. He worked best alone and he liked it that way. That was the reason he had come to Maine. She would just have to learn to accept it.

Bethany opened the oven to check her peach pie and decided it was done. The crust was golden brown and the juices were bubbling up between the lattice strips. She pulled it out and placed it on the cooling rack at the end of the counter. She then lifted the lid on the pot of chili and sniffed the mouthwatering aroma. Using a spoon, she scooped up a sample and blew on it before tasting it. The deep, rich, spicy flavor was delicious but it needed a touch more salt. After adding two shakes, she stirred the pot and replaced the lid. All she needed now was the rest of her company.

Would Michael come? She hoped he would.

"It smells *wunderbar*," Gemma said as she set the plates on the table.

"Let's hope it tastes as good as it smells." Bethany walked to the window that overlooked the path up to the cabin. She had invited Gemma to join them as a defense against her attraction to Michael. Gemma's lighthearted and flirty ways were sure to liven the evening and keep Michael entertained.

"Any sign of him?"

Bethany dropped the window shade. "Any sign of who?"

"The person you're hoping to see. You realize you've been to that window ten times in the last thirty minutes. I can't imagine that you are this anxious to catch sight of Pastor Frank. Therefore, it must be someone else. I'm going to take a wild guess and say it is a man. A newcomer. Someone who walks with a cane." She raised one eyebrow at Bethany. "Am I close?"

"If you must know, I did invite Michael Shetler. He

plays chess and I know that Pastor Frank misses the games he used to have with Elijah."

"That was very thoughtful of you. Why am I here? I don't play chess."

"You're here because I didn't want it to look like I had invited Michael for personal reasons. You know what I mean."

"You didn't want him to think you were angling for a return date? Or were you hoping I would catch his interest?"

"Both. When he sees I invited a single woman from our community to join us, he won't think I have designs on him myself."

A sly grin curved Gemma's lips. "What if this back-fires and he *does* like me better?"

"Then I will be happy for both of you and you can name your first daughter after me."

Gemma laughed and returned to setting the table. Bethany resisted the urge to look out the window again. It was possible Michael had made his way to the cabin without her seeing him, but she hoped he would at least stop by and let her know he had taken possession.

The rumble of a car announced the arrival of Pastor Frank. Bethany went to the front door to greet him and saw Michael turning in from the highway in a small cart pulled by a black-and-white pony. To her chagrin, he simply waved and went past the house on the track that led to the cabin. She tried not to let her disappoint-ment show. She stepped aside to allow Frank to enter the house and closed the door against the chilly after-noon. It was clear Michael wasn't eager to see her again.

After seeing Bethany's smile fade when he drove past her home, Michael almost changed his mind and went back. Almost. His best course of action was to see as little of her as possible. Out of sight, out of mind. He hoped. While he found her attractive, he couldn't offer her anything but a business partnership. To encourage anything else would be grossly unfair.

The cabin he had rented was set back in a small grove of trees up the hillside behind her place. As she had promised, the road up to it was well marked and had been plowed recently.

A small weathered barn came with the cabin and he stopped Jesse's pony beside it. A quick tour proved it would be enough for his two buggy horses and his buggy when he got one. The only drawback to the property was the steep hillside behind the barn. With his bum leg he'd never be able to get down to the bottom and lead his horses back up when he turned them out to pasture in the summer. He unharnessed the pony and led him inside to a roomy stall. Jesse had supplied Michael with enough hay and horse chow to last him a week.

He moved the horse feed inside and left the hay in the back of the small wagon. He was thankful to see a water pump stood near the barn. It would make keeping the animals watered easier even in the winter.

As he was heading to the cabin with his duffel bag over his shoulder, he saw the dog come trotting up the road. She had followed him from town as he'd hoped she would. He had tried to coax her into the cart, but she'd refused to have anything to do with it even after he lifted her into the bed. "You're a good girl. I'm glad to see you made it."

She ignored him and went to explore in the barn. Michael put his bag down on the porch and tried to open the door. It was locked. He was sure Bethany had told him it would be unlocked. He tried again to make sure the door wasn't just stuck but it wasn't.

He made his way to the back door with difficulty. The snow was deep enough in places to leave him unsure of his footing. If not for his cane and the wall of the cabin, he would have fallen several times. After all his struggles he found the back door was locked, as well. He could see that it had been opened recently by the arch of snow that had been pushed aside. A trail of footprints led from the stoop up the hill into woods. They were small footprints, those of a woman or a child.

Making his way back to the front porch was easier. The dog was sitting by the door waiting for him. He looked at the house below him on the hillside. It seemed he would have to face Bethany after all to get the key. He made his way down the road and knocked on her front door.

Chapter Five

The moment Bethany opened her door Michael knew he was in trouble. Her bright smile and the eagerness in her eyes pushed at the mental wall he had erected to keep people from getting too close.

He didn't want to shut her out. He wanted to be worthy of the friendliness she seemed so willing to share.

"You have decided to join us, after all. Come in, Michael. Please have a seat." She stepped aside and gestured for him to enter.

He shook his head. "I'm not here to eat."

Disappointment replaced the eagerness in her eyes. "Oh? What can I do for you, then?"

She moved back and he stepped inside. The dog squeezed in to stay at his side. Bethany frowned slightly but didn't say anything.

The house was typical of the Amish houses he'd seen all his life. From the entryway a door to his right led directly into the kitchen. Beautiful pine cabinets lined the walls. The floor was covered with a checkerboard pattern of black-and-white linoleum. The windows had simple white pull-down shades instead of curtains. The delicious aromas of Bethany's home-cooked meal filled the air. His stomach growled.

He resisted the urge to stay and make her smile again. "The cabin is locked. I can't get in."

Bethany cocked her head slightly. "Are you sure? Maybe the door is just stuck."

"I'm sure. The back door is locked, too."

"Why does he need in the cabin?" Ivan demanded, scowling at Michael.

Bethany gave her brother a sharp look. "Michael is going to be living there. Daadi rented the place to him. Do you know anything about the cabin being locked?"

"I don't know why you're asking me," Ivan snapped. "Every time something goes wrong I get blamed." He pushed to his feet and rushed out of the room.

Color blossomed in Bethany's cheeks as she glanced at her guests. "I apologize for Ivan's behavior. I thought he was doing better. Jenny, did you lock the cabin?"

Jenny shook her head, making the ribbons of her *kapp* dance on her shoulders. "I play there sometimes with Ivan and Jeffrey, but I didn't lock the door."

Bethany met Michael's gaze but quickly looked away. "I believe there is a spare key in Grandfather's bedroom. If you'll excuse me, I'll go find it. It may take me a moment or two. I'm not sure where Daadi kept it."

The dog suddenly left Michael's side. He made a grab for her and missed. "Mutt, get back here."

She ignored him and went to investigate the new people in the room. She gave the young Amish woman and the *Englisch* fellow at the table a brief sniff, then rounded the far end. Jenny had her hands out. The dog settled her head in Jenny's lap and looked up with soulful adoring eyes as the girl scratched her behind her ears.

"What a beautiful dog." Jenny stroked her soft fur. "I think she likes me."

Michael walked over and took hold of a length of black nylon webbing Jesse had fashioned into a make-shift collar. "I'm afraid she hasn't learned any manners."

"What's her name?" Jenny asked.

"Mutt." He still wasn't sure he would keep her, although she seemed to have attached herself to him. Maybe she would like Jenny better and stay here.

The slender man in *Englisch* clothing rose to his feet. "Mutt is not much of a name but it's better than Cat. I'm Pastor Frank Pearson. You can call me Frank." He swept a hand toward the young Amish woman seated across from him. "This is Bethany's friend Gemma Lapp and you must be Michael Shetler."

The pastor held out his hand. Meeting new people made Michael uneasy. He rubbed his sweaty palm on his pant leg before taking the man's hand in a firm grip. "I take it you are the chess player."

Frank's expression brightened. "I am. Do you play?"

"Now and again."

"We'll have to arrange a match someday. I'm sorry you didn't get to meet Elijah. He was a true master of the game. He told me quite a bit about you."

Michael grew cold. "Is that so? I don't know what he could have told you. We never met."

The pastor's expression didn't change. "He said you came highly recommended by an old friend of his. I believe it was George Meyers and that you grew up near Sugarcreek in Ohio. My grandmother was from the Sugarcreek area, but she left many years ago. Please, have a seat."

It had been a long day and Michael just wanted to

get settled in a place of his own. He accepted the invitation mainly because his leg was aching.

"Would you like some *kaffi*?" Gemma asked.

He nodded. She rose and brought him a cup and saucer with three pale yellow cookies on the plate. "These are lemon crinkles. My specialty. I hope you like them."

"Danki." The coffee was black and bracing. The cookies were light, tart and delicious.

"You can't call her Mutt," Jenny said from the other end of the table.

"Why don't you name her?" Gemma suggested.

Jenny peered into the dog's eyes. "I'm going to call you Sadie Sue. Do you like that name?"

The dog barked once and everyone laughed.

"That settles it," Michael said. "She is now and forever Sadie Sue."

"How are the cookies?" Gemma gave Michael a smile every bit as sweet as the pastry.

"They're delicious. They remind me of the ones my grandmother used to make." He prayed Bethany would hurry up before he was subjected to more questions. She came back in the room a few seconds later.

"Found it." She held the key aloft.

Michael grimaced as he stood and leaned heavily on the table. He had been sitting just long enough for his leg to stiffen. When the sharp pain subsided he picked up his cane.

"Are you all right?" Bethany asked, reaching a hand toward him.

Her sympathy irritated him. He hated when people treated him as if they expected him to topple over at any second. "I'm fine."

"How were you injured?" Gemma asked softly.

His throat tightened. He couldn't draw a full breath.

The walls of the house started to close in. He needed to get outside. "I've got to get going."

He saw the confusion in Bethany's eyes, but nothing mattered except getting enough air. He pushed past her and went out the door. On the porch he stopped to scan the yard and outbuildings for signs of danger. Was someone lurking in the woods beyond the road? He took a step to the side and backed up to the wall of the house so that no one could get behind him. Sadie followed him out and sat at his side, nuzzling his hand. He stroked her head.

After a few deep breaths of the cold air, Michael's panic receded. It was okay. There wasn't any danger. He took one step away from the safety of Bethany's house and then another, glad to escape without having her watch him fall apart.

Gemma propped her elbow on the table with her chin in her hand. "Did that seem odd to anyone else?"

Bethany had to admit Gemma was right. "He acted like he couldn't get out of here fast enough."

"I hope it wasn't my cookies." Gemma sat back and folded her arms across her chest.

Pastor Frank took a sip of his coffee. "I don't think it was anything we said or did. Michael has been through a rough time."

Bethany turned to Frank. "What do you know about him?"

"Only a few things that your grandfather shared with me. I don't feel it's my place to repeat what was said."

Gemma arched one eyebrow. "Okay, now you've made me curious."

Frank smiled but he shook his head. "Many people tell me things in confidence. I take that responsibility seriously. I think it's enough to say that Michael came to New Covenant seeking privacy and a chance to heal in body and mind."

"Is there anything we can do for him?" Bethany asked.

"We can invite him to our Thanksgiving dinner," Gemma suggested. "He shouldn't spend the holiday alone."

Pastor Frank nodded. "Good idea. Treat him like you would anyone else. Be friendly, be kind, be compassionate, don't pry. I suspect he will discover soon enough if he truly belongs here."

Gemma rolled her eyes. "One winter was enough to convince me I didn't belong here. I don't mind snow, but when it gets so deep you can't see the cows standing out in it, that's too much snow."

Bethany chuckled. "And yet here you are facing another winter in northern Maine."

"I can't. What would you do without me?"

"I honestly don't know," Bethany admitted. Gemma was a dear friend and she would miss her terribly if she ever left New Covenant.

"Gemma, will you serve the peach pie and ice cream for me? I must speak with Ivan. His behavior tonight was not acceptable." Bethany braced herself for a verbal battle with Ivan as she climbed the stairs to his bedroom. She knocked softly. He didn't answer.

She opened the door and discovered he wasn't in his room. Her conversation with him would have to wait but it would take place. He wasn't getting out of it this easily. She checked the other rooms and the attic, knowing he sometimes liked to hide in those places, but she didn't find him.

When Bethany came downstairs she joined the others

and enjoyed a slice of pie and ice cream. When everyone was finished, Gemma began clearing the table.

Pastor Frank patted his stomach. "That was a very good meal. Invite me more often, Bethany."

She summoned a smile. "Come anytime. I'll feed you."

He laughed as he rose and got ready to leave. She handed him his gloves after he finished buttoning his coat. "I'm glad you came tonight, Frank. We have missed your company."

"I'm glad I came, too. What did Ivan have to say for himself?"

She clasped her hands together. "He wasn't in his room. He must have slipped out the back door. What am I going to do with him?"

"He's a troubled boy. All you can do is show him you care about him, give him the opportunity to confide in you and pray he finds the courage to tell you what's bothering him."

"I know he doesn't want to be sent to live with our uncle. I had hoped learning that he only has until Christmas to mend his ways would be incentive enough."

"Unfortunately, it may only add to the pressure he's under."

"Will you talk to him?"

"As a family friend or in my official capacity as a psychologist? Would your bishop approve of that?"

Bethany squeezed her fingers together tightly. She wasn't sure but she was willing to risk more of the bishop's disapproval. "I think he would allow it but I'm asking as a friend."

"Then I will be happy to see Ivan. Bring him by my home any day after school this week. If he'll come."

"I will do that."

He started out the door but stopped and looked back. "One more thing. Will you give a message to Michael Shetler for me?"

"Of course."

"Tell him my door is always open if he needs someone to talk to. That's all. Good night."

"I'll tell him. Good night, Frank." Bethany closed the door behind him. What did Frank know about Michael's past that he felt he couldn't share with her?

Michael unlocked the front door of the cabin and stepped inside. Instantly he knew someone had been there before him. The back door was open a crack. He was sure it had been locked earlier. He crossed the room and closed the door, uneasy at the thought of someone having access. His anxiety level climbed as he thought about trying to sleep in an unsecured place. He thanked God for the dog at his side. A dead bolt and new locks for the doors were a must first thing in the morning.

The dog stayed by his side as he searched the building. Her calm attitude reassured him that the visitor was long gone. The place was neat and cozy. The cabin was a single room with a tiny kitchen in one corner. A bump out beyond the kitchen contained a modern bathroom with a shower and a propane hot water heater. Two big windows on the south wall let in plenty of evening light. A metal bed frame in the far corner held a bare mattress with a sleeping bag on it. A glance around the room gave him the impression that someone visited often. There were empty food wrappers and several magazines beside the fireplace. Perhaps Ivan and Jenny played here. He walked back to pick up his bag near the front door.

Glass shattered, startling him. Michael saw two boys

through the broken window before his leg gave out and he hit the floor. Instantly, he was back in the jewelry store, in the middle of the robbery. He had to get out. He crawled toward the door and pulled it open, expecting another bullet. Someone was screaming. Sirens grew closer. Red lights flashed on the ceiling overhead. The smell of gunpowder choked him.

A dog started barking. There hadn't been a dog there that night. He tried to concentrate on the sound. The dog was real. The rest was a nightmare, so realistic he could hear the robbers' voices, he could see their mask-covered faces, he felt the impact of the bullet and the burning pain in his leg. He kept crawling to get away from them.

"Mister, are you okay?"

The new voice, like the barking dog, wasn't a part of the past. Michael struggled to focus on it. Bethany's brother was kneeling beside him. He didn't want anybody to see him like this. "Go away."

"I'm going to go get help." The boy jumped to his feet and ran toward the house down the hill. Michael crawled after Ivan but couldn't stop him.

Not Bethany. Don't bring Bethany.

It was his last thought before the nightmare sucked him back into the past and made him relive the unbearable. He screamed in pain as a bullet shattered his thigh. He wept as his coworkers were murdered one by one. The wail of sirens grew louder. He knew he was next.

"Michael, can you hear me?"

Another voice not from the past.

"Don't shoot," Michael begged, but the gunshots came again and again. He jerked each time.

"Can you tell me what's wrong? Are you hurt?" The

different voice was insistent. Michael tried to hold on to it. He reached out his hand. Someone took hold of it.

"It's Pastor Frank Pearson. We just met. What's wrong, Michael?"

"He's killing them. He's killing them all. Don't shoot."

"Michael, I want you to listen to me. You're safe. No one is shooting. You're in Bethany's cabin in Maine. No one can hurt you here. You're safe. Michael, you're safe."

"I'm in Maine." Harsh panting filled his ears. He knew he was making that sound but he couldn't stop.

"I want you to listen to my voice. No one is hurting you."

Michael turned his head and tried to focus on the man kneeling beside him. He wanted out of this nightmare, but he didn't know how. "Help."

"I'm here to help you. I think you are having a flashback to something bad that happened before. It's not happening now. It's all in the past. Do you understand? You are safe. No one will hurt you."

Michael had no idea how long he lay on the snowy ground listening to Pastor Frank's voice, but slowly the cold air began penetrating the nightmare. The cold was now. The cold was the present. He took a deep breath and then another. He was looking up at darkening sky. There was a single white cloud drifting overhead. It looked like a catcher's mitt. He heard soft whining. Turning his head slowly, he focused on Sadie Sue. She lay beside him with her head on his thigh.

Michael's pounding heart began to slow. He laid a hand on her head. *"Goot hund."*

"Are you feeling better?" Pastor Frank was still kneeling at Michael's side.

Embarrassed that anyone had seen him like this, Michael struggled to sit up. "I'm fine."

"I'm glad to hear that. If you would like to tell me about what happened, I will be happy to listen."

"I don't want to talk about it." Michael struggled to get up. Pastor Frank gave him a hand and helped him to his feet.

"That's perfectly understandable."

Michael looked around. "Where is my cane?"

Sadie sat at his side, her wagging tail sweeping the snow from his doorstep. She leaned against him as he patted her head.

Pastor Frank located Michael's cane inside the door and handed it to him. He smiled at the dog. "The Lord provides comfort for us in many amazing ways."

Michael wanted nothing more than to retreat inside the cabin and lock the door. "Thanks for the help. I was fortunate I fell at your feet."

"Actually, you didn't. You fell at Ivan's feet. I had just finished having supper with Gemma and Bethany. I was getting in my van when Ivan raced up and said you needed help."

Ivan was standing a few yards away from them. His pale face and wide eyes revealed how frightened he was. Michael rubbed his hands together to warm them. "I'm sorry I scared you, Ivan."

"You may have done more good than harm," Frank said softly and beckoned Ivan closer. "He insists he was the one who threw a rock through your window, but I have my doubts."

"I saw two figures," Michael said.

Ivan approached slowly. "I thought you had been hit in the head or something. I thought you were dying."

Michael managed a half smile. "As you can see, I'm not."

"Why did you break the window?" Frank asked.

Ivan stared at the ground and shifted from one foot to the other. "I don't know."

"I think you do," Frank said.

"Jeffrey and I like to hang out here. We were mad that we couldn't use it as a meeting place anymore. I guess we thought you might not stay if the window was broken. We didn't mean to hurt you."

"Actions have consequences," Frank said sternly. "Your wrath served no good purpose. Before you act in anger again, you must think about this day."

"I will. Are you going to tell Bethany about this?"

"No," Michael said emphatically.

Frank placed a hand on Ivan's shoulder. "You'd better go home. Your sister was looking for you."

"To scold me again, right?"

"To talk to you about what's really bothering you. Your sister loves you. You know that."

"Sure, that's why she's sending me away." The boy turned and walked toward the house with lagging steps.

"He's got a chip on his shoulder," Michael said.

"He does, but right now I'm more concerned about you."

Michael grew uncomfortable under Frank's intense scrutiny. "I told you I'm fine."

"How often do you have these flashbacks?"

"I don't know what you're talking about."

"Yes, you do. Why deny it? What's important is that I know exactly what you are going through. I used to be in your shoes. I dealt with PTSD for three years before my symptoms improved. I haven't had a flashback for five years now."

"How?"

"How did I get better? Time and therapy. Why don't we step inside out of the cold?"

Michael limped into the cabin. The dog followed him in and went to lie in front of the fireplace.

"I don't have much in the way of furniture yet. I'm having some stuff shipped from home." There was an overstuffed green leather chair by the fireplace and two straight-backed chairs that came with the cabin. Michael lowered himself into the upholstered chair and glanced at Frank. "What caused your PTSD?"

Frank turned one of the wooden chairs around and straddled it. "I served in the military right out of high school. I saw some brutal fighting and horrible situations at a very young age. I married while I was in the service. I thought I was tough. I thought I was okay but a few months after I got home I started having episodes where I relived the most frightening events I went through. I started having nightmares, panic attacks. I became moody, bitter and depressed. My wife didn't know how to deal with me, and we divorced. Thankfully a fellow veteran recognized what was wrong with me and got me help."

"You stopped having them?" Michael wanted desperately to believe it was possible.

"In time they went away. I found God and He changed my life. I wanted to do His work, but I also wanted to use modern medicine to help people suffering with mental health issues. I went back to school to become a psychologist and counselor, and then I became a minister. Michael, what triggered your episode today? Do you know?"

Michael shook his head. "It just came out of the blue."

"It may seem that way but there is often a trigger associated with an episode. It can be a sensation that recalls the trauma, such as pain. Strong emotions, feeling helpless, trapped or out of control can bring on a flashback or panic attack. A trigger can be as simple as a smell, a phrase, a sound."

Michael turned to look at the window. "The glass breaking. That's what triggered it today." One of the thieves had broken the glass jewelry case and triggered the alarm.

Michael gazed at Frank. "You said I can get over this."

"Recovery is a process. It takes time and there are often setbacks. It's important to stay positive, but yes, the majority of people with PTSD recover in time. For a few it is a lifelong battle. Therapy can help enormously. Talking about your trauma in a safe environment is a way to lessen the hold it has on you. How often do you have these flashbacks?"

"Three or four times a week. Sometimes every day. This is the first one since I arrived here. That was three days ago."

"And how long do they last?"

"It feels like an eternity but maybe ten minutes." Michael rubbed his thigh. It always ached worse after an episode.

Frank nodded. "And how long does it take for you to recover from one?"

"Twenty minutes or so. Will you have to tell someone about what happened today?"

"I don't but I wish you would let me help. I have a survivors' support group that meets every other week at my church. I invite you to check it out. You aren't the only one dealing with a traumatic past."

Michael shook his head. "I'd rather no one knows about this."

Especially Bethany. It shouldn't matter so much what she thought but it did matter.

Pastor Frank didn't argue. "As you wish. Please let me know if I can be of help in any way. Don't get up. I'll see myself out. I've got some plywood to cover the window. I'll be back with it in half an hour."

"I appreciate that. And for all your help earlier."

After Frank left, Michael set about building a fire in the fireplace. He was surprised that the ashes were still warm. Ivan or his friend had recently had a blaze going here. When Michael had a decent fire burning to drive off the chill, he sat down to wait for Pastor Frank's return. It wasn't long before there was a knock at the door. He got up to answer it.

Ivan stood on his doorstep looking dejected. Bethany stood behind him with her hand clamped on his shoulder.

Michael tried to disguise his rising panic. What had the boy told her?

Chapter Six

Michael didn't look happy to see her. Why should he be?

Bethany kept her chin up in spite of the mortification that weighted her down. Her brother was bent on making it harder for him to remain with her. He should be improving his behavior but he wasn't. Instead he had shown that she couldn't keep him in line. Once again she was forced to apologize for his actions.

She took a deep breath. "Good evening, Michael. I understand that Ivan broke one of the windows here. I'm truly sorry. I will have it replaced as soon as possible. In the meantime, my brother has something he wants to say to you."

"I'm sorry," Ivan mumbled.

It wasn't much of an apology, but she let it pass. "He also told me you were hurt."

"I was startled. I tripped and fell but I wasn't hurt. As you can see."

She couldn't read Michael's reaction. His face was blank. How upset was he? She wanted this awkward episode over as quickly as possible.

"I'm sure that you and I can find a way for Ivan to make amends and decide on a punishment."

"That won't be necessary."

Her brother wasn't getting off the hook so easily this time. "I insist. He needs to take responsibility for what he has done."

"I agree, but Ivan and I will work out the details. He is old enough to decide what's appropriate."

She pressed a hand to her chest. "As the adult in the family, I feel I should have a say in this." Surely he wasn't going to disregard her position as head of the family?

"Ivan and I can reach an agreement that's fair."

Her brother peered up at her. "I am old enough."

Michael nodded and stepped back. "Come in, Ivan, and we will discuss this. I'll send him home after we get the window boarded up. The pastor has gone to get some plywood."

Ivan went inside the cabin and Michael closed the door, leaving Bethany standing on the porch feeling foolish as well as incompetent.

She stomped back to the house but she couldn't stop thinking about Michael's high-handed attitude. *She* was responsible for Ivan. *She* should be a part of any discussion that involved her brother, not dismissed by some stranger as if she were a child.

Inside the house she went to the linen closet and pulled out sheets, pillows and several quilts, knowing there weren't any in the cabin. With her excuse for returning in hand, she headed out of the house. Michael Shetler had a thing or two to learn about dealing with her.

Ivan looked nervous but ready to accept his punishment. Michael walked over to the chair and sat down.

The dog moved to sit beside his knee and leaned against his leg. He waited for the boy to speak first.

Ivan stuffed his hands in his pant pockets. "I'm sorry about the broken window."

"It can be fixed. What sort of punishment do you think you deserve?"

A flash of bitterness crossed Ivan's features. It was gone before Michael could be certain of what he'd seen. He leaned forward. "Why didn't Jeffrey stick around? Why didn't he stay to make sure I was okay? He has been staying here, hasn't he?"

"His dad gets mad real easy. Jeffrey sometimes hangs out here when he does. He took off tonight because he was afraid of getting in trouble at home."

Ivan took a seat beside the dog. "What happened to your leg?"

Michael wasn't prepared to have the tables turned on him but something told him that Ivan could be trusted with at least part of the truth. It might be what the boy needed to hear. "I will tell you on one condition. I don't want this mentioned to your sisters. Okay?"

The boy nodded.

"I was shot during a robbery."

"Are you joking?" Ivan's eyes grew wide.

"No joke."

"Wow. That's—I mean—you are the only person I know who has been shot."

"I would rather you didn't share the story with your sisters or your friends. It's not a pretty memory for me and I don't like pity."

"Sure. I can see you wouldn't want people talking about it. Does it still hurt?"

"All day every day but I was blessed. Other people died."

"People you knew?"

"They were my friends." Michael could feel his anxiety level rising as it did every time he thought about that night. Sadie Sue tried to climb in his lap and lick his face. He stroked her head and grew calmer.

Ivan shook his head in disbelief. "That's awful."

"The man who shot me, what kind of fellow do you think he was?"

"Evil."

"You would think so, but he wasn't much more than a scared boy pretending to be tough. Do you know what his first crime was?"

"What?"

"The first time he was arrested it was for stealing money from a neighbor. He was fourteen."

Ivan pinned his gaze to the floor. "Maybe he didn't have a choice."

Michael pushed Sadie Sue off his lap. She sat quietly beside his chair and watched him intently.

"We all have a choice. Your sister is mighty worried about you, Ivan."

The boy reached out and stroked the dog's head. "What's her name?"

Michael let him skirt around the issue of his sister's concern, knowing the boy would come back to it sooner or later. "I called her Mutt. Your sister, Jenny, named her Sadie Sue."

Ivan chuckled. "Sadie Sue. Only Jenny would think a dog needed a middle name."

"I like your little sister."

"Me, too."

"Bethany has treated me with kindness. She strikes me as a good woman."

"She treats me like I'm a little kid."

"Stop acting like one."

Ivan shot him a sour glare. "I don't. She should treat me like the man of the family."

Michael shrugged. "Being the man of the house isn't about how people treat you. The man of the family takes care of the people in his family. What have you done to take care of Bethany or Jenny lately? Think about it."

Ivan was silent for a few minutes. Finally, he looked up. "I don't have the money to pay for a new window, but I'll split wood for your fireplace for two weeks."

"A month."

"Okay, a month."

"And you are not going to skip school again, not even if Jeffrey asks you to do it."

Ivan tipped his head to the side. "How did you know Jeffrey asked me to skip with him?"

"Because Jeffrey took off tonight and left you to face the consequences alone. Something tells me he is at the bottom of some of your troubles."

Ivan scrambled to his feet. "He's my friend. You don't know anything about him."

"You're right. I don't and I'm sorry. I was wrong to say that."

Ivan relaxed his stance. "My grandfather used to say a wise man is the one who can admit when he is wrong."

"I wish I'd had the chance to meet your grandfather. I owe him a lot."

"You would have liked him."

"I'm sure of it. Ivan, you value your friend Jeffrey and rightly so, but don't value your sisters less because of that friendship. Do you understand what I'm saying?"

"I think so."

"Catch up on your schoolwork and don't skip."

"Okay."

"You should get on home now. Remember, take care of your sisters. Don't expect them to treat you like you're the man of the family. Be that man. The same way your grandfather was. They will respect you for that."

"I'll try."

Sadie Sue rushed to the door and barked once. Michael got up and went to open it, expecting Frank. Bethany stood on his doorstep, her arms loaded with linens. "I knew you would need sheets and blankets."

"Come in." He glanced at Ivan. Would the boy keep his secret? He hoped his trust wasn't misplaced. "Ivan and I have come to an agreement."

Turning to Ivan, Michael held out his hand. "We have a deal, right?"

"Right." Ivan shook on it. "I have some homework to finish. See ya." The boy went out the door, leaving Michael and Bethany alone.

Suddenly alone with Michael, Bethany stepped past him, determined to show him she wasn't intimidated by his presence. "Where would you like these?"

"On the bed will be fine."

How silly of her. Of course he would want sheets and pillows there. She crossed the room and tossed her burden on the foot of the bed. "I see you have a sleeping bag. You came prepared to rough it."

"It's not mine. I think it belongs to Ivan's friend Jeffrey. Apparently he stays here sometimes when his father is upset with him."

"I wasn't aware of that. Was that the reason the doors were locked?"

"It would be a good guess. What do you know about the boy?"

"Not much. He's been friends with Ivan since we arrived. His family lives over the ridge about a half mile as the crow flies but farther by road. His father drives a delivery truck. I don't think the mother works." She crossed her arms as she faced him. "But I'm not here to talk about Jeffrey."

"You want me to know you are in charge of Ivan, and you don't want me to interfere."

He had practically taken the words out of her mouth. Some of her bluster ebbed away. "That's true. I'm the head of the household."

"I understand and I respect that," he said softly.

His intense gaze left her feeling exposed and vulnerable. Could he tell she doubted her ability to keep her family together? That she felt backed into a corner by the bishop's words? There was no way he could know what was in her mind yet she was sure that he did. She started for the door. "I hope you will be comfortable here."

"I hope so, too. Good night, Bethany."

The gentle way he said her name with such longing brought goose bumps to her arms. She hurried out the door before she could change her mind and stay to learn more about her unusual new neighbor.

Early the next morning the sound of someone chopping wood woke Bethany from a restless sleep. Knowing it would be useless to stay in bed, she got up and dressed for the day. Downstairs she put on a pot of coffee and enjoyed one cup in solitude. As she watched the eastern sky grow lighter, her thoughts turned to Michael. Her annoyance had vanished in the night.

Was he right to exclude her from his talk with Ivan? Last night she didn't think so, but now she was able to look at the situation without embarrassment clouding her thinking. She had been prepared to be a buffer between Ivan and Michael. She wanted her brother to make amends, but she didn't want his punishment to be unjust. Perhaps it was better that she stayed out of it and let Ivan face the consequences of his actions alone.

She glanced at the clock on the wall. Once the children were off to school she still intended to have a talk with Michael. Rising to her feet, she started on breakfast. When the eggs and oatmeal were ready, she called up the stairs. "Ivan, Jenny, time to get ready for school."

She returned to the kitchen and set plates and bowls on the table. It wasn't long before Jenny came down still in her nightgown. She made a beeline to the stove, where she warmed her hands. The upstairs bedrooms weren't heated. Hot flannel-wrapped bricks helped stave off some of the chill, but they didn't last all night. The heavy quilts only helped as long as a person stayed in bed.

When Ivan didn't appear, Bethany went to the staircase again. "Ivan. Time to get ready for school. Did you hear me?"

As she was waiting for a reply, the back door opened and he came in bundled from head to toe in his work clothes. He bent to pull off his boots. "We got four more inches of snow last night. The snowplow just went by on the road and left a huge pile of snow on our side."

She stared at him in amazement. "What were you doing outside?"

"I was chopping wood for Michael, and I shoveled the path to his house. I fed and watered our animals, too, but I didn't gather the eggs. Jenny should do that for you. I'm really hungry. What's for breakfast?"

"Scrambled eggs and oatmeal. It is nice of you to make sure Michael had wood for his fireplace."

"I have to do it for a month." He didn't sound resentful at all. He was actually smiling as he sat down at the table and pulled off his stocking cap.

"How long is he making you do my chores?" Bethany asked.

"He isn't making me do them, and they are my chores now."

Somewhat taken aback, Bethany filled their plates and took her place at the foot of the table. She looked at Ivan. "Would you like to sit at the head of the table and lead the prayers from now on?"

Both his eyebrows rose. "Really?"

It was the responsibility of the male head of an Amish household to signal the beginning and the end of the silent blessing before meals. Their grandfather had always been the one to lead prayers. After his death Bethany took over the task, never once considering that it should have fallen to Ivan. To her, he was still a child, but he wasn't little anymore.

She realized her brother was waiting for her reply. "Of course you may."

He moved his plate and sat down opposite her. Bowing his head, he clasped his hands together. Bethany did the same and silently repeated the blessing. When she was finished she waited with her head bowed for Ivan's signal. He unfolded his hands and picked up his fork. Jenny had her eyes closed. Ivan cleared his throat.

Jenny peeked at him with one eye. "Are you done?"

He nodded once. "I am."

"Goot." She reached for her glass of milk.

Ivan poured honey and milk on his oatmeal. "Jenny, I want you to gather the eggs for Bethany every day."

Jenny looked puzzled. "I do it when she asks me to."

"It will be your chore every morning before school, starting tomorrow. Bethany has enough to do."

Jenny shrugged. "Okay. Pass me a piece of toast, Ivan."

Bethany couldn't understand this sudden change in Ivan. What had Michael said to him? She wanted to ask but she didn't want to discuss it in front of her little sister. Jenny had a habit of blurting out things she had overheard.

Later, when the children were ready to go meet the bus, Bethany brought out their lunch boxes. "Ivan, did you complete the homework your teacher gave you?"

"Not all of it, but I'll stay in at recess and get the rest of it done."

"I'm pleased to hear you say that." But could she trust that he meant what he said?

"And you won't skip school again. Is that clear?" she said firmly.

"Michael and I talked about it last night. I won't skip." Ivan took his lunch box from her. "He's a *goot* fellow."

"I like him and his dog." Jenny grabbed her lunch box and headed out the door. Ivan followed close behind her, leaving Bethany more curious than ever about what Michael had said to inspire her brother.

After dressing warmly, she hiked up the hill to the cabin and knocked. She waited and knocked again but he didn't answer. She checked the barn and found his pony and cart were gone. Disappointed, she went back down the hill. Her talk with him would just have to wait.

For most of the next day and a half Michael wrestled with the notion of leaving New Covenant. He came here because he hoped the remoteness of the settlement and a change of scenery would put a stop to his anxiety attacks and flashbacks. To have such a profound episode occur within a week of his arrival was deeply disappointing. In the end he decided he had to stay. There was nowhere else to hide. He didn't want his decision to be emotional. As much as he tried to dismiss one important factor, he couldn't. Bethany was here.

If he was going to stay, he needed to work. He had a choice between building sheds with Jesse and the bishop or doing what he loved. The only drawback with repairing timepieces was that he'd be working for Bethany. He liked her. A lot. But there was no future there as long as he could fall apart at any second. His episode Sunday night had driven that fact home.

He would go back to his original plan. Bury himself in his work and remain apart from people as much as possible. He walked down the hill and found Bethany hanging wash on the line at the side of the house. Her clothesline stretched from the back porch to a nearby pine tree. A pulley system allowed her to pin her clothes on the line and move them out without stepping off the porch into the snow.

He nodded to her. "*Guder mariye*, Bethany. May I see your grandfather's workshop?"

She hesitated a fraction of a second then nodded. "Of course. It's this way."

She walked through the house into the kitchen and opened a door. "This was my grandfather's workroom."

His disappointment must have shown on his face. She tipped her head slightly. "Is something wrong?"

He didn't want a workshop attached to the house where family members could come and go as they pleased. He wanted a space all to himself. "I thought the workshop was one of the other buildings on the farm."

She shook her head. "Grandfather liked being close

to us. He usually kept the door open, but if you're thinking that we will disturb you, you can keep it closed."

"I don't like interruptions while I'm working."

Her smile was forced. "That's understandable. We will make it a point to not interrupt you. You may add a bolt to the door or a lock if you prefer."

"That will not be necessary. As long as everyone's aware that I'm not to be bothered while I'm working, that should suffice." He stepped through the doorway into a tidy room with a long workbench in front of a large window. The workbench itself was made of oak. It had four shallow drawers across the front.

He opened the first drawer. Numerous screwdrivers were lined up by size in a wooden holder that had obviously been custom-made. The next drawer held a jeweler's loupe and several magnifying lenses all nestled into cotton batting. The third drawer held an assortment of gears and springs Elijah must have scavenged from clocks of all types. The fourth drawer held ledgers, receipt books, stationery and padded envelopes.

Michael looked around the room at the dozen or so clocks hanging on the walls, some in various stages of repair. The running ones ticked softly. "Your grandfather was obviously a man who took great care with his tools." He ran his finger along the top of the workbench. It was satin smooth.

"Daadi believed in a place for everything and everything in its place. He liked to use authentic old tools. He said they simply do the job better than the new ones."

"I have to agree." Along the back of the workbench were several dozen books stacked on top of each other. Michael picked up one and read the title. *"Clocks of the 1800s."*

She picked a book up and ran her fingers over the

colorful cover. "Daadi would spend his free time reading about the history of clocks. I would often find him in here late at night poring over antique books on the ancient practice of clock making. I could never understand how he knew what all those little gears and wheels did."

"Repairing a clock can be complicated work, but it can also be simple when the pieces speak for themselves."

"How so?"

"Everything inside of a clock's mechanisms has a purpose. Everything is there for a reason. If you work backward, if you understand what part connects to another part and then another, the clock will tell you what each part does."

She swept her hand through the air, indicating all the timepieces on the walls. "I think you love the art of this the way he did."

"There is something fascinating and beautiful inside each clock I open. I'm happy when I can return it to someone who has treasured it. Often I see them smile when they hear a clock chime again because it brings back good memories."

She smiled softly and swiveled the old leather chair around to face her. "Good memories are important."

She looked at him. "Now that you have had a chance to see the workshop, what do you think? Are you interested in a partnership?"

"I can work in here."

She held out her hand. "Do we have a deal?"

He hesitated a second but then accepted her handshake. "We have a deal."

He held on to her fingers a few seconds longer than he needed to. She blushed as she pulled her hand away.

* * *

Bethany couldn't ignore the attraction she felt for Michael. The amazing thing was she had only known him a few days. Maybe letting him work here wasn't a good idea. For some reason she felt off balance when he looked at her with that penetrating gaze of his.

She gave herself a hard mental shake. She was being ridiculous. He needed the work and she needed the income. It wasn't like antique watch repairmen grew on trees. She would have to make sure she kept the relationship strictly business.

"Are you comfortable in the cabin?"

"It's snug. Or it will be when the new window gets in. Pastor Frank took the measurements last night. He's going to order a replacement for me."

She slipped her hands in the pockets of her apron. "Make sure the bill is sent to me. Ivan mentioned that you encouraged him to remain in school. I don't know what else you said to him but he is a changed boy. He's doing chores without being told. He's catching up on his schoolwork. Is he still splitting wood for you?"

"Without fail."

"Good. However, I still think I should have been included in the conversation."

Michael faced her. "Ivan said you treat him like a little child and not like the man of the house. I doubt he would have spoken so plainly about it if you had been in the room. I told him if he'd act like a man he would be treated as such."

"I don't agree with his assessment."

Michael grinned. "I didn't think you would. You have to admit that you don't treat him like a grown fellow."

Of all the nerve. "You haven't been around this family long enough to make an assumption like that."

"It wasn't my assumption. It was Ivan's." He smiled broadly as if inviting her to share the joke. She didn't find it funny.

"And if Ivan's change of heart wears off in a week or two, I imagine I'll be the one to blame." What possessed her to imagine she was attracted to this man? She knew from the first time they met that he was laughing at her. He was still laughing at her.

His smile faded as he seemed to realize she was upset. "I'm sure he will backslide a time or two. That's only natural. No one is looking to assign blame to you."

"That's just it. Men are assigning blame to me. The bishop, my uncle, they assume I can't control a boy Ivan's age. They want to take the problem off my hands. He isn't a problem. He's my brother. I don't know what we will do if the bishop insists on separating us, but I can tell you I won't stand still for it."

"Defying the bishop could get you shunned."

"There are other Amish communities in Maine. As much as I loved my grandfather and shared his vision for New Covenant, I will move lock, stock and barrel before I give up my brother. You don't need to worry about putting a lock on this door. I will not set foot in this room while you are here."

She walked out and slammed the door behind her.

Chapter Seven

"You should invite Michael to eat with us," Ivan said at the dinner table three days after Michael had moved into the cabin.

Bethany had spent much of the time regretting her outburst. She owed him an apology. Michael wasn't the cause of her problem. She shouldn't have taken her ill temper out on him. He had been trying to help.

Michael *had* helped although the bishop might not be able to see the improvement in Ivan's attitude. She was also certain he wouldn't simply take her word for it.

"Why can't Sadie Sue eat with us, too?" Jenny asked.

Bethany leveled a don't-be-ridiculous look at Jenny. "Because I won't allow a dog in the house at mealtime. I don't care how much you like her. As for Michael, I haven't asked him because he specifically said that he likes working alone and he likes his privacy. Now that he is going to be working in Grandfather's shop, I want you both to understand that when that door is closed you are not to go in there."

"But what if I need something?" Jenny asked.

Bethany put down her fork to stare at her sister.

"What could you possibly need from Grandfather's workshop?"

"I don't know. I might need to play with Sadie Sue. She likes to fetch sticks."

Bethany tried not to smile at her sister's cajoling tone. "I'm sure there will be plenty of times that you can play with her. Just not while Michael is working."

Ivan helped himself to another dollop of potatoes. "Michael might like to work alone but that doesn't mean he likes to eat alone. You should ask him."

"I'll consider it." That was all she was going to say on the subject. "Are you excited about having Thanksgiving dinner tomorrow at the Lapp farm?"

Jenny held her hand high in the air. "I am. No school for four days."

Bethany looked at her brother. "What about you, Ivan?"

"Jeffrey won't be there. I won't have anyone to hang out with."

"I'm sure that the Miller boys will include you in any games they start." The trio of cousins were in their late teens but they normally included Ivan in their group sports during church get-togethers. There were so few people in New Covenant yet. She wasn't sure that all of those would stay after enduring a Maine winter.

"Is Michael going to be there?" Ivan looked at her hopefully.

Bethany thought back over the times she and Michael had spent together. "I don't believe I mentioned it to him. Jesse may have told him about it."

Ivan pushed back his chair. "I'll go invite him."

"After you finish your supper." Although Bethany hadn't liked hearing that she treated Ivan as a child, she had to admit there were some things their grandfather had done that Ivan could take over.

"I thought perhaps you could read some passages from the Bible for us tonight. I have to work on Jenny's Christmas program costume."

"You really want me to?" He looked amazed.

"Absolutely."

"Sure. I'd be happy to do that. When I'm finished eating can I invite Michael to the Thanksgiving dinner?"

She glanced at the door and then back to her brother. "You'll have to go outside and check if there is a light in the workshop windows. If there is, wait until he is finished working. If there isn't a light, go ahead and go up to the cabin. But first, how was your day at school?"

"I'm caught up on my work." His comment lacked enthusiasm. He wouldn't meet her gaze.

"I'm happy to hear that. What else happened today?"

"Somebody said I stole money from their locker. I didn't but I'm not sure the teacher believed me. She looked through my desk and didn't find anything."

"Oh, Ivan, I'm sorry."

"It's okay."

It wasn't okay but Bethany didn't know how to deal with it. Her brother had built himself a bad reputation. Repairing it would take time. Time he might not have. The bishop would be at the dinner tomorrow. Could she convince him that Ivan had seen the error of his ways after the bishop had heard Jedidiah's tale?

Michael's input might sway the bishop if he could be convinced to attend the dinner. He knew Ivan was chopping wood each day and doing his chores and doing better in school.

She pushed the chicken casserole around on her plate

as her appetite vanished. The bishop wouldn't hear Michael's observations if Michael didn't speak to him. She was going to have to apologize to Michael and then ask him to speak on Ivan's behalf as a favor.

Her chicken casserole might as well have been crow. That was what was on the menu for later.

"Ivan, I'll invite Michael to the Thanksgiving dinner at the Lapps' tomorrow. I want you to help your sister practice her lines for the Christmas program."

He looked ready to object but nodded instead. "Okay. I will."

She rose from her chair. "*Danki.* The two of you clear the table. I'm going to speak with Michael."

"Invite Sadie Sue, too," Jenny said.

"*Nee*, I will not invite the dog. If you wish to do something special for her you will have to do it here."

"Can I bake her some cookies?"

"Learn your lines for the Christmas program first."

"All right," Jenny said, but she didn't look happy about it.

Bethany checked the workshop first. The light was off. He must've gone home. She trudged up the hill, bemoaning how quickly it got dark this time of year. As she drew near the cabin she saw Michael was filling a pair of pails at the pump in the yard. His dog sat by his side. She woofed several times, causing him to look around. He caught sight of Bethany and stopped. He watched her with a hint of uncertainty in his eyes. She couldn't blame him.

She forged ahead. "It seems like I am apologizing every time I see you."

He just stared at her.

He wasn't making it easy.

"I wanted to say that I'm sorry for the way I behaved the other day. Although it isn't really an excuse, I am very concerned about my brother. I do not want to send him to live with our uncle. Onkel Harvey is a good man, don't get me wrong. He has a fine family. My reason for wanting to keep Ivan with me is a selfish one. I love my brother. I promised my mother as she lay dying that I would take care of Ivan and Jenny. I don't want to break that promise."

"That's understandable. You are forgiven. There was no need for you to come and apologize."

She pressed a hand to her chest. "I *needed* to apologize."

He picked up one bucket of water and started toward the barn. Bethany picked up the second bucket and followed him. He frowned as he glanced at her. "I can manage this."

"Many hands make light work. Did you find everything you need in my grandfather's workshop today?"

"I did, plus I have many of my own tools."

"I guess that makes sense." In the barn she put the bucket down as he poured the first one into a small tank in the pony's stall. He handed her the empty pail, picked up the full one and poured it into the tank, as well.

He walked out of the barn and Bethany followed him. It appeared that he wasn't in the mood to talk. She followed him anyway.

"I don't know if Jesse mentioned it but our church community is having a Thanksgiving dinner tomorrow. I wanted to make sure you knew you were invited."

"I'll be working."

"It will be a great opportunity to get to know the other Amish families here."

"I'll meet them in time."

"Why wait?" She tried to sound cheerful not desperate.

"Because I'm working tomorrow."

She had hoped she wouldn't have to beg but he left her no choice. "All right, I have a favor to ask of you."

A slight smile curved his lips. "Really? I can't wait to hear this. Has Clarabelle given you the name of a new marriage prospect that you want me to check out?"

"I wish you would forget about the cow."

"I've tried but I can't. It's stuck in my brain."

"Oh, never mind." She turned to go. She'd only taken a few steps when he spoke again.

"Wait. What is it that you need?"

She stayed where she was with her hands pushed deep into the pockets of her coat, so he couldn't see how tightly clenched her fingers were. "The bishop will be there. I need your help convincing him that Ivan has had a change of heart. That he's doing better." She stared at the ground, afraid to see him refuse. "Will you do that? Please?"

Michael groaned inwardly. She had no idea what she was asking. A dinner with dozens of strangers in an unfamiliar house. A crowd. The noise. He grew tense just thinking about it.

Why did she have to look so dejected? So vulnerable? Why was she pinning her hopes on him? It would be amazing if he didn't end the dinner as a babbling ball of fear hiding under the table. He couldn't do it.

She glanced at him from beneath lowered lashes.

How could he not do it?

She wanted to keep her family together. He prayed for strength for the first time in months. Sadie Sue whined as she gazed up at him. "I know, I know. It's a bad idea."

He crossed the few steps between them and stopped inches from Bethany. He lifted her chin so she would look at him. "Okay, I'll do it, but you must understand that my words may not carry much weight. I'm new here. I'm not even a member of your congregation yet."

He would speak to the man and then leave. He didn't have to stay for the meal. He would come home and work in peace.

The joy on Bethany's face was almost worth the discomfort he knew he was going to endure. Beneath his fingers her skin was soft as the silk cloths he used to polish his work. Her beautiful eyes were damp with unshed tears. Her lips were red because she had been biting them. He wanted to soothe them with a kiss.

As sure as the sun would rise again tomorrow, he knew one kiss would not be enough.

He stepped away from her. She blinked rapidly and swiped at her unshed tears with both hands. *"Danki."*

"Please tell me I don't have to cook something and take it to eat."

Her laugh was shaky. "I'll make enough for both of us."

"Where is this party taking place?"

"At the Lapp farm. It's about a half mile from here. You met Gemma the other night. The farm belongs to her parents. We might as well ride together, don't you think? I have to take some tables and chairs for them to use. I'll pick you up at noon. That should give you plenty of time to meet people before they start serving at two o'clock."

A half mile wasn't too far. He could walk that distance home alone.

Bethany grabbed his hand. "Bless you. I mean that from the bottom of my heart. Bless you and the good you are doing for my family."

"I'm doing it for Ivan. The kid deserves a break."

She let go of him and pushed her hands deep into her coat pockets. "Of course. He may not realize it yet, but you are a true friend."

As she hurried away he shook his head. Thanksgiving Day would end in disaster for him. He looked down at Sadie Sue. "I am an idiot. Did you know that? You've adopted an idiot for a master."

Michael waited on the porch with his back against the side of the cabin as Bethany drove up in a large wagon the next morning. The children were sitting beside her. His nerves had been on edge since he woke well before dawn. Sadie Sue was shut inside the cabin. He wished he could take her with him.

"Happy Thanksgiving," Bethany called out. The children echoed her greeting. They were staring at him.

All he had to do was walk down the steps and get in her wagon. His palms were damp; his heart was racing. He counted to three and pushed away from the wall. Bethany had Ivan and Jenny get in the back, giving him more room. Getting up onto the seat was easier said than done. The wagon seat was much higher than a buggy. It wasn't graceful but he finally hauled himself up and onto the padded wooden bench.

"All set," he muttered between his clenched teeth.

"Thank you again for doing this."

"Sure, no problem." He hoped.

"I don't see Sadie," Jenny said.

"I locked her in the house." He couldn't believe how much he'd come to rely on the dog. She alerted him when someone was near. When she was at ease, he was at ease.

Bethany spoke to the team and the wagon lurched forward, jarring his leg. Out on the roadway the going was smoother. He let go of his death grip on the side of the seat.

Bethany glanced his way. "Is your leg paining you?"

"Some. I think there's a change in weather coming."

"The newspaper this morning said we could expect a significant snowstorm over the next three days."

"What is 'significant' to the people of Maine?"

"Two, maybe three, in places."

"Inches?"

"Feet," she said with a smile. "Don't worry. Jesse plows our lanes open with his big team but you should invest in some snowshoes before long."

Snowshoes and a cane. How was that going to work? Maybe moving here had been a mistake.

It didn't take long to reach the Lapp farm. Bethany drew the horse to a stop by the front door. The children jumped off the back of the wagon and ran inside. Bethany turned to him. "Can I help you get down?"

He shook his head. "I don't need help. Besides, if I fall I only want one person to get hurt."

She ignored him, jumped down and came around to his side. "I won't let you fall."

"I should believe a woman who talks to cows? Stand aside." He grimaced as he swung his bad leg over the side.

"Nope. Keep one hand on the seat and put your other hand on my shoulder and lower your weight slowly."

"I'm not getting down until you're out of the way."

"You will get very cold sitting here when the sun goes down."

"Stubborn woman."

"I've been called that before."

"Why am I not surprised." He searched for a way to get down without help. It was a long drop. "Okay, I hate to admit it, but your idea looks like my best option."

He gave her his cane and she leaned it against the wagon wheel. Placing his hand on her shoulder, he scooted over the edge of the seat and started to lower himself to the ground.

One horse took a step forward. The cane fell, clattering against the wheel spokes. The other horse tossed her head and took a step, jerking the wagon. Michael lost his grip on the seat and pulled Bethany off balance.

The second he started to fall Bethany wrapped her arms around him and threw herself over backward, trying to take the brunt of his weight. Her head struck the ground with a painful-sounding thump. She didn't make a sound.

"Are you okay? Bethany, are you okay? Speak to me." Michael was holding himself above her on his forearms. His face was inches from hers. Her lids fluttered up. She looked at him and blinked twice.

"You have pretty eyes." Her voice was a bare whisper.

"What?"

She closed her eyes. "Nothing. I'm okay. Are you hurt?"

At least she was talking. "My pride has a big dent in it, but I don't think anything is broken."

"Then could you get off me? You're very heavy." She winced in pain.

"What is going on here?"

Michael looked up to see an older Amish man with a graying beard glaring at him. Jesse stood at his side.

"Hi, Jesse." Michael rolled off Bethany and lay sprawled beside her. His bad leg was on fire, his shoulders ached, and he had skinned both hands trying to keep his full weight from crashing down on her.

"Michael?" Jesse's eyebrows rose until they touched the brim of his black hat.

"It's me. Happy Thanksgiving."

"What are you doing on the ground?"

Michael laughed even though it hurt. "I put my trust in a woman who has conversations with her cow. Big mistake." He turned his head to gaze at Bethany. "Are you sure you aren't hurt?"

"I'm still checking." She pressed a hand to the back of her head.

Her friend Gemma came out of the house. "What has happened? Bethany, is that you?"

Bethany pushed herself into a sitting position. "Hello, Gemma. Happy Thanksgiving."

Jesse was still frowning at Michael. "I don't understand what you are doing on the ground."

"Bethany kindly gave me a ride here, and when I was trying to get out of her wagon, I fell on her. It was an accident. I think she hit her head pretty hard."

Gemma helped Bethany to her feet. "You poor thing. Are you injured?"

Bethany managed a half-hearted smile. "Only bumps and bruises. I'm afraid Michael is the one who is hurt."

Michael struggled to his feet with Jesse's assistance and leaned against the wagon. "I'm fine. Where's my cane?"

The elderly Amish man beside Jesse picked it up and handed it to Michael with a scowl on his face. "I am Bishop Schultz."

"Just the man I wanted to see. I'm Michael Shetler. I'm a newcomer to the area."

The bishop stroked his beard as he stared at Michael. "Jesse has told me about you."

"I need to unpack the tables and chairs," Bethany said.

"Someone else can take care of that. You need a few minutes' rest to regain your wits," Michael told her in a stern tone.

She scowled at him. "My wits are not scattered."

"That's open to debate. You hit your head pretty hard. You could have a concussion. Gemma, make her go inside and rest."

Michael caught the sidelong glare Bethany shot at him. She wasn't happy to have him telling her what to do. Too bad. In his opinion, she was too pale. He didn't want her keeling over and spoiling the party. That was his job.

Gemma smiled kindly at Michael as she took Bethany's arm. "He is right. Come in. I have some fresh brewed sweet tea and my special lemon cookies, and I'm going to fix an ice pack for your head."

"I would speak with you, Bethany, when you are recovered," Bishop Schultz said. Bethany grew a shade paler.

Inside the house the mouthwatering smells of roasting turkey, fresh baked breads and pumpkin pies filled the air. Michael saw Ivan seated beside two teenage boys looking through a hunting magazine. He beckoned to the boy. "Ivan, can I see you a minute?"

Ivan came over. "What's up?"

"Ask your friends to help you bring in the tables and chairs from the back of the wagon and take care of the horses."

"Sure." He went back to the boys and they all walked outside. A few minutes later they came in carrying the extra seating. Gemma's mother directed them where to set up. Another family arrived with baskets of food, and a festive air began to fill the room as happy chatter and laughter grew in volume.

Michael stayed beside Bethany, who was seated in a wingback chair near the fireplace. She soon had a plate of cookies on her lap and a glass of tea in her hand. Her color was already better when Gemma brought her the ice pack. Michael knew Bethany had taken the brunt of the fall trying to protect him. It should have been the other way around.

His gaze was constantly drawn to her. Her color returned to normal, but the longer he watched her the more flushed she became. Every time he caught her eye she looked away.

After ten minutes, Bethany set her empty glass aside. "I should be helping in the kitchen."

Bethany couldn't take Michael staring at her another minute. Didn't he realize everyone was noticing his attention? She blushed at being the recipient of so many speculative looks. She was about to get up when the bishop approached her with Jedidiah a few steps behind him.

The bishop settled himself in a nearby chair. "Are you feeling recovered, Bethany?"

"I have a headache that I'm sure will get better quickly. Jedidiah, did you get my letter and the check?"

"I did. It was a fair price, though the cost was not the issue. I trust Ivan will repay you?"

She clasped her hands together. "I want you both to

know that my brother has improved his attitude one hundred percent since that incident."

"Even if that is true, it is too little too late." The bishop's stern look chilled her.

She gestured to Michael. "This is Michael Shetler. He has taken over Grandfather's watch repair business. He can attest to Ivan's improvements. He has seen it firsthand."

"In what way?" Jedidiah asked.

"The boy broke a window in the cabin I rented from Bethany. I had a talk with him. We settled on his punishment. He has split wood for me every morning, has taken over many of Bethany's outdoor chores, and he has improved his grades at school. I believe his friend has been the instigator of much of the trouble Ivan has been in."

The bishop folded his arms over his chest. "If that is true, the boy has shown bad judgment in his choice of friends."

Jedidiah shifted his weight from one foot to the other. "I spoke with his teacher yesterday evening. We happened to be in the grocery store at the same time. She tells me some of the *Englisch* children have accused Ivan of stealing money."

"One child did. She searched his desk and didn't find anything. It wasn't Ivan," Bethany insisted.

The bishop's face grew somber. "I wish I could give him the benefit of the doubt, but there have been too many instances where he has been involved. Jedidiah has offered to take the boy until his uncle arrives. He feels he can give Ivan the supervision he needs. I have agreed to this."

"*Nee*, you can't take him from me. You can't."

"What if I were to take responsibility for the boy?" Michael offered.

Chapter Eight

Michael was certain that he had lost his mind. The look on Bethany's face told him she thought he was her hero.

The bishop regarded him intently. "Are you sure you understand what this means?"

"I do. I will oversee the boy's discipline. I will stand as substitute for his father. Any person who has difficulties or accusations against the boy can address them with me. If you will allow me, then the boy does not have to leave Bethany's care or his home. Should he go to live with Jedidiah now, he will be unable to complete the bargain he has with me."

The bishop nodded slowly. "I appreciate what Jedidiah has offered. I didn't feel right taking the boy from his sister's care, but I saw no other choice after Jedidiah told me about the theft of his goods. You have given me one. You are new to us but Jesse has vouched for your character, Michael, otherwise I would not agree to this, but I trust his judgment. This arrangement will be only until the boy's uncle arrives at Christmas," the bishop added. "I want to be clear that this isn't a permanent situation, and that you are accepting financial responsibility as well as a moral responsibility to see that Ivan behaves himself."

"I understand that."

Bethany's hopeful gaze was pinned on Michael. "You don't have to do this."

He considered retracting his offer but he wasn't prepared to see the Martin family split up. "I understand that. I want to do it. I'll speak to Ivan about it when we get home today."

"Agreed." The bishop smiled broadly. Even Jedidiah looked relieved. The two men walked away.

"I can't thank you enough," Bethany said with tears in her eyes.

"Let's hope Ivan feels the same way." He was already regretting his rash gesture. His intention was to spend less time with Bethany and her family, not more.

Bethany heard the hesitancy in Michael's voice. "You won't be sorry you did this. It proves that you believe in my brother and that is priceless to me."

Michael rubbed his hands on his pants. "I think I need some fresh air."

He left the room. Once he was out of sight, Gemma hurried over to sit beside Bethany. "What was that all about?"

"Ivan."

"I was afraid that's what the bishop had on his mind when he cornered you. Is he still sending the boy away at Christmas?"

"He wanted to send him to live with Jedidiah until then, but Michael volunteered to be responsible for him."

"How did you manage that?"

"It was his own idea."

Gemma leaned forward eagerly. "Tell me all about your mystery man."

"There isn't much to tell. Apparently, he corresponded with Daadi about working for him. He had already paid the first and last months' rent on the cabin. He likes to keep to himself. And he's from Sugarcreek, Ohio."

"I don't mean the dry details. Does he have a girlfriend back in Ohio? Is he looking to marry? Does he have money?"

"How would I know that?"

Gemma chuckled. "You don't know how to snoop. I could find all that out in ten minutes."

"I'm not so sure. He doesn't like to talk about himself."

"Then he is hiding something. I wonder what it is. How did he know your grandfather?"

"He didn't really. A jeweler by the name of George Meyers recommended Michael to my grandfather and that's all I know. He and Ivan get along. I'm grateful for that."

"You like him, don't you?"

Bethany was wary of the eager look in her friend's eyes. "He's nice enough."

"I'd say he's a lot better than Jesse Crump or Jedidiah. I can't believe he fell into your lap and all you can say is that he's nice enough. He is the answer to your prayers."

"What are you talking about?"

"You need a husband by Christmas and Michael Shetler appears out of the blue. God moves in mysterious ways."

"You're being ridiculous. There is nothing between us."

"I wouldn't say that. I noticed the way he looked at you when he was sitting beside you. We all noticed. He's interested. The man has potential. With a little effort on your part, you could have him eating out of your hand. I've got to go help Mamm. Can I get you anything else?"

Bethany shook her head and winced. She pressed a hand to the back of her aching head. "I'm gonna sit here with my ice pack for a little longer."

Gemma patted Bethany's knee. "Let me know if you need anything."

Jenny came running to Bethany's side along with Sadie Sue. "Look, sister. I didn't invite her. She came all by herself."

"I wonder how she got out." Bethany stared at the dog. She was sure Michael had locked her in.

Sadie's attention turned to the tables where the food was being set out. She licked her chops. Bethany foresaw a disaster. "*Nee*, Jenny, take her outside."

"But why?"

"Because I asked you to."

"Okay. Come on, Sadie Sue." Jenny headed toward the back door, taking Sadie within a few feet of the table and a steaming plate of sausages. The dog stopped and eyed the dish as Jenny went out the door. No one else was near the dog.

Bethany rose from her chair. "*Nee*, Sadie Sue. Don't do it."

Jenny opened the back door and looked in. "Sadie, come on."

The dog gave the sausages a forlorn glance and trotted out the door. Bethany sank back in her chair with a sigh of relief.

"Was that my dog?" Michael asked as he came in from outside.

"*Ja*, it was Sadie Sue." Remembering Gemma's comments, Bethany found herself tongue-tied. Did he find her attractive? Or was his attentiveness just part of his makeup that had nothing to do with her? Bethany wished she could tell what he was thinking.

He scratched the back of his head. "I wonder how she got out of the house."

Bethany shrugged.

"How are you feeling?" he asked.

"Better." She kept her demeanor cool. Were people watching them and speculating? She caught sight of Gemma smiling widely. Her friend winked.

"I'm glad to hear you are better. I'm going to go take Sadie home and see how she escaped. I hope we don't have to replace another windowpane."

"Will you be coming back?"

"*Nee*, you stay and enjoy your friends. I have work to do."

She didn't want him to go. She was torn by her conflicting feelings. "Don't you even want something to eat?"

"I have plenty back at the cabin. Get someone to drive you home if you aren't feeling better."

"Ivan can drive the wagon."

Michael nodded and walked away. When he opened the door he glanced back at her with such a look of longing that it startled her. Was there something between them and she had been too blind to see it?

Bethany decided the family would walk to the church service on Sunday instead of taking the buggy. The preaching was being held at the home of Nigel and Becca Miller. Their farm was little more than a quarter of a mile beyond the Lapp place. Nigel was a carpenter who made furniture in the off-season.

An unexpectedly warm southern wind was melt-

ing the snow, making the sunshine feel even brighter.
Rivulets of water trickled along the ditches and flowed
out of the snow-covered fields. Amish families—some
on foot, most in buggies—were all headed in the same
direction. Cheerful greetings and pleasant exchanges
filled the crisp air. Everyone was glad to see a break
in the weather.

Bethany declined numerous offers of a ride, content to stretch her legs on such a fine morning. The
icy grip of winter would return all too soon. Jenny and
Ivan trudged along beside her, enjoying the sunshine.

She turned in at the farm lane where a dozen buggies
were lined up on the hillside just south of the barn. The
horses, still wearing their harnesses, were tied up along
a split-rail fence, content to munch on the hay spread
in front of them or doze in the sunshine.

The early morning activity was focused around the
barn. Men were busy unloading backless seats from
the large gray boxlike bench wagon that was used to
transport the benches from home to home for the services held every other Sunday. Bishop Schultz was su-
pervising the unloading. When the wagon was empty,
he conferred with his minister.

Bethany entered the house. Inside, it was a flurry of
activity as the women arranged food on counters and
tables. Several small children were being watched over
by the Millers' niece. She beckoned Jenny to come help
her. The Miller boys were outside playing a game of tag
and Ivan went to join them.

Catching sight of Gemma unpacking baskets of food,
Bethany crossed the room toward them and handed over
her basket of food for the lunch that would be served
after the service. "*Guder mariye*, Gemma."

"Good morning, Bethany. Isn't the weather wonderful?"

"It is." Turning to Becca Miller, Bethany grinned at the baby she held. Little Daniel was six months old with a wide toothless grin and a head of white-blond curls. "Wow, how this little boy is growing. May I hold him?"

"Of course. I hate to admit it but he gets heavy quickly these days." Becca handed the baby over with a timid smile.

Bethany took Daniel and held him to her shoulder, enjoying the feel of a baby in her arms and his wonderful smell. "You're not so heavy."

"He should be. He eats like a little piglet." There was nothing but love in Becca's eyes as she gazed at her son.

Gemma said, "I see the bishop and minister coming. We'd best hurry and join the others in the barn."

As she spoke, Bishop Schultz and Samuel Yoder entered the house and went upstairs, where they would discuss the preaching that was to be done that morning. The three-to-four-hours-long service would be preached without the use of notes. Each man had to speak as God moved him.

Bethany handed the baby back to Becca. The women quickly finished their tasks and left the house.

The barn was already filled with people sitting quietly on rows of backless wooden benches with the women on one side of the aisle and men on the other side. Tarps had been hung over ropes stretched between upright timbers to cordon off an area for the service. Behind them, the sounds of cattle, horses and pigs could be heard. The south-facing doors were open to catch what warmth the sunshine and wind could provide.

Bethany took her place among the unmarried women. Gemma and Jenny sat beside her. In front of them sat the married women, several holding infants. Becca slipped a string of beads and buttons from her pocket. She handed them to her little one. He was then content and played quietly with his toy. Her older boys sat beside their father.

From the men's side of the aisle, the song leader announced the hymn. There was a wave of rustling and activity as people opened their thick black songbooks. The *Ausbund* contained the words of all the hymns but no musical scores. The songs, sung from memory, had been passed down through countless generations. They were sung slowly and in unison by people opening their hearts to receive God's presence without the distraction of musical instruments. The slow cadence allowed everyone to focus on the meaning of each word.

At the end of the first hymn, Bethany took a moment to glance toward the men's side. She spotted Michael sitting behind the married men with Ivan. Her brother squirmed in his seat, looking restless. Michael, on the other hand, held his songbook with a look of intense devotion on his face.

He glanced in her direction and she smiled at him. He immediately looked away and she felt the pinch of his rejection. She hadn't spoken to him since Thanksgiving. Was something wrong? Was he regretting his decision to mentor Ivan? Her brother was thrilled. He didn't object to Michael standing in his father's role.

The song leader announced the second hymn, "O Gott Vater, wir Loben dich" ("Oh God the Father, We Praise You"). It was always the second hymn of an Amish service. Bethany forgot about Michael and her brother as she joined the entire congregation in singing God's praise, asking that the people present would receive His words and take them into their hearts.

At the end of the second hymn, the minister and Bishop Schultz came in and hung their hats on pegs set in the wall. That was the signal that the preaching would now begin. Bethany tried to listen closely to what was being said, but she found her mind wandering to the subject of Michael. What might he be looking for in a wife?

Michael sat up straight and unobtrusively stretched his bad leg. He was still stiff after his fall on Thursday. The wooden benches were not made for comfort. At least he hadn't fallen asleep the way their host Nigel Miller was doing. A few minutes after the preaching started, the farmer started nodding off in front of Michael. When Nigel began to tip sideways, Michael reached up and caught his arm before he tumbled off his seat.

Nigel jerked awake. *"Danki,"* he whispered as he gave Michael a sheepish grin.

Michael ventured a guess. "Working late?"

Nigel shook his head. "Colicky baby."

He leaned forward to look over at the women. Following his gaze, Michael saw Nigel's wife sitting across the aisle. Becca Miller held the baby sleeping sweetly in her arms. Her face held an expression of pure happiness when she caught her husband's glance. Bethany sat behind her.

What Michael wouldn't give to see Bethany look at him with a similar light in her eyes.

He quickly focused on his hymnal. Such daydreaming was foolishness. He wasn't husband material. He might never be. He tried to push thoughts of Bethany aside but they came back to him at odd times and more often than he cared to admit. He hadn't had another flashback or panic episode since the previous Sunday, but that didn't mean he was well.

Three hours into the service, the bishop stopped speaking and the song leader called out the number of the final hymn. Michael ventured a look in Bethany's direction. She held her songbook open for Jenny seated beside her. She pointed out the words as she sang them.

Bethany should have children of her own. She would make a good mother. He couldn't imagine why God had chosen not to bless her with a husband and children of her own. It didn't seem right.

The song drew to a close. Ivan was up and out the doors the second it ended. Teenage boys were expected to sit at the very back. Michael always assumed it was so their late arrivals and quick getaways didn't disrupt others. He followed more slowly. His eyes were drawn to Bethany as she walked toward the farmhouse with the other women.

How much of his life would he spend like this, watching her from afar, wishing for something that could never happen? Months? Years? What if he never got well?

On Monday afternoon just before the children came home from school, Bethany got out her crafting supplies and spread them on the table. She made a batch of oatmeal cookies and a pot of peppermint hot chocolate and left it simmering on the back of the stove.

She was cutting and folding card stock paper when Ivan and Jenny came in the door. Jenny's eyes lit up. "Is it time to make our Christmas cards?"

"*Ja*, it is time. Do you have your lists of the people you want to send them to?"

Both children were well prepared and provided a list

of more than a dozen people each that they would hand-craft a greeting card for. Bethany had her own list that included every family in the New Covenant congregation as well as Pastor Frank, the children's teachers, bus driver and many of the merchants in town that she did business with.

After two mugs each of the hot chocolate and a plate of cookies, they were laughing and sharing ideas for cards. Jenny loved to draw a snow-covered tree branch with a cardinal sitting on it. She added silver glitter to the snow and red glitter to the birds. Ivan liked making construction paper cutouts of a horse and sleigh and gluing them to the card stock. He covered the snowy foreground with glitter. Bethany enjoyed making snowmen out of cotton balls glued together inside the card.

Before long there was glitter on the table, glitter on the floor and glitter on the children, but Bethany didn't care. She had to make this Christmas a special one in case they weren't together next year. "Ivan, you didn't tell me what song you'll be singing at the community Christmas program." Since religious-themed programs could no longer be held in the public schools, the community had decided to keep the Christmas pageant alive and well in the community center. The children and their teachers who wished to participate were eagerly welcomed.

Ivan didn't look up from crafting his card. "I'm going to sing 'O Come, O Come, Emmanuel.'"

"That's one of my favorites. Will you sing it for me now?" she asked with a catch in her throat.

He did and there were tears in her eyes by the time he finished. "That was fine. God has blessed you with a wonderful singing voice."

Jenny laid down her scissors. "I want to sing a song."

Bethany blinked away her tears and smiled. "What song would you like to perform?"

"'Go Tell It on the Mountain.'"

"That's a fine song. Let's all sing it together." Bethany hummed the first note and they all joined in singing at the top of their lungs to the very last verse.

"I don't know how you expect me to get any work done with all the noise and the delicious smell of hot chocolate coming from this room."

Bethany looked up to see Michael standing in the doorway with an indulgent smile lighting his face. Sadie Sue ambled over to Jenny. She got a hug and a pat before settling to the floor beside Jenny's chair with a sprinkling of red glitter across her head.

Bethany pointed at Michael. "That door is to remain closed while you are working."

He held his hands wide. "I'm done for the evening."

"In that case, pull up a chair and start making your Christmas cards. They have to go in the mail by the end of this week if you want them to arrive on time."

"I haven't sent many cards in the last few years, but I will definitely take some of that hot chocolate. Is that peppermint I smell?"

"Help yourself. I will make a list of people for you. Let's start with your mother and father. They will get a card, right?"

He nodded as he filled a white mug from the pot. "I have three brothers and two sisters."

She wrote down the names and addresses that he gave her. She sat poised with a pen. "Grandparents?"

"Gone, I'm afraid."

"Mr. Meyers at the jewelry store where you used to work? Grandfather always sent him one. How about some of the people you worked with? Are you still friends with them?"

He paused with the mug halfway to his mouth. He slowly lowered it. "I don't have friends there anymore."

He put the mug down, walked back into the work-room and closed the door.

Bethany didn't know what to make of his abrupt retreat. She looked at Ivan. "Did I say something wrong?"

Ivan shrugged. "He was shot during a robbery there. He doesn't like to talk about it."

Bethany stared at her brother, unsure she'd heard him correctly. "Michael was shot?"

Ivan nodded. "That's why he limps. I wasn't supposed to tell you. You won't tell him I mentioned it, will you?"

Bethany shook her head. "I won't say anything."

No wonder Michael didn't like to talk about his injury. Someone had robbed him at gunpoint and shot him. Was he the only one? Or were there others, too? She thought back to something her grandfather had mentioned. He told her the man who sent him watches to fix had a store robbed. Somewhere she had her grandfather's correspondences. He kept everything in case he had to prove the work had been done and the time-pieces had been returned.

Some things about Michael began to make sense. The way he was always vigilant. He didn't like crowds. He often stood with his back to the wall. She assumed he was leaning against the wall to rest his leg, but he might just as easily have been doing it to assure himself there was no one behind him.

She looked at Ivan and Jenny. "Let's make Christmas cards for Michael's family. It can be our Christmas gift to him. What do you think?" They both agreed and got to work.

Later that evening, Bethany carried a lantern into her grandfather's room. She put it down on his bedside table and pulled a large box from under his bed. She opened it and began to search for letters from George Meyers. She found the one she was looking for. Holding it in her hand, Bethany was torn by the feeling that she was invading Michael's privacy by snooping into his past. Would it tell her what she needed to know about Michael and what troubled him? Like her brother, she didn't know how to help Michael if she didn't know what was wrong.

She opened the letter and began reading.

Chapter Nine

Michael peered through his jeweler's loupe at a tiny screw he was attempting to insert into the mechanism of an antique gold pocket watch. His concentration was broken by the thump-thump-thump of Sadie Sue's tail against the floor. It was her signal that he wasn't alone but the visitor was someone she knew.

He couldn't believe what a difference having the dog had made on his anxiety level. He was confident in her ability to alert him to strangers. He didn't feel the need to constantly scan his surroundings for danger as often. When he did get agitated, she would distract him by nuzzling him for affection or bringing him the red ball she loved to fetch and dropping it in his lap.

"What are you doing?" Jenny asked as she came up beside him. His workbench was just high enough to allow her to rest her hands and chin on it.

"I'm working. Are you supposed to be in here?"

"I can't come in when the door is closed."

"Is the door closed, Jenny?" He turned the loupe up so that he could see her face. She was the perfect picture of boredom.

"It was closed but then it opened, so I came in."

He tipped his head to the side. "Did it open because you turned the doorknob?"

"Maybe. Are you mad?"

He sighed heavily. "What do you need, Jenny?"

"I want someone to play hide-and-seek with me. Will you, please?"

"I'm working. Ask your sister to play with you."

"She's doing the laundry."

"Then perhaps your brother would enjoy playing with you."

"He says I'm too little and that I'm just a pest. I'm not a pest, am I?"

Michael put down his screwdriver. The tiny screw popped off the magnetized end and went rolling off the workbench onto the floor. He pressed his lips into a hard line. "You are not a pest, but I don't have time to play, Jenny. I have work to do."

Her hopeful expression dissolved into a serious pout.

He got off his stool and awkwardly dropped to one knee to see under the bench. Jenny picked the screw up and handed it to him. "No one wants to play with me."

He paused and thought for a minute. "Why aren't you in school?"

"'Cause the teachers have to go to meetings for two days."

He got back on his work stool. "Play with Sadie."

"Sadie Sue can't play hide-and-seek. She can't count."

He put his loupe back on. "I'm sure Sadie can learn to play hide-and-seek with a little help from you. You go hide, and I will send her to find you." If he was fortunate, he could have ten or twenty minutes of uninterrupted work time before she came looking for the dog.

Bethany opened the door. "Jenny, I thought I told you to stay out of the workroom while Michael is in here."

"He wants me to play with Sadie Sue."

Bethany folded her arms across her chest. "Then bring the dog with you and leave Michael alone."

"We're playing hide-and-seek. I'm going to go hide. Michael, you count for her." Jenny took off at a run.

He waited a long moment, then looked at his dog. "Ten." She wagged her tail.

Bethany grinned at him. She had the most contagious smile. It boosted his spirits every time he saw it. "I'm sorry Jenny bothered you. She has been out of school for the past two days because of teachers' meetings. I think she has a touch of cabin fever."

"I'm ready," Jenny called from somewhere in the house.

Michael looked down at the dog. "Go find Jenny."

Sadie Sue didn't move. He patted her head. *"Goot hund."*

Bethany arched one eyebrow. "I see your plan. Jenny stays hidden and you get some work done?"

"It was the dog's idea." He put his tools down. "What are you baking that smells so good?"

"It's a turkey-and-rice casserole for supper. Is your compliment a sly way of asking if you can join us for supper?"

"You read me like a book."

She tipped her head to study him. "I wish that was true."

He looked away first. He would be in deep trouble if she actually could read his mind. At the moment he was wondering what it would be like to kiss her.

"You are always welcome to eat with us, Michael. You never need an invitation." She paused, looking as if she wanted to say something else. Her indecision vanished. She smiled softly. "If you'll excuse me, I have to go find Jenny."

She clapped her hands together. "Come on, Sadie. Let's leave Michael to finish his work." Sadie rose and followed Bethany out of the room.

Michael picked up his screwdriver but working had lost its appeal. He laid his equipment aside and went out to the kitchen.

Bethany was diligently checking hiding places for her sister. He was the one who happened to notice that the door to the cellar was open a crack.

He clicked his fingers and Sadie trotted to him. He whispered in her ear and then gave her a small push toward the door. She trotted right past her quarry without seeing her. Jenny would've been safe if she hadn't giggled. Sadie spun around and pushed her nose in behind the door.

"Aw, you found me." Jenny patted the dog's head and looked to Michael. "Keep her here while I go hide again."

"Wait a minute." He turned to the refrigerator and opened it. There were several links of cooked sausage left over from breakfast. He picked up the plate and looked at Bethany. "Is it okay if I give this to the dog?"

"Feed *goot* food to a dog? Are you serious?"

"Please?" he cajoled. He used the same tone on Bethany that Jenny had used on him. To his surprise, it worked.

"Very well, but I don't see why the dog needs sausages. She's filled out fine on dog chow."

He motioned to Jenny. "Come here. We are going to teach Sadie Sue to find you so you two can play hide-and-seek and leave me alone."

Bethany's eyes brightened. "That might work. Good thinking. Where did you learn how to train dogs?"

"I've never owned a dog before. This will be trial and error." He crumbled the links into pieces and gave them to Jenny. "Put these in your pocket. When I say 'find Jenny,' I want you to hold out a piece in your hand. Got it?"

"Sure."

"Sadie, find Jenny." Sadie cocked her head to the side as she stared at him.

Jenny fished a piece of sausage out of her pocket and held it out to the dog. "Here, girl."

Sadie never needed a second invitation where food was concerned. She ambled over to Jenny and gently took the piece of meat from her hand.

"That was fine," Michael said. "Now I will take her a little farther away. This time, Jenny, don't say anything. Just hold out your hand."

He took Sadie by the collar and led her to the other side of the room but her eyes were still on the little girl. He turned the dog so she was facing the other way. "Sadie, find Jenny."

Sadie spun around and made a beeline for Jenny, gulped down the piece of meat and barked.

Jenny laughed. "I think that means she wants some more."

"She will have to earn another piece." He took the dog by the collar and led her to the other side of the room.

Bethany regarded him with an amused expression. "You have taught a dog to eat sausage. Everyone will be amazed."

"Don't be a doubting Thomas." This time he took Sadie out into the workroom. "Sadie, find Jenny." The dog galloped from the room straight to Jenny and claimed her tidbit.

He was pleased with his experiment so far. "Now comes the real test. Jenny, I want you to go into the other room where Sadie can't see you. I want you to be quiet. Don't call her. Let's see if she will go look for you."

Jenny hurried out of the room. Bethany smothered a giggle. "I think the command should be 'go find sausage.' If I ever lose my breakfast meat I'll know who to call on. Michael and his amazing Sadie Sue."

"Scoff all you want. This is going to work." He looked down at the dog. "Sadie, find Jenny."

Sadie remained at his side watching him intently with her whole back end wagging. Bethany started laughing. She swung her arm out, pointed toward the doorway and yelled, "Find sausage!" Sadie started barking at her.

As much as he enjoyed the sound of Bethany's laughter, he didn't appreciate her lack of confidence. "She is going to get this. Jenny, come back here."

Jenny walked in the room looking confused. "Did I do it wrong?"

He shook his head. "You did fine. It is Sadie who needs a little more work. Why don't you go put on your coat and boots and we will take this outside, where there aren't so many confusing smells for Sadie and fewer people who want to make fun of her."

Jenny put her arms around Sadie's neck. "You'll get it. I know you will. You're the smartest dog in the whole wide world." Sadie licked her face, making her giggle. Jenny headed for the coatrack. Sadie Sue followed with her nose pressed to Jenny's pocket.

Michael met Bethany's gaze and saw her affection for him in the depths of her eyes. His heart tripped over itself. She cared for him. He knew it as surely as if she spoke the words out loud.

He was falling for this amazing, beautiful, caring woman and he had no idea how to change course.

He had little to offer. He was a broken man. Nothing more than a jumble of pieces like some of the watches that came to him. Sometimes a boxful of gears and a dial couldn't be assembled to work properly no matter how much the owner wanted it repaired.

Bethany tipped her head slightly. "What?"

He shook his head and looked away. "Nothing. I was thinking about a broken watch I received the other day."

"Why does that make you sad?"

"Who said I was sad?"

She leaned closer. "I read you like a book, remember?"

Then she should be able to see how much he had grown to care for her. "It's sad because the watch can't be fixed."

"Why not?"

He turned away, afraid she could see what he was thinking. "An important part is broken. It can't be mended." He was the broken timepiece and could never forget it.

"Do you think another watch repair business might have the part you need?"

"It's not likely."

"If you really want to restore it, you should ask if someone else can help you. What about asking Mr. Meyers for help?"

Michael heard something in her voice he didn't understand. He looked at her sharply. "What do you know about George Meyers?"

She rubbed her hands together. "He supplied my

grandfather with the majority of his work. He also suggested my grandfather write to you and offer you a job here."

Michael tensed. "I told you that."

"I was going through some of Grandfather's things last night and I found the letter George Meyers sent to Grandpa."

Michael swallowed hard. What else was in the letter? "Was it informative?"

"He said you were injured during a robbery at the store."

He shouldn't be surprised. It was newsworthy. "What else did the letter say?"

"That three of his employees were killed by the robbers," she said gently.

He closed his eyes. "That's true."

"I'm so sorry. It must have been terrible for you."

He couldn't speak. Did she pity him now? He couldn't look at her. "What else did George tell your grandfather?"

"Mr. Meyers wanted you to have a chance to start over. I'm glad he asked Grandfather to contact you."

Michael glanced up at her. She meant it. If George had mentioned that Michael was off in the head, Bethany didn't share it. Michael relaxed. George Meyers had given him more than a chance to continue his work. He'd given him a chance at a new life. It had been nearly two weeks since his last PTSD episode. Perhaps he truly was getting better here.

Was his new life one that could include Bethany and the children?

The thought was almost unimaginable. His skin grew clammy. The idea that Bethany might one day love him was terrifyingly wonderful. Was it possible?

Did he deserve such a gift? If only he could be sure he would get well.

"I'm ready," Jenny called from the front hall.

"I'll meet you on the back lawn." He was glad of the distraction. He needed to forget about a relationship with Bethany that was anything other than professional. He went out to the workroom, grabbed his coat, pulled on his overshoes and went out the side door with Sadie at his heels. He didn't want Bethany drawn into the darkness that hid inside him, waiting to spring out.

Jenny, dressed in her dark blue coat and bright red mittens, was waiting for him on the snow-covered lawn. She had a red-and-blue knit cap pulled over her white prayer *kapp*. Scooping up some snow, she formed a snowball and tossed it from hand to hand.

"Fetch it, Sadie." Jenny threw the ball, and the dog made a dive for it into a drift, leaving only her back legs and tail visible. She pulled out of the snowbank and shook vigorously, pelting Jenny with clumps of snow. Jenny stumbled and fell. Sadie started licking her face, making Jenny giggle as she tried to fend off the determined pooch. "Stop it, Sadie, stop it."

"She must think you're a sausage," Bethany called from the doorway. She had her arms crossed over her chest and her shoulders hunched against the cold.

Michael packed a snowball and threw it. It smacked against the side of the house above Bethany's head, sending a shower of snow her way. She ducked and brushed the crystals from her clothes. "Hey, that's not fair. I'm not dressed for a snowball fight."

"Then go back inside. Sadie needs to concentrate. You're distracting her." In truth, he was the one distracted by her presence.

"Well, don't expect to get any more sausage from

me." She was smiling as she shut the door. A few seconds later he saw her draw the shade aside at the window so she could watch them.

For the next hour he and Jenny worked at teaching Sadie to find the girl. By the time they were both too cold to continue, Sadie was getting it right about half the time. She was still more interested in hunting among the trees than she was in finding Jenny even for a piece of sausage.

"I say we call it quits," Michael said as he sat down on the back porch steps and rubbed his aching thigh.

"She's almost got it." Jenny sat beside him.

"If we work with her a few more days I think she will find you most times, as long as a rabbit doesn't run in front of her."

Jenny tipped her head to smile at him. "Maybe if I had a rabbit in my pocket instead of sausage she would do better."

"You may be onto something. Where can we get a bunch of pocket-size rabbits?"

"You're funny, Michael."

"You are, too, Jenny."

"Are you going to stay with us a long time?"

He shrugged. "That's a hard question to answer."

"Don't you like it here?"

"Truthfully, I don't like the cold."

"Wait till summer. Then you'll really love it here."

He brushed snow from the top of her hat. "I will be here that long, anyway."

"Why don't you have a wife?"

He leaned back to stare at her. "That's kind of a personal question."

"Well? Why don't you?"

"I guess because I've never met someone that I wanted to marry."

"Gemma says my sister needs to be married so Ivan can stay here and not have to go live with our *onkel* Harvey."

"I know your sister loves Ivan just like she loves you. But when people get married it has to be because they love each other and not for any other reason."

"You don't have a wife. You could marry Bethany and you'd sort of be my *daed*."

"It's not that simple.

"All the kids in my class have *daeds*. Sometimes they feel sorry for me. There is going to be a father-daughter program in the spring. It would be nice if you could come as my *daed*."

"Jenny, Bethany and I are not going to get married, but I will take you to the father-daughter program anyway. How's that?"

She smiled brightly. "You will?"

"I promise."

"That makes me happy. Can we go in now? My toes are cold."

"Excellent idea. My everything is cold."

She got up and took hold of his hand to pull him to his feet. To his surprise, she hung on to his hand as they walked into the house.

Bethany was sitting beside the window, mending one of Ivan's shirts, when Jenny and Michael came in. "How goes the training?"

"We've decided that to be one hundred percent effective Jenny must have a rabbit in her pocket when she gets lost. Sadie Sue likes hunting rabbits a little bit more than she likes tracking down Jenny even for a bite of sausage."

The dog, who had been sitting quietly beside Michael, suddenly took off toward the front door. She barked several times when someone knocked.

Bethany got up and went to answer the door. Her *Englisch* neighbor, Greg Janson, tipped his hat. "Good evening, Ms. Martin. I would like a few minutes of your time to discuss something that happened on my farm last night."

A sense of foreboding filled Bethany. "Does this have anything to do with Ivan?"

"In fact it does. I've come to you first. But I'm not opposed to going to the sheriff."

Bethany invited him in. Michael stood in the hallway. Bethany indicated him with one hand. "Michael, this is Greg Janson. He has the farm south of here. Mr. Janson, this is Michael Shetler. He is a business partner."

Mr. Janson nodded. Bethany led the way into the kitchen. "Would you like some coffee, Mr. Janson?"

"No, thank you, ma'am. I'll get right to the point. Last night someone broke into my henhouse and stole three laying hens. The commotion woke my son. He looked out and saw Ivan running down the road with a gunnysack slung over his back."

"If it was nighttime, how was your son able to recognize Ivan?" Michael asked.

"My boy is in the same class as Ivan. He knows him pretty well. They've even been in a scuffle or two together. Plus, the boy was dressed Amish with those flattop black hats you folks prefer."

"I appreciate you coming to me first," Bethany said quietly.

"We have heard a lot of good things about having the Amish for neighbors and for the most part you folks have lived up to your reputation. I don't want to bring the sheriff into this if I don't have to. Things like this can get blown out of proportion. Anybody who has a pig or goat come up missing, they can point a finger at the Amish without any proof. You folks just accept that and forgive the accusers. Nothing gets solved and folks keep on thinking you're guilty. I don't want to see that get started here."

"We appreciate your attitude, Mr. Janson. Would you like to speak to Ivan?" Michael asked.

"I'll leave that up to you."

"I will pay you what the hens are worth." Bethany got up to find her checkbook.

Michael stalled her with a hand to her shoulder. "I'm responsible for Ivan now. I will take care of this."

Mr. Janson held up one hand and shook his head. "I could just as easily have lost them to a lynx or coyote. I don't want to be paid for them. I came here because I want your boy to know that he was seen and that next time he comes on the place I will call the sheriff."

The outside door opened and Ivan came in. He stopped and his eyes grew wide when he saw Mr. Janson. Bethany beckoned to him. "We were just talking about you."

"About me? Why?"

"Because my boy Max saw you stealing our chickens last night," Janson said.

Ivan shook his head. "It wasn't me."

"Max knows you. He was certain."

Ivan looked at Michael. "Honest, I didn't go out last night. Why would I take chickens?"

Michael laid a hand on Ivan's shoulder. "Do you know who might have done it?"

Ivan stared down at his feet. "I only know it wasn't me."

Bethany turned to Mr. Janson. "Thank you for bringing this to our attention."

"Like I said, I don't want it to get out of hand." He tipped his hat to her and left.

Bethany waited until the door closed and then she turned to Ivan. "How could you do something so foolish?"

"I knew you wouldn't believe me."

Michael kept his hand on Ivan's shoulder. "I believe you. Why would someone want to make it look like you are the one who took them?"

"I don't know."

"But you do have an idea who it was, don't you?"

Ivan turned his pleading eyes to Michael. "I can't tell. I promised I wouldn't tell."

Chapter Ten

Bethany was shocked that Michael believed Ivan. Even she doubted her brother's innocence. Yet the crime didn't make any sense. Why would Ivan steal three chickens?

Why would anyone? The vast majority of farms in the area had their own chickens as she did.

"Go on and get ready for supper, Ivan." When her brother left the room, Bethany looked at Michael. "What are we going to do with him?"

"The next time there is a report about something Ivan is suspected of doing, I think it would be best to involve the police."

"The bishop would not agree to that. Our community has taken great pains to avoid any involvement by the *Englisch* law."

"The police can easily rule out Ivan as a suspect by fingerprints or by DNA. Their findings will carry weight with the *Englisch* community."

"You really think someone is deliberately blaming Ivan?"

"I do."

She wished she could be so positive. This setback

was crushing. "I'm not sure I can simply wait for another incident to occur."

"It's the only choice we have unless Ivan can be convinced to break his promise and tells us what he knows."

"Do you know who he's protecting?"

"I think I do but I have no proof. I think you know, too."

"Jeffrey?"

He nodded. She shook her head in bewilderment. "But why? Do you think we should tell the bishop about this?"

Michael took his time answering her. "I'd rather not, but if you feel you should, then I'm okay with it."

"What do we do?"

"We keep to a normal pattern of activity. And we keep a good eye on Ivan. What are your plans for this week?"

"I have a lot of things that need to be done. Christmas is getting closer by the minute. I have a ton of baking to get finished. On Saturday I plan to send the children out to collect fir branches and winterberries for the house and for wreaths. I was hoping that you would go with them."

"I can."

"On Sunday Pastor Frank is coming to supper."

"Why?" He looked at her suspiciously.

"Because he's a friend. We enjoyed his company. He frequently drives us and other Amish people in his van at no charge."

"I see."

She walked to the window and stared out at the low gray clouds scuttling across the sky. A few snowflakes floated down from them. She wound the ribbon of her *kapp* around one finger. "I had asked Frank to speak with Ivan about his behavior but I never took Ivan to see him. He's been doing so much better lately. You have been a good influence on him. But now this."

Michael walked up to stand behind her. She could see their reflection together in the window. She was becoming dependent on him for advice and for comfort. She longed to rest her head against his shoulder and feel she wasn't facing this problem alone.

"I know you're worried," he said quietly.

If she leaned back, would he take her in his arms? It was a foolish thought. "To worry is to doubt God's mercy. I try not to, but it seems to be my best talent."

He chuckled. "I thought speaking Cow was your best talent."

She smiled. "Don't tell Frank I get my advice from Clarabelle. He went to many years of school to become a psychologist and counselor so he could advise folks."

"Jenny thinks you should marry. That way Ivan won't be sent away."

Bethany looked down as her face grew hot. "She's been listening to Gemma. Husbands don't exactly grow on trees in New Covenant."

"Anyone you chose would be getting a fine wife."

She looked up to study his reflection in the glass but it wasn't clear enough to let her see what he was thinking. "Are you making me an offer?"

"You would be getting a very poor bargain if I was."

She turned around so she could look into his eyes. "Why do you say that?"

"Because it's the truth."

There was so much pain in his voice and deep in his eyes that she wanted to hold him and promise to make everything better. She couldn't. She knew that, but it didn't lessen her desire to help him.

The letter from Mr. Meyers hadn't told her why Michael didn't return to work in his store or why he left his family in Ohio to come to Maine. He could have easily fixed watches for Mr. Meyers there the same way he was doing here. "What's wrong, Michael?"

He laid a hand against her cheek. "Nothing that you can fix."

"How do I know that if you can't tell me what troubles you?"

"Trust me. You don't want to know." He turned and walked down the hall and out the back door.

He was so wrong. She wanted to know everything about Michael Shetler. Her mother's voice echoed from the past. *If you don't know a man inside and out, don't marry him. He'll bring you nothing but pain.*

Michael was up early on Saturday because he knew Ivan and Jenny would be over as soon as they could. He hoped that Bethany would accompany them on their trek into the woods to gather winterberries and fir boughs for wreath making but he wasn't sure that she would. It was hard for him to believe that he had only been in New Covenant a little over two weeks. So much had happened. So much had changed. He hadn't had a flashback for thirteen days and not a single panic attack. Maybe his PTSD episodes were behind him for good. He prayed it was true.

Sadie alerted him that the children had arrived by scratching at the door and woofing softly. He opened the door and she shot outside, barking and bounding around Jenny. The girl was pulling a red toboggan. She dropped to her knees and threw her arms around Sadie's neck. The dog responded by licking her face. Jenny's giggle was so much like Bethany's that anyone could tell they were related. Ivan stopped to pet the dog, too.

Bethany came up the hill behind the children. Her bright welcoming smile was like the sun breaking through on a dreary day. He was happy to see her smiling again after the depressing visit with Mr. Janson.

Michael's refusal to talk about his past troubled her, too. He knew that, but his decision would never change.

Bethany pulled a blue toboggan with a bushel basket on it. Like the children, she was bundled for the outdoors with a heavy coat, mittens and snow boots. The red-and-white-striped knit scarf around her neck was identical to the one Jenny was wearing.

Ivan patted Sadie and then hurried to Michael's door. He was pulling a yellow disk sled. "*Guder mariye*, Michael."

"Morning, Ivan. So where are we going?"

The boy pointed up the ridge. "I know the perfect place to get pine boughs. It isn't far."

Michael looked at the pine-covered forest stretching up into the mountains. "I hope that's true. I'm not sure my leg will hold up in all this snow. Besides, don't we have about a million trees to choose from close to home?"

"It has to be balsam fir and we will pull you on the sled if you get tired." Bethany stopped beside Ivan.

"I give up. Why balsam?" Michael returned her smile. The darkness of his past was etched deep in his soul, but just being with her gave him hope that he could be healed. He prayed that God would show him mercy.

Michael couldn't plan any kind of family life until he was sure, but he could dream of the day when he had the right to tell Bethany how he felt about her.

"I want balsam fir because of its wonderful, spicy scent, its lovely color and its short dense needles."

Michael looked at both of their sleds. "Are we planning to bring back a lot of branches? I was thinking we'd have an armful or two."

Bethany began counting on her fingers. "Gemma and her mother want some. We need enough for our house and for your cabin. Plus, I will make some for friends and I also plan to sell a few at the grocer's. Mr. Meriwether lets us set up a display in front of his store. Last year I sold thirty-eight of them and made almost a thousand dollars."

"I didn't know you operated a seasonal business."

"We have to make ends meet any way we can. Are you ready?"

He nodded even though he wasn't looking forward to the hike. Sadie Sue took off after a rabbit.

Ivan put Jenny on her sled and pulled her along as he walked beside Michael. Ivan met Michael's gaze. "The snow might get too deep for her. A man takes care of his family, right?"

Michael smiled. "Right."

When Sadie Sue returned without a bunny, Jenny coaxed her to sit on the sled with her. She and Ivan took turns pulling the dog along. Sadie wasn't sure she liked the ride and kept jumping off and then back on. Their antics had Michael and Bethany laughing as they made their way up into the forest.

Ivan was true to his word. He led them to a small grove of the fir trees less than three hundred yards beyond Michael's cabin. The trees were almost all the same size at about eight feet tall and evenly spaced.

Michael glanced at Bethany. "Someone planted this grove. Do we have permission to harvest these?"

She gave him a reassuring grin. "We do. This land belongs to Pastor Frank. We are free to use what we like. If we take a whole tree, he asks that we replant one to replace it."

"He's a generous man." Michael hadn't seen him since the night of his flashback. Although he had been tempted to attend the survivors' group meeting, he wasn't ready to have others know about his problem.

Bethany distributed clippers to everyone and they set about filling the sleds with piles of the wonderfully pungent branches. When the children had finished cutting, they went exploring while the adults cinched down the loads with lengths of rope.

Michael tied off the last knot, dusted the snow from a nearby fallen log and sat down to rest. Bethany came over to join him. The view spread out before them was breathtaking. They could see the winding course of the river down below, the silver ribbon of highway that paralleled the river's course and the houses of Fort Craig. In the distance the Appalachian mountain range provided a beautiful backdrop. It was a lovely spot and he had a beautiful woman beside him.

She rubbed her hands up and down on her arms. "It's getting colder."

He slipped his arm around her and she moved closer, making his heart beat faster. Not with fear but with joy.

"How long have you been taking care of your brother and sister?" Michael asked gently. He leaned forward to see her face.

Bethany smiled. "A long time."

"What happened to your parents? Does it bother you to talk about it?"

She shook her head. "My mother passed away shortly after Jenny was born. The doctor had a medical reason but I think she died of a broken heart. My father had left us about a month before that."

"I don't understand."

"Neither did I. If you are thinking that my father died, you are mistaken. My father packed up and moved away. He didn't want to be Amish anymore. It was the third time he had come back into our lives, begged for forgiveness, and was welcomed by our Amish community. I would like to give him credit for trying to shoulder his responsibilities, but I'm not sure he tried very hard."

"He left your mother twice before that? Left her and his children?" Michael could barely believe what he was hearing.

"The first time he went away I was six. I woke up on my sixth birthday to find my mother crying and my father gone. Just gone. He didn't bother to tell me goodbye."

"I'm sorry. That was cruel."

"He came back two years later, said he was sorry and begged Mother to give him another chance. She did. I was overjoyed. Mother was, too, but only for a while. He stayed for three years but even as a child I could see they weren't happy together. He left again. The next time he came back he only stayed a year."

"Did he ever tell you why he couldn't stay or what he did when he was away?"

"Not to me. He refused to talk about his other life. He did come to Mother's funeral. I thought he would take care of us but he said he couldn't. I was sixteen. He left me with a brokenhearted little boy and a newborn babe. We haven't seen or heard from him since."

"It's hard to believe a man could cast aside his responsibilities that way." No wonder she was so committed to keeping the children with her.

"Fortunately, our mother's father, Elijah, stepped up to take us in. My father's brother, Onkel Harvey, was willing to accept us but I wanted to stay with Grandpa. That's how I ended up helping Elijah look for a place to start his new Amish community. Each fall after the farm work was done, we would travel to different locations, looking for a place to settle. When we received a letter from Pastor Frank telling us about New Covenant, we decided to visit during the winter to see just how bad it was going to be. The road leading to our farm was merely a tunnel plowed through four feet of snow."

"I'm sorry about your father."

"Our faith requires a strength of character that he didn't possess. My mother could have gone with him, but she refused to abandon her faith and break her vows to God."

"She must've been a strong woman."

"She was, but each time my father came back and then left again, it was like he took pieces of her strength with him until there was nothing left."

"You have inherited your strength from her."

"I hope so. She wanted Father to come back so badly. She prayed for it. When she knew she was dying, she made me promise I would keep the family together. She didn't say she wanted it for him in case he came back, but I think that's exactly what she hoped for."

"It was a big burden to place on a young girl." He bent and kissed her lips gently.

He felt her sharp intake of breath and he drew back. "Maybe I shouldn't have done that."

"I didn't mind."

He looked away from the comfort she offered. "Did you ever consider leaving the Amish?"

"I think we all question at one time or another if this path to God is the right one for us. I never seriously considered leaving. What about you?"

"I did more than question. I left the Amish life behind and lived in the outside world for five years."

She gave him a funny look. "You did? What made you come back?"

"That is not something I care to talk about." His answer seemed to take her by surprise.

"I'm sorry. I'm just trying to understand. You say you want to live alone but you spend almost as much time with my family as I do."

"Ivan and Jenny can be hard to resist." As was their big sister. He rose to his feet and held out his hand to her. "We should head back."

"Will you remain Amish?"

He could tell it was important to her to know the answer. "I will."

Bethany allowed him to help her up but she pulled her hand away from his quickly. She had shared the most painful part of her life but he was unwilling to speak of his past. Until this moment she considered him someone she could count on. Someone dependable, but was he? He'd left the Amish once. What if he decided to leave again? A seed of doubt had been sown in her mind.

She shouldn't have let him kiss her. There was no promise between them. No plan for the future. That knowledge alone should help keep her emotions from carrying her away where he was concerned.

Ivan came through the trees with a big bundle of

winterberry branches in his arms, leaving a thin trail of red berries on the snow behind him. Sadie Sue walked beside him. He laid the branches on top of the blue sled. Bethany looked around. "Where is Jenny?"

"She said she wanted to play hide-and-seek with Sadie Sue. She's gone to hide."

Michael patted the dog's head. "Let's hope she has a bunny in her pocket."

Bethany didn't look amused. "Let's pray we can find her if the dog can't."

"That will be easy. We'll just follow her footsteps in the snow," Ivan said.

Michael took Sadie Sue's head between his hands. "Find Jenny."

Sadie took off into the trees. He looked at Bethany. "Do we follow the dog or just hope she finds Jenny before it gets dark?"

"I'm going to follow the dog." She pointed to the log they had been sitting on. "You don't need to do more hiking than you have already. Rest."

Ivan sat on the log. "I'm going to wait here."

They heard Sadie barking in the distance. Bethany started toward the sound. She hadn't gone far when she saw Jenny and the dog coming toward her. Jenny was covered with snow but she was smiling from ear to ear. "She found me. I buried myself under the snow and she found me. She's the smartest dog in the whole wide world."

Bethany smiled at her sister. "Well, for that she deserves a whole sausage. Are you ready to go home?"

Jenny nodded and they began to walk side by side. She glanced up at Bethany. "Can I ask you something?"

"Sure."

"I've been thinking that you should marry Michael."

Bethany arched one eyebrow. "You've been thinking that, have you?"

Jenny cocked her head to the side as a serious expression settled over her face. "I like him. Ivan wouldn't have to go away and you could have babies."

"I see you have this all figured out. How many babies do you think I should have?"

"Three or four. Mostly girls but you could have one boy if you wanted to."

It hurt Bethany's heart to know her little sister was worrying about Ivan, too. She managed a reassuring smile. "I don't believe the bishop is going to send Ivan away, so I'm not going to marry Michael or anyone else until you and Ivan are grown up. You are my family. I don't need anyone else."

Jenny kicked at the snow. "Ivan said you would say that."

Bethany patted her sister on the head. "Then Ivan is smarter than I gave him credit for."

On Sunday evening Michael was reading Elijah's book on the history of clocks when Sadie perked up and thumped her tail on the floor. She kept her eyes on the front door. A knock followed. Michael knew who was there before he opened the door.

"Good evening, Frank."

"Evening, Michael. I thought I would stop by and see if I could interest you in a game of chess." He had a case under his arm.

"I have a strong suspicion that I'll be outclassed, but sure, come in."

Frank looked at Sadie. "Is this the same dog you had before?"

"It is."

He bent to pat her head. "Living with you certainly agrees with her. I don't see a single rib sticking out anymore. Her coat is gorgeous. Such a pretty golden color." He glanced at Michael. "How have you been?"

Michael led the way to a small table and two chairs set in the corner. He clicked on the floor lamp and took a seat. "Sadie is not the only one improving. I've come a long way."

"Really?" Frank opened his case and lifted out a chessboard and pieces. "Tell me about it."

"I haven't had a flashback or a panic attack since the last time we spoke. I've never gone so long without an episode."

Frank glanced at Michael. "I'm glad to hear it. I've been expecting you to show up at one of my support groups but you keep disappointing me."

"I don't see the need for therapy if I'm getting better on my own. You said some people get over it by themselves."

"I did say that. What do you think has made the difference?"

"Sadie Sue, for one thing. She always alerts me if someone is near. I depend on her sharp nose and ears. If I start getting edgy, she will come over and distract me. She's amazing."

"So instead of being hypervigilant, you rely on the dog to do that for you. I don't want to belittle your progress, but isn't that substituting one kind of crutch for another?"

"Maybe it is but it makes life bearable."

"Bethany tells me Ivan has been in trouble again but that you are sticking up for the boy." Frank began to place the chess pieces on the board.

"I think the saying is 'innocent until proven guilty.'"

"Sadly that is sometimes forgotten in today's society. Have you thought more about your flashback triggers?"

Michael shifted uncomfortably in his chair. "Like I told you, I haven't had one since the night we met."

"I'm glad to see you are improving but I hope you understand that recovery is a slow process. There will be setbacks. They may not be as severe as what you've had in the past but you should be prepared for them. Being prepared ahead of time makes it easier for you and for anyone with you to get through an episode. Black or white?" He held out two chess pieces.

"White. How can I be prepared for one if I never know when they will occur?" Michael positioned his men on the board.

"That's a good question. Since you are working and living close to Bethany, she might benefit from learning about this, too."

Michael glanced up sharply. "I don't want her involved."

"Is that wise? She has a good head on her shoulders. She won't panic."

"No!"

"Okay, but I think you're making a mistake."

"It's mine to make." He was aware of Bethany's withdrawal at the pine branch gathering. Was it because of his kiss or something else? It had been hard for her to relate the story of how her father bounced in and out of her life and then abandoned them. When Michael admitted that he had left the Amish once before, it touched a nerve for her.

Maybe her coolness was for the best. He was better. He knew he was better, but he wasn't sure if it would last.

After beginning the game in silence and playing for

a while, Michael realized he wasn't outclassed by Pastor Frank. They were evenly matched and he began to enjoy the game.

"Do you have plans for next Saturday evening?" Frank asked.

"Nope. Why?"

"The city of Presque Isle puts on a holiday parade every year that's worth going to see. I'm getting together a vanload of Amish folks and driving them up to enjoy it. Would you like to join us?"

A big outing, crowds—he wasn't sure he was up to it. "Is it something Ivan and Jenny would enjoy?"

"Absolutely. It's fun for all ages and it's free. I've already asked Bethany and she said she would come."

"I'll consider it. I believe this is checkmate." Michael moved his queen to trap Frank's king.

Frank studied the board and sighed heavily. "I concede. Nice game."

"Another?" Michael asked.

Frank shook his head. "I should get going. I'll save you a seat in the van if you decide to go with us. Think about what I've said. Being prepared to endure a flashback or panic attack can make it easier on everyone involved."

"I'll keep it in mind."

But he wouldn't involve Bethany. Not ever.

Chapter Eleven

Bethany lifted Jenny to stand on a chair. The girl was wearing her Christmas costume and Bethany wanted to make sure the hem was straight. "Hold your arms out," she mumbled around the three straight pins she held between her lips. Two dozen more were stuck into the pincushion shaped like a tomato that she wore on her wrist.

The house smelled of pine and cinnamon. Green boughs graced the window ledges and the fireplace mantel. Christmas cards from faraway friends had started arriving. They were displayed nestled in the pine branches or hung from red yarn stretched across the windows. Christmas was fast approaching, and in spite of her assurance to Jenny, Bethany's last hope of keeping Ivan had crumbled. Her uncle had included a letter in his Christmas card. He strongly believed the bishop was right and Ivan should return with him. It was a bitter blow. It seemed to be God's will to separate her family.

She folded the material of the white gown under and pinned it across the top of Jenny's feet. "Is this how long you want it?"

"I don't know," Jenny said quietly.

"Did the play director tell you if you had to have wings?"

"I can't be an angel without wings."

"But you are the narrator. Should your costume be different than the other angels or the same?"

Jenny put her arms down. "I don't know." Her lower lip trembled.

Bethany took a hold of her sister's hand. "Don't cry. This is for your Christmas pageant. This should be fun. I'll make it long enough to touch the floor and if the director says it should be shorter then I will shorten it. You don't have dress rehearsal for a few days, so I have plenty of time to change it."

"Good thinking." Michael stood in the open doorway to his workroom. "If you cut it too short you won't be able to lengthen it."

She rolled her eyes at him. "Have you had a lot of experience as a seamstress?"

Michael had been joining the conversations more often in the past few days. The workroom door hadn't been closed all week. She welcomed his interactions with her family but she couldn't forget the all-too-brief kiss they'd shared. What did it mean? Did it mean anything to him? During his time in the outside world, had he kissed lots of women?

"As a matter of fact, I have had some sewing experience," he declared. "My brother and I made a camel costume for our Christmas pageant when I was in the sixth grade. We were told it was very lifelike."

Bethany looked around for her fabric marker and realized she had left it in the sewing room. "I'll be right back, Jenny."

She left the room, grabbed the marker from the sewing machine and started back into the kitchen. She was in the hall when she heard Michael say, "Of course you can ask me anything, Jenny. What's wrong?"

Bethany waited in the hall to hear what Jenny had to say. Why was her sister confiding in Michael instead of in her?

"I don't want to be the narrator," Jenny said.

"You don't? Why not? I think you will make a fine narrator."

"Mrs. Whipple says my voice is too small. I didn't know I had a small voice. How do I get a bigger one?"

"I don't think there's anything wrong with your voice, Jenny. Who is Mrs. Whipple?"

"She's one of the ladies helping our director, Miss Carson. I heard her tell Miss Carson that someone else should be the narrator because she couldn't hear me in the back row."

"That made you feel bad, didn't it?"

Bethany didn't hear anything. She assumed Jenny was nodding.

"Jenny, I will be happy to help you make your voice bigger."

"You will?" Jenny sounded thrilled.

"Absolutely. We will practice once your sister is finished with your costume. Just come into the workroom when the two of you are done."

"I'm not supposed to bother you in the workroom."

He chuckled. "That's only when the door is closed. When the door is open you can come in whenever you like."

Bethany walked into the kitchen and saw Jenny had her arms around Michael's neck. He pulled her arms away as a fierce blush stained his cheeks.

"I have to get back to work," he mumbled.

He was so good with children. He should have a dozen of his own.

When she realized where her thoughts were taking her, she pushed them aside. He wasn't the one for her. How could she consider a relationship with someone whose past was so full of secrets, with a man who didn't feel he could confide in her?

Michael closed the cover of a grandmother clock after setting the time. He waited as it ticked its way to the top of the hour. The chimes rang out in clear pure tones. He wiped his fingerprints from the glass. Tomorrow he would pack it up and mail it back to George Meyers. His former boss had been sending a steady stream of work his way, and Michael was grateful.

Jenny appeared in the doorway. "Can I come in?"

"Sure."

She came in and climbed up on his work stool. She opened the drawer and lifted out one of the tools. "Will one of these tools make my voice bigger?"

He smiled and took the pliers from her. "We will save those as a last resort. You stand on a stage, don't you?"

She nodded. He lifted her onto the workbench. "There are a few things you have to do to get a bigger voice. Right now, I want you to close your eyes. And I want you to whisper your first two lines."

Movement caught his eye and he glanced over to see Bethany watching him. He beckoned her to come in. She did but she stayed by the door.

"How was that?" Jenny asked.

"Fine. I want you to keep your eyes closed and pretend you need Ivan to come in from the other room. He's pretty far away but you can't yell. Want to try it? Talk loud. Say your lines."

"Ivan, a long time ago, in a land far away, there were shepherds tending their flocks in the hills near the little town of Bethlehem. Can you hear me?"

"That's pretty good. Now I want you to try telling him again but this time he is upstairs."

She shook her head. "I don't think he can hear me upstairs."

"Bethany, will you go to the stairwell and see if you can hear Jenny?"

"Of course." She turned and walked out of the room.

Jenny repeated her lines in a loud voice. A few moments later Bethany returned.

"Well?" Michael looked at Bethany for confirmation.

"I heard her, but just barely."

"Hmm. I wonder what will help. Bethany, do you have any suggestions?"

They conferred and with some practice they were able to get Jenny to be heard by someone standing on the stairwell. Jenny was excited that she wouldn't have to give up being the narrator and promised to speak loud enough to be heard on the roof. As she went to change out of her costume, Bethany stayed in the workroom.

She opened one of the drawers. "I've often wondered what all these things are for."

He sensed that she wanted to talk about something else. He would let her work up her courage. "It looks like a lot of stuff but there are just different sizes of the same items. Gears and pins. Pliers and screwdrivers. Tweezers and little magnets to retrieve dropped pieces of metal."

She picked up his jeweler's loupe. "And this is to let you see things more clearly, isn't it?" She held it to her eye and turned so she was looking at him.

"Is it working?" he asked gently.

"I'm not sure." She pulled it away from her face. "Every time I look I see something different." He knew she was talking about him.

"That is one of the drawbacks of looking too closely."

"I think the problem is I didn't have my subject in focus. What can I do about that?"

"Not much, I'm afraid, if your subject is unwilling to cooperate." He wasn't ready to risk her knowing the whole truth.

"So the loupe is for seeing small pieces in great detail. How do I see the whole picture in greater detail?"

"The trick is to take a step back," he said bluntly. Their relationship had progressed so quickly he wasn't sure of his own feelings or of hers.

She laid the lens down. "I think that's what I need to do."

"I think it would be best if we both did that."

A wry smile curved her lips. "I agree."

She started to walk past him but he caught her arm. "Can we still be friends?"

"I don't see why not," she replied, but he couldn't tell if she meant it.

Bethany expected her next meeting with Michael would be awkward. To prolong the inevitable, she went to visit her friend Gemma after the kids were off to school the following morning.

Gemma welcomed her with a hug and then intense scrutiny. "Okay, out with it. What's troubling you?"

Bethany turned away from her friend's sharp eyes. "The same thing. Ivan." It was true but it wasn't the whole truth.

"I know you are worried about your brother but

something else is on your mind or you wouldn't be here."

Bethany began to remove her bonnet and coat. "You make it sound like I never come to see you unless I'm in some kind of crisis."

Gemma poured two cups of coffee and sat down at the table with them. She pushed one across to Bethany when she sat down. "You visit me without a crisis often, but I know you well enough to see you are deeply troubled. What is it? I'm here to help."

Bethany prided herself on being in control. She didn't believe women were weaker than men, but when she looked up and saw the sympathy in Gemma's eyes, Bethany's pride flew out the window. Tears welled up and spilled down her cheeks. "I'm so confused."

"Oh, you poor dear." Gemma was around the table in a moment and gathered Bethany into her arms. "It's okay. Go ahead and cry."

"I can't abide women who act like watering cans." She sniffled and continued to cry.

Gemma patted Bethany's back. "No one could accuse you of being a watering can. You are one of the strongest women I have ever had the privilege to know."

"Then why do I feel like such a fool?" Bethany wailed.

"Because love makes glorious fools of us all."

"I'm not in love. I can't be in love."

"And yet here you are crying on my shoulder because your mystery man has stolen your heart."

Bethany drew back to stare at Gemma in amazement. "How can you know that?"

"Because I have been in love myself."

"You have? With who?"

"A fellow who is denser than a post. But never mind

about me. This is about you. First I have to know how bad it is. Has he kissed you?"

Bethany buried her face in her hands and nodded, unable to speak.

"Did you kiss him back?"

"Maybe just a little," she whispered.

"Do Ivan and Jenny like him?"

"Jenny adores him. Ivan looks up to him and tries to emulate him."

"All right. Has he told you that he loves you?"

"*Nee*, we've not spoken of our feelings."

"So you haven't professed your love. Okay. Things aren't as bad as you are making them out to be."

"How can you say that? I spend my days and nights thinking about him, wondering if he's thinking about me."

"That's normal in any new relationship. I know that you are a wonderful catch for any man. I don't see the problem on this end. Why is he all wrong for you?"

Bethany wiped her face with both hands and drew a ragged breath. "Because I don't know anything about him."

"You know a lot of things about him."

"You don't understand. Something bad happened to him. He has told me in general terms what happened but I know there is something else. Something he won't talk about. He's so secretive. I'm worried that I really may not want to know what he did."

"Bethany, you have to ask yourself what is the one sin that you can't forgive."

She frowned slightly as she looked at Gemma. "There is no sin that cannot be forgiven."

"You believe that with all your heart, don't you?"

"Of course I do. Jesus died on the cross for all men's

sins. We are instructed by God to forgive those that have trespassed against us."

"What is the one thing in Michael's past that you could not forgive?"

That made her pause. "I would forgive anything."

"Then why do you have to know what he has done?"

Bethany pulled her coffee mug close and took a sip. It was lukewarm. "It's not that I can't forgive his sins great or small. It's that I believe you can't love someone that you don't trust. How can he love me if he doesn't trust me enough to share his burdens?"

"Has he said that he loves you?"

"*Nee*, he has not."

"But you are in love with him?"

Bethany gave her friend a beseeching glance. "Maybe. I don't know. What would you do in my place?"

"Sell the farm and move to someplace warm."

Bethany managed a half-hearted smile. "You know I'm being serious."

"I do. I trust your judgment, Bethany. Therefore, you should trust your own judgment. You have so many things vying for your attention and that keeps you from thinking straight. You and I both know that you won't marry anyone before Christmas, even if it is the only way to keep Ivan with you. You're much too smart for that. An Amish marriage is forever. Ivan will return to us when he is older. It will be a hard separation, but it won't be forever. If you like Michael Shetler, even if you think you love him, you still need time to get to know one another."

"He asked me if we could be friends."

"Did he mean it?"

Bethany thought back to that moment. "I believe he did."

"That's a good sign. It means he cares about you and he values the relationship the two of you have. What did you say?"

"I said I didn't see why not."

"Well, that should give him some hope. Can you be his friend even if he never confides in you?"

Bethany pondered the question. She liked Michael. More than that, she cared deeply about him. He made her laugh. He understood Ivan better than she ever could. Jenny adored him and looked up to him. Bethany realized her life would be poorer if Michael Shetler wasn't in it. If his friendship was all that she could have, she would gladly hold on to it.

She nodded. "I can be his friend. You, Gemma, are such a wise friend. You give much better advice than Clarabelle."

Gemma looked appalled. "I should hope so. Isn't that your milk cow?"

Bethany chuckled. "Someday I will tell you the story. I will take your advice. I won't rush into anything. I still believe that Ivan is better off with me. I'm not letting him go without a fight."

Gemma took a sip of her coffee and made a bitter face. "That sounds like the Bethany I know and love. How about a fresh cup of hot coffee?"

"And a lemon cookie?"

"Absolutely. They come free with all my advice. How would you like to stay and help me bake cookies for the holidays? I need eight dozen."

"I would be delighted to repay even a small portion of your kindness."

Bethany spent the entire day with Gemma, enjoying her friendship, sampling new cookie recipes and making several dozen of each type to take home. Chocolate chip cookies, oatmeal cookies, gingerbread men, moose munch, sugar cookies and lemon crisps because she knew Michael would enjoy them. With several large plastic containers in her arms, she paused outside Gemma's front door.

"Thank you again."

Gemma waved aside Bethany's gratitude. "Someday I will need your shoulder to cry on."

"It will be available day or night. Are you going with Pastor Frank to see the Christmas parade in town?"

"I am. So are my folks. What about you?"

"The children and I are going for sure. I don't know about Michael."

"We will enjoy it with him or without him, right?"

"Right."

Bethany waved goodbye and headed home. As she approached her lane, she saw the school bus pull away. Four of the local schoolchildren went swarming up the mounds of snow left by the snowplows on her side of the road. She noticed Jeffrey was one of them but she didn't see Ivan.

She stopped to watch them playing king of the mountain. The one who obtained the summit then had to keep others from claiming his throne. There was more pushing and shoving than she liked to see, but all she did was caution them. "Make sure you don't push anyone toward the road. Stay on the outside of those piles."

"We know, Ms. Martin," one of the younger boys replied.

She left them to their fun and walked up her drive. Pastor Frank's van sat parked in front of the house. The sound of laughter and the smell of pizza greeted her as she entered. She stepped into the kitchen to see Pastor Frank, Michael, Ivan and Jenny seated around the table, making Christmas wreaths. All of them wore pine branch crowns around their heads. Michael's held two long branches upright like antlers. Jenny had two small upright branches near the front of her head. Ivan had two bushy branches hanging down. The pastor had red winterberries woven into his.

Bethany shook her head. "What is going on in here?"

"We're making Christmas wreaths to sell at the market," Jenny said.

Bethany set down her containers of cookies. "I see. Who are you supposed to be?" she asked, looking askew at all of them.

"I'm a bunny," Jenny said with a giggle. She got down from the table and hopped around the room.

Ivan slid off his chair. "I'm a hound dog." He started barking and chasing Jenny. Sadie Sue immediately got up from her place under the table and started barking at them as they ran up the stairs with her close on their heels.

Bethany looked at Michael and tried not to laugh. "I assume you are a Christmas reindeer?"

He shook his head, making one of his antlers fall off. He picked it up and tucked it in again. "I am a Maine moose."

"Of course you are. Pastor Frank?"

"I'm a pastor with a limited imagination wearing a pine branch wreath on my head decorated by Jenny." He gave her a big smile.

She looked at the number of wreaths stacked against the wall. "You have been busy. I know the children just got home a little while ago, so, Michael, did you make these by yourself or did Frank help you?"

"Those were all done by Michael," the pastor said. "I just brought the pizza. It's baking now. You are always feeding me. I thought I'd return the favor."

Michael stretched his neck one way and then the other. "I was tired of fixing clocks and decided to try my hand at wreath making. What do you think?"

She picked up several and checked the construction. "Not bad at all. I'm sure these will sell well with a little more decoration added."

"Did you have a good day?" he asked with a shade of uncertainty in his eyes.

She smiled. "I did. I went to visit Gemma and we baked cookies all day."

"Are there samples?" Pastor Frank's gaze slid to the counter and her plastic containers.

"There are. Pastor Frank, I know you enjoy oatmeal cookies. I have two dozen set aside just for you." She handed him a full plastic baggie.

"These are going straight out to my van so I don't forget them later." He removed his crown before heading out the door.

Bethany held out a container. "I actually made some moose munch if you want to try that, Michael the Moose."

He got up from his chair. "You don't have to ask me twice."

Opening one of the containers, he took a handful of the mix and turned to face her with his hip leaning against the counter. "How are you today?" he asked.

She cocked her head slightly. "I'm better. I had a wonderful time with Gemma and I've come to realize how truly valuable a great friendship can be."

"Present company excluded?" he asked.

"Present company included," she assured him. His smile warmed her all the way through.

Pastor Frank returned a few minutes later. The children thundered down the stairs when he called out that the pizza was ready. Bethany smiled as they crowded around him eagerly. This was the way it had been before her grandfather died. Friends stopping by. Storytelling, good food and good company. It was comforting to know it didn't have to change.

After supper Bethany and Jenny rehearsed her lines as the men decided to teach Ivan the game of chess. The boy had an aptitude for it and was soon intent on learning more moves. It was almost ten thirty when Bethany called a stop to the game.

"It's a school night and it is way past Ivan's bedtime." She had tucked Jenny in hours ago.

Pastor Frank pulled on his coat. "I apologize for keeping you all up so late. It was like old times and I guess I got carried away. Good night, all."

Bethany and Michael watched him leave from the doorway. When he drove out of sight, she closed the door.

"I'd better leave, too," Michael said. "I had a fine time tonight, Bethany. I've forgotten how satisfying an ordinary night with friends can be."

"I'm glad you enjoyed yourself. We'll do it again soon."

He put on his hat and coat, but instead of leaving he seemed to come to some decision. "The weather isn't bad and I've been sitting too long. Would you care to take a walk with me?"

"That would be nice." She put on her coat and gloves and walked out the door to stand beside him. "Which way?"

"You have lived here longer than I have. You choose the direction."

"There is a path that leads to an overlook. It's not too steep."

"I'll keep up. Don't worry about me."

She took him at his word. They walked in silence for a time with Sadie Sue ambling alongside Michael. The crunch of their boots in the snow was the only sound. It was cold, but Bethany was warmly dressed and exercise kept her from getting chilled. "What do you think of New Covenant?" It was a safe subject and she was interested in his opinion.

"It's a long way from being a self-supportive community."

"What do you think we need here?"

"You don't have a blacksmith or wheelwright."

"We have a blacksmith coming in the spring. A man with three boys."

"You don't have an Amish school."

"Once we reach ten school-age children in the community, the bishop will allow us to hire a teacher and open a school of our own."

"You need a grocer. Mr. Meriwether's prices are too high."

She chuckled. "Tell me something I don't know. I shop there every week."

"And where is the nearest pizza parlor? What is an Amish settlement without a pizza parlor?"

"There is one in Fort Craig. They even deliver."

"I'll have to get their number. What about you, Bethany? What do you want out of New Covenant?"

"I want to see a happy, healthy, thriving community. We are so few and far between right now. I pray the community survives."

"And if that doesn't happen? What if there is a split in the church? It happens all the time. You won't be immune because of your remoteness."

She shrugged. "I guess we'll just have to face that issue when it comes, if it comes. I like to expect the best that life has to offer."

"Isn't it better to expect the worst and then be pleased when it doesn't show up?"

"I reckon you and I simply look at life differently. Here is the overlook I mentioned. I don't see anyone around now, but it's a popular place with young lovers in the spring and summer."

They came out onto a rock ledge that jutted out between two old pine trees. Below was a stunning view of the Aroostook River. It was a silver ribbon winding its way through the countryside illuminated by a full moon just rising. She pointed east. "See where the farmland stops and the forest starts?"

"I do."

"That is Canada."

"Good to know in case I ever want to leave the country in a hurry."

"It is farther than it looks. Shall we go back?"

"Are you getting cold?"

"A little," she admitted.

They walked back to the house in silence. Bethany was overwhelmed by the smell of pine boughs when she entered the front door. The scent would always remind her of Michael in the future. She turned to face him. "Good night, Michael."

"You take care," he said as he went out into the night with Sadie Sue at his heels. Bethany sighed as she watched him walk up the hill. Being friends was truly the best path for them. Wasn't it?

Only the ache in her heart said it might not be enough.

Chapter Twelve

Bethany rose from bed feeling more rested than she had in weeks. Her first thought was to wonder if Michael shared the same feeling of relief that they were remaining friends, or did he hope for more one day?

She was fixing herself coffee when she heard a truck pull up in front of the house. She looked out the window. Mr. Meriwether got out of his delivery van and started for the house. The sheriff's SUV pulled up behind him. The look on their faces said it wasn't a social visit.

Bethany clutched her chest. "Oh, Ivan, what have you done now?"

Since he wasn't out of bed yet, he couldn't very well answer her question. She opened the door before Mr. Meriwether knocked. He inclined his head. "Good morning, Ms. Martin."

"Good day to you, Mr. Meriwether, Sheriff Lundeen. What can I do for you gentlemen?"

"I'm afraid we are here on an unpleasant errand," the sheriff said.

Mr. Meriwether nodded. "It sure is. Last night a little after midnight someone broke into one of my warehouses. They took several thousand dollars' worth of mechanic's tools, and brand-new toolboxes."

"What does that have to do with me?" she asked, fearing she knew the answer.

The sheriff removed his hat. "Is your brother, Ivan, at home?"

"*Ja*, he is here, though he is still abed."

The sheriff came in, forcing Bethany to step out of his way. "We're going to need to talk to him. The perpetrator was caught on a surveillance camera. It appears to be your brother arriving on foot and then he begins loading the stolen merchandise into a white panel van that pulled up just outside the fence. We didn't get a good look at the driver or the plates."

"It was an Amish boy fitting your brother's description," Mr. Meriwether added as he followed the sheriff inside.

Bethany led them into the living room with her heart pounding so hard she thought they must be able to hear it. This was serious. Thousands of dollars' worth of tools? This wasn't three chickens. She grew sick at heart. "I will go upstairs and get my brother. I'm sure he had nothing to do with this. Please have a seat."

"Thank you for your cooperation, ma'am." The sheriff sat on the edge of her sofa.

She hustled Ivan out of bed with only the briefest of explanations. She went into Jenny's room. "Jenny, get up and go get Michael. Tell him I need him right away."

"But I haven't had any breakfast."

"You can eat later. Now go."

The shock on Ivan's face when he saw the sheriff waiting for him told her he knew nothing about what was going on.

She stood beside Ivan. The sheriff began questioning him. Michael arrived twenty minutes later. "Can you fill me in?" he asked the law officer.

The sheriff looked him up and down. "Are you the boy's parent?"

"I'm not. I'm a friend."

"Then I don't see how this concerns you."

"I gave my word to our bishop that I would assume responsibility for Ivan's action. Anything that concerns him concerns me. If not, we must ask you to leave until the bishop and church elders can join us."

Bethany could see the wheels turning in the sheriff's mind. Did he want one Amish man or a whole roomful of them present for his questioning? Reluctantly he agreed to have Michael present and filled him in on what was known.

Michael was the one who picked up on a discrepancy. "You say the robbery took place a few minutes before eleven. We were here with Pastor Frank Pearson until ten thirty. We all saw Ivan go upstairs."

"But you admit that he could have left the premises after you did," the sheriff pointed out.

"You say a boy arrived on foot and a second perpetrator in a white panel van pulled up a few minutes later. Even if Ivan left here at 10:31, he would have been hard-pressed to run three miles in very cold temperatures and then calmly walk into Mr. Meriwether's warehouse and carry out the tools you claim were stolen."

Bethany could see the sheriff wavering. He said, "It's not outside the realm of possibility. He could have gotten a ride with the person in the van."

"But it is reasonable doubt," Michael insisted. "Were there fingerprints? Do you have a full view of his face on tape?"

Bethany was grateful for Michael's presence. He seemed to know exactly what to say.

The sheriff leaned forward on the couch and stared at Ivan. "We can't make a positive ID but it appears to be a boy wearing gloves, a dark coat and a black Amish hat."

Michael turned to Ivan. "Did you do it?"

Ivan shook his head. "*Nee.* I did not."

The sheriff sighed as he rose to his feet. "I don't have enough to hold the boy at this point. I have to wait for my forensics team to process the scene. Ivan, you can't leave town. Do you understand?"

Ivan nodded. Michael said, "Believe me, we want you to find this guy as much as you want to find him."

After the sheriff and Meriwether left, Bethany knelt in front of her brother and took his hand. "What do you know about this?"

"I think I can get the tools back, but I'm not going to turn anyone in."

"You can't protect Jeffrey forever," Michael said softly.

"You don't understand. I have to help him."

"Do you know who was driving the van?" Michael asked.

He shook his head. "I'm not sure."

Ivan left the room and Bethany didn't think twice about throwing herself into Michael's arms. She needed him. And he was there for her. "What should I do? I thought sending him to live with my uncle was terrible, but sending him to jail is unthinkable."

"It won't come to that. He's a juvenile. Besides, the evidence they have is circumstantial."

She leaned back to look at his face. "How do you know so much about police proceedings?"

"You know the store where I worked last year was

robbed. I answered questions from the police for weeks on end. I can't believe I was able to listen to his interrogation without breaking down. I guess I really am doing better," he mumbled more to himself than to her.

She gazed at his dear face. "Thank you for everything."

He held her away and took a step back. "That's what friends do."

Early the following morning, Bethany heard a car turn into her drive. It was the sheriff again. Had he come to arrest Ivan? He stopped a few feet from her walkway and got out. She opened the door as he reached the porch with her heart in her throat. "Good morning, Sheriff."

"Good morning. Is Ivan here?"

"I hope so. I haven't seen him yet. Has there been another robbery?" She braced herself to hear the answer.

"No. In fact, just the opposite has occurred. Sometime during the night all the tools and equipment stolen from Mr. Meriwether's property were left outside his gate. There doesn't appear to be any damage. Nothing is missing. Mr. Meriwether is dropping all the charges."

Relief made her knees weak. "That's wonderful news." It wouldn't keep Ivan from being sent to live with Uncle Harvey, but it was so much better than having him go to jail that it didn't seem horrible anymore. She couldn't wait to tell Michael.

After the sheriff left, Bethany pulled on her coat and boots, intent on seeing Michael, but a knock on the door stopped her. She opened it and saw Mrs. Morgan, Jeffrey's mother, on the porch. The woman had a large bruise on her face and a split lip.

"Mrs. Morgan, what happened? Come in. Do you

need to go to the hospital?" Bethany put her arm around the woman and helped her inside.

"Don't mind me. This is nothing. Is Jeffrey here? He didn't come home last night."

"He's not here. You must be out of your mind with worry. Let me get Ivan. Maybe he knows where Jeffrey is. Come in and sit down." The woman entered the kitchen and sat down as Bethany raced up the stairs to Ivan's room. She sagged with relief when she saw he was still in bed. She shook his shoulder. "Ivan, wake up. Mrs. Morgan is downstairs. She says Jeffrey is missing. Do you know where he is?"

Ivan sat up, rubbing his face. "I thought he was at home."

"When was the last time you saw him?"

"About midnight."

"Midnight? You went out last night?"

"Yeah. I'm sorry. I had to."

Bethany considered sending him to fetch Michael, but she realized there was nothing Michael could do. She went downstairs and found Mrs. Morgan with arms crossed and her head down on the kitchen table, weeping.

Bethany sat down beside her and put her arm around the woman's shoulders. "It's going to be all right. Ivan hasn't seen him since last night."

Michael appeared in the workshop doorway. "What's going on?"

Bethany quickly filled him in. He came and sat down across from Mrs. Morgan. "I think you should call the police."

Mrs. Morgan looked up and clutched Bethany's arm. "No. I can't do that."

* * *

Two nights later, Sadie's low growl brought Michael wide-awake. She left his bedside and trotted to the door. He sat up in bed. "What's wrong, girl?"

Sadie whined, looked back at him and whined again. Michael slipped out of bed, pulling the top quilt over himself against the cold night air. "I'm coming."

He made his way to the window beside the door. He used the corner of the quilt to wipe the frost from the center of the glass. He was expecting to see a lynx or coyote. Instead he watched a human figure approach the back door of Bethany's home and disappear into the shadows. His heart started pounding. Was she in danger?

He tossed the quilt aside, quickly pulling on his clothes and boots. He grabbed his coat from the hook by the door and pulled it on as he stepped outside. Sadie stood by his side but she wasn't growling. She looked at him. He nodded. "Go find him."

She started toward Bethany's house with Michael close behind her. The beam of a flashlight shone from the open back door. Michael couldn't see who was holding it, but he did see the person the light settled on. It was Jeffrey Morgan. The boy entered the house and the light went out. When the kitchen light came on, Michael decided to investigate further. Sadie was already at the back door, scratching and whining to be let in. Michael stood in the shadow of the pine tree off to the side and waited. When the door opened it was Ivan. "Sadie, stop it. You'll wake everybody. Go home."

Michael stepped out of the shadows. "Good evening, Ivan."

The boy's eyes widened in shock. "Michael. What are you doing here?"

"Sadie alerted me to a prowler. You've got some explaining to do."

"I reckon I do. Come into the kitchen." He turned and walked down the hall. Michael followed him.

Jeffrey was at the kitchen table, eating baked beans straight out of the can. As Michael watched Jeffrey tear into his food, it reminded him of the first time he saw Sadie gulp a sandwich down in one bite. Michael looked at Ivan. "What's going on?"

Jeffrey stopped eating to glance at Ivan and shook his head no.

Ivan spread his hands wide. "We can't do it by ourselves. Michael will help."

"He'll make me go back."

Michael took a seat across the table from Jeffrey. Ivan sat beside his friend. "Jeffrey can't go home. He isn't safe there."

Jeffrey had stopped eating and was staring down at the table. "I won't go back."

Michael reached across the table and put two fingers under the boy's chin. Jeffrey flinched but didn't pull away. Michael lifted the child's face until Jeffrey looked at him. "I know a lot about being afraid. I won't make you do anything that you don't want to do. Why don't you tell me about it?"

Jeffrey compressed his lips into a thin line. It was Ivan who spoke. "His dad beats him."

"He hits my mom, too," Jeffrey added in a small voice.

Michael sat back. He had suspected as much after Mrs. Morgan refused to call the police or go to the hospital, but this was beyond his ability to help. He wished Bethany was here.

Jeffrey stuck his fork in the empty can. "That's why

I got so mad when I learned you were going to be staying in the cabin. I used to stay there when things are bad at home. I'm sorry I broke your window."

"I thought Ivan threw the rock." Michael glanced between the boys.

Jeffrey looked at Ivan. "He took the blame for me. He sticks up for me a lot."

"The stolen supplies from Jedidiah—was that your doing or Ivan's?"

The boys exchanged guilty glances. Ivan wrinkled his nose. "It was sort of my idea. The bishop preaches that we have to share with those in need. I figured Jedidiah would share if he knew, so I took what I thought he could spare. I didn't know he'd be so upset about it. I was going to leave him a note but I didn't have paper or a pen with me."

"He only did it to help my family. Sometimes my mom and my little brother and sister don't have enough to eat. I helped him carry the stuff," Jeffrey added. "We're sort of both to blame."

Michael sighed. "I see you are equal partners in crime, as it were."

The boys nodded.

Michael shook his head in disbelief. "It's always better to ask first. And the chickens?"

"Mom had to cook our laying hens a few weeks ago. The little ones missed having eggs in the morning. I only took what we needed to eat."

"How did you boys get the tools returned to Mr. Meriwether?"

Jeffrey looked pleased. "I sort of borrowed my dad's van. I know how to drive it. He hadn't sold the stuff yet." The boy's grin faded. "He got real mean when he found the stuff was missing. I had to get away."

Ivan locked his pleading gaze on Michael. "What are you going to do now? You can't make him go home."

Michael rubbed his aching leg, stalling for time. He didn't know what to do. If Jeffrey was a member of the Amish faith, he would take this to the bishop. This required someone with a level head and a compassionate heart. "Ivan, I think you should go wake your sister."

"I'm up." Bethany came into the room, pulling the belt of her pink robe tight. "I overheard most of this conversation. Jeffrey, do you know your mother is worried sick about you?"

He shrugged one shoulder. "I left her a note tonight. She'll know I'm okay when she reads it."

Michael exchanged a knowing look with Bethany. She sat down beside him. He was glad of her presence. She smiled softly at Jeffrey. "You're a thirteen-year-old boy and it's winter in Maine. How are you surviving? Where are you staying?"

Jeffrey wouldn't look at her. "Here and there."

"And how often in the past two days have you had a decent meal?"

He lifted the empty can. "Tonight."

Michael shared a speaking glance with Bethany.

"What should we do?" she asked, speaking Pennsylvania Dutch. "He isn't Amish. The *Englisch* have many rules about children."

"They do have complicated laws about child custody. I know that much from my time in the outside world. We could be in trouble for not telling the police he is here."

Jeffrey surged to his feet. "I don't know what you're saying but I won't go back."

Michael held up one hand to reassure him. "We are not suggesting that. I think going to Pastor Frank is our best option. He will listen to you, Jeffrey, and he will make the right decision. He will not put you in harm's way."

Jeffrey sank back onto his chair. Ivan laid a hand on his shoulder. "Pastor Frank is a good fellow. You can trust him."

Bethany leaned forward and took Jeffrey's hands in hers. "You have to trust us. We want what is best for both you and your mother. You can't stay out in this weather. You could die."

"That would be better than going back to him."

Michael stood up. "You and I are going to go see Pastor Frank and tell him the situation. I know he will do the right thing. You can try running away again, Jeffrey, but you will be easy to track in the snow. I don't think you'll get far."

Jeffrey put his head down on his folded arms and began to cry.

Bethany waited for Michael to return. She left a lamp on so he would know she was up. It was almost four thirty when he stepped through the door. He looked tired and he was limping heavily. She wanted to throw her arms around him and help him to the sofa but she wasn't sure he would appreciate that gesture. "How did it go?"

He sat down on the sofa beside her with a deep sigh. "Children are complicated creatures. I'm surprised parents choose to have more than one."

"That's a very cynical thing to say. Humans are indeed complicated creatures. Since the good Lord made more than one of us, I assume He sees something wonderful in each of us."

"Even Mr. Morgan?"

"Even him. He deserves forgiveness and our prayers as much if not more than anyone."

Michael sighed. "I know you're right. That is what our faith teaches us. That is what our Lord commands us to do, but sometimes it is hard living by those words. That boy was covered with bruises."

"Pastor Frank didn't make Jeffrey go back to his father, did he?"

"He knew exactly what to do. He notified the police and reported the child abuse. Jeffrey and his brother and sister were taken to a children's home where they will be well cared for until permanent placement can be found. Frank is sure they'll go back to their mother when she is ready. Jeffrey's mother chose to go to a women's shelter."

"And Jeffrey's father?"

"Mr. Morgan was arrested and taken to jail. He is wanted in another state for burglary and arson. Apparently he often made Jeffrey steal stuff for him. It was his idea to dress Jeffrey in Amish clothing in case he was seen. Jeffrey said it was his father who damaged Greg Janson's tractor and let Robert Morris's cattle loose. He felt both men owed him more money for work he'd done for them last summer. It seems they fired him and hired two Amish fellows instead."

"At least everyone will know now that Ivan wasn't to blame for those things. I hope the bishop will reconsider letting him stay with me now. I'll speak to him tomorrow."

"Ivan still made some poor decisions but his heart was in the right place."

She reached out and covered Michael's hand with her own. His fingers were cold. "I was truly glad that you were here to help tonight. I have no idea what I would have done without your guidance."

A small smile lifted one corner of his lips. "You would have figured it out."

She shook her head. "I don't think so. When that little boy started crying at the table, I just wanted to wrap him in a warm blanket and carry him up to a soft bed. He broke my heart."

Michael laced his fingers with hers. "I know just what you mean. It was like finding Sadie all over again. Speaking of which, where is she?"

"Jenny had a nightmare about an hour ago. Sadie is sleeping with her."

He drew back a little. "You let a dog sleep in Jenny's bed? This from a woman who says dogs don't belong in the house?"

"I can admit when I am wrong. Sadie will always be welcome in my house. Provided she has had a bath and that she doesn't have fleas."

"I knew I was forgetting something."

"What?"

"Flea powder for her. Did you notice her scratching a lot?" He began scratching the back of his head.

Bethany popped him on the shoulder. "You are not as funny as you think you are."

He winked. "I'm funny enough to get a smile out of you."

As he gazed at her, his grin slowly faded. She sensed a change come over him. Her heart began beating heavily. He moved closer and she didn't pull away. He cupped her cheek with one hand, sending her pulse pounding and stealing her breath. She waited for his kiss. He caressed her lips with his thumb. "I should go."

She couldn't think clearly, let alone come up with a single objection.

He rose abruptly and left the house.

Chapter Thirteen

Bethany spoke to the bishop the next afternoon at his business. Michael wasn't with her. She relayed her brother's involvement and stressed his innocence. "He believed he was protecting Jeffrey from his father's foul temper. You have to respect him for trying to do good."

"I'm sympathetic to your position, Bethany, but I haven't changed my mind. Ivan followed too eagerly after this *Englisch* boy and he had made poor decisions. You can't deny that. I still feel the boy will benefit from a full-time male role model."

"Michael is providing Ivan with guidance. The two of them get along well and Ivan has improved so much." She held her breath, praying the bishop would see things her way.

"My mind is made up on this. The boy will benefit from his uncle's counsel evermore."

She pressed her hands together. "Please reconsider—"

He cut her off. "Bethany, go home and raise your sister. Your brother will return to you in time if it is God's will."

She had lost. Bethany left the bishop's workplace devoid of hope. If she wanted to keep her family together, the only thing left for her to do was to move away from New Covenant and start over somewhere else, but she had no idea where to go and no money to start over with.

The evening of the community Christmas play was chilly with overcast skies that promised more snow. Ivan insisted they use the sleigh to travel to the community building. He said it was more Amish and it felt more Christmas-like. Both children were excited because there would be a small gift exchange after the program that the bishop had agreed they could participate in.

Michael brought the sleigh to Bethany's front door and spread a thick lap robe over her when she got in. "I don't want you to catch cold."

"Ivan! Come on," Jenny shouted from the back seat, causing the patient horse to toss his head and snort. Ivan came out the door, letting it slam shut behind him. He had been trying to act as if the program was no big deal, but Michael could see he was excited, too. The teenager piled in the back seat with his sister.

After a second or two of getting settled, Ivan said, "Scoot over, Jenny, and give me some room."

"I'm cold and you have more of the blanket."

"I do not."

"You do so."

"Enough," Bethany said, putting an end to the rising family squabble.

Michael lifted his arm and laid it along the back of the seat to give Bethany more room. She moved closer. As much as he wanted to slip his arm around her shoulders, he knew it would be a bad idea. He was already having far too much trouble remembering to treat her as a friend.

"Ready, everyone?" Michael asked. Three confirmations rang out. He slapped the lines and the big horse took off down the snow-covered lane.

Sleigh bells jingled merrily in time to the horse's footfalls. The runners hissed along over the snow as big flakes began to float down. They stuck to Michael's and Ivan's hats, turning their brims white. Jenny tried to catch snowflakes on her tongue between giggles.

Michael leaned down to see Bethany's face. "Are you warm enough?" She nodded, but her cheeks looked rosy and cold. Michael took off his woolen scarf and wrapped it around her head to cover her mouth and nose.

"Danki," she murmured. "Won't you be cold?"

"Nope. It's a perfect evening, isn't it?" The snow obscured the mountains. The fields lay hidden beneath a thick blanket of white. Pine tree branches drooped beneath their icy loads. A hushed stillness filled the air, broken only by the jingle of the harness bells. It was a picture-perfect moment in time and Michael wished it could go on forever.

The community building was only a few miles from the farm in a converted brick factory not far from the city center. For Michael, they reached their destination much too quickly. As they drew closer they saw a dozen buggies and sleighs parked along the south side of the building out of the wind while the parking lot in front of it was full of cars and trucks.

As the kids scrambled out of the sleigh, Michael offered Bethany his hand to help her out. When she took it, he gave her an affectionate squeeze. She graced him with a shy smile in return.

Inside the building, the place was already crowded with people. What had once been the factory floor held rows of folding chairs facing a small stage at the front.

Swags of fragrant cedar boughs graced the sills of the tall multipaned windows. A Christmas tree stood in one corner, decorated with colorful paper chains, popcorn and cranberry strands, and handmade ornaments made by the children. A table on the opposite wall bore trays of cookies and candies and a large punch bowl. An atmosphere of joy, goodwill and anticipation permeated the air.

Several *Englisch* people Michael didn't know approached Bethany to tell her how happy they were to learn Ivan had been cleared and how glad they were to have Amish neighbors. Everywhere Michael looked there were welcoming smiles. He had been prepared to feel uneasy in the crowd but he didn't. The Martin children hurried to join their classmates behind the stage. Michael and Bethany found seats out front a few minutes before the curtain rose.

The children performed their assigned roles, singing songs and reciting poetry. Then it came time for Jenny to narrate the Christmas story. She walked out on stage in her white robe with her long hair in two golden braids. Michael glanced at Bethany. Her eyes brimmed with maternal pride. He squeezed her hand and together they watched the community's children bring the story of the first Christmas to life.

When the play was over, Jenny held one hand high. "*Frehlicher Grischtdaag*, everyone. Merry Christmas!"

The curtain fell and Michael clapped until his hands hurt. The last song of the evening was Ivan's solo. To Michael's surprise, the boy had a beautiful voice. His a cappella rendition of "O Come, O Come, Emmanuel" brought tears to a few eyes, including Bethany's.

Later, when everyone had a plate of treats, Jenny

squeezed in between Bethany and Michael. He said, "You did well, Jenny. Your narration was very good."

"Danki."

Bethany slipped her arm around the child and gave her a hug.

Michael rubbed Ivan's head. "Who knew you could sing so well?"

The boy blushed with happiness. Everyone seemed happy, only Bethany's joy appeared forced.

It was full dark by the time the festivities wound down and families began leaving. Michael brushed the accumulated snow from the sleigh's seats and lit the lanterns on the sides. The horse stood quietly, one hip cocked and a dusting of snow across his back. Michael stepped back inside to tell Bethany they were ready.

Scanning the room, he saw her with a group of young Amish women. Two of them held babies on their hips. Bethany raised a hand to smooth the blond curls of a little boy. As she did, her gaze met Michael's across the room.

In that moment, he knew exactly what he wanted. He wanted Bethany to have the life she was meant to live and he wanted to be a part of it. He wanted to spend every Christmas with her for the rest of his life. If only he could be certain his PTSD wouldn't return.

"Is it time to go home? I'm tired." Jenny, sitting on the bottom bleachers, could barely keep her eyes open.

"Yes, it's time to go home." He picked her up and she draped herself over his shoulder. Bethany joined them a minute later. In the sleigh, Michael let Ivan take the reins while he settled in with Jenny across his lap and Bethany seated beside him. The snow had stopped. A bright three-quarter moon slipped in and out of the clouds as they made their way home.

Snuggled beneath a blanket with Bethany at his side, Michael marveled at the beauty of the winter night in the far north and at the beauty of the woman next to him. When they pulled up in front of her house, Michael carried Jenny inside and up to bed while Ivan took the horse to the barn.

Michael stepped back as Bethany tucked her sister in. "I had a wonderful time. Thank you for inviting me."

"I'm glad." She closed the door to Jenny's room and faced him in the hall.

He stepped closer. She didn't move away. Reaching out, he cupped her cheek. "Good night, Bethany."

"Good night, Michael." Her voice was a soft whisper. Slowly, he lowered his lips to hers and kissed her.

Bethany melted into Michael's embrace. His kiss was gentle and so very sweet. Their mutual decision to take a step back and simply remain friends vanished from her thoughts as she slipped her arms around his neck. He briefly pulled her closer, and then he let her go and took a step away. "I'll see you tomorrow."

She pressed a hand to her lips to hold on to that wondrous moment. Ivan came walking up the stairs and passed them on the way to his room. Embarrassed, Bethany wondered if he had seen her in Michael's arms. He muttered a polite good-night and went in his room. Maybe he hadn't seen anything.

She mumbled a quick goodbye to Michael and fled into her room. She closed the door and leaned against it. There was no way they could go back to being just friends now.

Could she accept him without knowing the secret part of his past he wouldn't share? His kiss seemed to indicate he wanted to be a part of her life, but he hadn't said anything about what kind of future he saw and if she had a place in it.

Christmas was less than two weeks away, and she was going to lose her brother if she failed to convince the bishop to change his mind. Was Gemma right? Was Michael the answer to her prayers?

Chapter Fourteen

Sadie rose from her spot beside the fireplace the next morning and trotted to the front door, wagging her tail. She looked back at Michael and whined. A second later he heard a timid knock. He sprang out of his chair, hoping it was Bethany, and twisted his bad leg in the process. There was so much he wanted to say to her.

He pulled open the door. Jenny, not Bethany, stood on his stoop. She was dressed in a dark blue snowsuit and coat with bright red mittens on her hands. The ribbons of her *kapp* dangled out from beneath her hood. Behind her stood four other bundled-up children. Two boys wore flat-topped black hats, so he knew they were Amish *kinder*. They were all pulling colorful plastic toboggans.

Jenny grinned eagerly. "Can Sadie come out and play with us?"

He glanced down at the dog standing beside him. She wiggled with excitement but she didn't dash out the door. She looked to him for instructions. "I reckon."

He held the door wider and tipped his head toward the outside. "Go on. Have some fun."

Sadie bounded out of the house, jumping in circles around the children and barking.

"*Danki*, Michael," Jenny shouted as they headed toward his barn. He noticed that she was pulling two sleds, one red and one yellow. Why two? Every other child had one. Perhaps they were meeting someone else. They'd only gone a few more feet when he saw Jenny give the rope of one sled to Sadie. She held it in her mouth and trotted along with the group.

They disappeared behind the barn where the ground dropped away sharply, making a perfect hill for sledding. Although he couldn't see them, he could hear them calling encouragement to Sadie. The day was warmer than the past two weeks had been. He glanced back at the business paperwork waiting for him and decided it was time for a break.

He grabbed his hat and coat, put them on and closed the cabin door behind him. A walk in the fresh air was exactly what he needed. Maybe he would walk down and see Bethany. He smiled at the memory of their kiss last night. He was head over heels for her and he believed she felt the same but they hadn't discussed their feelings.

Maybe he was reading more into a kiss than he should. Bethany didn't know about his PTSD. Would that change her feelings toward him? He was better, it had been almost a month since he'd had a flashback, but was he well enough to consider a future with her? How would he know when he was healed?

A freshly shoveled path led from his cabin to Bethany's house. Ivan kept it open for him when he came to chop wood. That was the direction Michael wanted to go but he didn't have an excuse to see Bethany. He didn't want to appear too eager or pushy. The tracks of the children and dog led the other way.

He followed along, trying not to slip and fall in the new snow. When he reached the edge of the barn, he had an excellent view of the children sledding down the hill. Sadie was at the bottom with Jenny. They began to trudge back up, taking care to avoid the others flying down the hill toward them. Jenny was pulling her sled while Sadie pulled the other up the incline. He had never seen a dog do that.

At the top of the hill Jenny positioned her sled, sat down and pushed off with her hands. To his amazement, Sadie jumped on her own sled and went flying down the hill with her ears fluttering backward.

"Michael?"

He turned at the sound of Bethany's voice and saw her walking toward him. She held a package under her arm. He beckoned her closer. "You have to see this."

She smiled as she approached him. "This came for you in the mail. I thought it might be important and you weren't in your workshop."

"I was catching up on some paperwork. You need to see what the children are up to. Jenny stopped by to ask if Sadie could come out and play."

Bethany giggled. He would never tire of hearing her mirth. It always made him smile. He stepped to the side so that she could have his vantage point. He stumbled and would have fallen if she hadn't grabbed his coat to steady him. It was a good reminder that he wasn't fit. Sometimes he forgot how damaged he was when she was around.

She didn't say anything but set his package on a stone by the barn door. She stepped to where he had been standing and looked at the children. "Your dog is sledding all by herself. Did you teach her to do that?"

The wonder and amusement in her voice eased the embarrassment he felt. "*Nee*, this is the first time."

"Oh, she's pulling it back up the hill. I don't believe it. It's like she's one of the children. That is a remarkable animal."

And you are a remarkable woman. For a second he was afraid he had spoken aloud.

"What are you two looking at?" Ivan asked as he walked up beside them. Jeffrey was with him. The boy, his younger siblings and his mother had returned to their home a few days after his father's arrest.

"We are watching Sadie use a sled," Bethany said.

"Are you fooling me?" Ivan walked to the edge of the slope and Jeffrey followed him. They began packing the snow into a ball and rolling it around to make it bigger. When they had one about a foot in diameter they pushed it down the hill toward the group of children.

"Not a good idea." Michael shouted, "Look out below!"

The snowball quickly gained size and speed. Both boys sprinted after it as did Bethany. Michael watched helplessly, knowing he wouldn't be of any use.

Sadie barked and raced up the hill to meet the ball. She leaped to the side and tried to bite it as it rolled past. Her actions changed the direction just enough to let it roll harmlessly past the little girl who fell trying to scramble out of the way.

The snowball came to rest a few feet away from the trees that separated the field from the road. Michael heard Ivan apologizing. "I didn't think it would get so big. I thought it would break apart."

Bethany eyed him sternly.

"Honest, sister. I wasn't trying to hurt anyone. I thought we could make a snowman faster by rolling the balls down the hill to make them bigger."

She looked up at Michael as if seeking his opinion. He didn't think the boys meant any harm, either. He nodded slightly. She turned back to her brother. "Okay. It was almost a good idea. It just shows that you have to consider all parts of a problem before you decide on a solution. The easy way is not often the best way."

The younger children eagerly began creating snowmen of their own.

Jenny beckoned to Michael. "Help me make a tall snowman, Michael."

He wanted to join them. How many happy memories would it take to make him forget the horrible ones? Even if he wanted to, there was no way he could get down the hill without falling and arriving at the bottom inside a massive snowball. He shook his head and held up his cane.

Jenny pulled her sled over to Sadie and whispered something in her ear. Then she gave her the rope. Sadie came charging up the hill, pulling the empty sled. She skidded to a stop in front of Michael, dropped the rope and began barking furiously.

He looked at his dog. "You can't be serious. You want me to sled down the hill." He took another look at the terrain. It actually wasn't a bad idea. He looked at all the people beckoning him to come down. Getting down was the easy part. Getting up the slope would be the real challenge.

Sadie jumped up and put her paws on his chest. He ruffled her ears. "What kind of Amish man gives in to the whims of children and dogs?"

She barked once and looked downhill.

He followed her gaze and saw Bethany watching him. "Good point. She is down there. I was looking for an excuse to spend some time with her. When an opportunity falls into my lap I shouldn't waste it."

He awkwardly lowered himself into the red plastic sled and used his cane to pull himself to the edge of the incline. He looked at Sadie. "If I break my other leg I'm going to blame you." He pushed off and went flying down the slope.

He remembered how much fun it was to go sledding down a hill when he was a child. As an adult, he was a little more concerned about arriving at his destination in one piece.

Bethany held her breath as Michael shot down the hill with more speed than any of the children had obtained. To her relief, he used his cane as a drag to slow down when he neared the bottom. He came to rest a few feet in front of her. All the children applauded. Ivan jumped forward to help him to his feet. Michael was laughing like one of the *kinder*.

She had never seen him so lighthearted. It seemed that whatever had plagued him when he first came to New Covenant was giving way to a happier man.

She turned around with a snowball in her hand. "I've been wanting to do this for quite some time." She threw the ball and it hit him in the chest.

He brushed at his coat. "I refuse to get in a snowball fight with you. It's not dignified."

"You're right." She scooped up another handful of snow and packed it together. "I wouldn't want you to do something undignified." She let fly and this one struck him on his shoulder.

He brushed the loose snow away with one hand. "You are asking for trouble."

"I don't think so. I'm pretty sure I can outrun you."

"That was a low blow."

She tossed a newly formed snowball from one hand to the other. "You said you didn't like being treated differently because you need to use a cane."

"I think I will have to make you pay for that remark." He advanced menacingly.

She scuttled backward. "Forgiveness is the foundation of our religion. You don't want me to tell the bishop that you threatened me, do you?"

He kept coming and she kept backing up. "I think he would understand," he growled.

She took another step and tripped over the snowball Jenny had left unfinished. Michael scooped up a handful of snow. Standing over her, he dumped it on her face. She shrieked and rolled away. Surging to her feet, she shook her head to get rid of the snow and then glared at him. "That was just plain mean."

She was adorable. Her cheeks were bright red from the cold. Snow sparkled on her hair and eyelashes. The joy that filled his heart caught him off guard. Meeting her was the best thing that ever happened to him. How had she managed to worm her way so firmly into his heart in such a short amount of time?

"I apologize. I promise no more snow in the face, but I must remind you that you started it."

She looked as if she wanted to argue but gave in. "Okay, that is true. Now I have had my comeuppance and we are even, right?"

"I'd say so."

The boys had managed a haphazard snowman with a ragged straw hat, but they decided to go on to other adventures, leaving the slightly crooked fellow leaning into the wind.

"He looks lonely," Bethany said.

Michael put his hands on his hips. "I think he just looks homely."

Bethany moved several paces back. "I've been told I need to look at the whole picture."

"And what do you see?"

"A homely, lonely snowman. Let's fancy him up."

They found some winterberry and holly to decorate his straw hat. Bethany used a handful of red berries pressed into the snow to form his mouth. Michael supplied the branches for his arms and he sent one of the children to get a carrot for his nose.

Bethany withdrew a pace to look at him when he was finished. "There's still something missing."

"What?"

"I know." She pulled the red-and-white-striped scarf off and wrapped it around the snowman's neck. "There. He looks great."

Michael chuckled. "He looks like a mighty fancy Amish fellow. Is he one of your suitors?"

"He is and I will accept his offer." It was now or never. She smoothed the snowman's rough cheeks with her mittens, knowing Michael was listening. She'd never been so bold in her life, but she had to try. "The bishop understands why Ivan acted as he did when I explained things to him the other day, but he is still convinced a firmer hand could have prevented much of the trouble Ivan became embroiled in. He won't reconsider sending my brother away. I need an Amish husband before Christmas and the Lord has provided. That is, unless another suitor speaks up and asks me for my hand in marriage." She couldn't look at Michael.

He stepped close to her. "I don't think you should marry this fellow."

She looked into Michael's troubled eyes. "Do you think I'll get a better offer?"

He shook his head and walked away from her. "I wish I could be the man you need, but I'm not, Bethany."

"I think you are."

"You make it so hard to say no."

She moved to stand in front of him. "If it's hard to say no, then maybe you should say yes. I won't make any demands on you. Your time will be your own. You can have one hundred percent of the business. I need your help, Michael."

"I'm sorry."

Jenny came walking back to see what they were up to. She clapped her hands when she saw the snowman. "He's beautiful. He can be Bishop Schultz come to marry Michael and Bethany." Jenny looked at her sister.

Bethany gave Michael a sidelong glance. His face could have been carved from stone. She leaned over and forced a smile for her little sister. "There isn't going to be a wedding. I told you that."

Jenny's face fell. "Okay. I'm going to help Jeffrey and Ivan build a snow cave."

Michael glanced at Bethany and then quickly looked down at his boots. "Are you going to the Christmas parade in the city with Pastor Frank?"

"Yes, we are. What about you?" She avoided meeting his gaze.

"I think I will go." Maybe during the Christmas parade would be a good time to gauge how she felt about them.

Bethany retreated a pace. "I'd better get started on

lunch. They're going to be a hungry bunch when they come in."

"I've got some work to do, too."

She regained some of her composure. "That's right. A box came for you. I left it at your barn."

He looked up the slope. "I might work on something that's already in the workshop."

"I'll get the box." She grabbed the empty toboggan that Jenny had left by her snowman's head and trudged up the hill. She picked up his box, got in the sled and pushed off.

When she came to a stop two feet in front of him, he arched one eyebrow. "Show-off."

"I'm just using the gifts God gave me." She handed him the box and walked beside him all the way to his workshop, but the awkwardness between them persisted. Had she ruined their friendship with her desperate attempt to keep Ivan?

A half hour later Bethany was at the kitchen sink, peeling potatoes for French fries, when Jeffrey came in. "I'm hungry. Can I have a sandwich?" Sadie Sue followed him in and plopped down in front of the fireplace with her tongue hanging out.

His cheeks were rosy red from the cold but his lips were tinged with blue. "I think you should stay in for a while. Take off your boots and let me check your feet."

She had learned her first winter here that frostbite was nothing to be trifled with. He did as she instructed. His toes were bright pink but there was a patch of white skin on the back of his left heel. "You are definitely not going back outside. I'm going to get a pan of cool water and I want you to keep your foot in it until I tell you otherwise."

"But we just finished a great snow cave. Ivan is expecting me to come back."

"I'll explain to him why you have to stay in."

Michael had been working in his shop but apparently he had overheard her conversation. "I'll go tell Ivan what's going on."

"Danki," Bethany said and smiled at him. He was always willing to lend a helping hand. In many ways he reminded her of her grandfather. He had the same kind of gentle soul. She fixed a pan of water and had Jeffrey soak his foot.

Michael put on his coat and hat. "Where is your snow cave?"

"Out by the highway. The snowplows have made huge piles there." The snow the previous night had left four more inches on the roadways.

Michael stepped out onto the porch. "I see the piles, but I don't see the kids."

Bethany came out and stood beside him. She shaded her eyes with one hand against the glare of the sun off the white snow. "I don't see them, either."

Mike took a pair of snowshoes off their hooks on the porch. As he did, Bethany heard the grading rumble of the snowplow coming down from the ridge. The truck with a large blade on the front blasted through the new snow, easily making bigger drifts along the side of the road. It was headed down to the intersection where Jeffrey said Ivan and Jenny were playing.

The snowplow driver couldn't see the children for they were on the far side of the high snowbank away from him. She saw a flash of red in the snow and thought it must be Jenny's glove. The snowplow hit the side of the big pile and pushed it farther off the edge of the highway, adding a huge new supply of snow on top of what was already there. The place where she had seen Jenny's glove was completely covered. She started screaming and ran toward her sister.

Michael saw the whole thing happen and was helpless to stop it. How much time did they have? A few minutes? Maybe more if the children were in any kind of air pocket. He turned around and hurried to the house. "Jeffrey, get your shoes back on and run to the neighbors. Jenny and Ivan have been buried by the snowplow. We need everybody who can get here to dig. Go."

Jeffrey rushed to do as he was told. Michael ran to the tower of snow. Bethany was on her knees, digging with her bare hands. Michael grabbed a snow shovel from the porch and rushed to her side. He gave it to her and began using his cane as a probe into the snow, hoping to come in contact with a body. Each time his cane sank all the way in, he prayed harder.

It seemed like hours but it could've only been minutes when he heard the sounds of shouting from up the road. A dozen Amish men came rushing toward them with shovels and rakes. They spread out on either side of Bethany and Michael and began digging. Jeffrey was digging frantically with them. Bethany was crying. She kept saying "no, no, no."

He kept probing inch by inch, knowing Jenny and Ivan were under there somewhere and running out of time. He had never been so scared in his life. Not even when he knew the gunman was going to kill him. Suddenly Sadie Sue was beside him, whining. Bethany stopped digging and looked at the dog and then at Michael.

"It's a long shot," he said. He knelt beside Sadie and said, "Find Jenny." She whined and didn't move. Bethany came to stand beside Michael. "Find Jenny, please."

The dog trotted away from where they were digging

and Michael's hopes crashed. He went back to probing and Bethany returned to digging.

Twenty feet away, Sadie Sue started barking and digging at the snow.

Bethany looked at Michael. "I saw her glove here. I know I did." She kept digging and uncovered a red plastic candy wrapper.

Jeffrey had returned. He took Bethany's shovel away and raced over to the dog. He began frantically scooping the snow aside as she dug her way in. Suddenly the dog disappeared completely.

Bethany heard crying and knew at least one of them was alive. Praying as she had never prayed before, she stumbled to where Jeffrey was kneeling. The rest of their neighbors gathered around the hole and began widening it. Sadie came backing out, but she was dragging something. With two strong tugs she emerged from the hole, pulling Jenny out by her coat. Ivan crawled out on his own.

Cheering broke out from everyone. Bethany grabbed up her sister and held her tight and threw her other arm around Ivan. "Thank you, merciful Lord."

She looked at Michael and held out her hand. He came and embraced them all. He never wanted to let them go. As his frantically beating heart slowed, he added Sadie Sue to the group hug. She started licking Jenny's face, making the child giggle.

Ivan looked at Michael. "I knew you'd find us."

Not once during the emergency had Michael thought about the robbery or its aftermath. He had faced a life-and-death challenge without triggering a flashback or a panic attack. He had worked side by side with Bethany to save her family. A family he wanted to be a part of forever.

He caught Bethany's eye. "If you haven't said yes to the snowman, I'd like to reconsider your offer."

"You would?" Hope brightened her face.

"I would."

"Is that a yes?" A grin spread across her face.

"If you'll have me."

"I will." She hugged Ivan and Jenny harder. "I most certainly will."

Chapter Fifteen

On the Saturday evening before Christmas, Bethany, Michael and the children climbed into Pastor Frank's twenty-passenger van with sixteen other members of their Amish community, including the bishop, Jesse, Gemma and her parents.

Bethany kept Jenny close to her. The child had been subdued since the accident and wanted to constantly claim Bethany's attention. Michael didn't seem to mind. Bethany loved him for that. Ivan seemed far less affected.

As the van rolled down the highway Ivan began leading them in song. Michael joined in with his pleasant baritone voice. Christmas hymns new and old filled Bethany's heart with the joy of this most holy season. She knew how blessed she was to have Jenny and Ivan with her and how easily it could have turned out differently. Every time she caught Michael's eye he smiled at her. She hoped it was just a matter of time before he declared his love.

When they reached the city Pastor Frank parked the van on a side street and everyone made their way to the parade route. The streets were lined four deep with bundled-up people all sharing the holiday spirit on a frosty evening. Lavish holiday lights decorated the buildings along Main Street, blinking red and green and ice blue. Lit displays filled every business window.

Jenny, standing at Bethany's side, tugged on her coat. "I can't see."

Jesse leaned down to her. "Would you like to sit on my shoulders? I can see everything and you'll be even taller."

Jenny glanced at Bethany and then took Jesse's hand. "Okay."

He hoisted her to sit piggyback on his shoulders and she laughed. "Ivan, look at me."

"Hey, that's not fair," her brother shot back, but he was smiling.

Bethany reached for Michael's hand and gave it a squeeze. "She's feeling better."

"Kids are resilient and there is nothing like seeing a parade from the back of a giant to perk someone up."

Bethany chuckled and leaned against him. "You can always make me laugh."

Michael knew a depth of joy he never thought he would experience. His PTSD had improved enough for him to believe he was finally over it. The stress of searching for Jenny and Ivan hadn't triggered a flashback. He hadn't even had a nightmare afterward. That horrible part of his life was well and truly over. He smiled at Bethany and took her hand. Although she hadn't said that she loved him, he was sure that love would blossom in time to match his. And he did love her. With all his heart.

A PA system announced the parade was about to start and the crowd pressed forward. The canon across the park boomed and fireworks lit up the sky. The red streaks in the darkness held his attention. A shiver crawled down his spine. He couldn't shake the sight of red streaks on the floor and red flashes lighting up the night beyond his window.

Sirens sounded. People cheered as the local police and firefighters led the parade in their new machines with lights and sirens. The crowd behind him pressed closer. Michael couldn't breathe. He started hearing a scream and knew it was coming from him. He couldn't shut out the screams. Someone was talking to him, asking him what was wrong. A hand grabbed him and he swatted it. He had to get away.

He felt the impact of the bullet hitting his leg. He fell to the ground and started moaning.

Bethany had no idea what was wrong with Michael. She cried out for help as she knelt beside him. People gathered round, pressing closer, staring, uncertain how to help. Michael gazed wide-eyed into the space, hitting at her when she touched him. Bethany didn't think he knew she was there. Suddenly Pastor Frank was beside her.

"It's okay, Michael. It's Pastor Frank. You're having a flashback. It isn't real. You aren't in any danger. You're safe. Can you hear me? Bethany is here beside me. Is it all right if Bethany holds your hand?"

Michael's hand opened and closed on the sidewalk. Bethany took hold of it. "It's all right, darling. I'm here. I'm with you."

Pastor Frank patted her shoulder. "Keep talking to him. He needs to know that what he is seeing and hearing isn't real. I think we're going to need to get him away from this noise and commotion. I'm going to bring the van up."

Pastor Frank summoned a police officer who went with him.

Bethany held Michael's hand but he kept moaning and muttering people's names. She had no idea how to help him. She'd never felt more useless in her life. She didn't understand what was wrong. Was this what he was afraid of? Jenny was on her knees beside Bethany, crying. "What's the matter with Michael?"

Ivan took his little sister by the shoulders. "He's going to be okay. He'll get over this soon."

Bethany prayed Ivan's words were true.

Michael refused to come out of his cabin the next day. He didn't want to see anyone. He didn't answer the door although he knew both Frank and Bethany were outside. What was the point? Everyone knew now that he was just a shell of a man who looked normal but wasn't. Pastor Frank had been right. He wasn't going to be able to heal himself. He needed help. If he had tried to get help earlier maybe he could've salvaged something of his relationship with Bethany.

When the sun started to set, he went out and harnessed the pony. Pastor Frank's survivors' support group was tonight. Michael wasn't sure he was a survivor, but he definitely needed support.

At the church, he left his horse and cart and walked around the back of the building. A set of steps led to the basement. The door of the room where support group meetings were held stood open. A hand-lettered sign on the wall said Welcome to a Safe Place.

He wasn't sure what a safe place felt like anymore but if he was ever going to find one he had to start somewhere. He stepped inside and stopped in surprise. There were eight *Englisch* men and women seated at a round table with the pastor, but there were a dozen chairs lined up across the back of the room filled with the men and women of his Amish community. Jesse and the bishop. The carpenter Nigel Miller and his wife, Becca. Gemma Lapp and her parents, plus a dozen other Amish people he didn't know by name.

Bethany rose from her seat and came toward him. She held out her hand but he didn't take it. "What are you doing here?"

"I'm here to learn about PTSD and how to help the man I love cope with and overcome this disorder. We all want to be able to help you when you need us."

"The man you love? How can you still say that after what you saw? I was on the pavement, sobbing like a frightened child. I wasn't even aware that you were beside me. How can you love someone who is so damaged? 'The man that you pity' is what you really mean to say. You pity me."

"How can I not love you? In all the world you are the man who opened my heart so that I could clearly see God has chosen you to be my beloved. Are you a perfect man? *Nee*, for only God is perfect. Are you a good man? I believe, I know that you are."

Michael tried to swallow the lump in his throat as tears stung his eyes. "I don't deserve your love."

She smiled at him softly. "I have news for you. God and I believe you do."

Pastor Frank came to stand beside Bethany. "I am delighted that you came tonight, Michael. I wasn't sure that you would, but all of your friends have expressed a sincere interest in learning about PTSD and about how to deal with someone who suffers from it."

Michael started backing away. "I can't do this. Not yet. Not here. I'm sorry, Bethany."

"Michael, please." She held out her hand.

"*Nee*, whatever you thought was between us is over. I'm no good to you." He turned and walked out the door.

Bethany watched helplessly as Michael turned his back on her and left. She didn't understand why he wouldn't even try to accept their help. She looked to Pastor Frank. "What do I do?"

"That's why you're here. To learn about what you can do."

"Should I go after him?"

"No. I'm going to ask everyone to have a seat and I'm going to talk a little about PTSD and what it means to a person suffering from that disorder."

Bethany returned to her seat. Gemma grasped her hand.

Frank smiled at the crowd. "Some of you know exactly what I'm talking about. Others are just learning about the existence of this cruel disorder. Someone with PTSD will experience horrible events over and over again in a way that is so real they believe they are back in that situation."

Bethany listened and tried to learn all she could, but the magnitude of the problem was daunting. After the meeting was over she stayed to talk to Frank alone.

"Tell me how I can help Michael. Why did he push me away? I believe he loves me. I know he does."

"Michael considers himself weak. He is fearful that others, that you, will see him that way, too. Yet he can't hide from what has happened to him. He has tried to run away from it by moving to this remote settlement, but the change of scenery hasn't changed the disorder. But there is help and there is hope. I believe that shining God's light into the dark recesses of our pain will take away the power the trauma has over us."

"What do I do now?"

"When someone you love suffers from post-traumatic stress disorder, it can be overwhelming. You may feel hurt by your loved one's distance and moodiness. However, it's important to know that you're not a helpless bystander. Your love and support can make all the difference in Michael's recovery. Don't try to pressure him into talking. It may make things worse. Just let him know you're willing to listen when he wants to talk."

"I'm frightened. I'm not sure what I'm walking into but I love him. I have to help."

Michael had to leave. He couldn't stay and see the woman he loved look at him with pity for the rest of his life. He couldn't do it. He didn't own much. Just a few tools, some clothes and a big yellow dog. It should be easy to pick up and go, except it wasn't easy.

He was in the workshop, carefully packing up his tools, when the door opened. He knew who it was without looking. His eyes filled with tears but he refused to let them fall.

She spoke softly. "Please don't leave us."

"You must be out of your mind to want me to stay."

She stepped closer. "I don't think so. I think you're the man I need. You also happen to be the man I love."

His gaze flew to hers. "You don't know what you're saying."

"I know exactly what I'm saying. I am in love with you, Michael Shetler. My heart tells me you are the man I have been waiting for all my life."

He turned away and continued packing his tools. "You want a man who can fall apart in the blink of an eye because some sound or smell triggers a flashback? Is that your idea of an ideal mate? What if I'm driving a team and the children are with me and I don't see the train coming when I cross the tracks?"

"Michael, I know your problem looms large to you, but for me it is only one part of who you are. You are a kind, loving man. You are hardworking. You try to live your faith by caring for those around you. You are great with children and with dogs. You walk with a cane and you have PTSD. I won't pretend to understand what that is like for you. But do you really want to give up a woman who loves you, two children who adore you, and a mangy mutt that thinks you hung the moon?"

He put down his screwdrivers. "Sadie Sue isn't a mangy mutt."

"You're right. She is a very special gift sent by God to help us. She saved Ivan's and Jenny's lives, but I would trade places with that dog in a heartbeat. Do you know why? Because you accept that she loves you regardless of the difficulties you face. I wish you had half that much faith in my love. If you don't, then maybe I am wasting my breath."

Michael wanted to deny his love for Bethany but he couldn't. He knew it took a great deal of courage for her to come to him this way. She was the most remarkable woman he'd ever met.

"Bethany, I don't want to burden you with my weakness. You deserve a strong and stable man."

"I do." She gave him a sly smile. "Unfortunately, Jesse won't have me. That leaves you."

He grinned in spite of himself. "Jesse wouldn't stand a chance against your wit."

"You once told me that you would help me with anything I needed if it was within your power. Did you mean that?"

"I did."

"Then here is what I want. I want to be the person beside you the next time you have a flashback if you ever have one again. I want to know and understand what you are going through, what you are seeing and hearing so I can lead you to a safe place. Tell me what happened to you. Make me understand."

Michael shook his head. "I will never do that to you."

Her eyes filled with disappointment. "Why won't you let me help you?"

"You don't understand."

"Make me."

He stepped close and took her hands in his. "Bethany, if I share with you the pain and guilt and the horrible events that I lived through, then they can become your nightmare, too. You will be haunted by the things I tell you because you love me. I don't want you to know even a small part of the horror I endured."

"I'm a strong woman."

"I know you are."

"Frank told me he suffered with PTSD for many years after he came back from his military service. It destroyed his marriage and almost took his life. He found a way to deal with it by helping others. He also told me that talking about what happened to you is a way to decrease the power it has over your mind."

"He may be right. I will share my story with him but not with you."

"Don't you trust me?"

"I trust you with my life and all that I have. You must trust me when I say there are some things you are better off not knowing."

"I guess you are asking me for a leap of faith. Okay. I will not ask about it again. Are you going to marry me?"

He shook his head in bewilderment. "You are too bold to be a *goot* Amish maiden."

"I'm an Amish maiden who knows what she wants. You think that marrying me will ruin my life. I'm going to tell you that the only way you can ruin my life is to not marry me. Don't break my heart."

She stepped closer and slid her arms around his neck. "Please, Michael, say that you love me or don't say it— because it doesn't matter. I already know you do. I see it in your eyes. I feel it in your touch. I know it by the way your heart calls to mine."

He groaned and wrapped his arms around her to pull her close. "I can't believe I'm about to give you the opportunity to tell me what to do for the rest of my life."

Michael leaned close. Bethany knew he was going to kiss her. She had never wanted anything more. His lips touched hers with incredible gentleness, a feather-light touch. It wasn't enough.

She cupped his face with her hands. To her delight, he deepened the kiss. Joy clutched her heart and stole her breath. She'd been waiting a lifetime for this moment and never knew it.

He pulled her closer. The sweet softness of his lips moved away from her mouth. He kissed her cheek, her eyelids and her forehead, and then he drew away. Bethany wasn't ready to let him go. She would never be ready to let him go.

"I love you, Bethany," he murmured softly against her temple. "You make me whole. I am broken but you believe I can be mended. You make me believe it. I have lived in despair, ashamed of what I don't understand.

I thought I was beyond help. And then you came into my life and I saw hope."

"I love you, too, darling, but it is God that has made us both whole. Will you marry me?"

"To keep Ivan with you?" he asked.

She rose on tiptoe and kissed him. "To keep you by my side always. Will you?"

"Can't you hear my heart shouting the answer?" He kissed her temple and held her close.

Bethany had never felt so cherished. The wonder of his love was almost impossible to comprehend. Emotion choked her. She couldn't speak.

"Did he say yes?" Jenny's whispered question was hushed by Ivan.

Michael choked on a laugh as he realized they weren't alone. He looked up at the ceiling to compose himself. Bethany shook silently in his arms. He knew she was trying not to laugh out loud.

He mustered his most authoritative voice. "Eavesdroppers are likely to be sent to bed without their supper for a week."

Jenny popped up from behind the desk. "I wasn't eavesdropping. I just came in to ask my sister a question."

Michael kept his arm around Bethany as she turned to face her sister. "Ivan, what is your excuse?" she asked.

Ivan rose more reluctantly. "I came in to keep Jenny from interrupting the two of you."

"And what is the reason the two of you were hiding behind my desk?" he asked.

"I wasn't hiding. I was scratching Sadie's tummy," Jenny announced with a smile at her brilliant excuse. "But I did happen to hear my sister ask you to marry her, Michael. I thought men were supposed to ask first. Did she do it backward?"

Ivan took her hand and started to lead her from the room. "You have a lot to learn, sis. Women like to let men think it was their idea."

Jenny tried to get her hand loose. "Wait. We didn't hear his answer." Ivan didn't let go of her. She grabbed the doorjamb and held on as she looked over her shoulder. "Please, Michael, say you want to marry us."

A tug from her brother propelled her out of the room. He shut the door with a resounding bang.

Bethany turned and leaned against Michael's chest as she shook with laughter. "I'm the one who should tell you to run and get as far away from us as fast as you can."

"I'm afraid that no matter how far I went I wouldn't survive long."

She leaned back to look at his face. "Why is that?"

"Because my heart would remain here in your keeping and a man can't live long without a heart."

"Then you will marry me?" she asked hopefully.

"On one condition."

A faint frown appeared on her face. "What condition?"

"That I also get to ask the question. Bethany Martin, will you do me the honor of becoming my wife?"

"I will."

"Then I promise to love and cherish you all the days of my life," he said and bent to kiss her once more.

The door flew open and Jenny charged in with Sadie at her side. "He said yes and she said yes. We're getting married!" Sadie started barking wildly as she bounced around Jenny. Ivan stood in the doorway with a bright smile on his face.

Bethany gazed up at Michael with all the love in her heart. "Are you sure you want to marry all of us?"

He kissed the tip of her nose. "I want an Amish wife for Christmas, two fine Amish children, a fine house with a workshop and a *goot hund*. What more could a man need?"

"Maybe another kiss from his Amish wife?"

"My darling Bethany, you read me like a book." He leaned in and kissed her again, knowing no matter what trials he faced, he would never face them alone. God and Bethany would be with him always.

Chapter Sixteen

The morning of Second Christmas, December 26, dawned clear and bright in New Covenant, Maine. Bethany and Michael stood in the entryway of her house and greeted their wedding guests. Bethany's aunt and uncle had arrived on Christmas Eve and had helped take over the preparations for the wedding. Ivan and Jesse showed the guests to their seats.

Bethany glanced at her soon-to-be husband. He looked very handsome in his black suit and black string tie. He smiled back at her. "It's not too late to call it off."

She shook her head. "I think it was too late the day I met you."

He snapped his fingers. "That's who we forgot to invite."

"Who?"

"Clarabelle."

Gemma entered with her parents. "A blessed Christmas to you and may you have a blessed life together."

"Thank you for agreeing to be my sidesitter," Bethany said.

"I am honored to be your attendant at your wedding. Michael, who is going to stand up with you?"

"Jesse has agreed to do me the favor."

Gemma made a sour face. "That man is as dense as a post." She went in to take her place on the front bench where Bethany would sit during the ceremony.

"What does she have against Jesse?" Michael asked.

"Nothing, except he hasn't noticed her in all the time she has been trying to catch his attention."

"She likes Jesse? Are you sure?"

"Very sure. Do you think this is everyone?" She glanced into the full living room, where the church benches had been set out in two rows for the men and the women.

"I think so."

"Where are the children?" Bethany looked around. "I hope Jenny is not getting her new dress dirty."

"I think she's trying to figure out some way to smuggle Sadie Sue in."

"As much as I like your dog, I'm not going to have her at my wedding."

He laughed and pointed up the stairwell. "I wouldn't be too sure about that."

Jenny was kneeling at the top of the steps with Sadie Sue lying beside her. The two of them scurried back down the hall when they realized they had been spotted.

"Do you want me to speak to her?" he asked.

"*Nee*, she knows better. She will behave. I hope."

The bishop came up to them. "Are you ready?"

They smiled at each other and nodded. "We're ready," they said in unison.

While the preparations had been rushed, the ceremony itself went off without a hitch. The bishop was short-winded for a change and the preaching lasted only three hours. As Bethany stood beside Michael in front of the bishop, she couldn't help but realize how very blessed she was to have found the perfect man. She couldn't stop smiling.

Afterward, Bethany went upstairs to change her black *kapp* for a white one. In the corner of the room facing the front door, the Eck, or the "corner table," was quickly set up for the wedding party.

When it was ready, Michael took his place with Jesse and Ivan seated to his right. Bethany was ushered back in and took her seat at his left-hand side. It symbolized the place she would occupy in his buggy and in his life. Her cheeks were rosy red and her eyes sparkled with happiness. They clasped hands underneath the table. Michael squeezed her fingers. "You are everything I could have asked for and so much more."

"I promise to try and be a *goot* wife to you," she said with a meekness he distrusted.

"Just be yourself. That will be good enough."

"You realize you get to choose the seating arrangements for the single people this evening, don't you?" Gemma asked.

Michael shrugged. "I haven't given it much thought."

"This might be the first wedding in New Covenant but I'm going to make sure it isn't the last," Bethany said with a wink at her friend.

Jenny sat on the other side of Gemma. "Are you going to pick a husband for me?"

"I may just do that." She smiled at her sister.

Michael leaned back in his seat. "Are you taking up matchmaking now?"

She chuckled. "Clarabelle is my only local competition. I think I can do better than her."

He leaned close to her. "The old cow did right by me."

"I beg to differ. She never once mentioned your name."

"Do you know what?"

"What?" she asked, intrigued by the light in his eyes.

"I can't wait to kiss you again."

Bethany felt the heat rush to her face. "I can't wait for that myself, my husband."

* * * * *

If you enjoyed this story, look for these other Amish stories by Patricia Davids:

An Amish Harvest
An Amish Noel
His Amish Teacher
Their Pretend Amish Courtship
Amish Christmas Twins
An Unexpected Amish Romance
His New Amish Family

Dear Reader,

This is the first book in my new Amish series set in Maine. I hope you have enjoyed the story. In case you haven't noticed, I am a dog lover. The remarkable Sadie Sue was patterned after my own dog Sadie. Sadly she is no longer with us but we have wonderful memories of her happy personality and relentless drive to fetch the ball, fetch the ball.

PTSD is a disorder that has been in the news a lot in recent years. Many of our soldiers are returning to civilian life crippled by this devastating disorder. More research is needed to combat this problem but therapy dogs have been shown to have a positive effect on the men and women who own them. I have limited knowledge of the disorder and this is not meant to be a tutorial on the subject. Any mistakes or incorrect assumptions are purely my own.

Blessings to all,
Patricia Davids

SPECIAL EXCERPT FROM

Love Inspired®

When a young Amish woman has amnesia during the holidays, will a handsome Amish farmer help her regain her memories?

Read on for a sneak preview of
Amish Christmas Memories *by Vannetta Chapman, available December 2018 from Love Inspired.*

"What's your name?"

The woman's eyes widened and her hand shook so that she could barely hold the mug of tea without spilling it. She set it carefully on the coffee table. "I don't—I don't know my name."

"How can you not know your own name?" Caleb asked. "Do you know where you live?"

"Nein."

"What were you doing out there?"

"Out where?"

"Where was your coat and your *kapp*?"

"Caleb, now's not the time to interrogate the poor girl." His *mamm* stood and moved beside her on the couch. She picked up the small book of poetry. "You were carrying this, when Caleb found you. Do you remember it?"

"I don't. This was mine?"

"Found it in the snow," Caleb said. "Right beside where you collapsed."

"So it must be mine."

Caleb noticed that the woman's hands trembled as she opened the cover and stared down at the first page. With one finger, she traced the handwriting there.

"Rachel. I think my name is Rachel."

Rachel let her fingers brush over the word again and again. Rachel. Yes, that was her name. She was sure of it. She remembered writing it in the front of the book—she'd used a pen that her *mamm* had given her. She could almost picture herself, somewhere else. She could almost see her mother.

"My *mamm* gave me the pen and the book…for my birthday, I think. I wrote my name—wrote it right here."

"Your *mamm*. So you remember her?"

"Praise be to *Gotte*," Caleb's *dat* said, a smile spreading across his face.

"Is there someone we can call? If you remember the name of your bishop…" Caleb had sat down in the rocker his mother had vacated and was staring at her intensely.

They all were.

She closed her eyes, hoping to feel the memory again. She tried to see the room or the house or the people, but the memory had receded as quickly as it had come, leaving her with a pulsing headache.

She struggled to keep the feelings of panic at bay. Her heart was hammering, and her hands were shaking, and she could barely make sense of the questions they were pelting at her.

Who were these people?

Where was she?

Who was she?

She needed to remember what had happened.

She needed to go home.

Don't miss
Amish Christmas Memories *by Vannetta Chapman,*
available December 2018 wherever
Love Inspired® books and ebooks are sold.

www.LoveInspired.com